Islamic Dilemmas: Reformers, Nationalists and Industrialization

The Southern Shore of the Mediterranean

Religion and Society 25

MOUTON PUBLISHERS · BERLIN · NEW YORK · AMSTERDAM

Islamic Dilemmas: Reformers, Nationalists and Industrialization

The Southern Shore of the Mediterranean

Edited by

Ernest Gellner

MOUTON PUBLISHERS · BERLIN · NEW YORK · AMSTERDAM

Library of Congress Cataloging in Publication Data

Islamic dilemmas, reformers, nationalists and industrialization.

(Religion and society ; 25)
1. Islam—Near East—Congresses. I. Gellner, Ernest. II. Series: Religion and society (Mouton Publishers) ; 25.
BP63.A4N42437 1985 306'.6'091822 85-333
ISBN 3-11-009763-X

CIP-Kurztitelaufnahme der Deutschen Bibliothek

Islamic dilemmas: reformers, nationalists, and industrialization : the southern shore of the Mediterranean / ed. by Ernest Gellner. - Berlin ; New York ; Amsterdam ; Mouton, 1985.
(Religion and society ; 25)
ISBN 3-11-009763-X

NE: Gellner, Ernest [Hrsg.]; GT

 — Printing: Druckerei Hildebrand, Berlin. — Binding: Dieter Mikolai, Berlin. Printed in Germany.

Preface

Jojada Verrips (for the University of Amsterdam)
Daniel Meijers (for the Free University of Amsterdam)

Thinking up a conference is easier than setting one up, as Dr. John Davis discovered while serving as a Visiting Professor in the Department of European and Mediterranean Studies, Anthropology-Sociology Center, University of Amsterdam, in 1977-1978. In a recent book, which essays a critical synthesis of what anthropologists have written about the *People of the Mediterranean* (1977), Dr. Davis observes that little systematic study has been made of religion as Mediterranean people practise it. To help remedy this deficiency, Dr. Davis proposed to hold a conference on the subject attended by outstanding scholars of Mediterranean society, and drew up a list of prospective contributors. His collegues in Amsterdam received both suggestions enthusiastically, but finance was another matter. Hence it was only after Davis had left Amsterdam that funds were obtained to underwrite the gathering he had planned. Finally, in December 1979, two years after Davis first proposed his idea, the conference was held at the Free University of Amsterdam. For three days anthropologists and sociologists discussed each other's conference papers, most of which (suitably revised) appear in the present volumes, edited by Ernest Gellner and Eric R. Wolf, who chaired the proceedings. We are deeply indebted to Professors Gellner and Wolf, both for their splendid management of the discussion, and for the labours they undertook afterwards to prepare these books for press. They have our heartfelt thanks.

Their good work would have come to naught, however, but for the financial support graciously provided by the Subfaculty of Sociology, Cultural Anthropology, and the Sociology of Nonwestern Peoples at the University of Amsterdam; the Subfaculty of Social and Cultural Sciences at the Free University of Amsterdam; and the Netherlands Ministry of Education and Science. We also wish to thank Ir. J.H.H. Hasenack, chief administrator of the University of Amsterdam subfaculty and Mr W. Buitenhek, his counterpart at the Free University, for their personal interest and help in making this conference possible.

After John Davis left Amsterdam, we, the undersigned, took charge of organising the conference. Hence we wish to thank our colleagues in the Departments of European and Mediterranean Studies, University of Amsterdam, and the Anthropology of Religion, Free University, for their continuing trust and support - in particular Drs. Tom Nieuwenhuis (University of Amsterdam) and Drs. Miep Stam-van Ginhoven and Mrs Freeke Falkenhagen (Free University) whose assistance was indispensable.

After the conference Dr. Adrianus Koster, who already had been helpful in many ways, took over Daniel Meijers' responsibility for the publication of the present volume. At this stage Ms Gay Woolven, Department of Philosophy, Logic, and Scientific Method, London School of Economics; Dr. Katie Platt, Ms Hannie Hoekstra and Ms Nettie Westerhuis, University of Amsterdam, helped prepare the draft. Ms Marijke Kreuze, together with Ms Elly Molendijk and Mrs Grémina Hoekstra, Free University, typed this final manuscript. Thanks, too, are due to the Administration of the Free University for aid in translating several key contributions from the French language.

In addition, we owe thanks to Drs. Bertus Hendriks, Drs. Edien Bartels, and Professor Sydel Silverman, who rounded off the discussion with clear summaries and sharp comments.

Lastly, we wish to thank Professors Leo Laeyendecker and Jacques Waardenburg for their advice and support.

A conference like this can succeed only if the written contributions are of high quality and, moreover, if a certain community of interest develops among the participants. The reader can best judge whether the first condition has been met. As for the second, all we can say is that despite the multinational composition of the discussants, the division of the proceedings into two segments, concerned with religion on the Northern and Southern shores of the Mediterranean respectively, and the mix of Christian, Islamic, and Jewish traditions among us, our sense of academic community and shared scientific interest never flagged. On the contrary, if our experience suggests a general conclusion, it is that religion in Mediterranean society is an exciting subject, the study of which offers indispensable insights into how life is lived there. Hence we hope that these books will stimulate others to continue the work of improving our understanding of religious observance and commitment, and its significance for social existence, in the modern world.

Jojada Verrips
Daniel Meijers

Table of Contents

PREFACE — V
Jojada Verrips (for the University of Amsterdam)
Daniel Meijers (for the Free University of Amsterdam)

INTRODUCTION — 1
Ernest Gellner

LAW AND REALITY IN MODERN ISLAM — 10
Niko Kielstra

ISLAM AS A VEHICLE OF PROTEST — 22
Jacques Waardenburg

TOWARDS AN ECONOMIC MODEL OF VIRTUOSO RELIGION — 49
Bryan S. Turner

MILITANT ISLAM: A HISTORICAL PERSPECTIVE — 73
Jamil M. Abun-Nasr

THE ORIGIN OF MODERN CONSERVATISM AND ISLAMIC FUNDAMENTALISM — 94
Hassan Hanafi

TRIBAL PILGRIMAGES TO SAINTS' TOMBS IN SOUTH SINAI — 104
Emanuel Marx

THE ME^{c}RUF OF TAMJLOCHT OR THE RITE OF THE BOUND VICTIM — 132
Paul Pascan

THE DISCREDITING OF A SUFI MOVEMENT IN TUNISIA[+] — 146
Kenneth L. Brown

ISLAND PURITANISM — 169
Katie Platt

TRAJECTORIES OF CONTEMPORARY SUFISM — 187
Michael Gilsenan

THE CULT OF SAINTS IN NORTH-WESTERN TUNISIA[1]; AN ANALYSIS OF CONTEMPORARY PILGRIMAGE STRUCTURES — 199
Wim M.J. van Binsbergen

THE CONTEMPORARY SITUATION OF THE MUSLIM MYSTIC ORDERS IN YUGOSLAVIA 240
Alexandre Popovic

THE HISTORY OF RELIGIOUS POLITICS IN THE LEBANON 255
Anton Wessels

ASPECTS OF THE CHANGING NATURE OF LEBANESE CONFESSIONAL POLITICS: *AL-MURABITUN*, 1958-1979[1] 267
Marion Farouk-Sluglett
and
Peter Sluglett

Index 1: Proper Names 285

Index 2: Subject Matter 297

Index 3: Foreign Words 314

Introduction

Ernest Gellner

To discuss the religion of the southern shore of the Mediterranean is to discuss Islam. Though Islam does not have a monopoly of that region, given Jewish minorities in the Maghreb and both Jewish and Christian ones in the Near East, nevertheless it overwhelmingly dominates it. The departure of colonial settler populations, and the transformation of the Jews from a set of diaspora communities into the territorially compact national state of Israel, have further accentuated the Islamic hegemony. Only the Christian communities in Lebanon, Syria, Palestine and Egypt now constitute significant exceptions to this religious unity.

The papers assembled in this part of the volume reflect it. What remains of situations of religious pluralism is represented by the discussion of the highly significant but a-typical Lebanese case. Otherwise, they deal with problems, conflicts and developments internal to Islam.

Three great forces or processes are at work in this world: industrialisation, nationalism, and Reformism. By industrialisation, one means of course that entire syndrome of economic and social changes which is associated with the diffusion of modern technology, and which is sometimes referred to as 'modernisation', and which extends far beyond the methods of industrial production in any narrow sense. Its elements are as evident in agriculture and include features such as increased administrative effectiveness and hence greater centralisation, urbanisation, population growth, disruption of local communities, and increased literacy. By Reformism is meant that tendency towards a more scripturalist, fundamentalist, rigorous form of religion, which seems to be the central theme of the cultural history of Muslim countries for the past century. In a generic and non-prejudicial sense, it could also be called 'protestantism', in as far as it displays those traits which, in Europe, are associated with that term: stress on the authority of the written Word of the canonical text, distrust of spiritual middlemen and of the use of audio-visual aids to piety.

But in Europe, the age of the Reformation, and that of

industrialisation and nationalism, were separated by some two or three centuries. These great transformations were of course connected, but they were not simultaneous. The most famous theory of the genesis of industrial society makes extreme protestantism into a crucial precondition of 'capitalism' and modern rationality. The link between protestantism and nationalism is also close. Bernard Shaw commented on it in *St. Joan*: Cauchon speaking of the Maid, says:

> "Call this side of her heresy Nationalism
> if you will ... it is essentially
> anti-Catholic ..."

and Warwick replies:

> "Well, if you will burn the Protestant,
> I will burn the Nationalist ..."

St. Joan was ahead of her time in Europe, in being both 'Protestant' and Nationalist at the same time, but in Islam this conflation is now common. Nationalism and protestantism (I shall continue to use this term in a generic, sociological sense, without prejudice), constitute ideas, doctrines or values which have important, and overlapping, implications for the relationship of men to culture and society. Protestantism says, in effect, that the individual should heed and repect the recorded Word without excessive (or any) use of intermediaries, and that inner guidance and transcendent Authority suffice. Superficially, this might seem an anti-social doctrine, dispending as it does with the need for external sanctions and group feeling, and stressing instead the exclusive authority of something other-worldly and hence trans-social. But such a supposition neglects the far greater effectiveness of inner sanctions, especially when purified of reliance on external support, and when purged of contamination by compromise, haggling; and also of that special indulgence which socially incarnated, over-incarnated, all-too-human or all-too-social religion can hardly help showing to those who are loyal and generous to it and its representatives, irrespective of their purity of heart and faith. Paradoxically, 'protestant' religious styles cause men to internalise ideas and values more effectively, just because they do not employ more immediate, all-too-mundane reminders, reinforcements and bribes. Self-discipline is the most effective kind. *Innere Führung* may or may not work in the *Bundeswehr*, but it works admirably in religion. It defines a community, especially a large or anonymous one, better than more institutionally incamate religions.

And what has nationalism to do with this? A very great deal. A realistic definition of nationalism is this: It teaches that a man's real and binding loyalty is to a large, quite anonymous collectivity, the overwhelming majority of whom he does not and cannot know personally, men who are linked to him by nothing more than identity of culture, of style of thought and feeling (usually, but not always, of 'language', in the literal sense). A tribesman is a member of his tribe only in virtue of being first of all member of one of its clans, sub-clans, and so forth; his membership is mediated by membership of a nested set of subgroups, which assign him his social niche, which is an essential part of his identity. But a loyal member of a modern national state enjoys his membership without any such mediation at all. If he supports an enemy of his nation, he is a traitor, but if he chooses to support the foolball team other than that of his locality, he can do so with impunity and without compunction. The locality or local group is no longer a significant mediating link between him and the ultimate community, and it has no serious claims on him. There is a very significant parallel in the un-mediated nature of protestant worship and of nationalist political loyalty. The identification with a culture, whose adherents form a large, anonymous, mobile, (un?)organised mass, obliges him to be familiar with a standard, normative idiom, not with an idiosyncratic dialect, and to be literate in it. Protestant scripturalism imposes the same obligation.

For although, in its own terms, a protestant religion looks towards the Other, which is universal, yet that Other communicates with believers through the written Word, and that Word must, needs be drawn from some specific language. (It is this very literacy which facilitates this universality and openness - makes possible the elimination of spiritual middlemen.) But did God employ an *Ur-Sprache*, an eternal and unique proto-language, whose names for things are their 'real' names? If so, commitment to scriptural divine truth, and to that special and privileged culture associated with the language of scripture, would fuse. At least, one nationalism is in a position to hold such a view. We external observers, however, need not commit ourselves on this issue in theo-linguistics. For practical purposes, it doesnot make so much difference: either way, the stress on scripture links the believer to the language in which the Word is articulated, whether that language be unique or not.

In this respect, European protestantism and Muslim puritanism have gone in opposed ways: the former by making the Word accessible to all, endowed vernaculars with dignity, and fixed their forms, making them more usable for political-administrative purposes and for limiting the boundaries of cultural and later political communities. This option was theologically closed to Muslims. Within Islam, Arab nationalism is somehow more natural or fundamental than other nationalisms, though other nationalisms fused with Muslim feeling do exist, especially for Muslim nations bordering on non-Muslim ones (e.g. Somalis or Malays), and hence defining their ethnicity by their faith. In any case, through its scripturalism, protestant-style religion links the believer on the one hand to the far-flung culture with which the scripture is linked, and on the other, to the national state which alone is capable of maintaining the educational infra-structure which may eventually make the recorded truth accessible to all. Non-Arab states defined in terms of Islam, such as Pakistan, do of course notoriously face a dilemma about just how their patriotism is to be defined.

I have stressed the great parallel between scripturalist-puritanism and nationalism - the aversion to local mediation (whether by brokers or by sub-communities), and its replacement by loyalty towards and identification with large anonymous communities defined (in effect) by a shared culture, shared ideas and values transmitted not merely by daily life but above all by the written, impersonal word. A nationalist is nurtured on the literature of his land, and is not dependent on the idiosyncrasies of the local market story teller or the narrative powers of his personal grandmother (though his national literature may make a fuss of just such figures and endow him with, so to speak, a normative, all-nation, paradigmatic grandmother consecrated in writing). A scripturalist puritan checks the practices of local thaumaturge against the canonical prescriptions as interpreted by publicly tested scholars ...

But though this parallel may go some way towards explaining the link between the two phenomena of puritanism and nationalism, it does not on its own explain the emergence of either. Is there any reason to suppose that a spontaneous, self-generated aversion to mediation and particularism has swept the southern shore of the Mediterranean during the past centuries, causing men to turn against mediation, to repudiate *širk*, to note the imperfections of local rituals and mediators and the narrowness of local loyalties, and to turn to a purified faith and a wider identity? The question is not purely rethorical. Islam does in fact possess an in-built potential for such self-purification and regeneration, which has manifested itself from time to time, long before the operation of those modern factors which we are tempted to invoke in explaining the massive recent changes. For instance, there is no reason to suppose that the Wahabis in the 18th century, or Osman dan Fodio early in the 19th century, were impelled to their enthusiasm by an anticipatory reaction to the emerging world of Adam Smith and Karl Marx. They knew nothing of this emerging world; but the ever-ready potential of Islam to self-purification providentially made them ready and well prepared, when the shock-waves from that world eventually reached them.

Nevertheless, though such a 'spontaneous' or endogenous interpretation of the current turmoil of the Arab and Muslim worlds is not absurd and not excluded (and the fact that Islam has this ever-ready potential for purificationary, revivalist movements clearly is important and relevant), I do not think it will constitute a sufficient explanation for the great changes which concern us. For one thing, they do not altogether reproduce the old pattern. This is no longer merely an alliance between urban scholars, chasting a self-indulgent court which also over-taxes its subjects, with tribesmen from beyond the pale eager for access to urban sin in the name of extirpating it. The pattern is now more complex, and happens on a larger scale, and in a different social context.

From the inside, in terms of the message of the Reformers, the movement is indeed presented as spontaneous, as caused and justified by nothing else other than the manifest justice of its case. As we have stressed, in as far as this potentiality is ever-present in Islam and has manifested itself within from its inception - in fact the very emergence of Islam can be presented as the first instance of such renovation and self-purification - this view has an element of plausibility. But, as Edward Gibbon pointed out in connection with the rise of Christianity, the truth of a message is not always a sufficient explanation of its success:

> "Our curiosity is naturally prompted to inquire by what means the Christian faith obtained so remarkable a victory ... To this inquiry an obvious but satisfactory answer may be returned; that it was owing to the convincing evidence of the doctrine itself, and to the ruling providence of its great Author. But as truth and reason seldom find so favourable a reception in the world, and as the wisdom of Providence frequently condescends to use the passions of the human heart, and the general circumstances of mankind, as instruments to execute its purpose, we may still be permitted, though with becoming submission, to ask, not indeed what were the first, but what were the secondary causes ..." (*Decline and Fall of the Roman Empire, Ch. XV.*).

So, invoking Gibbon's precedent, we must also look for the subsidiary social factors. (Within Christianity, sociological explanation has long ceased to scandalise the theologians. Quite the reverse. They throw themselves at it with avid enthusiasm and practice it with eagerness, indulging, tacitly and often overtly, in a kind of auto-functionalism: functionality is intimately linked to truth, it appears, and the faith is functional in the life of the community, ergo the faith is true, and the question of its falsity does not even arise. Durkheim can hardly be exonerated from providing them with a rationale for all this, though there are plenty of others. The Muslims have not yet reached this stage, which might be a simple matter of time-lag, but could also constitute, as I suspect, one further piece of evidence for the unusual seriousness with which Islam is upheld in the modern world.)

The search for this social basis of the Muslim revival of course brings us to the third great force or process at present operative in this world: industrialisation or modernisation. The introduction of the new and very powerful productive, military and administrative technology has a number of consequences, amongst which the one most relevant for our purposes is the erosion of the small sub-communities which were *the* essential cells of social life in the traditional situation. The mediators with God were then in effect mediators between men and between human groups. Mediators are now out of fashion, because the stable local groups, between which they used to mediate, are being rapidly eroded. They are eroded in a number of ways, of which the most important is a great increase in the complexity of the division of labour (which is an immediate consequence in the use of the new technology), and the greatly enhanced power of the central state. The typical social structure of the traditional rural Muslim community was as follows: the majority of the rural population were ordinary tribesmen, i.e. participants in those local mutual-help and insurance associations known as tribes and clans, which, by threatening to enter into a state of feud with the community of any man who commits aggression against one of their own members, in great measure deterred such aggression, and thus provided their own membership with security; and which generally subscribed to an ethos which spurned the specialists and held up the unspecialised tribesman as the norm of humanity. Religious, political and economic specialists formed a minority, and were either above or below normal humanity. Even when they were above (the hereditary religious nobility), and thus entitled to formal respect and reverence, they were viewed with a touch of ambivalence and irony. If they were below (artisans/craftsmen, often Jewish or negroid), they were viewed with open and vigorous contempt. The characteristic religious life of such communities were conspicuously Durkheimian: the sacred, incarnated in holy lineages and in associated shrines, was fairly clearly distinct from the profane, and provided the profane with its punctuation in space, time and society. It marked, by its sheer presence by festivals, the boundaries of groups, the separation of seasons and seasonal activities, the identity and continuity of human associations.

But the new emerging socio-economic order impels men into a wide new diversity of occupations. Even the urban craftsmen, who had already been specialised, now pass through a standardising educational system, rather than a specific apprenticeship.

Occupational diversity and mobility, geographic mobility - *that* is the new order. At the same time, the newly powerful state completes the erosion of those local mutual-help associations called tribes or 'houses'; for the modern state, unlike its predecessor, is mindful of Max Weber's definition of the state, and jealously enforces and maintains its monopoly of legitimate violence. Private vengeance, communal military self-help, are out. A few untypical cases apart, where a kind of counter-eddy of modern trends has actually weakened the state (Lebanon, North Yemen), the power of the state has increased, is increasing, and will not be diminished.

But where does this leave the old forms of the sacred? Hanging suspended in thin air. They had once ratified and sustained and oiled social forms which have disappeared or are disappearing. So their function vanishes, only their personnel, and their doctrinal rationale, remains ... That doctrinal base is generally speaking feeble. In the days when they performed a valuable and essential function, this hardly mattered. Now that they are losing a large part of that function, they can easily be presented as pious, or rather impious, frauds. This is precisely the matter in which the Reformed message presents them.

The appeal of the new message, however, is not exhausted by the fact that it replaces the old in a more impersonal mass society, that it is better adapted to a more urbanised, increasingly literate, centralised and specialised society. It has a number of further important and attractive features. It is genuinely rooted in the historic past of the entire Muslim community. It is not imported from abroad. By the acknowledged highest norms of the local religious tradition (previously honoured more in the breech than in the observance, but honoured all the same), it is authentic. So, whilst extremely well adapted to the new order, it is at the same time well adapted to affirm the generic identity of the Muslims as against others, conquerors, settlers, intruders, outsiders. So progress, self-transformation and self-discipline can be presented, not as whoring after alien models, but as the affirmation of the truest and oldest local tradition, which had but temporarily been eclipsed by social decline or by the machination and aggression of enemies. The importance of this for societies which have endured collective humiliation during the colonial period is obvious. The painful option between westernisation and populism, between denial of own identity in order to gain equality of strength, or affirmation of local roots at the cost of continuing weakness, is thereby avoided. Reformed Islam is simultaneously a scourge of local weakness *and* an affirmation of the local identity.

And there are further advantages still. The new style enables the recently urbanised rustics simultaneously to disavow their rural past, of which they are openly ashamed, and to express their resentment of their opulent and questionably orthodox rulers, whom they secretly envy. Thus, one and the same style, serves simultaneously to define a new emergent Muslim nationality against the foreigner, to provide a charter for a self-disciplining and a disavowal of past weakness, for the elevation of rustics into townsmen, and for a critical stance towards the rulers, one which the latter cannot easily disregard ... So is there a mystery about the social bases of the puritanical, scripturalist Reformism which has swept Islam? The European Reformation preceded modernity and is said to have engendered it. It came from the religious periphery rather than the centre, it was more badly needed (in a faith more given, in its central form, to *širk*, to mediation and social involvement, than Islam), and it fragmented Christendom. The Islamic Reformation came later, was perhaps needed less badly in a faith already ever-inclined to reform, and it came from the centre of the religious establishment, though under the impact of extraneous forces; and it seems to have unified rather than fragmented the community of the faithful. It was also a precursor of nationalism, put closer to it in time, and sometimes indistinguishable from it.

That, as I see it, is the overall plot of the modern cultural and religious history of Islam and hence of the southern shore of the Mediterranean. Whether or not it is a correct account is for others, or perhaps for later history, to decide. But I cannot see the fascinating set of papers here assembled other than in relation to this general scheme, and so - very tentatively - I use this scheme as one way of linking these papers together in a continuous argument. Some papers exemplify it, some augment it, some contradict it and lead one to question and reconsider it. These tensions augment rather than diminish the interest of these juxtaposed arguments and material.

The papers fall into several groups, partly overlapping, and approximating to a kind of continuous argument - though of course individual contributors must not be assumed to be in agreement either with the background picture offered in this Introduction, or with each other. Initially, there is a set of fairly pure theoretical papers - Kielstra, Waardenburg, Turner - considering Islam globally against the background of history, the current world situation, or sociological theory. Abun Nasr and Hanafi, though still general, are slightly more specific, considering the historical roots of Reformism in one case, and the political deployment of Islam in a specific region, on the other. There follows a series of case studies - Marx, Pascan, Brown and Platt - describing either a traditional situation, or its transformation by the current wave of Reform, where all in all, seems to me to fit the argument I have outlined. (Though Platt's paper contains an interesting challenge to the view that the traditional self-renovating puritanism of Islam can be seen as continuous with the present wave of fused social radicalism and Islamic fundamentalism.) The next three papers present material which is more problematic. Gilsenan deals with a case of surviving Sufism which went against the current during the Nasserite period and which the present political authorities are unlikely to recruit for their present policies, notwithstanding nominal affinities. Van Binsbergen's material seems drawn from a region where rural society uses the old Little Tradition as a protest against the power elite, rather than, as seems to me far more common, learning and acquiring the erstwhile Great Tradition as an idiom of protest against a religiously lax elite. Popovic presents a study of the fascinating case of minority Islam which can not identify with nationalism (this having been preemted by another faith), and within which consequently the old particularist forms of faith maintain themselves more firmly. Their more orthodox Muslim rivals cannot accuse them of being anti-national, for Islam as a whole is already out of the running, in Yugoslavia, as a national creed. If the Balkans present an interesting instance of the separation of Islam from nationalism, then finally the Lebanon, in the papers by Wessels and by Sluglett & Sluglett, presents us with another controlled experiment: What happens if the state has become weaker rather than stronger? - And when it is linked to a sectarian community rather than a global one?

These papers were of course written before the beginning of the latest series of tragic developments in the Lebanon, but they do provide the background for that tragedy.

The material is rich, varied and well presented. If it does not definitively answer the questions which have been raised - nothing will presumably ever do that - it makes possible a clearer formulation of the issues, and it advances our comprehension of them.

Law and Reality in Modern Islam

Niko Kielstra

Since I have not done recent extensive fieldwork in the Middle East, I shall try to present a more general comparative paper. My point of departure is the fundamentalist revival in Islam, which has become evident during the last ten years. A number of national cases of this revival have been analysed in more detail in some of the other papers presented at this conference. Though a limitation to the "Mediterranean Area" makes little sense in terms of Islamic studies, I shall comply to the framework of this conference by leaving developments in Indonesia and Pakistan out of consideration. I have felt free, however, to include the Iranian case, which is the most spectacular recent example of the developments studied here, and concerns the Muslim country I know best. During the preparation of this paper I became acquainted with Jansen's recent book "Militant Islam" (1979), which presents a useful summary of factual information as well as an instructive example of the kind of analysis that has so far been applied to the phenomenon and the shortcomings of that analysis.

What has to be explained is not that traditional religious beliefs and practices have survived, nor that politicians try to justify their policies in terms of current religious norms. It is the fact that Islam is the only one of the major world religions which is experiencing a revival that could be called "fundamentalist". By the term "fundamentalism" I mean an approach to religion in which the prescriptions of its Holy Scriptures are taken literally and not just in a symbolic sense or as historical examples of more abstract moral or ritual concepts which are not necessarily to be applied under the present, rather different historical conditions. Western orientalists, even recent critical ones, have normally followed the example of Muslim apologists in supposing that the continuation of Islamic beliefs is a self-evident fact that needs no further explanation. (Such a culturalist view is not unknown amongst anthropologists either.) If we compare Islam with the other major world religions, however, such a continuity of fundamentalist beliefs is not self-evident at all. Fundamentalist groups within Christianity are mainly fighting rearguard actions, gradually losing their grip on the younger generations. "Radical Christianity" exists, (I do not intend to discuss here if that is a rearguard action, too, or if it has a future as a movement) but its theological tenets are diametrically opposed to fundamentalism. It intends, on the contrary, to reform Christian religion into a set of abstract moral norms. These moral norms can be applied to a large variety of social and historical events, but any specific application of them can only serve as a historical example and not as a fixed rule of conduct. Another characteristic aspect of "radical Christianity" is its tendency to a "secularization of ritual". Such few rituals as survive are no longer seen as meeting points between man and the supernatural but only as a confirmation of the unity and solidarity of the human cult-group itself.

Such tendencies are not limited to Christianity. In Judaism too the fundamentalist orthodoxy is on the defensive. It is noteworthy that, whereas Islam has played an important role in the nationalist movements in Muslim countries, the link between Jewish nationalism (Zionism) and orthodox Judaism is much more ambiguous. The Zionist movement has included both orthodox, liberals, sceptics and outright atheists, while some of the most extremely orthodox groups have kept aloof from it, considering that only the Messiah could reestablish the State of Israel and that any human attempts to constitute a Jewish state are irrelevant from a religious point of view.

In Hinduism and Buddhism it is much more difficult to speak of "fundamentalism", since their fundamental credo on which the various sects and cult-groups might agree is much more vaguely delineated. Even here, however, such recent developments as are taking place seem to go into the direction of a "minimum definition of religion" which shows a formal resemblance to similar "minimum definitions" in Christianity and Judaism. The characteristics of such a "minimum definition of religion" may be defined as follows:

1) There is an other-worldly reality, but little if anything can be known about its structure and attributes.

2) In prayer (and/or sacrifice) man can interrelate with this other-worldly reality, but the effect of such an interrelation is on a psychological and not on a supernatural level.

3) Such group rituals as persist accentuate the unity and solidarity of the group of believers and not the symbolic representation of other-worldly realities or any kind of supernatural efficiency.

Below such a minimum level the notion of religion disappears, when either the existence of an other-worldly reality or the possibility of human contact with that reality are denied, or it fades away into a purely private philosophy when there is no longer a community of believers. A religion stripped down to this minimum level may, however, have the best chances of surviving in a social and historical environment (modern urban life) where, as Mary Douglas has argued (1973), the fluidity of social groupings stimulates anti-ritualism, and where an intellectual context of technical rationality weakens interest in the "mythological" aspects of reality. With the term "mythology" I mean here: stories about events (as opposed to the formulation of norms and concepts) in which essential aspects of religious belief are symbolized, and which are claimed to be real (contrary to mere parables), but the historicity of which cannot be proven.

Islam, even in its traditionalist forms, is much closer to such a "minimum definition of religion" than any other of the world's major religions. The historicity of its Prophet and the major outlines of his biography are not subject to any historical doubt. A good deal of pious legend has been woven about Muhammad's life, but none of this is essential from a religious point of view (contrary to the importance of Christ's life history in Christianity). The definitive text of the Coran was established within twelve years after the Prophet's death from the (partly written) accounts of eye-witnesses. So there is much less doubt about the exact rendering of Muhammad's revelations than about the authenticity of Christ's words reported in the Bible. (From the point of view of textual criticism the Bible is much more comparable to the Hadith than to the Coran.) The Coran refers to a mythological background that is supposed to be known to the reader, including the main stories from the Bible, some stories about Arab prophets, the existence of non-human and non-divine categories of beings like *jinn* and angels, etc. From the point of view of the everyday believer, however, most of this may be treated as parables, the more so since he is not bound to any literal text for this background knowledge to the Coran. As long as the existence of an older monotheist tradition is recognized, historical detail is not particularly important.

Everyday ritual is limited to standardized individual prayers. The text of these prayers is simple without elaborate symbolism. They are supposed to be a sign of the submission of the believer to God, and are not supposed to have any other kind of efficacy. (For mystics prayer may mean much more than that, but one can be a perfectly faithful Muslim without any tendency to mysticism.) Prayers may be said collectively, but then they just express the community of believers and nothing more. The *Hajj* contains a much more elaborate ritual, but little effort has been made to dress this in elaborate symbolism; it is just a traditional way of carrying out the Pilgrimage, linking the participants with the Muslim past and little more than that.

Islam therefore contains a minimum of mythology, ritual and archaic symbolism. Theological speculation about the nature of the Divine is positively discouraged. Since the religious calendar follows the lunar year, religious celebrations have not become linked up with an agricultural year-cycle which means little to modern city dwellers. (Such agricultural ritual as survives in the Muslim world is tolerated by but not linked to Islam, and can thus be dropped without influencing more general religious beliefs.)

I think that factors such as these may help to explain why Islam has "kept" so much better than Christianity under the desintegration of traditional community structures and cultural patterns brought about by modern developments. Even in its traditional orthodox form it was much closer to the "minimum definition of religion" still palatable for the modern urban dweller than Christianity. Islamic rural folk religion has contained other elements, but these were at best tolerated by orthodox opinion, which had no objection whatsoever to the dropping of such additional beliefs and practices. In Christianity (and Judaism), on the contrary, some modern currents tend to go in the direction of a similar "minimum definition of religion", but they have to do so in a constant struggle with orthodox opinion, which considers the additional elements of traditional religion essential to the faith.

Such considerations may help to explain why we find much less outright religious unbelief or scepticism in even the most modernized and westernized sections of Muslim societies than in similar sections of Christian societies. They do not yet explain why modern Islam is developing in a fundamentalistic, legalistic direction while modernist tendencies in other world religions are developing just the other way. This problem can be split down into two sub-questions. In the first place: which are the social and political conditions that have made militant Islam into a major political force in some but not all Muslim countries? In the second place: why is it that no organized *liberal* reform movement has developed in Islam under any recent historical conditions? I define religious liberalism here as the tendency to translate traditional religiously based specific rules of conduct into much more general and abstract ethical concepts which may be applied in various ways according to the historical context. (Bahai-ism might have become just such a liberal reform movement, but it was most violently rejected by a Muslim community that had so far been relatively tolerant of sects, and subsequently it developed into a completely separate religion. It is, however, the only other religion that has made any appreciable number of converts amongst Muslims.)

Of course Islam has already since its earliest origins tended to prescribe ideal rules of conduct for a much wider range of everyday activities than Christianity (but not Judaism). We should not over-dramatize this difference, however. The substantial rules given by the *sharīʿa* are general enough to allow for a certain range of adaptation to changing social and historical conditions. Christian communities, on the other hand, have often developed "traditions" which are much more specific and detailed than anything written in the Bible itself, and such "traditions" have often been granted great moral authority, and have been defended with great tenacity. Islam has not, like Christianity, made a distinction between the religious and the political realm, but medieval popes have also claimed a political role as moral supervisors of the political rulers of their time. So we cannot reduce the different developments in Islam and Christianity to some original theological difference. "Absolutist" tendencies have existed in both religions, but they are dwindling away in Christianity and remain strong in Islam.

The role of Islam as an ideological counterweight to colonial or imperialist domination has often been accentuated as one explanation for its continuing vitality. Such anti-imperialist sentiments certainly inspired the reformers of the Salafīya-movement, whom the modern fundamentalists consider as their forerunners. These reformers (Afghānī, Abduh, Rida) were indeed not liberals. They claimed the right to develop new interpretations of the rules of the *sharīʿa*, more adapted to modern conditions, but they did not advocate the reduction of substantial rules to abstract ethical principles. In its own time, however, the Salafīya was not the predominant political movement in the Middle East. The cultural revival movement in the second half of the nineteenth century, known as *nahḍa*, and the various nationalist parties that became active after the First World War were not anti-religious, but they were looking forward toward a much more secularized type of society and culture than the Salafīya, and it were their opinions that were translated into the modernizing legislation of the period.

The mid-nineteenth century Turkish *Tanzimat*-reforms set the example. They limited the legal application of the *sharīʿa* to the field of personal status, where it was still generally accepted and used, and introduced secular, western inspired legislation in all other fields. The Iranian constitution of 1906 did the same, in spite of the fact that religious leaders had played an important role in the Constitutional Revolution. It did in fact provide for a committee of religious leaders, who should check if proposed legislation was not contrary to the *sharīʿa*, but even in the relatively rare periods in modern Iranian history when the constitution was taken seriously, this provision remained a dead letter. The constitutions of the various Arab countries that regained their independence since then have followed the same line. Only Atatürk in Turkey tried to go a step further and to abolish all religious elements in legislation, but his western type personal status legislation was quietly ignored by the majority of the Turkish population.

The progressive movements in various Arab countries in the nineteen fifties and sixties, known somewhat vaguely as Arab socialism, were the last example of this tendency. These movements, which took a somewhat different character in the various countries, tried to combine the solidarist economic policies of western social democrats with a much more authoritarian political system. They took great pains to argue that the socio-economic reforms they propagated were compatible with Islam and in fact reflected the original purity of early Islam, but the type of state they tried to establish was largely secular. (Colonel Ghadafi's regime in Libya does not belong to this tendency, but constitutes the first, somewhat atypical, example of the subsequent fundamentalist revival.)

What all these movements, from the *nahḍa* to Arab socialism, had in common, was that they were reform movements from above. During the period of active nationalist struggle they might mobilize large parts of the population, but leadership remained in the hands of a small westernized elite. Within this elite the relative importance of established aristocracies and of modern technocrats of more modest origins varied between countries, or between periods in the history of the same country, but the narrow social basis of these regimes remained much the same.

In many countries there was a rival elite, a more traditionalist and religiously more orthodox bourgeoisie. From a social-economic point of view this bourgeoisie represented an upper-middle class of well-to-do but relatively small bazar merchants and middle-size rural landowners. Religious professionals had traditionally often been recruited from these groups, or, if religious office ran in families, such religious families often belonged to this middle group in terms of wealth and education. In their style of life and religious convictions this traditional bourgeoisie was much closer to the mass of peasants and urban workers and to the fairly numerous lower-middle class of small shopkeepers and craftsmen than the ruling westernized elite. (Western style working class radicalism was limited to small groups of highly skilled industrial workers.)

In the political arena this traditional middle bourgeoisie was at a disadvantage. It had no control over the army, which was often the decisive factor in domestic political struggles, nor did it have the international connections from which support might be obtained for a long drawn-out liberation struggle. Socio-economic reforms (nationalisations, land reform, price controls, etc.) hit this group hardest, since it had neither the material means and the legal sophistication to organize its economic activities in more modern forms (which might escape the negative effect of the reforms) nor the political influence that might enable one to flout the law. So they often carried the burden of reforms with which the ruling elite might attempt to pacify popular discontent.

Political alliances began to change when it became evident that reforms by the ruling elite were definitely falling short of popular expectations. In countries like Turkey and Egypt economic development policy evidently failed. (The question if any other regime could have done much better, given the social and economic structure of these countries and the international context, is not relevant here.) In Libya a corrupt and inefficient monarchy could not satisfy the expectations raised by a sudden and unexpected access to oil wealth. In Iran there was in fact a quite rapid economic development, but in such a way that it increased the already large social inequalities. The ignomonous military defeat by the Israelis in 1967 shocked political confidence in the institutions of the state in the Arab countries concerned. Similar developments can be traced in Indonesia and Pakistan, which fall outside the context of this conference, however.

Under such conditions an oppositional coalition between the disgruntled traditional middle bourgeoisie and part of the proletariat becomes possible if such groups can find a common program. Protest against the religious laxity of the ruling elite constitutes such a program. Such a phenomenon has also been known during the First Industrial Revolution in the West. In the various non-conformist or dissenting groups that split off from the Church of England, or in the various nineteenth century split-offs of radical Calvinists from the official Dutch Reformed Church we also find elements of class antagonism expressed in terms of protest against the religious laxity of the ruling elite. Such a development was possible in a social context where orthodox religious faith was still alive and vigorous in large sections of the lower classes of the population, while some middle groups shared this faith and were willing to use it to recruit a political following. When large parts of all classes of the population lost their religious faith altogether and others turned to increasingly liberal interpretations of it, things began to change. Surviving Christian Democratic political formations in Europe have essentially become centre parties in which the religious element has become relatively minor, and the legal reinforcement of fundamentalist tenets has become a smaller and smaller part of their program.

Similar political-religious movements in modern Muslim countries can still appeal to the same kind of religious fervour as their seventeenth to nineteenth century Christian counterparts. (One has to go back to Cromwell to find the kind of revolutionary rhetoric used by Khomeyni.) I have already argued in the first part of this paper that Islam as a religion with a minimum of ritual and mythology may better be able than Christianity to resist the two main sources of unbelief in a modern social context: intellectual scepticism and urban working class insensibility to the archaic symbolism of an agricultural society. Jansen (1979) mentions a third recent threat to Islamic culture from the side of what he calls "the international youth culture". This youth culture is not inherently anti-religious, but it includes as an essential part a degree of free social intercourse and sexual experimentation between boys and girls which is absolutely incompatible with either the Islamic cultural tradition or the literal text of the Coran. This western youth culture has influenced students and some modern educated young workers in Muslim countries, but even within those groups it does not seem to lead towards any disaffection from Islam. It is in fact so incompatible with both the Islamic ideology and the actual social reality that it becomes something quite different and much less menacing for the Islamic tradition.

You cannot have a pop-culture without girls, and the number of girls who are allowed to mix freely with boys, let alone to run wild, in Muslim countries remains limited to an extremely small number from westernized upper class families who have become completely alienated from the culture of their own country. Outside this narrow social circle there is nothing to start with. In western societies, but also in some non-Muslim African and Asian societies there existed generally accepted patterns of dating and courtship, which may gradually be extended till they finally include an almost completely free and unsupervised pattern of intercourse between the sexes, but in Muslim societies there is no such generally accepted starting point. Formal or informal associations of young men, however, are nothing new or shocking in the Muslim world. A certain degree of sexual frustration, and the kind of sexist reactions to which such frustration leads, have probably always characterized such groups, but such frustration is maximized in the framework of a modern urban consumer society, in which such young men surround themselves with all the material attributes and symbols of a sexually much more permissive society. Such frustrations are easily mobilized not against the moral restrictions that caused them but against the cultural influences that made people conscious of them, i.e. against the west and against attempts to westernize the style of life of Muslim societies. Iranian revolutionary propaganda and rhetoric have paid much more attention to the libertarian sexual mores in court circles (of which ex-empress Farah Diba was rightly or wrongly made a symbol) than to the repressiveness, cruelty and corruption of the Shah-regime, and Khomeyni characterizes westernized intellectuals as "individuals who want to look at naked women".

The influence of western permissive youth culture may in fact have delayed a weakening of the traditional social segregation between the sexes in Muslim societies, and may have made it possible that at least part of the educated young people with left-wing sympathies in those societies became participants in or sympathizers with Muslim fundamentalist movements. It has charged any possible cultural alternatives with such a symbolic load of sexual phantasies, which are far from general reality even in the West, that they have become both practically unattainable and psychologically unsupportable. Even some girl students, often educated in a moderately westernized style of life, are now turning back to Muslim fundamentalism, which at least can offer them an established and socially accepted social role instead of saddling them with all the symbols and paraphernalia of sexual permissiveness in which they are not allowed to indulge anyhow.

Orthodox religious leaders seem to be conscious of the fact that they have to establish a rigid degree of sexual repression to maintain their influence over the modernized section of the young generation. The traditional and religiously sanctioned punishments for sexual misdemeanours: the public flogging of fornicators and homosexuals and stoning (or at least public execution) of adulterers, had in fact long been abolished everywhere outside the Arabian Peninsula, and prostitution and homosexual practices were silently tolerated as outlets. Now such tolerance has been abolished and the "canonical" punishments have been reestablished in those countries where an "Islamic" regime has been established, and similar measures are demanded by the fundamentalist movements elsewhere.

The major problem for all politico-religious movements, however, is how to come to terms with the harsh realities of politics. Moral exhortations are very fine, and the punishment of moral wrongdoers may even become a popular form of public entertainment, but they cannot become a permanent substitue for material prosperity and administrative efficiency. Some kind of Muslim socio-economic doctrine exists. It prescribes some kind of moralized market economy, in which speculation and usury are abolished, and the obligatory redistribution of specified parts of all types of income for public charity and for institutions of public interest. When it comes to applying this doctrine to the management of a modern national economic system the doctrine is rather vague and general, however. Many different interpretations are possible, and it remains to be seen if and how any of these possible interpretations could work in practice.

The fact that Islam does not admit the separation of politics and religion, and that it does at the same time not recognize any form of institutionalized "church" organization, may have constituted another safeguard against the danger of secularization. If *'ulama* took sides in politics, or if politicians claimed to act on religious principles, they were rarely all on the same side in actual controversies. So people could not get the idea that religion had no relevance for the problems of everyday life, neither could they become disappointed in religion as such because of disappointment in a political movement. (The Christian churches destroyed religious belief in large parts of their former working class adherents by their institutionalized association with conservative politics.) If, as in Iran at present, the whole of the Muslim religious establishment becomes associated with one political movement, the not unprobable failure of that movement to solve the practical political problems of the moment may reflect negatively on the public image of Islam as such. The direct claim to political leadership of the Iranian *ayatollahs* is probably a unique *Shīʿa* phenomenon. The effect may be the same, however, when secular dictators try to establish an "Islamic State" (Libya, Pakistan) or when Islamic fundamentalists tend to become allies of a conservative secular government (Turkey, Egypt, maybe Tunisia). In very wealthy countries (Saudi Arabia, the Union of Emirates, Kuwait, Libya) the existing government may, at least for a while, be able to buy off large scale social discontent, and in that case its association with the existing regime may not harm Islam as such. In countries that are poor in natural resources (Turkey, Egypt, Tunisia) or where natural resources, though fairly abundant, are relatively small in relation to the number of the population (Iran), the establishment of an "Islamic regime" or the association of Islamic orthodoxy with a formally secular regime may satisfy popular frustrations in the short run, but it may lead to similar phenomena of working class disappointment in and disaffection from organized religion as in the West since the Industrial Revolution. In some other countries (Syria, Iraq) Islamic fundamentalism exists while political rivalry between religious groups makes any development toward an "Islamic State" unfeasable. In such cases Islam may become an outlet for all kinds of popular discontent, and while in that way it may remain a living force, its more intolerant and narrow-minded aspects may tend to become prominent. A stable, moderately progressive, secular regime, as in Algeria, which respects the Islamic tradition, but develops its own political program and ideology, may in fact offer the most favourable environment for the adaptation of Islam to the modern world.

It remains to say something about my second question: why has no liberal reform movement so far developed in Islam under any set of conditions? In the other world religions religious liberalism is the attribute of relatively well-to-do groups with a fairly high level of education, of people who possess and use well articulated, secular models of their natural and social environment. For such people religious faith, if they retain any, tends to become reduced to a general ethical code and a feeling of identification with a traditional institution and (sometimes) a personalized moral example. There remains a step to be taken, however, from privately acknowledging such a view of religion to publicly propagating it. In the Christian

West private religious liberalism is at least as old as the Renaissance, probably older, but it only became an explicit and organized religious movement in the nineteenth and twentieth century. By that time the rather elitarian groups who held such views no longer risked to isolate themselves socially and politically, because orthodox religion was also losing its grip on part of the lower sectors of the population for quite different reasons: insensibility to archaic agrarian symbolism, resentment of the association between the orthodox church and socially conservative politics. Such was, at least, the case for Christianity and Judaism. In Hinduism and Buddhism the traditional orthodoxy had never spread to the rank and file of the population, which had continued to mix the religious "great tradition" with all kind of folk beliefs of miscellaneous origins. The propagation of liberal views of religion was there not so much a response to a decline of popular religious faith as to a split and subsequent rivalry between a traditional elite and a modern, western educated technocratic elite.

In the Muslim world we still find a mixture of the religious "great tradition" with folk beliefs of non-Islamic origin amongst some of the most isolated rural groups like some of the nomadic tribes. The politically most relevant groups of the population, however, the urban masses and the more well-to-do peasants, have turned to orthodox forms of belief. If they still hold some beliefs of non-Islamic origin, they will never acknowledge them as such. Religious orthodoxy has become a status symbol, as it was for the "respectable" working class people of the European past. Amongst the modern educated, technocratic elites of Muslim countries, one meets quite a few people who hold fairly liberal views of their religion. The public propagation of such views, however, would alienate them from the masses whose political support or at least whose abstention from active opposition are essential for the long-term stability of any political regime.

Kemal Pasha, cashing in on his immense prestige as leader of the struggle for national independence, tried to secularize Turkish society, but his success was only skin-deep. After his death his successors were gradually losing popular support, until they found themselves obliged to reverse their policies and to establish an alliance with Islamic fundamentalists to assure their political survival. Part of the Iranian elite under the Shah, overestimating the strength and stability of the regime, went in for a display of religious liberalism and thereby provided their political opponents with an effective argument to mobilize the masses against them.

The relative simplicity of the scriptural core of Islam (in comparison with, for example, Hinduism or Buddhism) and the fact that Islam has, through its system of obligatory charity and unalienable religious foundation, provided for a certain minimum of popular religious education, have led to a fairly orthodox set of beliefs amongst all but the most isolated and politically powerless groups of the population. Its lack of archaic ritual and symbolism, and the fact that Islam as such has never become too closely associated with any specific political regime, have so far prevented working class disaffiliation from organized religion. The rationality of Islam has so far prevented that intellectual scepticism led to large scale unbelief amongst the elite, but tendencies to a liberal interpretation of religion exist in that elite. In face of the orthodoxy of the masses it would be politically inconvenient and even unwise to demonstrate such religious liberalism too openly.

In such a situation middle class groups, who see their social, political and economic position decline in comparison with the western educated technocratic elite, can try to mobilize large masses of the urban (and sometimes also rural) population against that elite in the name of religion. The attraction of a modern western permissive style of life is diminished by the fact that it has become associated with a corrupt and oppressive national elite. On the other hand, the abyss between the reality of life in a present-day Muslim society and the permissive (especially sexually permissive) western style of life, reflected through the mass media and other consumer goods, has become so large and frustrating that even some young members of the western educated elite reaffirm their adherence to Islamic fundamentalism, which outlaws the sources of such temptations and frustrations.

This combination of factors has led to an Islamic fundamentalist revival that has become politically dominant in Iran, Pakistan, and Libya, while it has become a political power factor that can no longer be ignored in several other Muslim countries. The fact that Islam is now for the first time (in modern times at least) becoming directly associated with political regimes that show little prospect of solving the major socio-economic problems of their countries may, in the long run, when the popular expectations raised by these regimes becomes definitively disappointed, lead to a first wave of working class disaffiliation from organized religion in the Muslim world.

REFERENCES

Douglas, M.
1973 *Natural Symbols*, Harmondsworth:Pelican Books.

Jansen, G.H.
1979 *Militant Islam*, London:Pan Books.

Islam as a Vehicle of Protest

Jacques Waardenburg

A great number of studies have been concerned with Islam as a religion or as a normative social pattern in Muslim societies, and in particular with the way in which Islam can be used to legitimize a given situation or a given socio-political order. During the last ten years the current resurgence of Islam has attracted widespread attention to present-day Islamic movements of revival and reform and their social basis and political connections. The focus of interest here has been the way in which Islam can be instrumental in changing a given situation or overthrowing a given socio-political order, that is to say the critical use or function of Islam.

In this connection it is rewarding to look at the different ways in which an appeal to Islam is made to protest against a given situation or against given policies within or outside a Muslim society of which Muslims risk becoming victims. Such a protest implies in the first place a negative judgment and then an unambiguous rejection which may lead to militant action, resistance against a powerful enemy or an open struggle against what has been judged as wrong and rejected accordingly. Such a struggle may be solely of an ideological nature but it can also take on political and even military dimensions depending on the kind of danger perceived and the resources available for defense. In colonial times and afterwards too, the protest function of Islam was often played down on the grounds that it was potentially subversive or disturbing, which is an easy interpretation on the part of those who at a given moment speak of Islam from a position of power.

For an analysis of societies, however, the protest function of Islam, like that of other religions, is a valid theme of research. The case of Islam is all the more interesting since the very foundation of Islam as a historical religion, differing in this respect from Judaism and Christianity, had a marked reform and protest character (Waardenburg 1981), and since elements of protest go to make up so many currents in present-day Islam. Even conversions to Islam may reveal aspects of protest, for instance against religious practices existing elsewhere or against the West and the way in which Christianity has a legitimizing function for western behaviour in third world countries. Protests with an appeal to Islam are mostly expressed orally or in writing but also symbolically in ways of dressing for instance, or by ritual behaviour as in certain forms of public demonstrations.

The following inquiry is of a preliminary nature and seeks to survey some currents in recent history, and in particular in the Arab world, in which Islam has clearly served as a vehicle of protest. The many forms and aspects of Islam which lack such a clear protest character are not considered here. In principle a distinction should be made between protests based on specific norms and values to which Islam as a religion refers and which are held to be absolute, and protests made on other grounds where Islam has primarily an ideological role. In practice, however, these two kinds of protest which both appeal to Islam are closely interwoven and can hardly be distinguished, much less separated. Any protest which appeals to Islam can serve as an argument within the Muslim community and should be evaluated in this light. Although to outsiders an appeal which Muslims make to Islam can hardly be conclusive, Muslims tend to make such an appeal. In the following misunderstandings the simple rule holds that what is seen from outside as a "mere protest", is seen from the inside mostly as more than protest, that is as standing for the truth or for right moral action.

It is evident that in recent times, during and after the colonial period, different kinds of protest, against non-Muslims as well as Muslims and on different levels, have made a clear appeal to Islam. We shall first distinguish various levels of such protests and then give examples of religious movements in Islam in which a clear protest character on these various levels exists. This suggests the usefulness of the notion of "protest" for further analysis of a number of movements launched in recent times in the name of Islam. Some attention will then be given to the fact that in the Arab countries at least many protest movements of different kinds have articulated their protest in Islamic terms and thus were able to mobilize the masses. Finally, some considerations will be offered on the way in which Islam in particular can function as a symbol of protest. The symbolic meaning of Islam in Muslim societies, the defensive attitudes Muslim societies have had to take over against the power of the Western and Eastern blocks in order to survive in a scientific age, and the way Islam can be instrumental in defending basic norms and values which for the Islamic faith are unconditional and must not be betrayed all play a part here.

I. Levels of Protest

In a religion such as Islam it is possible to distinguish different levels on which a protest in the name of the religion can be expressed. For practical purposes we may distinguish three main levels:

- a "functional" level of a general nature which is not specific to Islam;
- a level of what may be called "religious culture" where religious movements or sectors, which express protest according to specific Islamic norms and values, can develop;
- finally what we would like to call the "religious dimension" of protest in Islam, in so far as it is connected with the very essentials of this particular religion.

On the second level, that of religious culture, two subsidiary levels can be dinstinguished depending on whether religious protest is expressed directly, in particular by specific religious trends and movements in history, or indirectly through the development of specific "religious sectors" in Islam, like that of Law and the mystical Path, which claim to transcend history even though they may influence it. We shall review briefly these four levels on which protests which explicitly appeal to Islam can be expressed.

1). Islam, like other religions, can be used in order to mobilize the believers for aims which are not derived from religion alone, and sometimes have nothing to do with it. Islam is then used functionally to reach certain goals which are not derived immediately from Islam itself. In this way Islam and the loyalty which Muslims feel towards it can be used for many purposes, among them the expression of protest, for instance as a defense against intrusion from outside (protests for instance against imperialism), or as a protection against grave forms of injustice within the community itself (protests for instance against the trampling underfoot of what we call human rights). In the first case such a protest can lead for instance to a straight-forward call to defend Islam, as in the call to *jihād* ("holy war") against an outside enemy, and in earlier resistance movements against Western intrusion. In the second case, within the Muslim community, it can lead for instance to the development of an ideology denouncing a tyrannical regime. The aim here, self-defense or self-protection, is of a general nature and is then qualified by an appeal to Islam. In other words: Islam is here a function of vital primordial needs and aims.

2). Within Islam as a religious culture there have always been appeals, movements and trends directly protesting against religious and social beliefs and customs judged as false or wrong, that is to say contrary to true revealed religion. This protest is most noticeable in what the Koran says about unbelief, various false beliefs, and forms of behaviour judged to be against God's will. Muhammad's preaching in this sense, both to non-believers and to believers, has remained alive throughout the history of Islam. It implies not only missionary activity but also the rise of movements rejecting what are judged to be corrupt forms of Islam and seeking to restore true Islam by means of a reform of the current sad state of religion. All these movements and their ideologies share a vivid protest against corrupt forms of Islam and the desire to realize by practical means the ideal society where true Islam reigns.

3). Within Islam as a religious culture there have also been from the beginning what may be called indirect forms of protest against the social and religious situation within the Muslim community. Other ways of expressing protest often simply were not possible. This indirect protest was of a religious nature and led to the development of specific "religious" sectors in Islam, something which had been unthinkable during Muhammad's lifetime. On the one hand a sacred Law was developed, the *Sharīᶜa*, the totality of rules for behaviour both individual and social, both ethical and religious. This was the work of the *ᶜulamā'*, scholars able to deduce from the Koran, the *Sunna* (early Tradition) and other sources an ideal pattern which they identified with Islam as such but which should rather be called *normative Islam*. On the other hand, after an initial stage of withdrawal from the world, which displayed ascetic features, various forms of a mystical Path were developed, the *ṭarīqa*, that is man's inner life as he moves through life and religious experience on his way to God. The elaboration of the Path was the work of the *Sūfīs*, mystics able to experience and describe the stages through which the relationship between God and the soul developed. Here not external behaviour but the inner life of man was stressed. *ᶜUlamā'* and *Sūfīs* both insisted on the need to realize a religious way of life communally as well as individually. Both the Law and the mystical Path which developed as a result of their efforts as specific religious sectors in Islam implied and expressed a critical attitude and religious protest against the way in which Muslim society in fact developed. In the name of either normative Islam or mystical Islam protests could be launched, and have been launched, by *ᶜulamā'* or *Sūfīs* against what has been seen as the betrayal of true Islam.

4). Finally, apart from the functional use of Islam to express protest and the direct in indirect ways of expressing protests with an appeal to specific norms and values of Islam, the Islamic faith by its nature appears to contain a strong element of protest. This may be termed the religious dimension of protest in Islam or the protest structure proper to the religion. This deeply religious protest is directed against any divinization of immanence or absolutization of things perceived, and against any imprisonment of man within a purely immanent world. The created nature of the world and its immanence are contrasted with God's creating activity and uncreated nature and his transcendence. We can speak of a dialectic between the Islamic protest against *shirk* as the sin of idolatry (or absolutization of things created) on the one hand, and the stress on *islām* or abandonment of oneself to God and carrying out his will on the other. The dialectic between abandonment of oneself to God and protest against anything perceived as divinization seems to be a basic feature of Islamic religion. Although the search for harmony is present in Islam as in all religions, elements of protest which appeal to Koran and *Sunna* but arise from a deeper, religious dimension of the faith itself have acquired in it a particular significance and militancy. This may account for the fact that on this level Muslims have always been able to say a radical "no" and take a militant attitude towards other religious and ideological forms conflicting with what was held to be true Islam, in extreme cases towards anything non-Islamic (Waardenburg 1979a).

II. Three Kinds of Religious Movements in Islam with a Clear "Protest" Character

The forgoing analysis of the different levels at which Islam can serve as a vehicle of protest not only makes a theoretical point more or less valuable in itself, but can serve to improve understanding of the religious background of a number of movements in Islamic history and the present time, in particular in the Arab world. Such movements should be studied in their particular socio-political and economic setting, and internal and external causes and influences should be taken into account. Attention should also be paid to the dynamics of the cultural tradition, where religious norms and values play such an important role, not only locally but also through the constant reference to Koran and *Sunna* as the basis for the "great tradition" or "normative" Islam. Even when there is a tendency to ascribe the real causes of Islamic movements to social and economic tensions and their political consequences, the fact cannot be ignored that it is precisely Islam which is used as an instrument and symbol of criticism and protest against the course of events in the world, including the Muslim world. The fact that it is Islam which is used to express and articulate protest, resistance and struggle has particular implications and consequences.

Does it make a real difference to say that socio-economic conflicts are expressed in Islamic terms, or that Islam as a religion and ideology contains certain militant aspects and intentions? Probably both statements are true but scholars have difficulty in combining them. A number of Islamic movements during the last hundred and fifty years or so have been both an expression of defense and resistance against Western domination and a protest against moral decline and disintegration within Muslim societies themselves. Even given the fact that, in the course of the 19th and 20th centuries, it has become ever more difficult to live according to the whole of traditional-religious values or to realize Islamic norms and ideals in their entirety, and also given the fact that a number of religious aspects of the older culture have now acquired a new and more secular meaning, nevertheless Islam, which had functioned in an age of political power as a symbol of glory and harmony, succeeded in the 19th century in becoming in many respects a symbol of hope and protest. But even in earlier times there were a number of "counter movements" with an explicit or implicit character of protest, which used religious arguments besides political or social ones. I would plead for serious consideration of these religious arguments in our analysis of these movements. A complete study of protest movements and ideologies in Muslim countries should of course also consider those which are "secular" or "nationalist" in the sense that they appeal to Islam neither directly nor indirectly. These are left out of consideration here.

1. The use of Islam for self-defense against outside domination and interference

In the course of the often conflictuous history between Europe and various parts of the Muslim world, the West has been very sensitive to protest and resistance movements which appeal to Islam and oppose western interference and domination. This, together with the history of warfare between European countries on the one side and Arabs and later Turks as well as more recently colonies with a Muslim population on the other, may be the main reason why Islam in the West has been, and often still is, considered as an eminently political and anti-western religion and ideology - a view which in a historical context certainly has been true in particular regions and among particular groups.

The most important variants of these natural protest and resistance movements are probably the following:

a. Local resistance by Muslims in a particular region to government by non-Muslims

In the 19th and early 20th century this led to a number of local insurrections and resistance movements against western penetration where often an appeal was made to Islam and sometimes *jihād* was proclaimed (Peters 1979). Such movements used then religious arguments in their resistance to domination not only by western Christians or westerners in general, but also for instance by Hindus, as is clear in the movement for the foundation of Pakistan. The resistance by Muslims against Jewish domination has been particularly fierce since Zionism is seen as a form of western imperialism using elements of Judaism for its purposes (Johnson 1982). This has led to a polemical literature in which both the religious roots of Zionism and their political abuse in the current state of Israel are vehemently denounced.

b. More coordinated calls for resistance to western domination in which Islam is appealed to

The different forms of the so-called Pan-Islamic movement, initiated by Jamāl al-Dīn al-Afghānī (1838-1897) and exploited by Sultan Abdül Hamid II, where the attempt was made to unite Muslims from different countries and regions in a common resistance to the West, are a case in point (Keddie 1968, 1972). Even if most of these forms were in fact more verbal than politically organized, the movement itself gave moral support to the instinctive and natural tendency among many Muslims to see western military and political domination, together with different kinds of western influence, as enemy number one. Even if this was only the initial phase of the various national independence movements which later, for the most part, almost ceased to appeal to Islam, this form of "Islamic protest" had a direct and more lasting effect in the spheres of culture and religion.

c. Defensive attitudes against foreign influence in Muslim countries

The defensive attitudes and action against English, French, Russian, Dutch and later also American influence in Muslim countries arise not only from the external political power structure at a given moment in a particular situation, but also and primarily from what is sensed as a threat to the Muslim way of life and to Islamic culture. To the extent that Islam is experienced as an integrating factor in that way of life - either as recognized norms or as experienced values lived out - and to the extent that the outside influence is felt to be threatening, a sharp contrast is perceived as existing between the foreign culture and Islam. This reinforces the feeling of being under threat, and it is only a small step to use Islam then as a basis for protest or resistance against the foreign culture which threatens it as a cultural whole. In this resistance Islam stands as a symbol of this cultural whole.

The many movements which have been launched in Muslim societies against certain western cultural influences have often been interpreted in the West as a kind of xenophobia inherent to Islam. In fact what is involved is a defense mechanism against outside influences which threaten norms and values which are considered to be essential and for the people concerned possess a religious nature. Islam can function as a defense and protest symbol precisely because it is the people's religion and stands for their deepest identity.

d. Israel

A well-known example of the ideological use of Islam against foreign occupation of what is felt to be the Muslims' own domain, against foreign domination and a threatening ideology, occurs in the resistance shown not only by the Arab countries but by the majority of the Muslim countries to the Zionist movement and the present state of Israel. The belief that the treatment meted out to the Palestianians inside and outside Israel (Lebanon!) and in the occupied territories infringes Islamic norms and strong feelings of solidarity among Muslims play no small part in this resistance, quite apart from all other humane, social and political factors which can and do play a role generally, unconnected with any particular religion. Among Muslims an additional appeal can be made to Islamic teachings in order to mobilize them against the state of Israel.

e. Missions
Another, perhaps more striking, example of a movement of protest and resistance which explicitly appeals to Islam as a religion occurs in the reactions of Muslims to attempts to convert them at any time or place, but in particular through Christian missions. Any attempt at conversion to another religion calls forth a fervent reaction, but in the case of Muslims particularly and certainly in the Arab world this reaction is strong and the number of converts from Islam to Christianity is negligible. Apologetic literature of Islam is abundant (Dorman 1948). Especially whenever Christian missions are viewed in connection with political interest, imperialism and colonialism and when they are seen as an attack on Islam, resistance to them is at least as strong as the resistance to political Zionism with its underlying ideology. In fact there are striking parallels in Muslim reactions to Zionism, Christian missions and certain forms of orientalism.

f. Orientalism
Anything which is felt to be an attack on or denigration of Islam obviously calls forth fierce resistance in the name of Islam. This applies not only to Zionist policies and missionary tracts and activities but also to scholarly studies which through their analytical procedures undermine the norms and values, the originality and essence of Islam. The scholarly analysis by non-Muslims of religious data pertaining to Islam is often perceived as intentionally destructive, and it is linked in the minds of many Muslims to deeper intentions of a religious, ideological and political nature which are inimical and aggressive to Islam. Scholarly research for instance on possible "borrowings" by Muhammad and the Koran from sources elsewhere, and on possible "fictitious" *ḥadīths*, traditions on sayings and actions by the Prophet, often constructed in later times but attributed to Muhammad, is then seen

as a perfidious attack by western scholarship on the truth and integrity of Islam. In response to this, apologetic movements of defense and polemics of denunciation arise. The subject of orientalism is a touchy one in the relations between the West and Islam on an intellectual level, as has been demonstrated not only by Muslim authors (Said 1978).

g. Islam and development

A last form of protest in a broader sense of the term, which appeals to Islam and is directed primarily at western but also at socialist countries has to do with development. It concerns the often heard reproach that Islam as a religion is largely responsible for the stagnation in development of Muslim compared to western countries (Waardenburg 1974). In particular the accusation that Islam, in terms of modern social and economic development, is a backward religion - even obstructing real development - has called forth various defensive positions. Their most important feature is a character of sharp protest and the elaboration of arguments meant to prove that Islam as a religion is essentially valid for all stages of social and economic development. Those forms of Islam which are an impediment to development are judged to be accidental, a result of particular historical situations, and not representative of true Islam.

In certain intellectual circles it is fully acknowledged that Islam itself undergoes a historical development apart from the eternal truths contained in the Koran, and socio-political changes are studied in this light (Esposito 1980). Other movements insist that, over against western social and economic development models leading to communism and capitalism, a specific Islamic notion of development distinct from - and in protest against - theories of development constructed in western and socialist countries should be elaborated. "Islamic" economics expresses then a protest against the weaknesses of other kinds of economics, just as an "Islamic" socialism, an "Islamic" nationalism or an "Islamic" revolution ought - ideally at least - to be free from the defects of any other kind of socialism, nationalism or revolution.

2. Direct forms of religious protest within Islam; the reform movements

It is noteworthy that throughout Islamic history there have been movements characterized more or less clearly by a religious protest against the course which that history was taking. Such "counter movements" identify this course as decline due to moral and religious laxity. The arguments they use are in the first place religious, mostly derived from Koran and *Sunna* and they favour the consequent application of the most important prescriptions contained in them. It is useful to make here a basic distinction between these movements according to whether they exhibit a direct or an indirect protest character leading to idealization. The former show the following main variants (Gibb 1947; Smith 1957; Işik 1974[2]).

a. Sunni traditionalists and revivalists
Ever since the first generation after Muhammad's death there have been movements of faithful Muslims observing Koran and *Sunna* and protesting on religious grounds against the political development of the community as it in fact took place under the caliphs: the Rashidūn caliphs in Medina, the Umayyads in Damascus and the Abbasids in Baghdad. By reference to Koran and *Sunna* it could be shown that government was not being conducted according to God's will, and sermons were a particularly suitable vehicle for this. Sometimes this led to armed insurrections and revolts, especially if such movements could serve specific interests of a political opposition; mostly, however, such movements condemned the current government practice as un-Islamic but maintained their obedience on pragmatic grounds, though without much inner loyalty to the government. Up to the 19th century two main types of such movements in *Sunni* Islam, keeping the Tradition (*Sunna*) of the Prophet, can be distinguished: the *traditionalists* who appealed in a broad sense to Koran and *Sunna*, and the *revivalists* who sought a literal and unconditional application of the religious prescriptions they contained and took action to achieve this. An example of the first are the Hanbalites who supported Ahmad b. Hanbal's stand against the philosophical theology of the school of the Muᶜtazilites in 9th century Baghdad. An example of the second are the Almohads with their strict puritan rule in 11/12th century North Africa and Spain. Ibn Taimīya (d. 1328 A.D.) and the Wahhābi movement in 18th and 20th century Arabia also represent this second stream of "revivalists" among the *Sunnis*.

b. Non-Sunni movements
As is well-known, since Muhammad's death there have been non-*Sunni* religious protest movements too. These have criticized current government practice and the course of history on the basis of an interpretation of Islam judged to be heredital by the *Sunnis* who, consequently, have not accepted this protest. Of these schismatic groups the most important have been the Kharijites and different kinds of Shīᶜite movements, especially the Ismailis or "Seveners" with their counter-caliphate of the Fātimids in Cairo (969-1171) and the Imamites or "Twelvers", who have had a separate history in Iran since the 16th century. It is here that since 1979 the religious leaders or *ᶜulamā'* have been in power but they had already participated in a national protest movement in 1891 (Keddie 1971; Bill 1982).

c. Mahdist movements
The various Mahdist movements in the Muslim world, proclaiming the end of time and the arrival of a reign of justice and peace under a *mahdī*, an eschatological figure, have also always denounced the existing state of unbelief and immorality in clearly religious terms and proposed a radical solution for it. They have always been short-lived but are in fact the most noticeable religious protest movements in Islam, exhibiting as they do a "messianic" character. Particularly known is the Mahdist state in Sudan of a century ago (Holt 1958).

d. The reformist movement
Especially striking for intellectual western observers has been the reformist movement founded in Egypt by Muhammad ᶜAbduh (ca. 1849-1905), one of the movements of internal enlightened protest against the state of Islamic religion in the middle of the 19th century (Adams 1933; Kerr 1966; Charnay 1966; Merad 1967). Over against the innumerable religious ideas and practices which were considered as "Islamic" at the time, sometimes without much foundation, the reformers went back very consciously to Koran and ancient *Sunna*, using them as a yardstick to judge existing ideas and practices and as the only source for a truly Islamic way of life and society. They attached great importance to the use of reason both in general and especially in the interpretation of religious texts, in the renewal of philosophical and theological thinking, and in modern science. Maintaining the highest respect for the Koran as well as for reason, they stressed a point made earlier in Islam, namely that there can be no conflict between reason and religion, and that Islam is the reasonable, more or less "natural" religion of mankind. Because of their stress on the use of reason and their puritanical attitude, reminiscent of that of the *Sunni* traditionalists and revivalists, the reformers were able to exert considerable influence among intellectuals who no longer felt at home in the scholastic formulas of law and doctrine or in the more emotional expressions of religious experience in the mystical orders. Starting out from the assumption of a pure, original and reasonable Islam they levelled a sharp protest at rigidified traditions and the following of doctrines solely on the basis of external authority. This pure Islam of revelation and reason, not depedent on time and place, was contrasted with local religious traditions and superstitions which could not be justified in Koran or *Sunna*. The movement returned to the original texts to achieve *iṣlāḥ*, reform, and this implied a movement of "scripturalism", a concommitant spread of literacy among the people and a continuous effort to improve education (Geertz 1968).

e. The Muslim Brotherhood
A more militant variant of the movements aiming at *islāh* is found in

a number of neo-orthodox movements which make a more limited use of reason as a critical and self-critical instrument on the basis of specific Koran and *Sunna* texts. They exhibit a stronger character of protest leading to more violent action than is the case with the reformist movements, which work more on an intellectual level. They too address themselves to a purification of Islam on the basis of the Koran and the ancient *Sunna*, but they are more politically involved and better organized to undertake political action than the reformers. The case of the *Salafīya* movement in Egypt provides an example of a development of reformism into neo-orthodoxy. In the case of the later Wahhabi movement in Arabia it was a revivalist movement which developed into neo-orthodoxy. But it is the *Ikhwān al-muslimīn*, the Muslim Brotherhood, in countries like Egypt, Syria and Pakistan which is most representative of this kind of *iṣlāḥ* (Husaini 1956; Mitchell 1969; al-Bannā' 1978; Aly & Wenner 1982). They wage an ideological struggle not only against what they consider to be a decaying Islam of laxity, scholastic rigidity and superstition but also against the secularizing ideas and practices which are part of the process of modernization striven for by most nationalist leaders and governments since independence.

f. Revolutionary movements

Following on from here a third, more radical, variant of *iṣlāḥ* movements may be distinguished, namely those movements which seek to do away with the modern nation-states with more or less secular governments which were established immediately after independence, replacing them by Islamic states based on the *Sharīᶜa*, religious Law. These movements undertake concerted action to bring about what is sometimes called an Islamic revolution, and may be considered revolutionary movements. They represent the most vital protest against the status quo and government policies in states which mostly became independent after World War II. The leaders of these states emerged in the nationalist struggle and tend to have a pragmatic, rather secular view of the way in which their countries can attain at least the necessary minimum of technical, socio-economic and political development. In most cases development has not gone as smoothly as hoped for and has demanded considerable sacrifices from the population. Political oppression and the processes of uprooting connected with modernization have provided an audience for those opposition groups which protest against the course of current secular policies. They call for the establishment of a radically different "Islamic" kind of state which will be the panacea for all existing problems.

Just as secular nation-states were established in protest at colonial foreign domination, so an appeal to establish Islamic states has arisen in protest at the practice of these very secular states. As is well-known, in countries like Lybia, Iran and in a sense also Pakistan "Islamic" revolutions have successfully been carried out, toppling more or less oppressive and corrupt regimes of older times. Even if the decisive action is often carried out by military men, such revolutionary movements mostly develop out of revivalist and neo-orthodox movements as described above. Their ideological force cannot be explained without reference to the appeal they make to profound hopes and ideals which have continued to exist among the traditionalist faithful who constitute the majority of Muslims everywhere. Though the majority of these people are not organized or mobilized into Islamic movements themselves, they nourish Islamic hopes and ideals which acquire a utopian force precisely in adverse situations and to which an appeal can be made then.

3. Indirect forms of religious protest within Islam; Law, the mystical Path and modernism

The movements brought together under this heading also embody a religious protest against the course of Islamic history and the practice of government in Muslim countries, but here the protest is indirect and in certain cases it is questionable whether the people concerned are themselves always conscious of the protest character of their particular movement.

a. The Law

The elaboration of religious law (*Sharīᶜa*) in the discipline of religious jurisprudence (*fiqh*), especially in the first centuries of Islam but also in later periods when it was refined, was not a pragmatic legal enterprise but represented the development of a normative pattern for the Muslim community's way of life which in many respects went clear against the actual pattern of behaviour of the society. This ideal character of the *Sharīᶜa* was strengthened by the deductive reasoning in its methodology (*uṣūl al-fiqh*) where social reality was only taken into account casuistically. Since the *Sharīᶜa* was held to be absolutely normative for all aspects of life, even if only a small part of it was in fact applied, there is reason to consider the attention given to its elaboration as an implicit but clear protest by the religious scholars against certain social realities and government policies. To the extent that reality deviated from what the norms prescribed, the elaboration of these norms and the declaration of their absolute validity implied a condemnation of and protest against reality as it existed in Muslim society.

b. The mystical Path

The contrasting attempts of the mystics and also the philosophers and gnostics in the course of Islamic history to fix inner religious experience or insight and interiorisation in general as the highest aim in life for the individual Muslim, equally implies an indirect protest against the way in which Islam was practised. Mysticism, philosophy and gnosis all three expressed a double protest: on the one hand against the worldly course of events and practices against which the religious scholars too protested in their own way, but on the other hand also against the external and formalistic character of the official normative religion as formulated and prescribed by these same scholars. As far as this latter protest was concerned, the mystics could count on the support of the traditionalist believers who equally, but more instinctively, rejected the "rationalization" of religion on the part of the scholars. And the different movements of *iṣlāḥ* (reform) later flourished in the ground prepared by the "purifying" mystics, although their own "puritanical" effort was directed towards the clear immediate meaning of Koran and *Sunna* rather than pure religious experience for its own sake.

c. Modernism

A singular kind of indirect protest against ideas and practices legitimized by Islam but which are held to be rejected on social or intellectual grounds are the various kinds of "modernist" movements prepared to accept values and norms from outside Koran and *Sunna* and often originating in non-Muslim cultures. These cultural movements in the 8th and 9th century which strove to assimilate Greek philosophy and science or Persian scholarship and government practices were the modernist currents of the time. The 19th and 20th century has seen the emergence of similar movements, which accept particular more or less generally accepted values as being either not incompatible with or even expressive of the true values of Islam. This can go so far that the claim has sometimes been made that these values are best represented or realized in Islam.

In the "liberal" period up to World War II Muslim modernists vindicated the tolerance, liberality and humaneness of Islam; later thinkers have claimed that socialism is best realized in Islam as a divine command of social justice which makes class struggle superfluous (Mintjes 1977). In the same way generally accepted values such as the dignity of woman and human rights may be claimed to be inherent in true Islam. In fact it is nearly always possible to find in the Koran hints of what may be called the humane values in a modern society, and so it is nearly always possible to appropriate values derived from elsewhere within the context of Islamic ideology thanks to an appeal to particular passages of Koran or *Sunna*. Apart from their ability to mobilize a traditional Muslim society in this way towards social development, such efforts of modernists also have an apologetic function; they defend Islam against reproaches made from outside that it is not tolerant, liberal, socialist, and so on, measured against "non-Islamic" norms and values. Such modernist movements and trends are often supported by governments which want to remove religious prejudices against generally accepted human values, like employment and public office for women, family planning and so on. The more pragmatic such modernist thinkers are, the more difficult it becomes to distinguish them from the more intellectual reformers who deduce the same values from Koran and early *Sunna* without alluding to the fact that they are also accepted outside Islam and are not due to influences by the latter.

4. Religious protest a structural feature of Islam?

It is significant that Muhammad's preaching and public activity as well as the prophetic movement resulting from it included an unmistakeable dimension of protest. In the first decades of its existence Islam was clearly a movement and a counter movement at one and the same time. The characteristics of Islam as a movement pursuing its own ends have been studied at great length. As a counter movement Islam protested against *jāhilīya* (pre-Islamic age of ignorance) practices and social injustices, against the particularistic concepts of salvation subscribed to by Jews and Christians, against what were felt to be misconceptions about the relationship between God and man and their essential difference. A radical protest was made against ideas and practices which conflicted with a universally valid truth of the unity and uniqueness of God and his commands to his creation carrying out his will. Islam as a religion never completely lost this protest dimension even in its later development thanks to its character as a prophetic religion, especially since the Koran, which contained the prophetic "protesting" in literal terms, has remained the basis of public and private preaching and religious life.

Consequently, the course of Islamic history has seen a number of movements which measure given realities against particular texts from Koran and *Sunna*; on their interpretation of these texts they base a direct or indirect religious protest against these realities. The fact that any absolutization of things perceived or imprisonment of man within the immanent world seem bound by their very nature to evoke protest may give a hint of the background of so many Muslim protest movements in the course of history with a religious appeal. If such movements rarely succeeded in seizing power in the more densely settled areas and regions, they still provided a fermentation of unrest and hope for better times, especially among the less privileged, who abandoned themselves to God. And absolute claims and absolutizations coming from outside Islam have in general been rejected more or less radically. Islamic ideologies and movements of the 19th and 20th centuries have expressed protest not only against mistaken interpretations of Islam, as previously described, but also against the many forms of political oppression, social injustice, and economic exploitation existing in Muslim societies and against the claims of other ideologies and religions to solve the woes of the time. Protest in Muslim societies seems to have a transcendent tendency, and in an Islamic cultural and religious framework it leads to the nostalgia for a religious ordering of things precisely as a protest against empirical realities: an Islamic society, an Islamic state. Any government choosing a secular ordering of affairs will always have an opposition which articulates the inevitable protests in the direction of Islamic norms and values, the ideal of a just society and the dream of an Islamic state.

III. Protest and Islam in the Arab Countries in Particular

There is a great variety in the political role and function of Islam in the Arab countries and the Middle East in general (Ahmad & Ansari 1979/1399; Ayoob 1981; Cudsi & Dessouki 1981; Curtis 1981; Dessouki 1982; Donahue & Esposito 1982; Hussain 1983; Voll 1983). What role then has Islam played in Arab movements of protest and what use have such movements made of Islam to express and legitimize their protest?

The great movements of protest in Arab countries over the last fifty years have been directed against foreign domination (colonialism, imperialism, cultural hegemony), Zionism and the state of Israel (interpreted in part as a form of imperialism), and feudal regimes (implying social injustice and corruption). These movements, however, with the exception of the Muslim Brotherhood and related groupings, have not given their protest an explicitly Islamic label, so that in general one cannot speak here of Islamic protest movements in the sense described above. The Arab nation and Arab culture, of which Islam clearly constitutes an intrinsic part in the consciousness of the people including most Christian Arabs, are however appealed to. More important, a call is also made for the defense of certain values as part of Arab culture and society, values which are very often linked to Islam, if not with reference to Koranic vocabulary than at least with strong emotional appeal to Muslim Arabs. Although this needs further investigation, our hypothesis is that in the great Arab protest movements since World War II Islam, if not explicitly mentioned, is closely associated in the mind of the masses with particular human values defended and, as the supreme value, lends force to the very defense itself. An attack on Arab values may well be felt by Arab Muslims as an attack on Islam too, since it forms part of their identity. In this case Islam seems to be essentially something to be defended by implication.

Within most Arab countries themselves, on a more limited scale, there are other kinds of protest movements which make a more immediate appeal to Islam. They are directed against ideologies from outside (liberal, capitalist, or communist which go against certain basic teachings of Islam and must be "islamicised" before being acceptable), the decline of morality and the decrease of traditional faith (often ascribed to negative influences like secularization from the West) and the dissolution of local Muslim tradition or the change of laws on personal status (perceived as abandonment of the duty to apply the prescriptions of Islam). Such movements are for instance in Egypt the *Ikhwān al-muslimīn*, the *Djamā^c at at-takfīr wa'l-hidjra*, *al-Djamā^c a al-islāmiya*, *al-Djihād*, *Shabāb Muhammad*, *Hizb at-tahrīr al-islāmī Djund Allāh*. In Pakistan the *Djamā^c at-i-islāmī* should be mentioned. Such movements call for the application of all Islamic prescriptions in full. Islam seems to be used here, basically, to formulate a demand and easily then becomes an ideal, however difficult to realize.

In both cases mentioned - with an indirect or direct appeal to Islam - protest movements, involving condemnation and rejection, are concerned. On a local or national scale certain movements may appeal openly and directly to Islam, whereas the movements which extend to the Arab world as a whole seem to imply that, when the Arab culture, nation and identity are to be defended, Islam and Islamic values are involved in a more indirect way. The very fact that the protest is couched mainly in words, though it sometimes takes an active form, suggests that power is often lacking in reality but may also build up with protest and resistance. For protests are always made on the basis of particular norms, values or truths, and if these are accepted by the audience and participants, the protest will develop further and may ultimately constitute a basis for resistance and struggle. It should be noted that in many situations in the Arab world and elsewhere an open protest is impossible, but a close analysis of cultural expressions in for instance literature will then reveal an indirect, even "symbolic" character of protest which may have great moral strength and can hardly be suppressed.

The way in which in the Arab world a protest which contains an appeal to Islam is articulated deserves further study of literary and social data to be analyzed for their references to Islam. The following distinction of four basic types of protest should be substantiated by considering the movements of protest in their precise context and by tracing their rise and further developments among particular groups (Berque 1966). It seems that in the Arab world a protest which contains an appeal to Islam can be articulated in at least four different ways:

a. it can acquire a militant political character involving intense action, e.g. in the struggle for independence or for the establishment of an Islamic state (Faouzi 1978);

b. it can have a marked ideological character, including

resistance to discrimination and injustice, with an appeal to Koranic norms of justice and a perfect but utopian Islamic society (Utrecht 1978);

c. it can have a predominantly cultural character when it addresses itself to resisting the influence of another culture, e.g. American, and when it serves to build up indigenous cultural values and guarantee the continuity of the indigenous cultural tradition (Waardenburg 1978);

d. it also can have a more unconditional religious character, e.g. in rejecting atheism, foreign ideologies and religions or in striving to overturn the existing situation in favour of an Islamic revolution, or just to strengthen and expand Islam as a religious faith, ideology or normative pattern.

Further research is needed into the role of particular religious leaders as *ᶜulamāʾ*, *shaykhs* and local preachers (Baer 1971; Keddie (ed.) 1972; Green 1978), in articulating protests in Islamic terms, and also into the function of organized religious groups as *ikhwān* and *ṭarīqa's* (Gilsenan 1973, 1983; De Jong 1978) and voluntary associations (Berger 1970). An important factor is the attitude taken by the authorities, who can admit or support, but also suppress and persecute these protest movements, generally according to the danger they represent to the state and its political interpretation and use of Islam. But even when they are suppressed, protest movements which appeal to Islam can in the long run exert considerable influence on traditionalist Muslims who recognize the absolute validity of the norms to which the appeal is made. Hence attention has been drawn to revolutionary tendencies in Islam and their preconditions (Hodgkin 1980; Johansen 1982) or to the potentials of Islam in the USSR (Bennigsen & Broxup 1983) or the psychological basis of the resurgence of Islam (Taylor 1983).

Before touching symbolic forms of protest we should mention the slower but continuous process of constructing and building up of Muslim societies (Abdel Malik 1972; Delanoue & Jomier 1976), of personality (Lahbabi 1964; Djaït 1974) and of intellectual vigour (Laroui 1967, 1974). Deep-seated structures in Muslim societies lend them their force to survive (Brown 1976; Eickelman 1976; Geertz 1968; Gellner 1969).

IV. The Use of Islam as a Symbol of Protest

On all the four levels which we have distinguished in the course of this paper, expressions of protest which appeal to Islam have a real as well as a symbolic character. The protest is made against a given, real state of affairs and should be seen as a response to reality.

It is expressed, however, often in religious Koranic terms referring to norms and values judged to have an absolute and universal validity, and the expression of the protest, consequently, is highly symbolic. This double nature, both real and symbolic, of any protest in the name of Islam is perhaps its greatest force, since people are encouraged to adopt attitudes of resistance and struggle not for material gains only but within the framework of a wider spiritual struggle of a community as well as of individuals, a struggle whose consequences extend beyond the grave.

In expressions of protest as considered above, Islam's symbolic function is apparently activated in the community at the moment that essential aspects of life are at stake or elements of it are felt to be threatened. These include fundamental norms of religious behaviour, relations between human beings and social organization, the unalienable terrain of family relationships and political autonomy, and of course the truth of the Islamic faith and the dignity of Islam. In Muslim societies, as elsewhere, the reaction to defend one's identity against threatening forces by appealing to one's religion is almost instinctive. The fact that in recent history use has been made of Islam to express a protest indicates the profound level at which Muslim societies have been threatened. Resistance has had to be offered on this level because it has been felt that something sacred is threatened; thus a militant appeal to religion is made. The protest is then followed by resistance and struggle concerned with concrete social and cultural realities but endowed with a profound symbolic dimension expressed in Islamic terms whose true meanings are difficult for an outsider to unravel.

In order to arrive at a semantics and perhaps hermeneutics of protests made in the name of Islam, some basic rules should be adopted. It must be admitted, for instance, that a protest which appeals to Islam has a definite religious meaning for Muslims, whatever other meanings it has. It should be admitted too that many protest movements which have arisen in Muslim societies have evident natural causes (for instance oppression or rivalries) but are articulated in Islamic terms, just as they would be articulated in other cultural contexts according to the religious and ideological framework which is valid there. And even when an appeal has been made to Islam (which is not absolutely necessary: many protests have been enunciated in Muslim societies without any direct reference to Islam) allowance must be made for the somewhat fluid character of Islam and the corresponding polyvalence of its elements. This, together with the absence of formal organization and representation, gives Islam a certain indefinable character and enables it to be used in many different ways, in particular when it is appealed to. On closer consideration we may be able to say that each protest movement can use Islam in its own way, but it is still Islam which is used to articulate the protest and move the masses. Even performing the rituals can imply protest and may be felt accordingly by the participants.

Some pertinent distinctions must then be made in the use of *the concept of Islam*. First, the Islamicists' use of the term to indicate a particular culture, system or religion as an object of investigation is different from the traditional use of the word by Muslims to indicate what they consider to be their religion which represents something sacred to them. We must recognize that Muslims use the word "Islam" generally not to indicate an object but to refer to what is held to be right behaviour or an expression of truth, that is to say a spiritual reality perceived and interpreted with certain intentions. Similarly, the social function of particular elements of Islam within a given society is quite different from what Muslims traditionally consider to be the function of Islam, namely to indicate an unconditional normative pattern which ought to be realized on earth. Unless such distinctions are made, the study of the use of Islam as a symbol of protest is doomed to misinterpret the ways in which "Islam", that is to say certain elements of Islam, are used to articulate a protest.

The question should be raised, finally, whether Islam as a religion and ideology might be in a privileged position to express protest, not only in the context of the protest of "Third World" ideologies in general against Western imperialism (Keddie 1982), but also compared to other religions and ideologies. Muhammad's preaching and the Koran in particular contain a criticism of any absolutization of earthly things and any imprisonment of man within the world and a continuous protest against all forms of *shirk*. This line has been pursued throughout Islamic history. Although recognizing the revelations said to have been given to Moses and Jesus (in a written and largely lost form), Muslims have generally taken a militant attitude to non-Islamic religious and ideological systems, intensely conscious as they are of the absolute character and superiority of Islamic norms. And an underlying nostalgia and longing can be felt for a truly Islamic society and state based on the *Sharīᶜa* and God's ordinances contained in it. This nostalgic longing nourished by the Koran gives a religious dimension to social protest movements in Muslim societies and political movements in general in so far as they appeal to Islam. It also sharpens the critical sense with regard to any man-made social order. As soon as such a social order is felt by Muslims to be oppressive, it may unleash a vigorous protest in words and action along revivalist and even revolutionary lines - unless, because of the nature of the oppression, the protest has to be silent or symbolic. Islam also lends itself to use as a symbol of protest by evoking greatness: the Arab conquests of the first centuries, the glorious period of the first "rightly guided" caliphs of Medina and the illustrious civilization of Islam, or its great empires - Ottoman, Safavid and Moghul - at the beginning of modern times (Waardenburg 1979b).

Conclusion

If Islam has been used in many instances over the last hundred years to express militant protest leading to resistance and struggle, this has certainly been connected with a position of powerlessness - political, economic and technological, but also social and cultural - *vis-à-vis* the dominating West. Islamic revival may be seen in the context of "thirdworldism" (Keddie 1982) or as providing a common discourse and an identity in a time in which traditional societies are dissolved or dissolving (Tibi 1981). When we pay attention to the features of protest accompanying them, Islamic culture and the present revival of Islam exhibit defensive features symptomatic of a struggle for survival. Once this survival is guaranteed, more creative attitudes may be expected to develop among the Muslim leadership, whether in Muslim countries or in countries where Muslims are a minority.

Whether or not processes of Islamization at the present display overtones of a spiritual *jihād* (as Sufi 1978), either in a broad or a deeper sense, as a protest against present-day forms of idolatry and religious laxity is a problem awaiting investigation. At all events we must speak of an overall process of ideologization of Islam in the late nineteenth and especially the twentieth century. Although a number of interpretations can be distinguished, they exhibit a common affirmation of Islam's absolute superiority over other religions and ideologies and contain a clear protest against what are considered to be the false claims of non-Islamic systems, ideologies and religions. Another subject which needs to be in investigated is whether, in this ideological struggle, an appeal to Islam is made as a system perfect in itself or as representing norms and values which are not confined to Islam as a historical religion and transcending it. It is quite possible that a religious protest may arise among critical Muslims against any absolutization of Islam itself as a religious system (al-ʿAzm 1969; Wild 1972).

In conclusion we would like to stress the urgent need for further study of protest movements not only against political oppression and social injustice but also against defection from what is held to be "true" Islam, yes both at the same time (Shari'ati 1980, 1982). Any transition from attitudes of protest to more creative approaches in this respect may be of decisive importance, and we need to be able to discern it.

REFERENCES

Abdel Malik, Anouar a.o. (Eds.)
1972 *Renaissance du monde arabe*. Gembloux (Belgium):Duculot. Reprinted in Tunis.

Adams, Charles C.
1968² *Islam and Modernism in Egypt. A study of the modern reform movement inaugurated by M. Abduh*. First edition 1933. New York.

Ahmad, Khurshid and Zafar Ishaq Ansari (Eds.)
1979/1399H *Islamic Perspectives. Studies in honour of Mawlānā Sayyid Abul Aᶜlā Mawdūdī*. Leicester:The Islamic Foundation, and Jeddah: Saudi Publishing House.

Aly, Abd al-Monein Said and Manfred W. Wenner
1982 "Modern Islamic reform movements: the Muslim Brotherhood in contemporary Egypt", *Middle East Journal* Vol. 36 No. 3, pp. 336-361.

Ayoob, Mohammed (ed.)
1981 *The Politics of Islamic Reassertion*. New York:St. Martin's Press.

ᶜAzm, Sādiq Djalāl al-
1969 *Naqd al-fikr ad-dīnī* (Criticism of religious thought). Beirut.

Baer, Gabriel (ed.)
1971 *The ᶜUlamā' in Modern History*. Special issue of *Asian and African Studies* as "Studies in Memory of Prof. Uriel Heyd", Vol. 7.

Bannā', Ḥasan al-
1978 *Five Tracts of Ḥasan Al-Bannā'. A selection from the Majmūᶜat Rasā'il al-Imām al-Shahīd Ḥasan al-Bannā'*. Translated from the Arabic and annotated by Charles Wendell. Berkeley & Los Angeles: Univ. of California Press.

Bennigsen, Alexandre and Marie Broxup
1983 *The Islamic Threat to the Soviet State*. London & Canberra: Croom Helm.

Berger, Morroe
1970 *Islam in Egypt Today. Social and political aspects of popular religion*. London:Cambridge Univ. Press.

Berque, Jacques
1966 "L'Islam d'après quelques témoignages récents", in: *Normes et valeurs dans l'Islam contemporain* ed. by J. Berque and J.-P. Charnay (Paris:Payot, 1966), pp. 247-265.

Bill, James A.
1982 "Power and religion in revolutionary Iran", *Middle East Journal* Vol. 36 No. 1 (Winter 1982), pp. 22-47.

Brown, Kenneth L.
1976 *People of Salé. Tradition and change in a Moroccan city 1830-1930*. Manchester:Manchester Univ. Press.

Charnay, J.-P.
1966 "Courants réformateurs de la pensée musulmane contemporaine", in: *Normes et valeurs dans l'Islam contemporain*, eds. J. Berque and J.-P. Charnay (Paris:Payot, 1966), pp. 225-246.

Cudsi, Alexander S. and Ali E. Hillal Dessouki (Eds.)
1981 *Islam and Power*. London:Croom Helm.

Curtis, Michael (ed.)
1981 *Religion and Politics in the Middle East*. Boulder, Colorado: Westview Press.

Delanoue, Gilbert and Jacques Jomier
1976 "Les Musulmans", in: *L'Egypte d'aujourd'hui: Permanences et changements 1805-1976* (ed. by the "Groupe de Recherches et d' Etudes sur le Proche Orient"), Paris:Centre National de la Recherche Scientifique, pp. 27-67.

Dessouki, Ali E. Hillal (ed.)
1982 *Islamic Resurgence in the Arab World*. New York:Praeger.

Djaït, Hichem
1974 *La personnalité et le devenir arabo-islamiques*. Paris:Seuil.

Donohue, John J. and John L. Esposito
1982 *Islam in Transition. Muslim perspectives*. New York & Oxford: Oxford Univ. Press.

Dorman Jr., Harry Gaylord
1948 *Toward Understanding Islam*. Comtemporary apologetic of Islam and missionary policy. New York:Teachers College, Columbia Univ.

Eickelman, Dale F.
1976 *Moroccan Islam. Tradition and society in a pilgrimage center*. Austin, Texas & London:Univ. of Texas Press.

Esposito, John L. (ed.)
1980 *Islam and Development. Religion and sociopolitical change*. Syracuse, N.Y.:Syracuse Univ. Press.

Faouzi, A.
1978 "Islam, réformisme et nationalisme dans la résistance à la colonisation française en Algérie (1830-1930)", in: *Islam and Society*. Special issue of *Social Compass*, Vol. XXV, No. 3-4,

pp. 419-432.

Geertz, Clifford
1968 *Islam Observed. Religious development in Morocco and Indonesia.* New Haven & London:Yale Univ. Press.

Gellner, Ernest
1969 *Saints of the Atlas.* London:Weidenfeld and Nicolson.

Gibb, H.A.R.
1972 *Modern Trends in Islam.* Chicago:Univ. of Chicago Press 1947. Repr. New York:Octagon Books.

Gilsenan, Michael
1973 *Saint and Sufi in Modern Egypt. An essay in the sociology of religion.* Oxford:Clarendon Press.

1983 *Recognizing Islam. An anthropologist's introduction.* London & Canberra:Croom Helm.

Green, H.
1978 *The Tunisian Ulama 1873-1915. Social structure and response to ideological currents.* Leiden:Brill.

Hodgkin, Thomas
1980 "The revolutionary tradition in Islam", *Race and Class*, Vol. 21, No. 3, pp. 221-237.

Holt, P.M.
1958 *The Mahdist State in the Sudan.* Oxford.

Husaini, Ishak Musa
1956 *The Muslim Brethren. The greatest of Modern Islamic Movements.* Beirut:Khayat.

Hussain, Asaf
1983 *Islamic Movements in Egypt, Pakistan and Iran. An annotated bibliography.* London:Mansell.

Işik, Huseyin Hilmi
1974[2] *The Religion Reformers in Islam.* Istanbul.

Johansen, Baber
1982 "Islam und Staat im 20. Jahrhundert. Soziale und ökonomische Voraussetzungen einer religiösen Protestbewegung", in *Islam und Abendland* (ed. Ary A. Roest Crollius). Düsseldorf:Patmos Verlag.

Johnson, Nels
1982 *Islam and the Politics of Meaning on Palestinian Nationalism.* London etc.:Kegan Paul.

Jong, F. de
1978 *Turuq and turuq-linked Institutions in Nineteenth century Egypt. A historical study in organizational dimensions of Islamic mysticism.* Leiden:Brill.

Keddie, Nikki R.
1968 *An Islamic Response to Imperialism. Political and religious writings of Sayyid Jamāl ad-Dīn "al-Afghānī".* Berkeley & Los Angeles:Univ. of California Press.

1972 *Sayyid Jamāl ad-Dīn "al-Afghānī". A political biography.* Berkely etc.:Univ. of California Press.

(ed.)
1972 *Scholars, Saints and Sufis. Muslim religions institutions since 1500.* Berkely etc.: Univ. of California Press.

1971 *Religion and Rebellion in Iran. The Tobacco Protest of 1891-1892.* London:Frank Cass.

1982 "Islamic revival as thirdworldism", in *Le cuisinier et le philosophe. Hommage à Maxime Rodinson.* Etudes d'ethnographie historique du Proche-Orient réunies par Jean-Pierre Digard. Paris:Maisonneuve et Larose, pp. 275-281.

Kerr, Malcolm H.
1966 *Islamic Reform. The political and legal theories of Muhammad ᶜAbduh and Rashīd Riḍā.* Berkely etc.:Univ. of California Press.

Lahbabi, Mohamed A.
1964 *Le personnalisme musulman.* Paris:Presses Universitaires de France.

Laroui, Abdallah
1967 *L'idéologie arabe contemporaine. Essai critique.* Paris:Maspero.

1974 *La crise des intellectuels arabes: traditionalisme ou historicisme?* Paris:Maspero.

Merad, Ali
1967 *Le réformisme musulman en Algérie de 1925 à 1940. Essai d'histoire religieuse et sociale.* The Hague & Paris:Mouton.

Mintjes, H.
1977 *Social Justice in Islam.* Amsterdam:Institute for the Study of Religion, Free University.

Mitchell, Richard P.
1969 *The Society of the Muslim Brothers.* London:Oxford Univ. Press.

Peters, Rudolph
1979 *Islam and Colonialism. The doctrine of jihād in modern history.* The Hague etc.:Mouton.

Said, Edward W.
1978 *Orientalism*. New York:Pantheon Books.

Shari'ati, Ali
1979 *On the Sociology of Islam. Lectures*. Translated from the Persian by Hamid Algar. Berkely:Mizan Press.

1980 *Marxism and Other Western Fallacies. An Islamic critique.* Translated from the Persian by R. Campbell. Berkeley:Mizan Press.

1982 "Intizar, the religion of protest". in Donohue and Esposito (Eds.) 1982, pp. 297-304.

Smith, Wilfred Cantwell
1957 *Islam in Modern History*. Princeton:Princeton Univ. Press (pb. 1977).

Sufi, ᶜAbd al-Quādir as
1978 *Jihad. A Groundplan*. Norwich:Diwan Press.

Taylor, Alan R.
1983 "The political psychology of Islamic resurgency", *American-Arab Affairs* Nr. 4 (Spring 1983), pp. 120-131.

Tibi, Bassam
1981 *Die Krise des modernen Islams. Eine vorindustrielle Kultur im wissenschaftlich-technischen Zeitalter*. München:C.H. Beck.

Utrecht, Ernst
1978 "Religion and social protest in Indonesia", in *Islam and Society*. Special issue of *Social Compass* Vol. XXV, No. 3-4 (1978), pp. 395-418.

Voll, John O.
1983 "Islamic dimensions in Arab politics", *American-Arab Affairs* Nr. 4 (Spring 1983), pp. 108-119.

Waardenburg, Jacques
1974 "Notes on Islam and development", *Exchange* (Leiden), nr. 4 (March 1974), pp. 3-43.

1978 "Official and popular religion in Islam", in *Islam and Society*. Special issue of *Social Compass*, Vol. XXV, No. 3-4 (1978), pp. 315-341.

1979a "World religions as seen in the light of Islam", in *Islam: Past Influence and Present Challenge*. Ed. by Alford T. Welch and Pierre Cachia. Edinburgh:Edinburgh Univ. Press 1979, pp. 245-275.

1979b "De Islam gebruikt als uitdrukking van protest", in *Het Islamitisch Midden-Oosten. Beweging en tegenbeweging*. Nijmegen: MOI-publicatie 3, October 1979, pp. 54-77.

1981 "Towards a periodization of earliest Islam according to its relations with other religions", in *Proceedings of the Ninth Congress of the U.E.A.I.* Ed. by Rudolph Peters. Leiden:Brill, pp. 304-326.

Wild, Stefan

1972 "Gott und Mensch im Libanon. Die Affäre Sādiq al-ᶜAzm", *Der Islam*, 48 (1972), pp. 206-253.

Towards an Economic Model of Virtuoso Religion

Bryan S. Turner

Introduction

Max Weber's sociology as a whole and his sociology of religion in particular are characteristically ambiguous in relation to Marxian materialism. Weber's studies of religion have been interpreted as a series of refutations, if not of Marx's own analysis of religion, then at least of the more vulgar reductions of religious phenomena to class interest by Engels, Kautsky and Bernstein. The comparative studies of Protestantism, Confucianism, Hinduism and Islam appear to demonstrate the autonomous role of religious ethics in shaping the economic organisation of society. However, it can also be claimed (Turner, 1977a and 1977b) that Weber's analyses are not only compatible with those of Marx, but that Weber's 'vision of history' is fundamentally deterministic and pessimistic. His sociology is grounded in the notion of the inevitable fatefulness of historical processes in which human intentionality is always undermined and denied by its social consequences. Marianne Weber (1975:337) writes that her husband's outlook was dominated by the belief that 'on its earthly course an idea always and everywhere operates in opposition to its orginal meaning and thereby destroys itself'. Illustrations of these self-cancellations in Weber's sociology are plentiful. Muhammed's inspired monotheistic and salvational prophecies were transformed by their very success 'into a national Arabic warrior religion' (Weber, 1966:262) with a distinctly feudal character. The spiritual *jihād* for salvation was translated into a feudal movement for 'world domination and social prestige' (Weber, 1964:148). All charismatic break-throughs are inevitably corrupted by the material interests of disciples and later reconstituted under the process of social routinisation. While charismatic authority calls for pure devotion, followers are motivated by mundane interests and everyday concerns. Furthermore, priests have an important role to play in diluting charisma before it can be served up as a mass religion. The teachings of Jesus 'contained passages of an ethical substance which first had to be explained away by priestly interpretation (and thus in part turned into their exact opposite) before they were suitable for the purposes of a mass church in general and a priestly organization in particular' (Weber, 1958:26). Within a broader canvas, Weber argues that precisely those features of Western history which promised to liberate men from the slavery of magic and enchantment produced the 'iron cage' of capitalist society. The anti-magical asceticism of the Protestant sects and secular instrumental rationality destroyed themselves in the disenchanted nightmare which Weber regarded as 'an unalterable order of things'.

Weber's pessimistic view of history is coupled with a deterministic model of society in which economic interests and political power occupy a dominant part. It is not surprising, therefore, that the metaphor of machinery is central to his sociological narrative. Weber's social universe is littered with 'cages','cogs','switchmen' and 'tracks'. Weber wants to avoid Marx's materialism, but his analysis of human society drives him constantly to a recognition of the centrality of economic and political interests. This ambiguity between his epistomology and his *Weltanschauung* is pre-eminently to be observed in his study of charisma, virtuoso religion and routinisation. On the one hand, the origins and distribution of charisma in society are apparently not determined by economic relations. On the other hand, material interests of the carriers and disciples of charisma shape and determine the outcome of charismatic movements. Pure loyalty is supposed to be the contraceptive device which protects charisma from debasement, but we find that at every level of Weber's analysis of charisma economic interests continuously penetrate the inner mechanism of charismatic relationships. The point of this commentary is not, however, to give the 'dry bones' of the debate between Weber and Marx yet another rattle, but to show that a discussion of Weber's concept of virtuoso religion provides an insight into the economic processes of sanctification. However, to demonstrate the relevance of Weber's virtuoso model is also to show that the *sanctum sanctorum* cannot be insulated against the profane effects of economic arrangements.

Virtuoso and Mass Religion

Although Weber's general conceptualisation of the charisma-bureaucracy distinction has been widely discussed, his more specific contrast between virtuoso and mass interests has not been systematically explored (Roth and Schluchter, 1979). Weber nowhere offered any sustained elaboration of virtuoso and mass religious styles, despite the centrality of this distinction to his view of Hinayana Buddhism, 'the god-suffused *bhakti* piety' of the Hindu cults and the importance of saints in Catholicism and Islam. Since Weber provided no sustained analysis, this dichotomy has to be picked rather carefully out of his text and to achieve this exegesis it will be valuable to quote from Weber's sociology of religion in some detail.

Weber observed that religion is a 'quality' which is unequally distributed through human society. As an 'empirical fact',

> "men are *differently qualified* in a religious way..... The sacred values that have been most cherished, the ecstatic and visionary capacities of shamans, sorcerers, ascetics and pneumatics of all sorts, could not be obtained by every one. The possession of such facilities is a 'charisma' which, to be sure, might be awakened in some but not in all " (Weber 1961:287).

Since these religious gifts or 'commodities' are in demand but, in the nature of the case, in short supply, there emerges in all religions various forms of religious inequality and stratification of grace. Thus,

> "all intensive religiosity has a tendency towards a sort of status stratification in accordance with differences in the charismatic qualifications" (Weber 1961:287).

Weber goes on to characterise these skills or qualifications of the adept by making an analogy between musical and religious capabilities. Heroic or virtuoso religiosity is contrasted with mass religiosity. The mass of the population are those who are religiously unmusical rather than those who stand at the bottom of the secular hierarchy.

Weber treated the 'drive for salvation' as one of the crucial dimensions of all world religions. Whether or not this religious quest was directed towards salvation in terms of inner-worldly asceticism or other-worldly mysticism had major implications for civilisation as a whole. All religions which place an emphasis on rebirth and spiritual renewal will create a religious 'aristocracy' since people are unequally attuned to religious impulses. Weber argues that it must be recognised that

> "not everyone possesses the charisma that makes possible the continuous maintenance in everyday life the distinctive religious mood which assures the lasting certainty of grace. Therefore, rebirth seemed to be accessible only to an aristocracy of those possessing religious qualifications..... In Islam there were the dervishes, and among the dervishes the particular virtuosi were the authentic Sufis" (Weber 1966:162-3).

Despite the very strong commitment to egalitarianism in religious matters in both Christianity and Islam, the unequal distribution of charisma produces an aristocratic hierarchy of virtuosi. These elites have been historically under pressure from the religious mass to water down, to simplify and to minimise the ethical and ritualistic requirements of 'authentic' charisma. There are, therefore, two aspects to Weber's model of virtuoso/mass religiosity. First, there is the stratification of populations into layers of charismatic capability. Secondly, there is the tendency for virtuoso requirements to be reduced to match the mundane limitations of the everyday life of followers, supporters and disciples.

Weber's analysis of virtuoso religion points to the economic support which is necessary for the cultivation and maintenance of a religiously musical elite. Since, especially in the case of other-worldly asceticism and mysticism, the virtuoso had to be free from employment in the economy and liberated from the mundane requirements of food and shelter, the virtuoso had to rely on the charity of their lay sympathisers. There developed, therefore, a set of reciprocal economic relations between the virtuoso, the inner circle of devotees and the outer circle of laity. In exchange for these mundane gifts, the laity received the charismatic blessings of the virtuoso. Weber notes that

> "As the peasant was to the landlord, so the layman was to the Buddhist and Jainist bhikshu: ultimately, mere sources of tribute. Such tribute allowed the virtuosos to live entirely for religious salvation without themselves performing profane work, which always would endanger their salvation" (Weber 1961:289).

Weber's musical model of the stratification of charismatic gifts has, therefore, to make the assumption that there is such a phenomenon as a religious 'talent' with the same sort of logical status as athletic, mathematical or musical talents. The notion is that certain individuals are better equipped to receive and to develop spiritual gifts than the inept mass of the population. To some extent this analogy raises a 'nature/nurture' debate inside religion as to the precise manner in which certain individuals 'are better equipped'. From a sociological perspective, it is important to argue that the distribution of charisma and religiously talented persons is as much determined by the social structure as the distribution of 'military talent' among Highland Scots is determined by the clan system, the political role of the chiefs and the absence of alternative employment. Given the economically fragile base of virtuoso religion, there are good grounds for suspecting that virtuosity will become associated with certain status groups. Since heroic religiosity requires freedom from economic want, the cultivation of this type of religiosity will be made easier for privileged social groups.

For the disprivileged, the transition from mass to virtuoso status or from the outer circle of followers to the inner circle of adepts, is problematic. This is especially true where the novice is already encumbered with work, familial and kinship responsibilities. The transition from a privileged social position to a privileged religious one is not only far easier but far more 'natural'. The humble occupational origins of Jesus and Paul are not necessarily an obvious refutation of my thesis that an employed virtuoso is a contradiction in terms, since both men abandoned carpentry and tent making in favour of lay contributions. In the case of other religious leaders, Gautama and Muhammad could draw upon existing wealth to finance the initial stages of their meditation and religious development. In particular, Muhammad's spiritual development would have been impossible without the economic support of his wife Khadijah. Additional support for the claim that religious and social status are closely connected can be taken from the fact that in Christianity the 'official' saints of the Church have been predominantly over-recruited from dominant, privileged classes (George and George 1953-1955). However, it is not just the upper class that moves naturally into adept or virtuoso religious roles for the same logic of availability applies also to such groups as widows, the young or the retired. Wherever there is no pressing, day-to-day requirement for direct employment in the labour market, leisure may be available for developing and joining in the supererogatory demands which are characteristic of virtuoso religious styles. Obeyesekere (1968) has made an analysis of the stratification of Buddhism to show how elderly villagers, particularly widows, become *upasaka*. This religious stratification occurs because widows are more able to fulfil virtuoso precepts than are villagers employed in demanding economic roles. Thus, while there is no necessary link between religious and social elites, there are good reasons for believing that there is a strong probability for such secular and religious linkage. In order for any heroic religiosity to appeal to the mass and to become a religiosity fostered by the mass, certain transformations of the pristine elitism of the virtuoso requirements must take place. Weber's virtuoso/mass dichotomy is not a static ideal type construct but a dynamic model of the continuous reconstitution of elitist religiosity into popular forms.

These transformations are, however, not to be conceived in a uniform or unidimensional fashion. The supply of charisma cannot be readily controlled and the demand for religious services is itself often specialised and differentiated. The production and consumption of charismatic gifts takes place in a competitive situation where the source of supply may well be elastic. In short, the language of conventional Samuelsonian economics provides an appropriate avenue for elaborating Weber's analysis of popular and elitist religiosity. Charisma is a 'commodity' which is exchanged for money, services and other commodities. The charisma at the inner centre of religious activity passes outwards bringing healing, comfort and teaching with it. The gifts at the outer lay circle pass inwards bringing the material conditions for charismatic reproduction. Given Weber's pessimism about the survival of 'true' virtuosity in a mass market, virtuosity is always forced to make concessions to popular demand. Thus,

> "With the exception of Judaism and Protestantism, all religions and religious ethics have had to reintroduce cults of saints, heroes or functional gods in order to accommodate themselves to the needs of the masses..... Islam and Catholicism were compelled to accept local, functional and occupational gods as saints, the veneration of which constituted the real religion of the masses in everyday life" (Weber 1966:103-4).

Overproduction of religious gifts in response to market demands results in inevitable devaluation of quality. However, it could be argued as a qualification to Weber's argument that what one might expect would be considerable charismatic specialisation and differentiation of religious gifts in response to existing social differentiation in the religious market. There may be 'up-market' and 'down-market' religious products which are consumed by various groups within the status hierarchy of the market place. Spiritually demanding, rigorous and theologically sophisticated charisma may satisfy the consumption wants of the social elite while remaining outside the 'income range' of the socially and religiously disprivileged.

Sufi Asceticism and Mass Religiosity

The history of Sufism has often been written as if it involved a unidimensional transition from elitist asceticism to popular religiosity. As Kritzeck (1973:153-4) brusquely observes, Sufism started out as a protest against Islamic worldliness on the part of 'high-minded ascetics' but under the influence of 'mediocre students' and the popular lodges it came to have

> "nothing to do with the original spiritual ideals. That was the point at which they started to take drugs, pierce their flesh, and whirl."

The word 'Sufism" was derived from 'suf', the undyed wool worn by Christian ascetics of the East. The woollen garment was later replaced by a patched frock which the sheikh gave to his novice. Sufis often referred to themselves as 'the folk' (*al-qawm*), 'the poor' (*al-fuqarā'*) or *darvīsh*. However, the original woollen garment was indicative of their asceticism and the Sufi movement was founded on

> "aversion to the false splendor of the world, abstinence from the pleasure, property and position to which the great mass aspires, and retirement from the world into solitude for divine worship" (Ibn Khaldun 1958, vol.3: 76).

From this ascetic and elitist withdrawal, many Orientalists treat the progress of Sufism as one of perpetual decline towards popular religion. The very success of Sufism as a social movement opened Islam up to the influence of indigenous beliefs and practices, heterodox attitudes and local customs (Gibb and Bowen 1957; Gibb 1969; Rice 1964). The popular saints became dependent on the alms of the laity but, in return, they had to demonstrate their magical and miraculous powers. The status of the saints came to depend on lay evaluations of their miraculous capabilities. Thus,

> "the purity of the saint's life or doctrine is of secondary importance; if he can work miracles, that is enough, he is a saint and therefore to be feared and one whose protection is to be sought. A saint without miracles is no saint at all" (Trimingham 1965:128).

According to this type of perspective, whereas heroic Sufism was based on the assumption that the goal of the religious path was extremely difficult to achieve and required strenuous training, in popular Sufism saintship was achieved by recognition in fire-eating, snake-charming, divination and wizardry. The other change was that the saint's *baraka* became almost entirely a matter of inheritance: the pure charisma of achievement was transformed into lineage charisma. In addition, popular Sufism came to include not only adherence to living saints but the cult of dead saints and their tombs. From these horizontal saints in their tombs, there appeared to be an endless flow of charismatic power.

There are a number of problems with this form of interpretation of Sufism and a particular difficulty connected with the distinction between popular and official Islam. It is difficult to make judgements about the purity of original Sufi asceticism without also raising traditional issues in Orientalism as to the 'authenticity' of Islamic spirituality as a whole and its dependence on Christian and other sources (Massignon 1922). The view of writers like Trimingham (1971: 26) that 'Sufism provided a philosophy of election which was diluted and adapted to the needs of the masses by the orders' certainly supports Weber's fatalistic history of self-cancellation, but it is not entirely adequate sociologically. Rather than treating Islam as a 'decline' from or 'corruption' of pure Islam, popular religion may be regarded as a form of 'practised Islam' (Waardenburg 1978) and the relationship between scholarly religion and its popular manifestations as an interaction between social groups interpreting their practices by reference to common formulae. Popular religion is not historically merely a vulgarisation of the Islamic mysticism of Ibn Al-Arabi and Al-Ghazzali since intellectualised mysticism and popular religion have always stood side-by-side oriented to different clientele with different social and religious interests. This is not to ignore the fact that the general societal status of popular religion has been fundamentally transformed by decolonisation, puritan reformism and nationalist ideology (L. Brown 1972). Returning to the analogy of economic and religious commodities, it is more accurate to regard popular and official religion as a form of differentiation and specialisation of religious services relevant to different lay markets than to treat 'mass religiosity' as the contaminated offspring of pure religious consciousness.

Class, Illness and Religion

As Weber (1966:101) notes, the disprivileged mass of the population, especially the peasantry, is not oriented towards an impersonal, rational theodicy. From the point of view of the religious elite, the rural peasantry were heathen (*paganus*) who obstinately clung to magic as a medium for manipulating local gods. In this social context, charismatic authority is particularly subject to mundane interests and needs of followers. 'Folk religion' is historically very closely connected with 'folk medicine' since one of the primary interests of the mass is the acquisition of remedies and cures in a situation where alternative forms of therapy are not available. While much of the contemporary discussion of Sufi brotherhoods has focused on their political functions (Geertz 1968; Gellner 1972; Wolf 1971), it is equally important to concentrate on what might be broadly referred to as the 'medical' or therapeutic component of transactions between saints and their followers in order to illustrate the specialisation of religion around the life-styles of various classes. In their traditional rural setting, it is difficult to distinguish the sheikhs from other practitioners within the folk system of spirit-possession and its treatment. Within the shantytown context, the religious 'clubs' function to integrate urbanised peasantry into a network of primary social relationships.

In general etymological terms there is, in any case, a close connection between social membership, therapy and religion. To save the soul and to salve the body are verbs which have their roots in the Latin *salvare*. The mediaeval summa and penitentials gave expression to the view that sin was an affliction of the body and soul which could be treated through the healing ministry of the sacrament of penance and through the grace monopolised in the Church.

In this respect, confession is a ritual of inclusion whereby the restoration of the individual to group membership involves a simultaneous healing of the body (Turner 1977b). While in Islam a comparable sacrament of penance was not fully developed (Gilsenan 1973), it is possible to identify similar mind/body conceptions in popular belief and ritual (Kennedy 1967:193). The notion of *baraka* also carries with it the meaning of plenitude and well-being in the symbolic form of bread.

While the social functions of *baraka* may depend on its systematically distorted meanings (Gellner 1970), there is also a consensus concerning its alleged therapeutic effects. Among the Hamadsha, Crapanzano (1973) reports that *baraka* is regarded as the force behind the cure of sickness, especially illness resulting from spirit-possession. However, the therapeutic effect of *baraka* cannot be analysed in isolation from the cathartic consequences of participation in the collective rituals of ecstatic dance (the *ḥaḍra*) and pilgrimage (*mūsem*). Participation in these collective events draws the individual into a network of supportive social relationships -

> "The ailing individual is not isolated and ignored, but becomes a patient who is the concern of the whole group. The group consists of family friends, and neighbors as well as the Hamadsha, not only offers the patient sympathy, encouragement, and the hope of cure, but also mobilizes itself to cure the patient of his troubles" (Crapanzano 1973: 215).

These rituals reorganise the social relationships which are in part the cause of the patient's stressful condition. Developing a Freudian psychoanalytic view of spirit-possession and their hysterical sequelae, Crapanzano goes on to argue that these 'socially generated tensions' arise from the psychological contradictions of male identity in a society which is organised around the subordination of women to men and the domination of men over boys. While masculinity is defined in terms of sexual virility, control of women and social dominance, sons are also expected to be subservient, dependent and obedient in relation to their fathers. The social role of young males is, therefore, like the social role of women in general. The social and psychological problem is consequently that of how men emerge out of these dependent 'feminine' roles. The symptomatology of being possessed or struck by a *jinni* include tremors, convulsions, mutism, paralysis and so forth. The symptoms are symbolic of the underlying tensions in the sexual division of labour. Being struck by *jinn* on the face is both the cause of paralysis and indicative of the problem of male identity. The cure for these afflictions involves an intensification of group membership (such as becoming an active participant in the Hamadsha) and participation in particular rituals which are aimed at discovery of the appropriate musical formula (*rīh*) which will extract the offending *jinn*.[1]

If therapy and health can be connected with the intensification of social interaction and renewal of social membership, then long-term occupation of a 'sick role' may be regarded as a form of social deviance (Parsons 1951). In a Middle East context, Morsy (1978) argues that illness behaviour may be a way of legitimising behaviour which contravenes traditional expectations. In the Egyptian Nile Delta, the *ma'zūr* or *ma'zūra* (possessed male or female) may exhibit a wide variety of symptoms of a medical character, but the social manifestations have a common theme, namely the breaking of social norms. A woman who suffers from *'uzr* may refuse to marry a particular man selected by her father, oppose her husband's intention to take a second wife or refuse to nurse a child. The importance of *'uzr* is that it provides an acceptable socio-medical label for deviant behaviour and at the same time provides some legitimation and institutionalisation for the behaviour. Thus,

> "the very term *'uzr* (excuse) provides the illness with a social definition. It offers the *ma'zūr* (excused) a temporary dispensation from the requirements of social canons"(Morsy 1978:603).

The onset of *'uzr* is closely related to conflicts within the family and to the exercise of power by men and elders such as a forced marriage or the threat of divorce. The sufferer from *'uzr* is able to retain a marginal status within the village and to avoid the social exclusion and punishment normally associated with serious deviance. The social role of the *ma'zūr* may, however, be terminated by involvement in a variety of collective, therapeutic rituals. The anxieties of female status may be aggravated by the existence of migrant labour conditions which denude these isolated villages of their male inhabitants. The saint cults and the *zār* ceremonies are both aimed at the 'return of husbands, marriage of children, material goods, cures and the like' (Kennedy 1967:189) in a situation where alternative institutions are not available. The *zār* helps 'to untie' depressions, apathy and withdrawal by involving these women in socially supportive activities.

In all human societies, sickness and its appropriate cures are not randomly distributed through the population, but are 'allocated' to human groups along channels which are determined by social criteria of class, occupation and sexual status. The social distribution of illness in industrial society may also have parallels in pre-industrial and developing societies.[2] While sickness in North Africa obviously has a very different cultural ambiance from sickness in European societies, it is still possible to conceptualise illness and its treatment in relation to the class and sexual characteristics of individuals. In the absence of a centralised professional monopoly of modern medicine, the various virtuoso religious groups, lodges and orders maintain important social functions in satisfying the religio-medical needs of their lay clients. In exchange for *baraka* and the therapeutic practices of dance and pilgrimage, the virtuosi are supported by alms, gifts and services. These gifts contribute to the separation of the religious elite from places in productive labour and their isolation from everyday routines. Through these exchange relations, the stratification of charisma is grafted onto the stratification of the population by social class.

The Differentiation of Religious Markets in Services

In general terms, the religious styles of North African Islam can be characterised by reference to two syndromes. In the towns, direct access to the Qur'an is associated with egalitarianism, a minimal role for saints, the scholarship and sobriety of the *ulama* and an absence of emotionalism and elaborate rituals in worship. In the countryside, there is a nonliterate, ritualistic and ecstatic religiosity, an emphasis on hierarchy, mystical states and the mediation of saints.[3] Where urbanised Sufi lodges develop, Sufi mysticism is an alternative to the *ʿulamā*-dominated religiosity, whereas in the rural areas it is a substitute for legalistic religion (Gellner 1968). Within this broad framework there is the interstitial development of Sufi lodges which cater to the needs of shantytown dwellers by developing specialised, competitive religious styles. The competition over clientele arises in part from the fact that there is an overproduction of saintly personnel in relation to local demand. Because Sufi saints were never required to adopt an official celibacy and their *baraka* could be inherited, the number of eligible saints tends to be in excess of available roles. These surplus descendants of saints could either become dormant virtuosi awaiting their turn in office or they could migrate from the countryside to the cities and *bidonvilles*. Innovation in social practices is often associated with competitive situations where over-production of personnel creates the need for new markets and audiences. The competitive religious market is no exception -

> "The migrant saint, in order to obtain new converts and to win members from the existing lodges, improved his competitive position by developing his own special technique which won new supporters and distinguished one lodge from another. The saint sold both himself and his commodity on the urban market and, as in other types of salesmanship, he developed a certain

> personal panache: the more unusual the commodity, the more likely it was to attract a new audience" (Mulkay and Turner 1971:50).

Where these saints are successful in establishing an audience or a new order, these religious 'clubs' provide mutual support and psychological security for their adherents in an urban context where most traditional forms of association have declined or collapsed.

This general distinction between rural and urban forms of Islam provides a general context within which to discuss the religiosity of the urban *zawiya* operating within an established town and the religiosity of the informal, loosely-structured teams or groups which function in the *bidonville*. Whereas the madina *zawiyas* are oriented to the support of the saint, the shantytown teams which perform public ceremonies such as the *ḥaḍra* are far more explicitly concerned with illness and the treatment of spirit-possession. The litanies and practices of the urban *zawiyas* are restrained and sober, while in the *bidonville* performances of the *ḥaḍra* tend to be dramatic, intense and violent. It can be argued that involvement as devotees (*muḥibbīn*) of the Hamadsha teams provides wider social involvement for the urbanised peasantry of the shantytowns by enlarging their circle of social contacts. Membership of these religious 'clubs' functions to integrate the rootless poor into primary groups in an environment which is anomic and uncertain. The 'underclass' of the *bidonville* (Worsley 1972) is able to find a psychological discharge in the head-slashing performances of the Hamadsha teams. The relationship between social deprivation and religious style can, however, be more subtly expressed in the following terms:

> "the concern for ritual differences seems to symbolize the differences between madina and bidonville inhabitants which the bidonville dweller senses. He prefers the bidonville teams because their devotees are very much in the same position as himself.... The foqra, who consider themselves city people, have never been anxious to develop a large following of bidonville muḥibbīn, despite the obvious increase in income these devotees would bring" (Crapanzano 1973:127).

Differences in religious styles can, therefore, be correlated with differences in rural and urban experiences, the deprivation of shantytown existence and the emotional crises associated with the power structure of the family. The religious practices are simultaneously symbolic of these social differences and cathartic responses to the personal difficulties which are generated by these structural arrangements. There is, in addition, an important economic dimension to this religious differentiation. In terms of Weber's virtuoso model, the supererogatory demands of an 'aristocratic' religious style are incompatible with the life-demands of mundane existence. The requirements of the 'elite' brotherhoods and *zawiyas* are incompatible with the demands of work and motherhood. Religious affiliation and practice correlate directly with the life-cycle, sexual status and socio-economic class position.[4] Throughout Islam the clientele for the curative and therapeutic aspects of the saint cults is predominantly drawn for women troubled by mundane problems of marriage, childbirth and divorce (Geijbels 1978). Their choice of saint is often restricted by the limitations on their geographical mobility and access to alternative systems of medicine may be closed. Women will also tend to select those orders and practices which will match the everyday requirements of domestic work. In

> "the Jilaliy order, for example, certain devotions and prayers need not be said exactly at the proper hour nor with undivided attention. Instead a Jilaliyya can gear her schedule more closely to household demands.... These feelings service to explain why most women carefully avoid membership in the Tijaniyya even into old age" (Dwyer 1978: 593).

While the Tijaniyya order has not been regarded as the most rigidly ascetic of Sufi orders, it has been closely associated with the wealthy and the politically powerful (Abun-Nasr 1965:47-379). However, the litanies of the order which have to be performed twice every day appear to make a particularly demanding inroad on the routine chores of domestic life of peasant women and on the work-schedule of ordinary men:

> "The hired hand at harvest time or the vegetable seller in the market cannot easily leave his work to perform the exacting Tijaniy devotions. Workers of this sort require greater flexibility. The Jilaliy, ben Nasriy and Derqawiy orders more readily meet these needs" (Dwyer 1978:596).

In order to fulfil the more exacting requirements of their orders or to change affiliation to one of the more rigorous orders, men and women have to wait until their old age provides some release from secular involvements and demands. [5]

The Religious Exchange System

All spiritual virtuosity depends on some element of withdrawal from mundane life and, in particular, from employment. Isolation from employment not only provides the opportunity for developing and adhering to supererogatory practices, it is also more seemly and in keeping with sacred activities. In order to maintain that isolation, the virtuoso requires some form of economic support. This economic aid can take the form of patronage as when one class pays a stratum of virtuosi to pray on its behalf (Rosenwein and Little 1974). More commonly, the virtuosi are maintained as an unproductive class out of lay payments, fees, gifts and the like. In the case of mystical virtuosi, this produces the paradoxical situation where the virtuoso flight from the sinful world is financed on the basis of the continuity of that profane environment.[6] Weber catches this paradox with his typical sharpness:

> "The contemplative mystic lives on whatever gifts the world may present to him, and he would be unable to stay alive if the world were not constantly engaged in that very labor which the mystic brands as sinful and leading to alienation from god" (Weber 1966: 172).

The Buddhist monk regards agriculture as a religiously meaningless occupation, yet it is precisely agricultural gifts which support the Buddhist virtuosi. In Islam perhaps the development of contemplative mysticism and hatred of the world has been less prominent than in Christianity and Buddhism. The ability of Islamic saints to marry and form charismatic lineages is one indication of this situation. There is, however, a clear pattern of exchange whereby the alms of adepts and devotees pay for the religious services of saints to lay people.

The saint/devotee relationship is both a system of exchange and ideally a system of redistribution. Gifts from the general population and *muḥibbīn* are given to the saint and/or his descendants (*wulād siyyid*) through the medium of the adepts (*foqra*) and the leader of the saint's lineage group (the *mizwar*). This wealth is then redistributed through the *wulād siyyid* to pilgrims, the poor and the sick. In return, both the poor and the general population receive the blessing of the saint's *baraka*. These acts of charity are the work of individuals who themselves are ideally without self-interest. In practice, both the *mizwar* and *ḥadra* team members were able to accumulate wealth.[7] On the one hand, team members extorted money and gifts from *muḥibbīn* and the general population by veiled threats of illness and unemployment resulting from the displeasure of *jnūn*. In this way, team members make a living from performance of the *ḥaḍra*. On the other hand,

> "the mizwars were able to maintain their economically advantageous position without losing, at any rate outside their descent group, the image of pious and charitable men endowed with great baraka of their own" (Crapanzano 1973:123).

The *baraka*-infested men of Islam follow the pattern of the mystics of Christianity and the Buddhist monks of Asia because, in Weber's terms, their lack of involvement in and disesteem for the world of labour are financed by a laity which is itself completely immersed in profane routines. Like academics, saints are unproductive workers who are maintained out of general revenue, charity and patronage.

In Christianity, Chirst's *baraka* flowed freely in his spittle at the pool of Siloam and his blood at Calvary.[8] Since the early Church was not a lineage system through which this *baraka* could be stored, the Roman Church developed a theory of the Church as a Treasury of Merit which could be opened by the keys of the episcopacy. In return for this fiduciary issue of charisma, the laity returned their penance and their tithes. As the system of penance was regulated in the thirteenth century, there appeared to arise an imbalance between the requirements of penance and the ability of the laity to pay up. Indulgences formed a sort of spiritual mortgage mitigating the immediate conditions of these penetential payments. The choice of the term 'treasury' by Cardinal Hugh of St. Cher in 1230 is indicative of the exactness and calculative precision with which the Church attempted to quantify the operation of charisma in the world. In Islam, Muhammad's *baraka* is distributed through kinship - or at least through a line of men who *claim* charismatic descent. *Baraka* is thus inherited by saints and the children of the saint (*wulād siyyid*). *Baraka*, however, is contagious and can be acquired by contact with a saint or his tomb. In Morocco, in particular, the existence of both personal and institutionalised *baraka* creates a potentially inflationary situation where grace might increase without an appropriate spiritual reserve. In his study of the legends of the Hamadsha, Crapanzano (1973:53) suggests that one resolution between the androgynous and the contagious principle is a feminisation of the saint who thereby passes from a personal to an institutionalised holy man. These legends thus attempt an ideological solution of the problem that institutionalised *baraka* can only be acquired agnatically, while personal *baraka* can be acquired contagiously. The treasury system in Christianity and the hereditary principle in Islam both have the effect of placing some institutional limits on the social distribution of a commodity which has a very high exchange value.

Conclusion

This attempt to provide an economic model of saintship raises some obvious problems, especially in relation to the argument that saintliness and labour are not easily conjoined. Obviously the dead saints have long vacated their secular roles in this world in favour of more ghostly callings. Among contemporary saints, Sheikh Ahmad al-Alawi the cobbler and Salama ibn Hassan Salama the government employee appear to create obvious difficulties for my thesis. In point of fact, Sheikh Ahmad turns out to be no real exception to the rule (Lings 1961). While he was apparently engaged in trade, most of the business became the responsibility of his friend and partner as the Sheikh began to draw a large following of adepts. The more he was drawn into his religious role, the more he was drawn out of his economic role and away from his secular responsibilities. At a later stage, the financial support from his business was complemented by the goods and services which came from his devotees. Salama, the founding Sheikh of the Hamidiya Shadhiliya, perhaps provides a stronger case against my economic model of virtuoso religion. Born into one of the poorer quarters of Cairo in 1867, Salama rose quickly from his post as a junior clerk to that of head of a department in the office of the State domains (Gilsenan 1973). He acquired a reputation as a reliable and effective employee. It was part of his teaching that the brothers should not avoid the responsibilities of work just as he himself had not withdrawn from his office and his this-worldly commitments. Indeed Salama

> "encouraged the brothers to work, and the most hateful thing to him was the idle man who would not go out and seek for his daily bread, but rather lived as a burden on other people" (Gilsenan 1973:18).

The fact that the Sheikh continued to work while also leading the *ṭarīqa* was a clear indication to his followers of the importance of having an occupation in society. Gilsenan (1973:139) points out that, while this did not constitute an ethic of asceticism driving the individual into a secular calling, it did provide a sober, moderate appraisal of the importance of work as a form of self-restraint and discipline.

I take the case of Sheikh Salama to be not so much a direct refutation of my argument as a striking illustration of the transformation of the role of saint and the functions of the brotherhoods in twentieth-century society. Given the changing relationships between the state and the rural hinterland, between the puritan scholars and the Sufi saints, both Sheikh Ahmad and Sheikh Salama were forced to walk a tight-rope between the enthusiasm of their urban working-class supporters and the criticism of *ʿulamāʾ* and government. The ethic of restraint, moderation and work is a product of changed circumstances. Sheikh Ahmad abandoned his early interest in fire eating, snake charming and the other practices of the Isawi *ṭarīqa* in order to develop a more spiritual path. In his reply to orthodox critics, he argued in *A Mirror to Show up Errors* that the dance and use of the rosary were perfectly acceptable orthodox practice of traditional Sunni Islam. In the Hamidiya Shadhiliya, there were definite limitations placed on the possibility of emotional, frenzied outbursts during communal rituals. Recent hostility against the *dhikr* and *ḥadra* of the various Sufi orders has led to various attempts at internal control and restraint of members. A number of laws of the Hamidiya Shadhiliya proscribe the use of certain instruments at the *ḥadra* and forbid the eating of glass, fire and cactus. The cautious work-ethic of Salama and the general sobriety of the order may thus not be evidence against the thesis that saints do not work, but rather evidence about radical changes in the character of sanctity in Islam and in the social function of religious lodges and orders.

Within a general context of secularisation and urbanisation, it seems probable that the volume of candidates who successfully meet the Church's criteria of translation, beatification and sanctification will decline. It has often been suggested that the religious and social conditions that gave rise to the need for saints in Christianity have largely disappeared (Mecklin 1955). In Islam, perhaps a similar process is taking place albeit for rather different social causes. In the rural areas, the saints may be less important as mediators between tribes. In the towns and *bidonvilles*, alternative forms of medicine, political allegiance and secular associations may also restrict the social importance and social role of the saint. The therapeutic role of the *zār* may in similar fashion give way to secular or Western treatment, while the generations of men and women who continue to seek out the advice of the *zār* practitioners may be inherited by their children (Fakhouri 1968:56). Social conditions therefore appeared to be stacked against the emergence of new saints. The dead saints

> "might continue to play a vital part in popular religion both in the mass pilgrimage and the private prayer. Secure in posthumous reverence they maintained their individual reputations for blessing and help. But the situational possibilities for new sainthood to be claimed or acclaimed by large numbers of Egyptians grew ever more restricted" (Gilsenan 1973:46).

Unable to secure an audience and hence to secure alms and gifts, there may be more pressure on men who claim personal *baraka* to remain within their secular occupations. At least in the urban areas, there may well emerge in popular Islam the worker-saint whose virtuosity is largely self-financed. Whether the worker-saint suffers the same fate as the worker-priest remains to be seen. These concluding observations should not be taken to be a criticism of saintship disguised behind a sociological vocabulary. In *Capital* Marx argued that the individual capitalist could not be blamed for exploiting workers, since every capitalist had to obey the laws of accumulation. The same could be said of saints. Unless they accumulate profane wealth, they cannot distribute their sacred blessing. Like capitalists, saints who fail to abide by Marx's dictum (Accumulate! Accumulate! That is Moses and all the prophets!) are obliged to leave the market.

At a more general level, the obvious theoretical objection to my argument is that the relationship between the saint and his followers does indeed involve exchanges, but these are of a symbolic rather than economic nature. By extension, my argument has imposed concepts of economic relationships which may have some relevance within a capitalist economy but have little or no applicability within rural, tribal, segmented, decentralised societies. Furthermore, it could be objected that I have concentrated illegitimately on the therapeutic aspects of these exchanges in order to give them a spurious concreteness, that is, the cure through the medium of *baraka* is exchanged for an economic reward. To answer this objection in full might involve a long detour through Lévi-Strauss' analysis of *'l'efficacité symbolique'* to Goux's analysis of multiple exchange systems (D'Amico 1978). My short answer is that in general I have no theoretical or moral objections to imposing my categories on unwilling subjects, but in the case of virtuoso religion it seems that the notion of economic (or at least, material) exchange is already embedded in the ways in which adepts and followers *themselves* conceptualise charisma and *baraka*. It has already been argued that, whatever else is involved, *baraka* and charisma carry with them ideas about well-being, plenty, health and wealth. In addition, followers of virtuosi often recognise that the exchange of gifts for charismatic blessing is not only economic but unequal. Sinhalese peasants often describe mendicant monks somewhat unflatteringly as 'rice-eaters', while the *bidonville* Hamadsha are referred to as 'exploiters'. If anything, my argument may in fact underestimate the macro-economic functions of Sufi lodges by limiting my considerations to micro-economic exchanges. The Sanusiya lodges were, for example, not only channels of *baraka* but great foci of trade, education and politics (Evans-Pritchard 1949).

The central theme of this discussion has been, therefore, that all virtuosity in religion requires economic support even where that source of economic support is highly despised by religious ideology. Weber thought that, while charismatic stratification did not parallel secular stratification, virtuoso standards were easily corrupted by mass religiosity because of the 'booty' mentality of followers and disciples. In this treatment of Islamic Sufism, the aim has been to elaborate and reinforce Weber's virtuoso/mass model in terms of an exchange theory of saint cults constructed around the idea that the virtuosi need the mass to finance their religious excellence. A number of variations on the problem of combining and separating religious and occupational roles has been institutionalised in religious history from the coenobitical communities of Christianity to the lineages of Islam. Perhaps the ultimate solution is a form of subterranean and covert virtuosity practised by men of the revived Malamatiyyah who

> "finding it necessary to pursue their sanctity through the very humiliation of not being able to display their unworldliness before the world, joined together in a regular tradition of concealed piety, which people should practice even while appearing worldly and without any Sufism at all" (Hodgson 1974, vol.2:457).

Such a strategy appears, however, to involve the preservation of a saintly role at the cost of any distinctive content, namely if one cannot beat them, one is obliged to join them.

NOTES

1. It is obvious that paralysis, catatonia, encephalitis lethargica and other disorders in European societies will have very different epidemologies and social significance from the cases of hysteria in Crapanzoni's Moroccan study. Nevertheless there are interesting parallels in that the social isolation of patients suffering from Parkinsonism intensifies their illness and in addition many patients respond favourably to music which provides a perspective to set against the disordered festination of Parkinsonism (Sacks 1976). Thus, the deeply Parkinsonian patient can be said to be 'possessed' by his hallucinations, tics and blocks.

2. In modern Britain, for example, standardised mortality ratios and rates of perinatal deaths are clearly influenced by social class membership. Similarly, various physical and mental illnesses are highly correlated with sexual status (G. Brown 1976). Differences in the treatment of illness, especially mental illness, according to social class position have been frequently observed (Dohrenwend and Dohrenwend 1969; Hollingshead and Redlich 1958).

3. Islamic saints thereby represent an interesting contrast to the saints of Christiandom. In the Roman Catholic Church, saints are

centrally and bureaucratically identified as paragons of orthodox faith and practice and therefore as suitable objects of veneration. The length of the process of canonisation normally insures that all saints are orthodox and dead. Their charisma cannot be inherited through the male line, although it may be contained in their tombs and relics. By contrast, Islamic saints are not centrally administered, not orthodox, not necessarily dead and their *baraka* can be transmitted both by contagion and by inheritance (Turner 1974).

4. The relationship of this pattern to the church-sect typology is obvious. While middle class, middle aged women are over-represented in churches, insofar as organised Christianity has any impact on the working class it is in the form of conversionist, emotional, fundamentalist sects (Niebuhr 1929).

5. The Demerdashiya Khalwatiya order provides an equally clear illustration of social and religious elitism (Trimingham 1971; Gilsenan 1973). Within an African context, the Mourides of Senegal have played a key role in the distribution of property and wealth (O'Brien 1971).

6. Weber's charisma/instrumental rationality distinction does, of course, bear a close relationship to Durkheim's categories of sacred and profane. Strict adherence to sacred prescriptions may drive men out of the profane world where the logic of these categories is that men 'are exhorted to withdraw themselves completely from the profane world, in order to lead an exclusively religious life. Hence comes the monasticism which is artificially organised outside of and apart from the natural environment in which ordinary man leads the life of the world, in a different one, closed to the first, and nearly its contrary' Durkheim 1961:55).

7. Since one of the tests of the possession of *baraka* is prosperity, it is important that the saints and their children *should* be wealthy. The redistribution of gifts from pilgrims to the poor must leave a considerable remainder since 'a poor *agurram* is a no-good *agurram*' (Gellner 1970:143).

8. Geza Vermes (1973) draws attention to the traditional healing significance of saliva and argues that Jesus had three main roles which in order were to heal the physically ill, to exorcise spirits and to forgive sins. Religion and healing, *baraka* and health appear to be closely interconnected in Judaism, Christianity and Islam.

REFERENCES

Abun-Nasr, Jamil M.
1965 *The Tijaniyya. A Sufi Order in the Modern World.* London.

Brown, G.
1976 Depression; A Sociological View, *The Maudsley Gazette*, 9-12.

Brown, L.C.
1972 "The religious establishment in Husainid Tunisia". In: N.R. Keddie (ed.) *Scholars, Saints and Sufis. Muslim Religious Institutions in the Middle East since 1500.* Berkeley, pp. 47-91.

Crapanzano, V.
1973 *The Hamadsha. A Study in Moroccan Ethnopsychiatry.* Berkeley.

D'Amico, R.
1978 Desire and the commodity form. *Telos* no. 35, pp. 88-122.

Dohrenwend, B.P. & B.S. Dohrenwend
1969 *Social Status and Psychological Disorder: A Casual Inquiry.*

Durkheim, E.
1961 *The Elementary Forms of Religious Life.* New York.

Dwyer, Daisy H.
1978 "Women, Sufism and Decision-making in Moroccan Islam". In: L. Beck & N. Keddie (eds.) *Women in the Muslim World.* Cambridge, pp. 585-598.

Evans-Pritchard, E.E.
1949 *The Sanusi of Cyrenaica.* Oxford.

Fakhouri, H.
1968 The Zar Cult in an Egyptian Village, *Anthropological Quarterly*, Vol. 41, pp. 49-56.

Geertz, C.
1968 *Islam Observed: Religious Development in Morocco and Indonesia.* New Haven.

Geijbels, M.
1978 Aspects of the veneration of saints in Islam with special reference to Pakistan. *The Muslim World*, Vol. 68, pp. 5-14.

Gellner, E.
1968 A pendulum swing theory of Islam. *Annales de Sociologie*, pp. 5-14.

1970 "Concepts and Society". In: D. Emmet & A. MacIntyre (eds.) *Sociological Theory and Philosophical Analysis.* London, pp. 115-149.

1972 "Patterns of tribal rebellion in Morocco". In: P.J. Vatikiotis (ed.) *Revolution in the Middle East and Other Case Studies*. London, pp. 120-145.

George, Katherine & C.H. George
1953 Roman Catholic sainthood and social status. *Journal of Religion* V, pp. 33-35.

Gibb, H.A.R.
1969 *Mohammedanism; A Historical Survey*. Oxford.

Gibb, H.A.R. & H. Bowen
1957 *Islamic Society and the West*. Oxford, Vol. 1, part I and II.

Gilsenan, M.
1973 *Saint and Sufi in Modern Egypt, an Essay in the Sociology of Religion*. Oxford.

Hodgson, Marshall G.S.
1974 *The Venture of Islam*. Chicago (3 Vols.).

Hollingshead, August B. & F. Redlich
1958 *Social Class and Mental Illness, a Community Study*, New York.

Khaldun, Ibn
1958 *The Muqaddimah, an Introduction to History*. London (3 Vols.).

Kennedy, J.G.
1967 Nubian Zar ceremonies as psychotherapy, *Human Organization*, Vol. 26, pp. 185-194.

Kritzeck, J.
1973 "Dervish Tales". In: L.F. Rushbrook Williams (ed.) *Sufi Studies: East and West*. New York, pp. 153-157.

Lings, M.
1961 *A Moslem Saint of the Twentieth Century*. London.

Massignon, L.
1922 *La passion d'al-Hosayn-ibn-Mansour al Hallaj, martyr mystique de l'Islam exécuté à Bagdad le 26. mars 922*. Paris (2 Vols.).

Mecklin, J.H.
1955 The passing of the saint, *American Journal of Sociology*, Vol. 60, pp. 34-53.

Morsy, Soheir A.
1978 "Sex differences and folk illness in an Egyptian village". In: L. Beck & N. Keddie (eds.) *Women in the Muslim World*, Cambridge, pp. 599-616.

Mulkay, M.J. & B.S. Turner
1971 Over-production of personnel and innovation in three social settings, *Sociology*, Vol. 5, pp. 47-61.

Niebuhr, H. Richard
1929 *The Social Sources of Denominationalism*. New York.

Obeyesekere, G.
1968 "Theodicy, sin and salvation in a sociology of Buddhism". In: E. Leach (ed.) *Dialectic in Practical Religion*, Cambridge, pp. 7-40.

O'Brien, Cruise D.B.
1971 *The Mourides of Senegal*. Oxford.

Parsons, Talcott
1951 *The Social System*. London.

Rice, C.
1964 *The Persian Sufis*. London.

Rosenwein, Barbara H. & Lester K. Little
1974 Social meaning in the monastic and mendicant spiritualities, *Past and Present*, Vol. 63, pp. 4-32.

Roth, G. & W. Schluchter
1979 *Max Weber's Vision of History; Ethics and Methods*. Berkeley.

Sacks, O.W.
1976 *Awakings*. Harmondsworth.

Spencer Trimingham, J.
1965 *Islam in the Sudan*. London.

1971 *The Sufi Orders in Islam*. London.

Turner, Bryan S.
1974 *Weber and Islam, a Critical Study*. London.

1977a The structuralist critique of Weber's sociology, *British Journal of Sociology*, Vol. 28, pp. 1-16.

1977b Confession and social structure, *The Annual Review of the Social Sciences of Religion*, Vol. 1, pp. 2-58.

Vermes, Geza
1973 *Jesus the Jew*. London.

Waardenburg, J.
1978 Official and popular religion in Islam, *Social Compass*, Vol. 25, pp. 315-341.

Weber, Marianne
1975 *Max Weber, a Biography*. New York.

Weber, Max
1958 *The Religion of India*. New York.

1961 *From Max Weber: Essays in Sociology*. London.

1966 *The Sociology of Religion*. London.

Wolf, E.R.
1971 *Peasant Wars of the Twentieth Century*. London.

Worsley, P.
1972 Franz Fanon and the 'Lumpenproletariat', *Socialist Register*, pp. 193-230.

Militant Islam: a Historical Perspective

Jamil M. Abun-Nasr

The militant Muslims, whose political influence has acquired great importance in the past few years, do not constitute a unitary movement. They are split into a large number of groups which seek different goals, by means of a rigourous application of the principles of Islam. Sometimes these groups are in opposition to national aspirations, and sometimes they merely express socio-economic grievances specific to their societies.

The only common ground which the militant Muslims seem to have, appears at first glance to be the rejection of European civilization, especially the political culture of Europe, in its liberal western as well as communist forms. The militant Muslim leaders who mobilized the Iranian masses against the Shah and still consider the United States as their arch-enemy, seek to crush the organized socialist groups in their country, who too contributed to the Shah's overthrow. Muslim groups of similar militant orientations have undertaken terrorist acts against the regime of President Asad of Syria, which enjoys the support of the Soviet Union, as well as against the pro-western regime of President Sadat of Egypt. Until about a year ago, Muslim preachers in Tunisia were causing much agitation directed against this country's pro-western political leadership, whose basis of power consists of a political party which, at least nominally, identifies itself with socialism.[1] And the militant Islamic ideology of President Qadhafi of Libya rejects both western liberalism and Marxist socialism (Muammar al-Gadhafi 1976).

Viewed in historical perspective, militant Islam would appear not only or even predominantly as a conglomeration of groups upholding a xenophobe religious ideology. It would appear rather as a continuous religious undercurrent, which recently acquired special significance to the Muslim masses because of the frustration of religio-nationalist hopes, in whose awakening the reformist Salafiyya movement played a decisive role. On the level of doctrine, militant Islam is a simplified version of the Salafiyya teachings, a version which derives its uncompromizing rigour predominantly from the fact that it has become a mass ideology, preached by popular religious leaders not bound, like the Salafiyya *ʿulamāʾ*, by the strict methodology of *fiqh* (science of the law) or indeed by any intellectual doubt.

The currents of thought and the historical situation which combined to bring about the first formulation of the Salafiyya doctrine in Egypt towards the end of the nineteenth century are, thanks to Albert Hourani's pioneering work (Hourani 1962) well understood. The shock which the Muslims experienced as they became confronted from the end of the eighteenth century with the great military superiority which the Europeans had over the Muslims, prepared the minds of an intellectually remarkable group of *ulama* to absorb the ideas reaching them from Europe and to work them out into a new Islamic synthesis. These *ʿulamāʾ* were scholars, versed in the traditional Islamic sciences and had a masterly knowledge of the technicalities of *fiqh*. As I shall show by reference to Rashid Rida, the Salafiyya *ʿulamāʾ* sometimes stretched the classical methodology of *uṣūl al-fiqh* (sources of the law) to its ultimate limits, but they did not ignore it in their endeavour to formulate a synthesis which was both Islamic and modern.

Although the method of reasoning of the Salafiyya *ʿulamāʾ*, especially the Egyptian amongst them, was classically Islamic, the new vision they evoked of Islam amounted to a reflection on the level of religious thought of the military retreat of the Muslims in the face of the Europeans. The Salafiyya leaders affirmed that the true Islam of *as-salāf aṣ-ṣāliḥ* (the pious forefathers) was a rational progressive religion. The model of progress which they consciously or unconsciously adopted was that of the economically prosperous, military effective, and politically stable European nation-state.

The retreat of *ʿulamāʾ*, who consider themselves to represent the religious conscience of the Muslims, before the advance of European civilization, can be accounted for by the fact that they did not perceive European civilization merely as an external ideological challenge. In the consciousness of the reformist *ulama*, who first formulated the Salafiyya doctrine as a religious-political programme before World War I, the European threat to Islam also consisted of the pervasive influence or European ideas, technical skills and material interests in Islamic lands. The reformist *ulama* were not intellectual recluses, but men who held public posts or had other positions in their societies worthy of being defended. The Salafiyya conception of reform cannot be properly understood in isolation from the fact that it was first formulated in Egypt after the material interests of the Europeans had penetrated the country on a large scale, the criminal law and the adjudication of business conflicts had been detached from the jurisdiction of the *qāḍīs*, and partly also after the British occupation of the country in 1882.

Changes in the structures of the administration and the army in

Islamic countries, the removal of important sections of the law from under the jurisdiction of the *qāḍīs*, and the economic transformations resulting from the penetration of European interests, were to lead in the long run to the undermining of the position of the *ulama* as a whole in society. In the early stages, the adverse effects of these transformations on the position of the *ʿulamāʾ* were felt only by the leading *ʿulamāʾ*, those who held the important judicial posts and enjoyed the benefactions of the rulers. There was an "expulsion from Olympus" for the *ʿulamāʾ*, as Daniel Crecelius has said (Crecelius 1972: 180), but at first it was an expulsion of only those who had olympian ranks. In order to explain what this fall meant, I shall attempt a description of the position which the men of religion had in the Muslim society before its penetration on a large scale by European influences. In making this description and in following the later development of the Salafiyya programme, I shall concentrate on the area of the Maghrib, partly in order to avoid vague schematized assertions, and because I am more familiar with the developments in this area than in other parts of the Islamic world. The developments in Egypt, the original homeland of the Salafiyya, will be held as a point of reference and comparison.

There seems to be a general agreement that the golden age of the *ʿulamāʾ* in Egypt was the last decades of Mamluk domination, the period of French occupation (1798-1801), and the beginning of the reign of Muhammad ᶜAli (Schölch, n.d.:40; Crecelius 1972:173-180). In this period, the *ʿulamāʾ* "performed the indispensable integrative functions that linked society with the government of the foreign élites" (Crecelius 1972:169). The *ʿulamāʾ* performed similar integrative functions in Tunisia during the Husaynid period until the reign of Ahmad Bey (1837-1855). The politically dominant stratum (the Beylical family, the élitist Turkish units of the army, the Beys' Mamluks, etc.) were of foreign extraction, and continued to lay emphasis on their foreignness even after they had become an integral part of the Tunisian urban society. All the members of the beylical family were born and brought up in Tunisia, and by the beginning of the eighteenth century, a large part of the élitist "Turkish" troops consisted of *kulughlis* (sons of Turkish soldiers and Tunisian women).[2] The ruling group distinguished itself from the native Tunisians (*ahl al-bilād*), who were barred access to key posts in the central administration (except as clerks) and in the army, through its identification with the Hanafite school of law, that of the Ottoman Empire. As an expression of the political domination of this group, the official supremacy of the judicial system was kept in the hands of a Hanafite: at first the Hanafite *qāḍī*, who until the middle of the 18th century was a Turk sent from Istanbul, and by the end of the century official supremacy passed on the the Hanafite chief *muftī*.[3]

Although the Husaynid Beys promoted the development of the Hanafite school of law and maintained formal supremacy of the judicial system in the hands of a Hanafite *ʿālim*, they also cultivated the goodwill of the leading Malikite *ʿulamāʾ* and Sufi *shaikh*s. Until towards the end of the eighteenth century, they allowed the posts of *qāḍī*, *muftī* and *imām*s of the major mosques in each town to be inherited within its notable *ʿulamāʾ* families. They made generous denotions to mosques and *madrasa*s, and from the reign of ᶜAli Bey (1759-1782) a special state fund was created from the revenue of the *jizya* (poll-tax) on the Jews and of certain *ḥabūs*-property, from which salaries to a chosen number of *ʿulamāʾ* and stipends to recognized students were paid (Hammuda b. ᶜAbdul-ᶜAziz 1970:204-205). The prominent *ʿulamāʾ* were granted estates, money to build houses, and an exemption from the payment of taxes. Mohamed el-Aziz ben Achour has shown, that the emergence of some of Tunisia's *ʿulamāʾ* as large landowners at the beginning of the nineteenth century was due to Beylical benefaction. In the first half of the nineteenth century the largest landowning family amongst the Hanafites was that of the Bayrams, descendants of a Turkish soldier. The Bayrams monopolized from the end of the eighteenth century the post of Hanafite chief *muftī*. At the same time, the largest landowning *ᶜālim* amongst the Malikites was Ibrahim ar-Riyahi, who held such posts as *imām* of the Zaytuna Mosque and Malikite chief *muftī*, and on several occasions served as ambassador of the Beys (M. el-Aziz ben Achour 1977:52-69). Ar-Riyahi came to Tunis as a poor student, and rose to prominence through ability as well as the favours of the Beys and the vizier Yusuf Sahib at-Tabaᶜ.[4]

The Husaynid Beys were not only interested in cultivating the goodwill of the leading *ʿulamāʾ* in the capital, but also of the men of religion in the countryside. Leon Carl Brown has pointed to the attention given by the Beys to maintaining good relations with the chiefs of the Sufi brotherhoods (Brown 1972:83-86), and Mohamed Hadi Cherif has shown that the founder of the Husaynid dynasty, Husayn b. ᶜAli, always had a *ᶜālim* from outside the capital as a religious counsellor, who received those coming from the countryside to complain against their governors and advised the Bey on dealing with their problems (M-H-Cherif 1979:477-496). My own research on religious learning in Tunisia in the Husaynid period has led me to the conclusion that the Beys pursued a conscious policy of linking all the important centres of religious learning - *madrasa*s as well as important *zawiya*s - to the state through the creation of *ḥabūs* for them and the making of regular grants of food and other supplies to them.

Islamists have become aware in the past few decades of the role which the religious leaders performed in Muslim society, before its penetration by western influences, as intermediaries between the rulers and the ruled. With regard to the gulf, which was to appear in Muslim society between the important economic and political forces and the religious leadership, as a result of these influences, it is specially important not to lose sight of the role which the men of religion played in economic life. In spite of the existence of a few exceptions[5], the holding of important religious and legal posts in Muslim society presupposed an urban family background and wealth. That the important *ʿulamāʾ* families intermarried with wealthy merchant and landowning families is also widely recognized amongst Islamists. But the integration of the *ʿulamāʾ* and other men of religion in economic activity did not arise only from these facts. It arose from the functions which they performed as *qāḍīs*, *ʿadls* (notaries) and *wakīls* (superintendents) of *ḥabūs*-property. The *qāḍīs* adjudicated conflicts arising from property ownership, inheritance, and business transactions. The *ʿadls*, who received the same training in Islamic law as the *qāḍīs*, drafted and certified contracts dealing with all sorts of property-transfer and business transactions. It was the practice, at least in Tunisia, that a prominent *ʿadl* be appointed as *shahīd* (witness, certifier) of expenditure on certain public projects or of the state revenue from certain sources (el-Aziz ben Achour 1977:103-112). On account of these economic functions and their position as custodians of religio-social values, Jacques Berque could write in the context of a study on the *qāḍīs* of Qayrawan, that the *ʿulamāʾ* acted more as social regulators than censors of morality (Berque 1973:108).

In the countryside the men of religion, more often the holymen (marabout or representative of a Sufi brotherhood) than the *alim*, also performed the functions of social regulators and were integrated into economic life. How the holymen performed these functions is starting to become clear through the work of such scholars as Berque, Evans-Pritchard, Gellner, Drouin and Pascon. However, one is not yet able to generalize about the role of the holymen in the countryside to the same degree as one can about the role of the *alim* in urban society. Two aspects of the association of holiness with economic activity can, however, be indicated. From the eighteenth century the Sufi brotherhoods started to replace the single marabouts in large areas as the spokesmen of the mystical tradition of Islam. This development was accompanied by the concentration of landed property in the hands of the Sufi *shaikhs*. The *shaikhs* of the Tayyibiyya brotherhood possessed large estates in northern Morocco and in Algeria, and conducted their dealings with the peasants cultivating them on the basis of contractual forms which, according to an official report by Berque in 1936, "*rappelle ... certaines modalités de notre vieux droit féodal*". Berque adds that through the system of tenancy they applied, the *shaikhs* of the Tayyibiyya were able to ensure for themselves "*une clientèle à la fois agricole et religieuse*".[6] Another example of the concentration of property in the hands of the *shaikh*s of the Sufi brotherhoods is that of the Qadiriyya and Rahmaniyya *zawiya*s in Nafta (south-west Tunisia). From the middle of the nineteenth century, reports of French officials in southern Algeria refer frequently to the trips made by agents of the *shaikh*s of these two *zawiya*s to gather the crops (cereals and dates) harvested on the lands they owned there.[7]

The second aspect of the association of holiness with economic activity relates to the functions of the maraboutic tribes, i.e. those tribes which claim descent from a marabout, in internal trade in the Maghrib. A report prepared in 1900 by the French intelligence services in Tunisia about one of these tribes, the Awlad Sidi ᶜUbayd, who had a *zawiya* in Nafta in the Tunisian Djerid, says that because these tribesmen were "*gens de Zaouia et aucunement hommes de poudre*", they travel with their camels "*entre le nord et le sud pour faire l'échange des produits de ces deux pays*".[8] There is evidence that other maraboutic tribes were active in the exchange of commodities between different regions of the Maghrib.

The temptation of idealize Muslim society before its penetration by European influences, describing it as an integrated one, with the men of religion acting as the custodians of its cherished values and the agents of inner harmony, should be guarded against. This picture is as misleading as that drawn by the Salafiyya leaders, of traditional Muslim society as a static one, with petrified religious institutions serving as the foundations of its moral and social stagnation. The controversy between the reformist *ʿulamāʾ* and the nostalgic traditionalists does not concern us here. What I tried to demonstrate through my reference to the roles of the men of religion in Maghribi society before its penetration by the influence of Europe is that the *ʿulamāʾ*, marabouts, and *shaikh*s of the brotherhoods were an integral part of the socio-political leadership. Their functions were not restricted to administering the cult and legitimizing political authority. They performed regulatory functions in social and economic life, and the more prominent amongst them derived, not only social prestige, but also relative wealth from the performance of these functions.

In Egypt and Tunisia the spread of European influence led to important changes in the army, the central administration and the legal system before the imposition of colonial rule. There is a parallel in the reaction of the leading *ʿulamāʾ* in these two countries to structural changes in the pre-colonial period: at first rejection, then from the 1870s, accommodation. In Egypt accommodation meant, among other things, the formulation of the Salafiyya doctrine. For understanding the difference between the Islam of the Salafiyya school and that of militant Islam, it is important to stress the point that the Salafiyya *ʿulamāʾ* at first conceived of reform as a concrete programme of action designed to transform the existing religious and political institutions. In spite of their apologetic affirmation that the true Islam is a rational progressive religion, these *ʿulamāʾ* did not devise a utopian programme for an ideal Muslim society, as the present militant Muslim ideologists do. The Salafiyya doctrine consisted of principles concerned primarily with the methodology of transforming Muslim law and relating it to a specific programme arising from a specifical historical situation. In order to illustrate this point and remain on familiar ground, I shall examine the development of the reaction of the *ʿulamāʾ* of Tunisia to pre-colonial structural changes in the central administration, while keeping Egypt as a point of reference.

By the beginning of the nineteenth century, the Husaynid state in Tunisia had achieved almost total control over the finances of mosques, *madrasa*s, and *zawiya*s. The practice of paying the leading *ʿulamāʾ* salaries from a special state fund, which had been initiated by ᶜAli Bey, was continued by his successors.[9] The appointment of the *wakīl*s of all *ḥabūs* property could take place only by Beylical decree. From the reign of Hammuda Bey (1782-1814), most of the *wakīl*s had become former army officers and other retired servants of the state.[10] Ahmad Bey's creating thirty new posts of *mudarris* in the Zaytuna Mosque endowed by the state, further consolidated the leading *ʿulamā*'s financial dependence on the state (Abi ad-Diyaf 1963/1966, IV:65-67). As I mentioned earlier, during the first half of the nineteenth century, only those *ʿulamāʾ* associated with Beylical authority were able to acquire large estates. It was therefore natural, that the leading *ʿulamāʾ* of Tunisia opposed changes in the structure of government upon which they had become dependent for their income and partly also for their influence in society.

The opposition of the leading *ʿulamāʾ* was immediately felt after Muhammed Bey (1855-1859) was induced to promulgate the fundamental law known as ᶜAhd al-Aman in September 1857 by the threat of French and British military intervention. The four *muftī*s of Tunis (two Hanafites and two Malikites), were invited by the Bey to participate in the work of the council set up in November 1857 to draw up a constitution based on this law. Muhammed Bayram IV, the chief Hanafite *muftī* and as such the Shaikh al-Islam of the country, agreed to attend the first meeting of the council only after the Bey ordered him to do so. After attending the first session, all four *muftī*s announced that they would no longer take part in the council on the ground that "their religious position was incompatible with the conduct of political affairs". They also said, that they would answer in writing any questions referred to them dealing with matters of Muslim law (Abi ad-Diyaf 1963/1966, IV:248). In 1860 a pseudo-parliamentary body called al-Majlis al-Akbar was constituted, consisting of state officials and notables, whose function was to exercise control over the Bey's ministers. This body did not include any of the leading *ʿulamāʾ*. The reformist minister Khayr ad-Din succeeded in persuading only three *mudarris*' to accept membership in it (ibid.V:33-38).

Ibn Abi ad-Diyaf points out that the argument put forward by the four *muftī*s to justify their refusal to become members of the new councils was an empty pretext (ibid.IV:248). For the four *muftī*s were the leading members of al-Majlis ash-Sharᶜi, a council which had judicial as well as advisory political functions. In the new councils the *muftī*s were ranked with state officials and city notables as ordinary members, and their participation in them served the purpose of legitimizing political institutions which usurped their authority as highly esteemed and rewarded spokesmen of Islamic law and as personifications of religio-political legitimacy. The reaction of the leading *ʿulamāʾ* of Tunisia to the structural changes resulting from European influence shows that, like that of the *ʿulamāʾ* of Egypt, they "first perceived modernization not as a set of foreign ideas, ... but as a set of hated new regulations, of odious and illegal seizures of their power and wealth" (Crecelius 1972:185).

In the last three decades of the nineteenth century, a group of reformist *ʿulamāʾ* appeared on the Tunisian scene. In Egypt at the same time, ᶜAbduh and al-Afghani were working out the main teachings of the Salafiyya, and the former showed readiness to cooperate with Lord Cromer in the hope of being able to use British presence to re-educate the Egyptian nation. Arnold Green has listed twenty-eight *ʿulamāʾ* who agreed to take part in carrying out the reforming programme initiated by Khayr ad-Din in the period when he was prime minister (1873-1877). Green points out that one of the factors which might have led these *ʿulamāʾ* to cooperate with the reforming prime minister was the "traditional desire to multiply one's positions and to increase one's income" (Green 1978:118-119). In other words, these *ʿulamāʾ* were coming to terms with the new realities. They came to terms with them through supporting a concrete programme put forward by a reformer who wielded political power. The reformist doctrine served as a set of guiding principles and as an ideological support of this programme. One of the reforming *ʿulamāʾ* who cooperated with Khayr ad-Din was Muhammad Bayram V, whose uncle Muhammad Bayram IV had staunchly turned his back on reform in the 1850s. Another was Ahmad b. Khunja who, through Khayr ad-Din's help, was appointed in 1877 as Hanafite chief *muftī*, i.e. as Shaikh al-Islam (ibid.:121).

Ahmad b. Khuja was a *ʿālim* of the solid traditional formation, well versed in *uṣūl al-fiqh* and in *tafsīr* (exegesis). He acquired a great reputation in Tunis as a teacher, and continued to teach the work on *tafsīr* by al-Baydawi even after he became Shaikh al-Islam. The renowned Malikite *ʿālim* Muhammad al-Fadil b. ᶜAshur extolled in a biography of Ahmad b. Khuja, the meticulous care with which he documented the *fatwā*s he wrote and which made him famous outside Tunisia. He was also a reformist thinker who, upon a suggestion from Khayr ad-Din, wrote two essays, showing the compatibility of Islam with modern civilization, and defending reform in general and Khayr ad-Din's programme in particular. According to Ibn ᶜAshur, Ibn Khuja played a determinant role in the changes introduced under the guidance of the Resident-General Paul Cambon in the early period of the French protectorate in the Tunisian system of law, and until his death in 1896 maintained excellent relations with French officials (ibid.:121-122; 136-137 and M. al-Fadil b. ᶜAshur 1970:93-101). Until World War I Egypt and in Tunisia, interest in religious reform remained restricted to a small group of *ʿulamāʾ* of the traditional scholarly formation, who held prominent religious posts. Reform remained a programme for transforming the central political institutions, some aspects of the Muslim law, and the main institutions of higher religious learning. As such it was a bridge between the *ʿulamāʾ* and the modern world, perceived not as an external ideological challenge, but as new structures emerging in the Muslim countries, whose scope was still sufficiently limited, that the *ulamāʾ* could hope to be able to come to terms with them. Albert Hourani is undoubtedly right in describing the impulse of reform at this stage as a liberal one, liberal not in the European sense, but in the sense of *at-Tasāmuḥ al-Islāmī* (Islamic tolerant openness) to which Ibn ᶜAshur ascribed Ibn Khuja's readiness to cooperate with French officials (Ibn ᶜAshur 1970:100). It was the tolerant openness of the cultivated Muslim upper classes.

By contrast with the last three decades of the nineteenth century, the teachings of the Salafiyya were transformed in the 1920s and 1930s into a nationalist ideology, whose spokesmen showed little interest in devising concrete programmes of reform. Three factors played a part in this transformation, which, being widely recognized, could be stated briefly here. The first was the consolidation of the colonial regimes along the lines which brought their economic exploitative character more clearly into focus. This recognition destroyed the remnants of the father-figure image that the pioneers of colonial administration had tried to project in the past. They were no longer seen to be bringing the superior skills and the legal principles of the more civilized nations to the colonized peoples. Persons like Lord Cromer, Paul Cambon, and Lyautey became out of place in the colonial structures whose foundations they had themselves laid.

The second factor was the wide-reaching transformation of the economic and political structures in the colonized countries in a way which rendered the politically integrative and legally regulative functions of the *ʿulamāʾ* in most areas of public life superfluous. No

ʿālim could any more reasonably hope, as ʿAbduh and Ibn Khuja had done, that through serving in the colonial structures he could influence them in a way compatible with his calling as spokesman of the religious conscience of the Muslims.

Thirdly, the rapid expansion of Islamic cities in the years after World War I made it no longer possible for politics in the Islamic world to remain the monopoly of small circles of notables. Unable to find a place for themselves compatible with their calling in the new structure, the spokesmen of the Salafiyya had either to withdraw from direct involvement in public life, or adapt their style of action and speech to the requirements of mass participation in politics. The ideology of the Organization of Muslim Brethren, about which I shall say more below, is the most concrete outcome of this adaptation.

The challenge which the spokesmen of the Salafiyya faced as a result of the emergence of the urban masses as a political force, led to responses which were influenced by the particular political situations in which they found themselves. But the trend towards simplifying the Salafiyya doctrine, and transforming it from concrete programmes of reform into symbols of national identity is noticeable in countries like Morocco and Algeria in which the spokesmen of the Salafiyya were *ʿulamāʾ* of the old scholarly formation. In both these countries, the leaders of the Salafiyya movement put much emphasis on the teaching of Arabic and Islamic culture in the schools which they founded. They took their tasks as educators of their peoples and as revivors of the true Islam as seriously as ʿAbduh had taken his. But in both countries the Salafiyya *ʿulamāʾ* had no offical positions to defend and from which to initiate reform, and had, therefore, to build a position for themselves by winning a mass following. They were also driven to adapt their style of action and public pronouncements to the requirements of mass mobilization by the fear, that the French educated Muslim leaders would become the only spokesmen of the economic and political aspirations of the urban masses.

The symbolic use of Islam to mobilize the masses in opposition to colonial policies in the Maghrib is a well known story. The *laṭīf* prayers in Moroccan mosques in 1930 were an effective means of mobilizing the masses against the Berber *zahir* (*dahir*) (Halstead 1967:178-190), the campaign led by Bourguiba in 1933 against the burial of Tunisians who obtained the French nationality popularized the conception that Islam was the basis of Tunisia's national identity (Bourguiba 1974:355-358; Moore 1965:32-33), and the use of the doctrine of *tawḥīd* (the oneness of God) by the Salafiyya leaders in Algeria as a symbol of national unity, was an effective means of combatting the argument of Ferhat Abbas and others, that the Algerian nation did not exist (Merad 1967:223-226; 276-278). These, as I said, are known facts which require no further elaboration here.

More relevant to the argument of this paper is the conclusion reached by Ali Merad, that the leaders of the Salafiyya in Algeria did not show any interest in drawing a concrete programme of social reform, and were satisfied with blaming the problems of their society on the colonial system. One of the reasons given by Merad for this failure is that the relationship between capital and labour in traditional Muslim society was regulated by *fiqh*, and none of the Algerian *ʿulamāʾ* of the Salafiyya school had any great competence in this field. These *ʿulamāʾ* were modernists, who evoked before their followers the image of a dynamic progressive Muslim society. They denounced the *marabout*s, accusing them of polytheism and of being responsible for social divisions in Algerian society. They denounced *taqlīd*, emphasized the need for a new *ijtihād*, and insisted that only through a re-examination of the original sources of the faith, especially the *Qurʾān* and *ḥadīth*, could the compatibility of the Islamic faith with scientific and technological progress become demonstrable. But they did not produce any new legal compendia, nor did they lay concrete programmes for the building of the modern Islamic state (ibid.:214-331). The Moroccan *ʿālim* politician ᶜAllal al-Fasi made a more serious effort than the Algerian leaders of the Salafiyya to analyse the problems of his society, discussing such questions as landownership, prostitution, and alcoholism. But here too the analysis is permeated by the desire to blame history and the colonial system for the appearance of these problems, and not to find workable solutions of them within a new Islamic structure (ᶜAllal al-Fasi n.d.).

In the Maghrib as in other parts of the Islamic world the spokesmen of the Salafiyya inculcated in their fellow Muslims the hope, that the independent Islamic nation-states, guided by the Salafiyya principles, would be prosperous and mighty, but also Muslim. They were the principal agents in making this hope a central element of the nationalist consciousness of the Muslim masses. But as they did not produce workable politico-economic programmes for the modern Islamic states, nor did they contribute to the effort of nationalist liberation in its crucial stages in a way which could have enabled them to acquire political power, they had little or no say in determining the course which politics was to follow in the Islamic countries after independence. The nationalist leaders, who made use of this hope in mobilizing the masses under their leadership in the confrontation with the colonial powers, used it after independence to consolidate and letigimize their political authority. But they assigned to the *ʿulamāʾ* who had aroused this hope only a subordinate function in public life. These *ʿulamāʾ* were called upon from time to time to issue formal statements in support of programmes of socio-economic development, which the rulers and their western-educated experts formulated. It was only on exceptional occasions that the *ʿulamāʾ* refused to issue such statements. The refusal of the *muftī* of Tunis J^{c}ayyit in 1960 to endorse Bourguiba's wish to exempt those employed in the public sector from the fast of Ramadan, is one of these rare exceptions (Gentz 1961:39-42). Furthermore the *ʿulamāʾ* did not attempt after the independence of their countries to restore the jurisdiction of the *sharī^{c}a* over aspects of public life which it had had in the past. As in the colonial period, questions of taxation and criminal and business law remained after the independence of the Islamic countries outside the jurisdiction of the *ʿulamāʾ*. In several Islamic countries - Egypt, Iraq, Iran, Morocco, Syria and Tunisia - restrictions were also introduced even on the provisions of the *sharī^{c}a* with regard to family law, especially those dealing with inheritance and divorce (Anderson 1976:38-42).

The readiness of the *ʿulamāʾ* to cooperate with the nationalist leaders, inspite of the maintenance of the gulf between the Islamic law and the economic and political life of the Islamic countries, seems to me to be part of a new Islamic orthodoxy which became consolidated in the Islamic world in the past thirty years or so. What I call the new orthodoxy amounts to subordinating the prescriptions of the *sharī^{c}a* to the nationalist interests of the Muslims and, with the exception of Iran, transforming the *ʿulamāʾ* into quasi-officials of the state, having no will of their own. The new orthodoxy arose from the requirements of realizing the religious-nationalist hope wich the Muslim rulers inherited from the Salafiyya leaders and corresponds to the dominant role which they and the technocrats, as opposed to the *ʿulamāʾ*, play in achieving it. This is a *de facto* orthodoxy, which is neither formally acknowledged nor openly defended. But the principle of *maṣlaḥa*, upon which it is based, in the new formulation of it devised by Rashīd Rida, is widely acknowledged.

The wide diffusion of the Salafiyya teachings and their acceptance by the *ʿulamāʾ* in many parts of the Islamic world was Rida's greatest achievement. Born near Tripoli in Lebanon, he lived in Cairo from 1897 until his death in 1935 and worked closely with ^{c}Abduh until the latter's death in 1905. The *al-Manār* periodical served as mouthpiece of the Salafiyya teachings, as consolidated and developed by Rida, and had an influence which went far beyond the boundaries of Egypt. Rida was driven by the pious aim of transforming the *sharī^{c}a*, so that it could become an all-embracing system of law for the modern Muslim society. But he was misled by the apologetic assumption, which is part and parcel of the Salafiyya teachings, that the true Islam was a rational religion compatible with progress, as well as by a high degree of wishful thinking, into a position which amounted to placing public utility before the scriptural texts as a source of the Islamic law. The assumption that the true Islam is a rational religion, led Rida into arguing that, with regard to the rules of the *sharīᶜa* governing man's life in society, as different from those dealing with ritual and devotion, a "broad measure of human interpretation and adaptation to changing circumstances" was admissible (Kerr 1960:102). He elevated *maṣlaḥa* (in this context meaning public interest) to a leading principle of *fiqh*, and combined it with another principle of the Islamic law, namely that "necessity makes legal what is forbidden", and in this way freed the new interpretation of the *sharīᶜa* from being strictly bound by the *Qurᶜān* and *ḥadīth*. Furthermore, Rida argued that the *sharīᶜa* should be developed through a new form of *ijmāᶜ* (consensus) based on consultation between the rulers and the *ʿulamāʾ* organized as a corporate body. He thus opened the way for recognizing the positive legislation of the rulers as part of the legal system of Muslim society (Kerr 1960:175; Hourani 1962:233-234). The wishful thinking in this attitude is that legislation not strictly bound by the exegesis of the scriptural texts, and guided by public interest, would remain compatible with the scriptural bases of the faith.

The militant Muslims reject what I have called a new orthodoxy. They reject the political authority of the modernizing nationalist élites on the ground that, even when working in the interest of the Islamic nations, they encroach on the prescriptions of the *sharīᶜa*. They also reject the religious authority of the *ʿulamāʾ* who accept to serve in the national structures which curtail the application of the prescriptions of the *sharīᶜa* to acts of devotion and norms of family life. Because of their scholarship, social background, and the functions they performed, the *ʿulamāʾ* belonged to the social élites in their countries. "*Porte-paroles de la 'grande culture', ils sont* (the *ʿulamāʾ*) *davantage l'expression de l'establishment urbain ...*" (Stambouli & Zghal 1972:207). This applies to the reformist as much as to the other *ʿulamāʾ*. Militant Islam is a popularized and simplified version of the reformist teachings of the Salafiyya, and it appeals specially to the urban masses. Until recently, mystical Islam, as interpreted and ritualized by the Sufi brotherhoods, had constituted the normal channel for the religiosity of the urban masses (Stambouli & Zghal 1972:207; Gilsenan 1973:93). The influence of the Sufi brotherhoods over the urban masses has been on the decline. The vacuum thus created has been filled by zealous Muslims preaching about a new Islamic millenium. The vision of the new millenium is implied in Salafiyya apologetics. In the hands of the militant preachers apologetics became the foundations of utopia.

The mystical religious drive and the popularization of the Salafiyya teachings, which combine to give militant Islam its dynamic character, are both reflected in the Organization of the Muslim Brethren (*Munazzamat al-Ikhwān al-Muslimīn*). The founder of this organization, Hasan al-Banna, was born in 1906 in the small town of Mahmudiyya, about 150 km from Cairo. He was the son of a religious teacher, who also practised watch repairing. During adolescence, al-Banna witnessed the *dhikr* (spiritual exercises) of the Hasafiyya Brotherhood. "Deeply impressed, he became involved in this particular order for the next twenty years, and with Sufism in a special way for most of his life" (Mitchell 1969:2). As a student in Cairo in the 1920s, al-Banna experienced at first hand the political turmoil through which Egypt was passing then. He also came into contact with spokesmen of the Salafiyya, including Rashid Rida. His intellectual formation was not Islamicly scholastic but modern: he studied not at the Azhar but at Dar al-ᶜUlūm. But he was a zealous dedicated Muslim and an organizer: before launching the Organization of the Muslim Brethren in 1928, he was involved in the foundation of a number of other associations (ibid.:3-6).

The teachings of the Organization of the Muslim Brethren, developed by al-Banna and others of its leaders, stressed that the revival of Islam would proceed not so much from the formulation of a new theology, but from the spiritual awakening of the Muslims. But principles which should give direction to this spiritual awakening are laid down. Three of these principles seem to me to have special significance in relation to the political role which the Organization played in the Arab world.

The first is the emphasis placed on the centrality of the *shariᶜa* in the life of Muslims, combined with stressing the need for reformulating it in the light of new circumstances. The reformulation of the *sharīᶜa* will proceed from a new *ijtihād* bound by the *Qur'ān* and *ḥadīth*, but some of the writers of the Organization admit the right of the head of the Muslim state to legislate in public interest (ibid.:236-241). The second important principle of the Organization is the refusal to admit any separation between religion and the state. One of the most influential of the writers of this Organization, Sayyid Qutb, sums up the attitude of the Muslim Brethren on this question as follows: "Islam is a word including in its total meaning religion, politics, economics, society, etc. ... *dawla* (state) is not the equal or opposite of *dīn* (religion); both are expressions of Islam" (ibid.:243). A third important guiding principle is the emphasis on the virtue of work. Institutionalized help to the needy in the form of *zakāt* (alms), and mutual help amongst the Muslims, are extolled; but labour is considered the only legitimate basis of property (ibid.:250-253).

The religiously simple but socially orientated teachings of the Organization of Muslim Brethren, as well as the dedication of its leaders, enabled it to attract the urban poor, as well as idealist intellectuals and university students. The uncompromizing insistence with which the Brethren pursued their effort to induce Muslim rulers to follow Islamic principles, and the public criticism which they directed against them, made the Brethren the enemies of the political establishments in the new Islamic nation-states. Although the charges made in connection with their implication in the assassination of Nuqrashi, the Prime Minister of Egypt, in 1948, and in an attempt on the life of President Nasser in 1954 have not been established, their drive to political power is real. It arises, as Mitchell has pointed out, from their belief "that the power to reform was inextricably tied up with the power to rule" (ibid.:308).

Although the Organization of the Muslim Brethren has had branches since the 1940s in most Arab countries, not all militant Muslims in these countries are members or sympathizers of it. The literature of the militant Muslim groups is vast, and it has not been systematically analysed. My reading of a small part of it,leads me to the conclusion that the militant Muslim groups in general, even those that reject any identification with the Organization of the Muslim Brethren, have in common with the Brethren a mystical vision of Islam, a utopian conception of modern Muslim society, and a disregard for the classical methodology of *fiqh*. To illustrate this point, I summarize the central points in a work on the subject of Islamic government by Taqiyy ad-Din an-Nabhani, the leading intellectual spokesman of *Ḥizb at-Taḥrīr* (the Liberation Party). This party has a great following amongst the Palestinians, and its followers often clashed with the members of the Organization of Muslim Brethren amongst the Palestinians.

An-Nabhani starts his analysis of the system of government in Islam by rejecting the separation of religion from the state, and affirms that the Islamic state is one governed according to the commandments of the religion. The revival of Islam does not depend only upon the building of mosques and the banning of alcohol, but upon the construction of a truly Islamic system of government. The principal functions of the Islamic state consist of applying the *sharīᶜa* in the Muslim society, and spreading Islam in other parts of the world. The development of the *sharīᶜa* should proceed from an *ijtihād* of the *ʿulamā*ʾ, endorsed and adopted as law by the *khalīfa*. The *khalīfa* himself should be chosen by the Muslims and should be held responsible for the strict application of the *sharīᶜa*. An elective consultative assembly (*majlis shūrā*) would advise the *khalīfa* in the name of the people on matters of public interest, but has no legislative authority. An-Nabhani goes into some detail in describing the organs of government and the judiciary in the Islamic state, always with the tone of someone who knows what belongs to Islam and what does not, and who feels no great need to justify his assertions. Revolution against rulers who do not follow the *sharīᶜa* is not only justified but a duty. Such a revolution is not an anti-Islamic act, but a liberational one, since its purpose is to restore the eternal Islamic order (Taqiyy ad-Din an-Nabhani 1953;in particular pp. 3, 7-8, 10-12, 79-83, 110-111).

As I said at the beginning of this paper, the militant Muslim groups do not constitute a unitary movement. Their ideology is neither original, nor is it uniform, inspite of its having the common characteristics I have already indicated. But the militant Muslims are all agreed on the necessity of reintegrating Muslim society through the restoration of the supremacy of the *sharīᶜa* in all spheres of life. Restoring the supremacy of the *sharīᶜa* would herald a new glorious era for the Islamic *umma*, viewed potentially as a united political entity. For the militant Muslims, while working for the revival of Islam in their own countries, they still hold on to the traditional concept that Muslims, wherever they are, constitute a single political community (Ansari 1961:28-38). But restoring the supremacy of the *sharīᶜa* is viewed also as a means of achieving social justice. The emphasis on social justice in the teachings of the militant Muslims, and viewing the strict application of the *sharīᶜa* in all spheres of life as its necessary basis, renders militant Islam politically dynamic, and gives its attack on the maintenance of the gulf between the *sharīᶜa* and the important economic and political forces in the Muslim societies an anti-establishment and anti-European character.

In the nineteenth century the *ᶜulamā'* at first rejected the structures which appeared in their societies as a result of European penetration, because these threatened their position. They then devised a doctrine which, they hoped, would serve as the basis for the reconciliation of Islam with the new structures and enable them to recover their influence. On the practical level, they failed. They could not obtain a new position of power in the Islamic nation-states and willy-nilly accepted a subordinate role in them. But they succeeded in making the hope for reconciling Islam with material and social progress a part of the religious consciousness of the masses. Through utopian ideological superstructures built upon the teachings of the Salafiyya, the militant Muslim leaders articulate an overwhelming mass resentment arising from the frustration of this hope.

The anti-European implication of this resentment arises from the fact that the politico-economic structures in the independent nation-states, which are held responsible for the frustration of this hope, are viewed as an extension of European civilization and Europian-American interests. These structures, it is true, are dominated by Muslims, but ones who are identified with European civilization, not only through the skills and socio-political ideas they channel into the Muslim society, but also through their style of life. When the militant Muslims attack the separation of religion from the state, describing it as a foreign plot against Islam, and denounce the style of life of the nationalist élites in their societies as being non-Islamic, they articulate the resentment of the poor upon being left behind in the process of economic development.

This economic resentment, upon which militant Islam feeds, accounts for the popularity of socialist thought with the militant Muslims. But it is a form of socialist thought which had to be harmonized with the religio-nationalist implications of this resentment. In this context, it will be relevant to note that one of the most widely read works on what is called Islamic socialism, was written by Mustafa as-Siba^{c}i (*Ishtirakiyat al-Islam* n.d.), one of most prominent leaders of the Organization of the Muslim Brethren in Syria in the 1940s and 1950s. As-Siba^{c}i's socialism, like that of President Qadhafi, amounts to social justice pursued in the nationalist interest of the Muslim. Through it, the Muslim affirm their independence from the west as well as from the communist world.

The religio-nationalist context of Islamic socialism should serve as a reminder that militant Islam cannot be explained only through an analysis of the economic problems of Muslim society. Economic analysis alone is not sufficient to explain the general phenomenon of militant Islam, nor even important episodes of it. The attempt, for example, to explain the occupation of the Grand Mosque of Mecca by Muslim extremists in November and December 1979, by reference to such problems, arising from the rapid economic transformation of Saudi Arabia, and the presence of uprooted tribesmen and poor immigrant labourers from the Yemen, leads to a dead-end if they were not viewed in relation to the latent religio-nationalist resentment, which these problems triggered off.[11] In Iran, the great economic gulf between the dominant groups associated with the regime of the Shah and the rest of the population, did not alone generate the forces which led to his overthrow. Socialist leaders articulated the economic grievances of the poor for several decades, but they could not make any headway against the political system which generated them. Only when the economic grievances were placed within the wider framework of the religio-nationalist grievances articulated by the religious leaders, were the Iranian masses mobilized on such a scale, that they dared to defy the Shah's modern army.

I have only touched briefly upon Iran, the country which witnessed an apocalyptic change through the agency of militant Islam, mostly out of ignorance of the historical background of the Iranian revolution. For the background of this revolution, I can do no better than to refer the reader to the two essays by Nikki Keddie and Hamid Algar in the collective work *Scholars, Saints and Sufis* (1972)[12] edited by the first of these two scholars. It is worth noting, however, that the *ʿulamā'* (*faqihs* in the *Shī^{c}ite* usage) in Iran could not be integrated in the structure of a modernist nation state as the

ʿulamāʾ in the Arab *sunni* part of the Islamic world. This is due to the *Shīcite-Ismacīli* belief that legitimate authority resides in the concealed *imām*, and the *faqīh*s have authority merely as his deputies, as well as to political developments in Iran during the twentieth century. A series of lectures, which Ayatollah Khomeiny delivered in Najaf in 1970 shows that, whereas he agrees with other militant Muslims in condemning the separation of religion from the state and restricting the jurisdiction of the *sharīca*, which he considers a western plot against Islam, he insists on the right of the *faqīh* to exercise political power directly in his capacity as deputy of the concealed *imām* (Ayatollah Khomeiny 1979:8-22, 45-62). In Iran, as in the Arab world, Islamic militancy feeds on a resentment which is religio-nationalist as well as economic. In Iran the resentment of the masses coincided with the resentment of an organized group of *ʿulamāʾ*. In the Arab world, the *ʿulamāʾ* are not organized, and the resentment articulated by the militant Muslim leaders works against them.

NOTES

1 For a detailed report on these preachers, see *Le Nouvel Observateur* of 17 December 1979.

2 See the references to the *kulughlis* in Muhammad as-Saghir b. Yusuf *Chronique Tunisienne*, tr. by Victor Serres and Muhammed Lasram, especially pp. 208-211.

3 Jamil M. Abun-Nasr "The Mashyakhat al-Islam in Tunisia", paper presented at the 9th congress of the "Union Européenne des Arabisants et Islamisants", Amsterdam, September 1979, and will appear soon in the Proceedings of the congress.

4 See inter alia ar-Riyahi's biography in Ahmad b. Abi as-Diyaf *Ithaf Ahl az-Zaman bi tarikh muluk Tunis wa cahd al-aman* 1963/1966, Vol. VII:73-82.

5 See Afaf Lutfi al-Sayyid Marsot (1972:157), who arrived at the conclusion that most of the prominent *ulama* of the Azhar in the eighteenth century were of peasant origin.

6 Jacques Berque "La Maison d'ouezzan - son attitude politique - ses relations avec l'Algérie et les Taybias Algériens - sa politique immobilière: Rapport de Mission", Archives d'Outre-Mer, Aix-en-Provence, 31 H-21.

7 Archives d'Outre-Mer, Aix-en-Provence, 16 H2-3.

8 Archives du Ministère des Affaires Etrangères, Paris, Correspondances politiques et commercials, Vol. 81, folios 7-60.

9 See the lists of the *ulama* paid salaries by the state in the 1820s in Archives Générales, Tunis, Dos. 703, Car. 63, Armoire 6.

10 Ibn Abi ad-Diyaf *op.cit.*, III, p. 57; and Archives Générales, Tunis, Dos. 989, Car. 81, Armoire 3.

11 For a predominantly economic analysis of the background of the occupation of the Grand Mosque of Mecca, see the article by A.H. "Hintergründe des Moschee-Aktion in Mekka", in *Neue Zürcher Zeitung* of 9/10 December 1979.

12 Nikki R. Keddie "The Roots of the Ulama's power in Modern Iran"; and Hamid Algar "The Oppositional Role of the Ulama in Twentieth Century Iran" in Keddie (ed.) 1972, pp. 211-229, 232-255.

REFERENCES

ᶜAbdul-ᶜAziz, Hamuda b.
1970 *al-Kitab al Bashi*. Tunis.

Abi ad-Diyaf, (ibn) Ahmad b.
1963/1966 *Ithaf Ahl az-Zaman bi tarikh muluk Tunis wa ᶜahd al-aman*. Tunis, Vol. III, IV, V.

Algar, Hamid
1972 "The Oppositional Role of the Ulama in Twentieth Century Iran". In: N.R. Keddie (ed.) *Scholars, Saints and Sufis*. Berkely & Los Angeles, pp. 232-255.

Anderson, N.
1976 *Law Reform in the Muslim World*. London.

Ansari, Zafar Ishaq
1961 Contemporary Islam and Nationalism, a case study of Egypt. *Die Welt des Islams*, Vol. III:28-38.

el-Aziz ben Achour, Mohamed
1977 *Les Ulama à Tunis aux XVIIIe et XIXe siècles*. Thèse de Doctorat de 3-ième Cycle. Paris-Sorbonne.

Berque, Jacques
1973 Cadis de Kairouan. *Revue de l'occident Musulman et de la Mediterranée* no. 13-14.

Bourguiba, Habib
1974 *Articles de Presse (1929-1934)*. Tunis, pp. 355-358.

Brown, L.C.
1972 The Religious Establishment in Husainid Tunisia. In: N.R. Keddie (ed.) *Scholars, Saints and Sufis*. Berkely & Los Angeles.

M-H-Cherif
1979 *Pouvoir et Société dans La Tunisie de Husayn bin ᶜAli (1705-1740)*. Thèse de Doctorat des Lettres. Paris-Sorbonne.

Crecelius, D.
1972 "Non-ideological Responses of the Egyptian Ulama to Modernization". In: N.R. Keddie (ed.) *Scholars, Saints and Sufis*. Berkeley & Los Angeles.

al-Fadil (Ibn) b. Ashur, Muhammad
1970 *Tarajim al-aᶜlam*. Tunis.

al-Fasi, ᶜAllal
n.d. *an-Naqd adhdhati*. Tetuan.

al-Gadhafi, Muammar
1976 *The Green Book, Pt. I, The Solution of the Problem of Democracy: The Authority of the People*. London.

Gentz, Jochen
1961 Tunesische Fatwas über das Fasten im Ramadan. *Die Welt des Islams*, Vol. III:39-42.

Gilsenan, M.
1973 *Saint and Sufi in Modern Egypt*. Oxford.

Green, A.
1978 *The Tunesian Ulama, 1873-1915*. Leiden.

Halstead, J.P.
1967 *Rebirth of a Nation, the origins and rise of Moroccan nationalism, 1912-1944*. Cambridge.

Hourani, Albert
1962 *Arabic Thought in the Liberal Age, 1798-1939*. London.

Keddie, N.R.
1972 "The Roots of the Ulama's Power in Modern Iran. In: N.R. Keddie (ed.) *Scholars, Saints and Sufis*. Berkeley & Los Angeles, pp. 211-229.

Kerr, Malcolm
1960 Rashid Rida and Islamic Legal Reform. *The Muslim World*, Vol. X.

Khomeiny (Ayatollah)
1979 *al-Hukuma al-Islamiyya*. Beirut.

Merad, Ali
1967 *Le réformisme musulman en Algérie de 1925 à 1940*. Paris.

Mitchell, R.P.
1969 *The Society of the Muslim Brothers*. London.

Moore, Clement Henry
1965 *Tunisia since Independence: the Dynamics of One-Party Government*. Berkeley & Los Angeles.

as-Saghir b. Usuf, Muhammad
n.d. *Chronique Tunisienne*, tr. by Victor Serres and Muhammed Lasram, Tunis, 2nd. Edition.

al-Sayyid Marsot, Afaf Lufti
1972 "The Ulama of Cairo in the eighteenth and nineteenth centuries". In: N.R. Keddie (ed.) *Scholars, Saints and Sufis*. Berkeley & Los Angeles.

as-Siba^{c}i, Mustafa
n.d. *Ishtirakiyat al-Islam*. Cairo.

Schölch, Alexander
n.d. *Ägypten den Ägyptern!* Freiburg.

Stambouli, F. & A. Zghal
1972 La Vie Urbaine dans le Maghreb Précolonial. *Annuaire de l'Afrique du Nord*, Vol. XI.

Taqiyy ad-Din an-Nabhani
1953 *Nizam al-Hukm fi 'l-Islam*. Beirut.

OTHER SOURCES AND DOCUMENTS

Archives d'Outre-Mer, Aix-en-Provence
31 H-21 (Jacque Berque, "La Maison d'ouezzan - son attitude politique - ses relations avec l'Algérie et les Taybias Algériens - sa politique immobilière: Rapport de Mission").

16 H2-3

Archives du Ministère des Affaires Etrangères, Paris
Vol. 81, folios 7-60 (Correspondances politiques et commercials).

Archives Générales, Paris
Dos. 703, Car. 63, Armoire 6.

Dos. 989, Car. 81, Armoire 3.

The Origin of Modern Conservatism and Islamic Fundamentalism

Hassan Hanafi

It is clear to anyone who watches the Muslim World that religious conservatism and Islamic fundamentalism have revived in the last decade. They continue to strengthen themselves beneath the surface and sometimes burst out as in Iran and lately in Saudi Arabia. This strengthening is still growing in the hearts of the masses and waiting for external occasions to explode. The sudden rise of Muslim groups shows only the tip of the iceberg. Many of them are still underground movements. The control of the mass-media by the state does not permit any free expression for these Muslim groups. They are filled up from the bottom and burst out when the safety valve is overwhelmed by internal pressure.

The 'awakening of Islam' as a giant who was asleep is a natural phenomenon. The Muslim World is now at the beginning of the fifteenth century. Popular tradition says that at the outset of every century a renewal occurs. Every Muslim now is waiting for that renewal. It is not millenarianism but centenarianism.

As nothing in history occurs merely by accident, the following three reasons can be identified behind this phenomenon which appears peculiar to the West but which is a natural and long awaited *parousia* to the Muslim masses.

I. THE FAILURE OF CONTEMPORARY IDEOLOGIES OF MODERNIZATION

All contemporary ideologies of modernization practised in the last quarter century failed to modernize Muslim societies. On the contrary, these ideologies perpetuated its backwardness, decadence and defeat. Gains on the surface such as economic development, increase of production etc. are annuled by losses in depth such as the moral regression of Islamic consciousness in the Muslim masses, fear, indifference, hypocrisy, etc.

Nothing was left for them except Islam, their holding tradition through all the vicissitudes of history. Even in its traditional form, Islam remained the only option for the Muslims. It has never been practised in modern times. It may be their own salvation.

a. The Failure of Western Liberalism

Before modern Arab revolutions, Western Liberalism ruled in Egypt. In spite of some gains in the economy, such as the national bank and in industry, in politics, including political liberalism and freedom of expression, it ended in a complete collapse on the eve of the Egyptian revolution. The king was a power intervening in the multi-party system, dissolving the parliament, abolishing the constitution, dismissing the elected prime minister, forming loyal parties to the palace, assassinating political leaders, etc. The multi-party system itself was a game played between the majority ruling party and the minority opposition parties. Both were eager to rule and to liquidate the opposition. Elections were falsified by the party in power, votes were bought and state machinery intervened. A *laissez-faire* economy was practised. Capital was controlled by a handful of *Pachas* playing with the stock market. Egypt was a cotton farm for the British textile industry, while national industry was in the hands of the same *Pachas*. Workers had no rights. Big landlords who represented 0.5% of the population owned more than 50% of the land. Peasants were almost owned by the landlord and bought and sold with the land. There was the extremely rich minority class and the extreme majority class.

Illiteracy was more than 85%. The highly educated were highly paid. Only the rich elite could afford advanced education, an alliance with the West was a permanent policy in foreign affairs in spite of the British occupation of the Suez Canal.

Muslim groups were persecuted. Hassan El-Banna, the charismatic figure and the leader of the Muslim Brethren was assassinated in February 1949. Before the masses, this total corruption demanded the remedy of Islamic Ethics. Islam offers solutions for economic, political and social problems in Egypt. The secret organization of the Brethren used violence as a defensive measure. The more difficult the political crisis gets, the more quickly Islam appears as the only salvation.

b. Failure of State Socialism

The revolution burst out in Egypt in July 1952 to implement radical changes in modern society. Its efforts included agrarian reform, development of the public sector, cooperatives, industrialization, worker's rights, free education, non-alignment, socialism, liberation, Arab nationalism, national struggle for all colonized nations, Afro-Asian people's solidarity, the three Continents Conference, etc. However, state socialism failed to modernize Muslim societies which later suffered a series of set-backs, including the defeat of 1967, Denasserization since 1970, socialist retreat, American alliance, Egyptian isolationism, recognition of Israel, etc. The failure is due to several reasons.

The revolution changed the economic system in terms of ownership and the means of production, but it did not change the mass-culture that remained in its traditional track. The categories used by the revolution were alien to mass-traditions: socialism, freedom, Arabism, production. These were all secular categories unable to make a large impact on mass behaviour. Party educational schools, youth organizations, powerful mass-media did not succeed in making these categories more convincing. Islamic socialism was a mere religious justification of the socialist laws of 1961 which were decreed by the political leadership. There was no real change in the traditional religious beliefs embedded in the culture. The disparities between slogans and realities, freedom in concept and despotism in reality, socialism in theory and the wealth of the ruling elite in reality, Arab unity in principal and Arab disunity in fact were very apparent. This dislocation between what people were told and what they saw resulted in the complete loss of credibility of all ideologies of socialism. The unity of words and actions is a religious dictum in mass-culture. The formation of a new class with the ruling elite at the top and the resurgence of a new feudalism in the countryside and a new capitalism in the private sector (e.g. construction, whole-sale trade) left the masses completely indifferent to the intellectual apparatus of the political regime. The absence of a popular political party to rally the masses behind the regime increased mass distrust. The masses moved away from any political activism, which was viewed as opportunism. The people were an easy target for the activities and the work of Muslim groups. The government clash with the Muslim Brethren and the smashing of this major Islamic group in Egypt made them appear as the real alternative to the failure of state socialism. The arrests, tortures and executions of its members rallied the masses behind them.

In the last decade, religion was used as an easy explanation of the defeat of 1967 in order to rally quick mass support for the failing regime. Had the people been closer to God and more steadfast in their faith, victory would have come. The victory of 1973 was due to the return to faith. The Prophet and the Angels even came and crossed the Suez Canal with the soldiers. The state of 'science and faith' became the model of the modern state. Religion has been used emphatically in the last five years as a means to discredit political opposition. All opposing groups, namely the Nasserites, Marxists, democrats, unionists, Muslim revolutionaries, were all dubbed as atheists. The frenzied zeal of Islam was used by political leadership as the only justification of its authority. Muslim groups, namely the *Jama'a Islamiyya* was used on the campus to clean out all progressive groups. Fanaticism became a common practice in daily life. The call for prayer five times a day in the mass-media, competition in mosques building, pushing the beards, dressing in the veil, praying in the middle of classes, etc. were all signs of 'Integrism'. The political leadership from its side propagated mystic values such as patience, resignation, reliance, predestination, love, peace, tolerance, etc. to subdue the masses and protect them against subversive rejectionist values. Obedience to the 'head of the family', the 'commander of the believers' was portrayed as the highest form of citizenship. Religious conservatism was used as the *opium of the people* by the political leadership, while Islamic fundamentalism served as the *cry of the oppressed* for the Muslim masses.

c. Failure of Traditional Marxism

Classical or dogmatic Marxism participated in the political struggle in the Muslim world. It has not succeeded in coming to power except lately in one or two Muslim countries. In spite its successes in leading national liberation against colonialism, obtaining national independence, attacking problems of underdevelopment such as illiteracy, poverty and industrialization, it also had its limits. The adopted ideology, the ideology of the working class (Afghanistan) or Marxism-Leninism (People's Democratic Republic of Yemen) is uprooted from the people's tradition. Like all other secular ideologies, it does not speak to the heart of the masses. Dialectical materialism, quality, quantity, contradiction, etc. are incomprehensible to the illiterate masses. That is why the ideology remained as prerogatives of the intellectual elite in spite of the claim that it is the ideology of the working class. The revolutionary intellectual elite may form strong mass leadership. However, ideological pedantism is different from religious populism. Moreover, the scientific ideology is almost impossible in a mythical society which is still operating through images, symbols, stories, narratives and all forms of anthropomorphic thought. Motivations in underdeveloped countries are a part of people's conceptual framework. A demagogue may rally the masses behind him more than a Marxist with a scientific outlook of the universe. Abandoning popular schemes is itself unscientific, once these schemes are operative at least for one or two generations. Rationalism, naturalism, democracy and humanism as metamorphoses of popular traditions may be more useful than a scientific ideology.

Traditional Marxism was applied literally without any adaption to the circumstances of particular Muslim societies. Class struggle, religion as opium of the people, the dictatorship of the proletariat or the priority of infrastructure over super-structure may not correspond with Muslim masses which believe in the *Umma* as an undestructable tie, in religion of the poor and oppressed and in the predominance of belief-systems for mass-behaviour. Studies of particular societies were absent as if the general theory were a magic key to all social problems.

Because of the absence of phases in social change and the desire to change the society in one shot, *coup d'état* was the means to power and launched the process of social change. Change from above always put Marxists in conflict with political regimes. They were easily accused of being atheist Muslims and agents of the Soviet Union.

The masses stayed away from the quarrel and left the leaders who had defended their interests arrested, tortured and jailed. It was an occasion for the leaders of the Muslim groups to have a free hand in the political scene as undisputed leaders.

d. Failure of Tribal Ritualism

Tribal ritualism, referred to in the West as 'Islamic fundamentalism', also failed to maintain an Islamic rule and to establish an Islamic State. Its authority has been shaken lately and challenged by fundamental Islamic groups in the recent attacks on the holy places in Mecca and Medina. The so-called strong 'Islamic Fundamentalist State' failed to maintain its power before the young zealots and pure Muslims.

This failure is due to several reasons. Islam has been transformed to pure ritualism without any social, economic or political content. This ritualism served as a cover-up to the most horrible exploitation and despotism. Rituals served as a licence for illegal deeds. The rule has indeed no Islamic justification whatsoever. It is a tribal rule which came about after the defeat of other tribes in the name of religious reformism (Wahhabism). That is why it is called *Saudi* rule. The royal family owned everything. The family princes are the absolute owners of the petro-dollars. All forms of corruption were on the front pages of western mass-media. Gambling, concubinage, polygamy, homosexuality, luxury, exuberance..... etc., all formed the image of the 'ugly Arab'. What is left to the people is charitable works.

Tribal ritualism opted for Western alliance. Military pacts, air and marine bases, money invested in American banks..... etc. were seen by Muslim masses as anti-religious. The wealth of the Saudi tribe was in shocking contrast with the poverty of millions of Muslims from Morocco in the West to Bengladesh in the East, from Turkey in the North to Chad and Sudan in the South. Tribal ritualism was the custodian of conservatism and reactionism in the Arab Muslim World. Socialism and progressism were real threats to it. After the failure of Arab socialism in Egypt after Nasser's death, ritualistic Islam was a common dominator in both Egypt and Saudi Arabia. It presented a common interest against all forms of radical change in the area. The call for the liberation of Palestine and for the recuperation of Jerusalem was addressed to Muslim mass feelings.

If religious conservatism played the role of consolidating reactionary regimes in the Arab World, Islamic fundamentalism played the role of opposing them in both Egypt and Saudi Arabia. Regenerated in underdeveloped societies, Islamic fundamentalism may still exist below the Muslim socio-political consciousness. It may still be the victim of formalism, fanaticism and westernization.

II. CULTURAL CONFRONTATION SUPERIORITY-INFERIORITY COMPLEXES

Religious conservatism and Islamic fundamentalism took another push from external factors. The Muslim World has been in confrontation with the Western World since the Crusades in the Middle Ages all the way up until modern colonialism and imperialism in contemporary Muslim societies. In order to dominate, the West, in the name of its culture, launched the most severe attacks on the source of power in the Muslim heart, namely Islam. Orientalism began to distort Islam as a revelation, a religion, a culture, a history and a people. Partial judgements were made which hurt Muslim consciousness. These misjudgements included the negation of Islamic revelation, the forgery of the *Qur'ān*, the epilepsy and polygamy of Mohammed, Islamic propagation by the sword, *Ahl El Dhimma* as second class citizens, imitation of the Greeks, the Persians, the Hindus and the Romans, deformation of Greek philosophy and science, confusion between Plato, Plotinus and Aristotle etc. Other judgements were directed at the Muslim soul itself as was the case in the distinction between the Semite and the Arian mind. Islam was held responsible for under-development in Muslim societies. Islam itself was said to be against progress, science and modern life. If Orientalism nowadays retracts some of these judgements, it still carries more subtle ones regarding the Islamic culture type, the cave-type (Spengler). Western social sciences took over and continued the same endeavour. Anthropology created *Islam observed*. The history of religion described Islamic rituals, *Sufi* practices and saints' cult. Theologians spoke of Islamic fatalism and predestination. Philosophers of history made the Western culture the peak and the model of all human cultures. Islamic culture was an ecclectic medieval one which prepared for the glorious advent of Western culture. Missionaries were not far away from this field. They stepped in participating in a process of acculturation.

These kinds of misjudgements, probably based on bad intentions, generated in the Muslims a strong desire to defend their spiritual patrimony and to hold steadfastly to their religion. They reacted against the misapprehensions of the West and found in Islam their own salvation. The desire to destroy Islamic identity in Algeria and Iran generated the opposite, the affirmation of Islamic identity in the most fundamentalist way. Islamic fundamentalism then meant anti-Western culture, good or bad. It presented a retraction from Islamic reformism which accepted good aspects in Western culture, namely science, progress, democracy, technology ... etc. The West which wanted to modernize the Muslim world generated religious conservatism and Islamic fundamentalism.

The alliance of Western powers with anti-Islamic leadership in the Muslim world against the interests of the Muslim masses gave practical evidence that Western powers were antagonistic to them. France supported Gallawi against the Moroccan people's interests. The USA supported the Shah against the Iranian people's interests. Western powers were behind all reactionary political leadership in the Muslim world. Muslim wealth was usurped by the consent and condescension of local leadership. In spite of military and technical aid to Muslim countries, Muslim masses felt pushed away from a real process of development. Muslims will always be imitators of progress and not its creators.

The West has always tried to convince the Muslim World that it will never be able to reach the last stage of development as in advanced, industrial and super-technologized societies. The rate of progress in the West is much higher than the rate of catching up of those countries undergoing development. Supposedly, the Muslim world will receive a cultural shock which will lead it finally to complete despair. Facing this inferiority complex, the Muslim world tried to find in Islam a source of power through which it could find compensation for this widening distance between itself and the West. The more productive the West becomes, the more attached to their own traditions the Muslims become. Muslim traditionalism is a natural reaction to Western modernism.

At the same time, the Muslim world sees itself a contemporary to what is called in Western literature 'the decline of the West'. Western thinkers themselves describe the phenomenon, attest it and warn against it. Supremacy in material production is contrasted by a spiritual vacuum and moral crisis. Many philosophers make declarations such as: reversing of values (Sheler), bankruptcy of the soul (Husserl) total nothingness (Nietzsche, Heidegger, Sartre), matter creator of God (Bergson). Conservatist and spiritual philosophies reacting against this nihilism were propagated in the Muslim world as inside witnesses from the West. The Muslims were right then to hold to their spiritual values which had been lost in the West. This call for the Spirit in underdeveloped societies appears in religious conservatism (ritualistic Islam) and in Islamic fundamentalism (religion rejecting group). If the glorious Western culture had this sad end, *a fortiori* progress is not a model to follow. To fold oneself is much sager than to stretch out. *Retour aux sources* is much better than *retour à la nature*.

III. DISCOVERY OF INDIGENOUS POWERS

Traditional Islam stayed in the heart of the masses as a stable and stagnant historical continuum. In the last seven centuries (7th-14th), Islamic culture lived on its own, modelling itself on its own golden age in the first seven centuries (1st-7th). This turning point in history marked the end of rational sciences (philosophy, *Usul El-Fiqh*) and the predominance of irrational sciences (mysticism and Fiqh). In theology, *Mu'tazilism* ended and *Ash'arism* dominated. Islamic culture became monolithic. The living tension between opposing trends: traditional and modernist, conservative and progressive ended in the victory of the first over the second. This victory was the historical reservoir of religious conservatism. The type of superstructure in underdeveloped societies may be added. The masses held Islam as a source of historical security for them, as a last resort, a custodian of their spiritual patrimony.

In the last two hundred years, Islam was seen as the only viable ideology for the Muslims. Reformist movements tried to rediscover Islamic rationalism, scientism and progressism. It went half-way until M. Abdou and then was returned to its traditional track by R. Reda. Islamic activism appears now in that line: conservatism in thought and fundamentalism in action. The downfall of the shah of Iran by a religious leader gave all young leaders of Muslim groups confidence in social and political change. Islam as ideology and motivation is still the sharpest weapon to be used in any mass movement.

Conservatism may be obscurantism in theory, but it is a source of energy which can burst out in any time. The Muslims began to discover their indigenous powers. Historical traditionalism, present conservatism (due to underdevelopment) and actual self-confidence generate Islamic fundamentalism.

Although the majority of the Muslim masses are still illiterate and depoliticized, they hear about their new wealth, oil, natural resources, vast markets, cheap labour, strategic areas..... etc. They read about the future of the world and the eminent place Muslims can have. Their glorious past can serve as a model for a more hopeful future. Traditionalism, "*Salafiyya*", meant *retour aux sources*. Under this impulse, formal Aristotelian logic in the past has been criticized and a new inductive logic has been discovered. Traditionalism in that sense implied rejectionism, the defense of authenticity against alien forms of thought. Once more, conservatism generates fundamentalism. Under the same impulse, modern conservatism discovered all the alien forms of political systems. Islam appeared as the only viable political system for the Muslims in the modern world.

The fragility of actual political regimes in the Muslim world gave Islamic activist groups more self-confidence. Some fell down and others are waiting to fall, some of these Islamic activist groups obtained success; a complete success in Iran or a relative success in shaking the regime in Saudi Arabia. Some gained popularity as in Egypt and others are on their way. *Mahdiyya* and *Sanusiyya* resurged in the Muslim mind. On the other hand, the Muslim masses are waiting for radical change in their life. The failure of ideologies, the crisis of leadership and the still indifferent masses are fertile land for generating Islamic activism more and more. Leaders and members of Islamic groups become more highly respected day after day. Their readiness for sacrifice and their zeal make them a model of behaviour in the eyes of the Muslim masses. It is very difficult to condemn them for the principles they believe in. Some of their judges sympathized with them during their trial and some others even adopted their ideals. They asked for dialogue, open discussion and free expression. They challenged the *ʿUlamā'* of *Al-Azhar* to confront them. Their strength in courts and the weakness of their prosecutors gave a glimmer of the relation between the present and the future.

Although Islamic groups are not experts in international affairs, their leaders as well as their members have a strong feeling for a new world order. The crisis of the West as well as of the East, in capitalism as well as in socialism, gave them an acute sense of the drama of the modern world. The crisis in the West, the lack of primary sources, energy, high wage labour, lack of markets, competition, exploitation, corruption, militarism, aggression..... etc. is without a solution from within. The superpowers are defeatable when confronted with the people's will for independence.

High principles and codes of ethics are only applicable within Europe. Outside, there is another code of ethics for the Barbarians. Words are different from deeds. The West did not offer any model of ethical behaviour. The moral crisis in the West left the youth in a complete spiritual vacuum.

The crisis of the East is no less great. It appears in collectivism, oppression of the individual, lack of production, imitation of the West, compromises on principles..... etc. In spite of all efforts of rehabilitation by borrowing from the West, the crisis was not solved. There is no solution from within.

Here, Islam appears as the only saviour of the world. It is the foundation of a new world order. It offers a solution of the actual world crisis in the East as well as in the West. The Islamic *Umma* is ready for it. It is the guardian of principles and the custodian of universal values. It commands the doing of good and the abstention from evil. Islam is still conserved in the heart of the masses. The baby has not yet been thrown out with the bathwater. Islam is the final revealed religion, the accomplished prophecy and the perfect model of life. The Muslims still have the sense of the message. They carry the deposit God offered to all nations, to do good on earth and to abstain from mischief. The educators of humanity in the past are still able to play the same role in the future.

In the past Islam found its way between two falling empires, the Persian and the Roman. Both were exhausted by wars. Both suffered moral and spiritual crises. Islam, as a new world order, was able to expand as a substitute to the old regime. Nowadays, Islam finds itself again as a new power marking its way between the two superpowers in crisis. Islam is regenerating, the two superpowers are degenerating. Islam is the power of the future, inheriting the two superpowers in the present. It is up to Muslim groups carrying Islamic fundamentalism to tell whether this prophecy will be fulfilled or will remain as pure messianism.

Tribal Pilgrimages to Saints' Tombs in South Sinai

Emanuel Marx

I

Every year towards the end of summer members of each of the Bedouin tribes in South Sinai congregate at a Saint's tomb in their area. There are about twenty well-known tombs in the southern half of the peninsula, and they are all located at major cross-roads and not far from water sources. Some are found close to centers of population, while others are far from them. Throughout the year individual Bedouin visit tombs whose resident saint, they think, can help them with their problems. Only at some of these tombs annual tribal gatherings take place. I intend to look closely at the annual pilgrimages of these tribes: the Muzeneh, who meet for three consecutive days and make the round of three holy tombs. From the tomb of their founding ancestor Faraj, they move to that of the prophet (*nebi* Saleḥ), and thence to that of Aron, the brother of Moses. The Awlad Sa'id, who gather once a year at the tomb of 'Ali Abu Taleb, the fourth Khalif. And the Jebaliyeh, sections of whom gather on separate occasions at the tomb of Sheikh 'Awad, a holy man whose antecedents are unclear, but may have been a member of the tribe.

Other saints' tombs at which tribal gatherings take place are: Sheikh Qra'i for the 'Alequat, Sheikh Suliman Nfe'i for the Qararsha, al-Hashash for the small Ḥamada tribe, and the female saint Shekha Swerḥa for the Sawalḥa. All these major shrines are classified by Bedouin as *maqām* (literally "place") a term widely used in the Islamic world to denote an important holy place, mostly, but not always, associated with a saint's tomb. Here, in Sinai, the *maqam* is a shrine whose patron saint is definitely not buried in it. It is contrasted with the *turbah*, a lesser shrine supposed to enclose the remains of a holy man. The shrines are surrounded by cemeteries, for it is assumed that the deceased are thus nearer to their God. Some of the tombs at the two major shrines, Nebi Saleḥ and Nebi Harun, have themselves become shrines of a kind. The ancestors of some Muzeneh descent groups buried at Nebi Saleḥ, and of the Jebaliyeh groups at Nebi Harun, are visited by their descendants on the *ʿid al-adḥā*, the Feast of Sacrifices. All the major shrines are surmounted by domed buildings, crowned with a crescent, the emblem of Islam. Near each shrine, an assembly-hut has been erected, which throughout the year serves as a rest-house for weary travellers. It is always equipped with cooking utensils, and a small supply of tea and sugar left by one traveller for the next. Tribesmen attend these gatherings in order to meet their friends, relatives and visitors from other tribes, to fulfil a religious duty, and to reaffirm their membership of the tribe and the right to use its resources. For the greater part of the year, tribesmen are dispersed in small groups and many men work most of the time outside their tribal area and even outside South Sinai. The tribal reunions are the culmination of their efforts to maintain the ties with other Bedouin. The variations in the reunions of the three tribes are connected to their different habitat and economies, as shown, among other things, in their annual migrations. Attendance at the tribal gatherings also fluctuates from year to year. This raises such questions as why tribes should celebrate an annual reunion, why the reunions of each tribe follow a different pattern, and why the attendance at them fluctuates from year to year. Another intriguing problem is why tribal gatherings should take place at saints' tombs. These questions were discussed by Robertson Smith nearly a century ago in his *Lectures on the Religion of the Semites* (1889). It will become evident that some of his views have stood the test of time, and that others are outmoded.

The cult of saints is found in many parts of the world, and assumes many shapes. In his study of cults in Spain, Christian argues that saints respond to the unrequited needs of people. One of his informants put this very eloquently, when explaining why people visit a famous image of the Virgin Mary: "God is simply not involved in our everyday activities, either because he chooses not to be involved, or because he does not have the power to act ... (But the Virgin) actively helps us, whether this be by intervention with God, or whatever. She is closer to us, does things for us in this world" (Christian 1972:147-148). God is so distant that this man even has doubts about his power to act. God is not concerned with the humdrum affairs of men, and cannot even be approached through influential human patrons. Therefore men take recourse to the mediation of saints.

Saints' cults are also prevalent in many parts of Islam (Levy 1962: 258), but Islamic leaders and scholars vary in their assessments. Some approve wholeheartedly of the practice, as in Linant de Bellefonds' (1974:355) claim that "the permissibility of visiting tombs was admitted very early on by *idjmāʿ*, consensual canonical law, : all the (law) schools ... even went so far as to recommend the practice." Goldziher (1967-1971,II:259) disapproves of it, but at the same time clearly perceives its causes: "The believers sought to create, through the concept of saints, mediators between themselves and an omnipotent Godhead in order to satisfy the need which was served by the gods and masters of their old tradition ... Here too applies what Karl Hase says of the cult of saints in general: that it 'satisfies within a monotheistic religion a polytheistic need to fill the enormous gap between men and their god'." Many commentators have followed Goldziher's lead. Thus Grunebaum (1951:67) views the cult of saints as "a striking deviation from the genuine prophetic tradition", and Lazarus-Jaffe (1976:223) describes even the pilgrimage to Mecca as a 'pagan heritage', although both writers are aware of the importance of these cults.

Some authors entertain a more favourable opinion of the cults, and treat them as an alternative to official Islam. Thus Gellner (1972:59) claims that it is practised in regions where "offical, genuine literate Islam ... is present only in a minimal form". Geertz (1968:48) interprets this as an "expression of that necessity ..... for a world religion to come to terms with ... a multiplicity of local forms of faith and yet maintain the essence of its own identity."

Statements such as these are based on the view that Islam is a strictly monotheistic religion; accordingly, the cult of saints is treated as either a pagan survival, as an aberration from orthodox religion or as a local custom, a small tradition. However, the cult of saints is found throughout Islam, and not only in places that are off the beaten track. It is practised in cities, villages, and even associated with mosques (Canaan 1927:2; Eickelman 1976:112). There is no difference between centre and periphery; the cult is essentially the same everywhere. The distant omnipotent God and the cult of saints exist side by side, and complement each other. For a distant God can be approached only through holy mediators. Individuals in need, who are unable to obtain the aid of their fellows, or whose problems are beyond remedy, commune with God through the saint. This is the practice throughout Islam, although periodically it is repressed by zealous governments or by "official" representatives of Islam, who view it as an infringement of their monopoly of temporal or spiritual power. The individual Muslim's belief in the efficacy of saintly mediation is the foundation of the communal pilgrimage. This can occur where whole populations or groups face the same intractable problems, and make the pilgrimage to the sanctuary both as individuals and as members of a larger entity.

However widespread the cult of saints is, it appears to be less common among nomadic pastoralists. Musil (1928:417) states categorically: "The Bedouins know of no communion with the saints. In the whole inner desert there is not a single holy grave or shrine erected in honour of a saint ... When they make short sojourns in the settled territory, where by every village the dome of a shrine rises above the real or imaginary grave of some man or woman whom public opinion considers to be a saint, they never pay attention to these domes."

But among the Bedouin of South Sinai and, incidentally, among those of Cyrenaica (Evans-Pritchard 1949:66-67; Peters 1976), and Morocco (Berque 1955:268ff), the visiting of shrines and pilgrimages are an important feature of social life. If we gain some insights into the sociology of the cult of saints in Sinai, we might improve our understanding of such cults elsewhere, and interpret their absence among some nomadic pastoralists.

II

South Sinai is the mountainous southern part of the Sinai peninsula up to the Tih Plateau. It covers an area of about 17,000 sq. km. Most of its interior is bare and rugged; high plateaus interspersed with mountains, build up to the Mount Sinai massif at the centre. The highest peak in the peninsula is Jebel Katarina, 2642 m, and other mountains are nearly as high. Asphalted roads run close to the sea shore round the tip of the peninsula. In the interior of the country there are only mud tracks, mostly running on an east to west axis. Some of these are suitable for trucks and other rugged vehicles. There is no regular public transportation of any kind, but the Bedouin car fleet, of over a hundred vehicles, mostly American and Russian jeeps, pickups and a few trucks, mostly in a bad state of repair, is up for hire. Parts of the peninsula are inaccessible to motor cars, and can be reached by camel or donkey, often only by circuitous routes.

The region is arid, with small amounts of rain-fall in the cool winter months, between November and March. In the coastal region, the annual average precipitation is about 10 mm, and in the high mountains about 60 mm (Ganor 1973:35). Rain-fall is very irregular, and in all parts but the high mountains there are often two to three consecutive years without rain-fall. The spatial distribution of rains is also very changeable, and in consequence there are few reliable pastures. Any sizable rain causes floods in the lower reaches of wadis and often results in serious damage to Bedouin property. Sometimes most of a year's rain-fall comes in a single downpour. Some of these torrential rains may occur in early summer. A flood that occurred in May 1968 destroyed hundreds of palm trees, houses and gardens, and ruined several major motor tracks. Others occurred in February 1975 and October 1979, with results almost as disastrous.

The winter months are usually cool. In the mountains there are each year cold spells, with temperatures occasionally falling as low as -10° (14°F). Summer temperatures are uniformly high, and in the low-lying areas often climb up to 40° (105°) during the day, and in the mountains to around 30°.

The vegetation is adapted to the harsh climate, and relies largely on ground water. During the long dry summer, most plants wither, and only the ubiquitous *baᶜtharan* (arthemisia), *ajram* (anabasis) and some other shrubs seem to withstand the heat successfully. But after rains colourful annuals appear. Some plants come to life even in the absence of rain; milder weather after a cold spell entices them out of the ground. There are few sources of surface water in the region, except immediately after rains. Water is mostly obtained from wells dug by enterprising Bedouin. In recent years government sunk several deep wells to which all Bedouin have equal access.

South Sinai is inhabited by over 6,000 Bedouin, giving a population density of less than one person to 2 sq. kms. A considerable part of this population lives close to the main east-west passage through the mountainous interior, Wadi Firan - Saint Catherine - Wadi Nasb. Although every Bedouin has a place or at least an area, that he considers his home ground, there are few permanent settlements of Bedouin and these have stabilised in recent years as local employment opportunities improved, and new wells were put in operation. The trend began in the mid-fifties when smuggling of narcotics accelerated and Bedouin invested some of the profits in wells and orchards. Some of these settlements, such as Bir Zrer and Bir 'Oqda, were established in relatively inaccessible places, for understandable reasons. The copious ground water supply in Wadi Firan allowed Bedouin to remain for many months in one place and to cultivate fruit and vegetables. The permanent employment found in Saint Catherine's monastery in the mountains gave rise to a Bedouin village in its vicinity. These trends were intensified since the Israelis took over in 1967. Though smuggling became almost extinct, more jobs became available locally, and new wells were dug. As a result, Bedouin households now tend to spend much longer periods in their home grounds.

Permanent settlements were few until the 50s. There was the little port of Al-Tur on the Red Sea with a population of about 500 souls, mostly sailors and fishermen. Some of these men were Bedouin. Near al-Tur there was a quarantine station for Egyptians returning from the annual pilgrimage to the holy places of Islam in Mecca, which provided seasonal work for many Bedouin. The other permanent settlement, Saint Catherine's monastery on Mount Sinai, is inhabited by 10-12 Greek monks. Founded in the sixth century and continuously occupied since, it is rightly viewed by Bedouin as the only stable institution in the region, more permanent and reliable than ephemeral governments. In the 50s, the Egyptians began to develop the region. They set up civilian headquarters in Abu Znema, north of al-Tur, built army camps and an air field, constructed roads along the Red Sea coast, and began to exploit on a commercial scale the oil fields, and the gypsum and manganese deposits found near the Red Sea coast. A few Bedouin were employed in these enterprises, but most of the workers were recruited in Egypt.

In the distant past, a small and highly mobile population of nomadic pastoralists could maintain themselves in south Sinai, provided they had access to all parts of the peninsula. It appears that some Muzeneh and Awlad Sa'id households subsist exclusively on their flocks. But for several generations the main source of the Bedouin's income has been wage labour, mostly in the cities outside the region.

No grain is grown in South Sinai, and the fruit and vegetables grown labouriously in small plots scarcely suffice for the needs of a household during a few weeks in summer. Practically all the food consumed in Sinai is imported from outside the region. In the past, when employment was scarce and communications slow and labourious, Bedouin devoted more attention to their gardens. Some households, especially among the Jebaliyeh, relied on them for their livelihood. Since the early 70's, wage labour became easily available and the incomes of Bedouin rose rapidly. As a result, Bedouin spend less time in their gardens, but still maintain them in reasonable condition.

III

When the Bedouin of South Sinai talk about the tribe, they may refer to three separate, partly overlapping entities. First, the Bedouin consider the tribe as a territorial organization, whose members control certain resources in that territory, and obtain rights to exploit resources in a larger area of subsistence. Membership of the tribe confers the right to "build a house" anywhere in their roughly defined territory, which in practice means settling in an oasis or in the valleys of the Mount Sinai region; preferential access to pastures and to employment in it; and to participate in smuggling activities passing through it. This last is a recent transformation of the former monopoly on conducting travellers through the territory (Niebuhr 1799, I:141,153). The tribe claims not so much to control a clearly bounded territory, but defined points in it and paths leading through it. When asked to describe their tribal territory, Bedouin present one with a list of salient points, such as oases, wells and pastures, but there is much disagreement between their statements about boundaries and considerable overlap between tribes. This is to be expected in a country whose practical value to the Bedouin is located in particular tracts. At any moment a considerable proportion of the men may be working outside the territory, and their flocks herding in the grounds of other tribes. This did not deter administrators and travellers from sketching tribal maps which neatly apportion all the South Sinai between the tribes (Murray 1935:247; Israel Army 1962:map 3; Glassner 1974:35).

The tribesmen are united by joint ownership of territorial resources, and some of them combine forces to prevent encroachments of outsiders. Thus I was told that some years ago an Awlad As'id man had constructed a stone house near a route which the Jebaliyeh claimed as their own. One of the Jebaliyeh elders warned him that he was welcome to set up a tent in that place, but not a house. The Awlad

Sa'id man moved away, and the house was then torn down.

Bedouin often migrate relatively short distances in their tribal territory. But they claim that "membership of the tribe also gives them access to all the pastures of South Sinai". They consider their tribes to belong to an alliance, which "in the past elected a common leader and moderator", and together they are called the people of Mount Sinai (*Tawarah*, s. *Turi*). The confederation is not represented in the genealogies by an apical ancestor. Government occasionally appointed one of the tribal chiefs as paramount chief, but this appointment was mainly ceremonial and the chief never exercised control over the population. Pastures are frequently shared by members of several tribes; whenever this happens, the herdsmen may camp together, irrespective of their tribal affiliation. Without this sharing of pastures, none of the tribes could engage in herding.

Six tribes are usually considered members of the alliance of *Tawara*: the Muzeneh and 'Aleqat who together constitute one moiety, the Sawalha, Qararsha and Awlad Sa'id - the other; and the Jebaliyeh, who are slightly inferior members of the alliance. Two other small tribes, the Hamada and the Beni Wasel, are viewed as remnants of the ancient inhabitants of the country who lost their land, but are tacitly accepted as belonging to the *Tawara*. Only the Huwetat tribesmen are thought to be intruders without right to land; and indeed most of them appear to have entered the area as late as after the first World War. They only do not perform the annual tribal pilgrimage.

Second, the Bedouin view the tribe as a political organization, an alliance of numerous patrilineal descent groups, whose purpose is to defend individual members and to protect the territory and its resources against intruders.

The political tribe is made up in this manner: each Bedouin is born into an agnatic descent group. The group is called a family (*'eleh*), is named after an ancestor who lived two to four generations ago and bears either his real name or his nickname (*naqbah* or *nabadh*). Some people cannot trace the details of their connection to this patronym. Bearers of the patronymic do not necessarily camp together or own joint property, and there is no formal leader. Some of the bearers of the patronymic, often close agnates, may, in company with cognates or even non-relatives, engage in joint economic ventures, for instance in smuggling. Others, and even the members of the economic partnership themselves, may then consider this as an activity of the agnatic descent group, oblivious to the fact that not all members participate in the joint activity and that some non-members are involved.

Several patronymic groups are affiliated to a large unit, which is at one and the same time considered a large descent group and a subunit of the tribe and which supposedly is associated with a not too clearly defined part of the tribal territory. This unit is called a quarter (*ruba*ᶜ, pl. *rubu*ᶜ) or branch (*fara*ᶜ, pl. *furū*ᶜ); these terms indicate that it is a subdivision of a larger unit, the tribe. Tribesmen freely admit that their patronyms are not necessarily descendants of the ancestors of the *ruba*ᶜ and that some tribesmen originated outside the tribe and joined the *ruba*ᶜ within living memory. The members of the *ruba*ᶜ do not all reside in the territory associated with their ancestor. A respected member of one of the constituent groups - not necessarily of a large or wealthy one - is elected elder, and his home becomes a meeting-place for members of the group. This man distributes resources allocated to the group by external agencies, such as work supplied by the government, and in this context acts as representative of the tribal chief. He also makes the arrangements for periodical reunions of the group. The tribe is conceptualized as a group founded by a single eponym, whose sons - and as the term *ruba'* implies, there are often four - are the ancestors of the *ruba'*. This tribe, as distinct from the administrative tribe headed by the chief, exists exclusively as an organization for the control of territory and initiates few joint political or economic activities. Bedouin often argue that the tribe as a whole pays blood-compensation (*dīyah*), but no instance has come to my knowledge.

And third, the Bedouin endorse the authorities' conception of the tribe as an administrative unit, headed by a chief and by headmen; these men are chosen by the tribesmen, and confirmed in office by the government. The authorities deal with, and provide some services for, the tribe through these representatives. In an economy based largely on wage labour outside the tribe, and with government services provided on a limited scale, the Bedouin do not attach great importance to their chiefs. Bedouin usually describe them as "government chiefs, who really represent only their personal interest". They do, however, admit that the chiefs act as liaison officers between the government authorities - and in the case of the Jebaliyeh also between the monks of Saint Catherine's - and the tribesmen.

Bedouin are well aware that the term tribe refers to different things, but consider them to be particular aspects of one entity. They conceptualize the tribe as a segmentary political organization. In this manner they explain under one head the territorial organization, the descent groups, political alliances and leadership. And all these aspects can be summarized in genealogical terms. The segmentary theory held by the tribesmen cannot, however, account for some other aspects of social organization, such as cooperation between members of different tribes, for instance in smuggling, for the wide-ranging networks of kinship ties, or for the organization of wage labour in towns.

In the annual tribal pilgrimage the three kinds of tribe merge and, what is more, for once the 'tribe' becomes a living reality. Its various aspects are represented in the ebb and flow of gatherings at the pilgrimage site, in the details of the ritual, and in the form of the saint's tomb itself. Here not only the aspects covered by the theory of segmentary organization are reflected, but also other sides of tribal life. Especially salient are the perennial problems of uncertain political conditions, the changing employment situation, and the hazards of life in a desert where drought and natural disasters are common occurrences.

Each tribe differs from the others in size, territorial resources and economic activities. I shall now briefly introduce the three tribes whose pilgrimages will be discussed: Muzeneh, Awlad Sa'id and Jebliyeh.

First, here is a list of tribes arranged by size. The figures are based on Ben-David (1972:113), taken from a census carried out by the Israeli authorities in 1968. Later information largely confirms these figures, and therefore I made only slight corrections.

Fig.1 BEDOUIN TRIBES OF SOUTH SINAI

Tribe		Population	Territory
Muzeneh		1,700	East and south of peninsula
Jebaliyeh		1,100	High mountains
'Aleqat		1,050	West coast
Qararsha		900	Firan to west coast
Awlad Sa'id		450	Mountains
Huwetat		390	Lower Firan
Hamada		250	North west
Sawalha		160	North west
Beni Wasel		100	al-Tur
	Total	6,100	

The Muzeneh are the largest tribe and also occupy the largest territory. Murray (1935:265) describes them as camel and sheep breeders many of whom "have lately taken to fishing". Their control of the east coast and part of the west coast put them in an ideal position for receiving narcotics from Saudi Arabia, and passing them on to other middlemen in Sinai. The final destination was usually Egypt. Smuggling thrived until about 1970, when it was stopped almost completely by the Israeli authorities. Some of the best known organizers of smuggling bands stem from this tribe, and Bedouin estimate that about 30 per cent of its income was derived from smuggling. There are some fishermen and sailors among the Muzeneh, but only few tribesmen own flocks of goats and sheep large enough for subsistence.

Bedouin claim that 50 to 60 animals are the minimum needed. One of the few men I met who owned a flock of that size claimed that he obtained an average monthly revenue of IL 400, in addition to which he obtained IL 200 from National Insurance. Altogether he had a monthly income of IL 600 (approximately £ 40). Most households live on the wage labour of one or more males, who earn IL 40 a day or more (nearly £ 3). While almost every household raises five to six goats or sheep, most people claim that they do not expect to make a profit on animals. For part of the dry season the animals are fed millet or corn, imported from outside Sinai. The small flocks are herded by women and girls. This seems to have been the situation for a long time, since H.S. Palmer (1906:69-72) found in 1869 that flocks were tended exclusively by girls, that men earned their living away from home (though not as wage labourers but as caravaneers), and that they bought corn with the money earned (similarly E.H. Palmer 1871: 81-82; Keller 1900:26).

While their movements are influenced by the needs of their animals, Bedouin must also take into account other requirements. Women and girls are expected to return home in the evening and to perform household chores. Therefore, they do not venture too far afield with their flock. Camps must remain close, but not too close, to water, usually at a distance of 2-3 kms from it, and near sources of firewood, such as broom (*ratam*), acacias (*seyāl*), or tamarisks (*tarfā'*), and amenities such as shops and roads. Therefore, they cannot provide the most favourable herding conditions for the animals, and cannot make their flocks pay.

The Awlad Sa'id live in the mountains west of Saint Catherine's monastery. They straddle all the roads along the east-west axis, and control some of the best pasture areas. Only a small area in the high mountains has been left to Jebaliyeh tribesmen. The Awlad Sa'id too used to engage in smuggling. They rely to a somewhat greater extent than the Muzeneh on flocks, and not a few of them possess small and relatively neglected orchards in the mountains. In the past their camels carried pilgrims from Egypt and supplies from al-Tur to the monastery. Now they too depend largely on wage labour.

The habitat of the Jebaliyeh is the high mountain. Their flocks are even smaller than those of the other two tribes, and there are households without animals. As their small territory includes no major mountain pass, they are more or less excluded from smuggling activities. They specialize in horticulture. Every tribesman owns an orchard in the high mountains, which is regularly watered and cultivated, even when its owners live elsewhere. Tribesmen claim that in the past they used to market their fruit in al-Tur and with the money they barely managed to buy a year's supply of grain, but could not afford other items such as tea, sugar and clothing. So the tribesmen sought employment in the area and outside it. Saint Catherine's monastery traditionally employs between 20 to 30 Jebaliyeh tribesmen and also a few Awlad Sa'id. While its workers are paid much lower wages than those in the labour market, it can offer them two advantages: work near home and work that is relatively secure. The monastery's employees often remain in their jobs throughout their working life, and even after retirement the monastery gives these men small but regular food rations. Tribesmen complain about the meagre pay, but remain in their jobs, for no one knows what the future has in store. The Jebaliyeh also used to supply guides for pilgrims who wished to visit the many sites in the vicinity of the monastery associated with the works of Moses.

Jebaliyeh 'explain' that their close ties with the monastery go back into history. Their ancestor was a Greek slave, named Constantine. When the monastery was established, he was one of a number of slaves sent out to serve the monks. This story both establishes the special link to the monastery and the tribe's claim that its territory "is owned by the monastery", and therefore cannot be touched. While individual tribesmen admit to various origins, their attachment to one of the tribe's four branches gives them a right to enjoy the advantage of being "children of the monastery" (*subṭān al-deir*), as they call themselves.

As their territory is too small for herding and as the monastery could employ only a few men, the Jebaliyeh were among the first wage labourers. As a result some of them acquired skills, and as builders and well-diggers worked all over the peninsula. They still rely on wage labour for most of their income and the men regularly work in the towns or the Abu Rudes oil installations. Between 30 to 50 men are usually employed by the Israeli administration.

Jebaliyeh households move as a rule between two locations: for most of the year, and especially during the cooler months, they stay in the "low-lying" areas at a height of about 1,600 metres; during the hot summer months they move into the mountains to enjoy the fresh air and the fruit of their orchards. A similar transhumance is observed by the Awlad Sa'id, but it takes place at a lower altitude. Their cool summer sites are at about the same height as the 'sheltered' winter sites of the Jebaliyeh.

All three tribes, then, depend on wage labour for their living, and men spend periods working away from home. At the same time, they tend their orchards and flocks of goats and sheep, although many people admit that they either make little money out of their flocks and gardens, or even lose on them. Why do the Bedouin behave as if they were gardeners and herdsmen, and not move their families nearer to the places of work? The answer is twofold. Bedouin who established themselves in secure jobs, settle in the towns and cities of Egypt, and are often followed by kinsmen. Many 'Aleqat and Qararsha, and some members of the other tribes have become townsmen. These people are generally out of the view of those who remain behind, although kin ties are not allowed to lapse. These tribesmen maintain the fiction that they are always drawn back to their homeland. This is true for the majority of Bedouin, whose employment is insecure. While most of their income is derived from wage labour, they know this is a short-term gain. They can lose their work at any time, through political upheavals and economic fluctuations, or because of illness and old age. Therefore they maintain a second economy, on which they can fall back in time of need. In order to operate this economy, the tribe is kept intact, and kinship ties are fostered. Bedouin often express this utilitarian behaviour as a sentimental attachment to their land. A Jebaliyeh man put it thus: "Our country is arid, nothing grows in it. Last night the dew froze and burnt (sic!) my tomato plants. The same happens to the almond and apple blossoms. Nor is it a good country for goats, you always have to supplement their food and lose money on them. Only its landscapes are beautiful and in summer the climate is good, but our livelihood (*rizq*) is obtained outside. I always return to it though, because my family lives here. And I do not leave because my country is dear to me. I am tied to it by my navel-string. For when a child is born, the father buries the navel-string and the placenta deep in the ground."

The sentimental attachment of this man and others to the land conveys its importance as a secure base. When compared to the income obtained by wage labour its resources are of little value. Yet they attach considerable importance to them, for if anything should go wrong, Bedouin could always fall back on the resources of their country. By some serious effort they could increase their garden produce, and they could migrate with their flocks so as to make the best out of the available pasture. Men keep their homes in the tribal area, and leave their gardens and flocks in the care of kinsmen. Should the need arise, these could be built up, and provide a small income. They do not balance the two economies very carefully. When they feel secure, they put less work into their orchards and flocks. When they fell threatened, they increase their efforts. But they never neglect the second economy altogether. The balance tilts with the news. This became evident late in 1975, during the negotiations between Egypt and Israel over an 'interim agreement' in Sinai. Suddenly there was a flourish of activity in the basic economy. Bedouin stopped the sale of animals and there was great interest in gardens. Some people acquired gardens, others dug wells and planted new gardens. Thus they prepared for the possibility of losing their work. When it became clear in 1979 that Israel would evacuate the Mount Sinai region, the phenomenon repeated itself.

Smuggling is to be viewed as a secondary accommodation to prevailing conditions. As people must stay in this wild and inhospitable country, they are available for any work that presents itself there.

In spite of high risks, and the not extravagant wages, numerous people were engaged in the business and viewed it as an accepted and respectable way of making a living. Only a handful of men made fortunes out of smuggling. Smuggling reinforces tribal allegiance as the control over routes is a precondition for entering the game.

IV

Uncertainty about the political and economic future then, ties these people to their country and to the tribe, and makes them behave as if they were pastoralists and gardeners in the accepted sense. Yet wage labour outside the tribal area is the main source of income. As a result, not only do many men spend a great deal of time away from their families and kin, but families are also widely distributed in small camps. While individuals move about a great deal, for much of the year they meet only some of the people on whom they depend for mutual assistance and reassurance. Relationships require maintenance. When persons do not interact regularly, they lose confidence in their relationship. Would it stand the test of a critical situation? Therefore each Bedouin strives to visit his relatives and friends, and the opportunity to see many of them at one time presents itself in late summer. At that time the dates ripen and the Bedouin congregate in the oases until the harvest is over. These large concentrations, in turn, form the basis for the organization of tribal gatherings.

Both the Muzeneh and the Awlad Sa'id go through annual migrations. Their pastoral year begins in spring (*rabīʿ*), the time when the weather becomes a little warmer and verdure springs up. This usually happens around February. In the mountains spring comes round every year, but in the lower areas only if there has been some rain in winter. Then the tribesmen leave their winter quarters, relatively large stationary hamlets of tin shacks and tents and some of them divide up into small camps of two-three tents in order to exploit the pasture wherever it is available. Even households with few animals may join in these movements, which are largely determined by the requirements of the larger flocks, because they wish to be close to relatives. Other camps may be larger and remain almost immobile. They are made up of households whose income depend on wage labour, and who put little emphasis on herding.

Spring pasture does not last long and the owners of flocks move into the few reliable early summer pastures, such as Wadi Rahaba and Wadi Slaf. The stationary camps move a short distance from the sheltered winter camping site to one that allows in the refreshing breezes.

The annual migratory cycle reaches the point of maximum concentration in summer. The pasture is exhausted and water sources dry up. People converge on the remaining wells in the oases or on the sea-shore and harvest their dates or, in the case of the Jebaliyeh, repair to their gardens in the mountains. Here tribesmen gather in large groups, there is much visiting and among the Muzeneh young men organize dances nearly every night. After the fruit have been picked and the time comes to move, the elders of the tribe call for a tribal gathering. The gathering not only fits into the seasonal pattern of maximum concentration of tribesmen, it also enhances it. This is the only occasion when the 'tribe' visibly becomes a group. At other times it does not operate as one political unit, though members are frequently aware that they act as tribesmen, for instance when they plant gardens, build houses or engage in smuggling.

The tribal gatherings, like the individual pilgrimages to Saints' tombs, are called 'visits' (*ziyāra*, locally pronounced as *zuwara*). This is the term used elsewhere too for pilgrimages to holy places, with the exception of that to Mecca, for which the distinctive term *hajj* is employed. While the pilgrimage to the summit of Jebel Musa is often compared with that to Mecca, it is nevertheless a *zuwara*. Each year a number of men and women make the still arduous and costly journey to Mecca.

What is it that makes a considerable number of tribesmen participate in the pilgrimage? There is very little persuasion involved; the organizers of the pilgrimage are respected members of their communities, but few of them are tribal chiefs or leaders with a strong hold on people. Their main preparations are to collect from the people in the neighbourhood contributions for the tribal sacrifice, which are eventually returned to the donors in the form of boiled meat, and jointly to set the date of the pilgrimage. An attraction of the pilgrimage is that the individual considers it as beneficial. The reputations of the major shrines have spread widely. Not only the tribesmen on whose territory they are situated believe in their powers, but also many others. All these places attract individual pilgrims from all over the region. The fame of some shrines has spread beyond the borders of South Sinai. Monday and Friday eves are considered as propitious for pilgrimage. On these days, throughout most of the year, individual households make their way to a shrine of their choice. In many instances this will be one of the holy tombs, but there are also a few other sites, among which the summit of Jebel Musa (where Moses is said to have received the Tablets of the Law) is the most venerated. Others are Jebel Meneja in Wadi Firan, and the uninhabited monastery of the Forty Martyrs in Wadi Leja, near Saint Catherine's (Levi 1977:175; 1978:18-19). In these pilgrimages people either redeem vows made when in danger or make requests. As the saint only mediates requests to allmighty God, a visit to any holy tomb, perhaps the closest one, should do. Yet, people are slightly sceptical, and trust their own experience and that of their relatives, which shows that some saints intercede more efficiently in some matters than in others. As individual experience varies widely, no real specialization has developed among the saints. But one result has been that people from all parts of South Sinai visit all the holy tombs, and that they often range far afield. Thus members of one patronymic group of the Jebaliyeh visited at various times during the last four-five years the following sites: a woman who had not conceived for two years ascended Jebel Musa with her family; a man wished to protect the wellbeing of his family by taking them on an outing to Sheikh 'Awad; two men took their flocks by car to Sheikh Habus in order to safeguard their health; one man carried his family by camel to Nebi Saleḥ, on recovering from an illness; an old lady regularly expressed her wish to make the expensive pilgrimage to Mecca 'next year'. Similarly, people all over South Sinai visit nearby and distant shrines, and all the saints are respected throughout the region.

This situation affects tribal gatherings in two ways. First, the commonly shared belief in saints' tombs, and in saints as intercessors with God, is one of the foundations of the tribal pilgrimage. Each of the individuals who participates in the gathering believes that he obtains a spiritual benefit. It must be added, however, that he may also expect material advantages, perhaps meet debtors or offer a car or a camel for sale. Bedouin see nothing incongruous in the seeking of spiritual and material benefits at the same time. They do not conceive of purely spiritual or purely material occasions, as found in specialised industrial societies.

Second, all the participants in the gathering, whether belonging to the celebrating tribe or not, respect the saint's tomb, and consider it the equal of the saints' tombs of other tribes. Even Nebi Saleḥ, whose tomb is the recognised centre of the tribal gatherings, is not considered superior to the others. Individual pilgrims do not prefer him in any way to the others, and often many weeks pass between one pilgrim and the next. This equality of saints expresses an important facet of the gatherings: that they are not held exclusively for the members of one tribe, but that people from other tribes can also attend. Indeed, people say explicitly that the gatherings are expected to attract visitors from other tribes. Thus, the meeting-place of the Bedouin of South Sinai shifts periodically from one site to another. At each gathering one tribe slightly dominates because of its numerical preponderance, but never becomes superior to the others. Not so long ago, people say up to 1965, at least five tribes, the Sawalha, Awlad Sa'id, Qerarsha, Muzeneh and Jebaliyeh, held separate annual tribal gatherings at Nebi Saleḥ. I can only surmise that the location turned this tomb into the central meeting place of the Bedouin of the mountains; it is situated on the intersection of the major east-west and north-south mountain passes, close to the main pastures, in an area frequented by Muzeneh,

Awlad Sa'id and Jebaliyeh. In view of the great importance of smuggling in those days, and of caravan traffic in earlier times, each tribe attached major significance to its rights of passage through the mountains, as well as to coordination of activities and maintaining peaceful relations with other tribes.

Today each tribe has its own meeting place, in its tribal territory. There are two clusters of such sites. In the west, not far from the sea, are the pilgrimage centres of the 'Aleqat, Qararsha and Hamada tribes. They are located close to the main concentrations of the population, whose employment is found in the towns in and around Sinai. Before the Israeli occupation, some people worked in the mines and industries of the area, but the majority worked all year round as migrant labourers, and approximately half of them eventually settled in Egypt proper. For these mobile people, the saint's tomb is close to home, as it points out their claims to the territory. The other cluster of pilgrimage centres, which will be examined in greater detail, are those of the Muzeneh, Awlad Sa'id and Jebaliyeh. They are located in the mountains, the former at the centre of the tribe's large territory, and the two latter at the edges of their tribal territory. Here pilgrimage requires most people to leave their homes and to move elsewhere. They go through a rite of passage, "beginning in a Familiar Place, going to a Far Place, and returning, ideally 'changed', to a Familiar Place" (Turner 1973:213). These tribesmen are already tied to the land, for here their basic economy lies. Here, where the attachment to the land is given, Bedouin seek in their pilgrimages to forge or maintain relationships in the tribe and outside it. The individual is drawn away from his round of daily life and its circumscribed field of relationships, brought to another place where he meets people from a wide area.

The date of the tribal gathering is set by a few elders, who take into account all the relevant factors. A Bedouin explained these: "The date of the gathering is fixed perhaps two months in advance, so that the news will get to all tribesmen. Conditions of work are taken into account, as well as the end of the date harvest (*masif*) in Wadi Firan (the dates there ripen later than in other oases), and the position of the stars. Only after canopus (*thraiah*) and other stars rise, the mutton becomes suitable for eating. Before that the goats are too lean and their meat is hard to digest." To complicate matters further, the feasts are held on Thursday afternoons, the eve of the Muslim day of rest, and during the full moon.

The dates of the tribal gatherings vary but little over the years. The earliest reported date gives the end of July (Burckhardt 1822:489). The gatherings I attended, or on which I possess details, all took place between the end of June and the beginning of September. In this respect there was no difference between the Muzeneh, the Awlad Sa'id and the Jebaliyeh.

My data on attendance are incomplete, but they do show that in recent years it varied considerably. Thus for the Muzeneh gathering at Nebi Saleḥ in 1970, 100-150 men are reported (Meshal 1971:95). In following years the numbers declined sharply, until in 1973 only 50 men were reported to be present. In 1975 the figure climbed up to nearly 200 men.

The Awlad Sa'id attended their tribal meet at Abu Taleb more regularly. At the gathering in July 1973 that I attended, about 70 men gathered in the rectangular open-sided hut opposite the saint's tomb. For the following year Kapara (1975:193) reports 40-50 men in the big hut, while others were still arriving. In contrast to the Muzeneh, whose attendance declined up to 1973, and went up again in the following year, the Awlad Sa'id pattern was stable. Most of the men attended each year.

The Jebaliyeh were different again. Tribesmen claimed that in the past they had had annual tribal gatherings which started at Nebi Saleḥ, who in the eyes of all tribes is the senior saint, and at whose tomb several tribes gathered, on separate occasions. From there they used to move on to Nebi Harun (the reputed tomb of Aron, the High Priest), near Saint Catherine's monastery. This gathering was held for the last time in 1965. After that there were no more gatherings of the whole tribe, but in August 1973 I attended a gathering of about 65-70 men of the Awlad Jindi sub-tribe at Sheikh 'Awad, and in August 1975 another one at the same place at which nearly all the Awlad Jindi men were present. A month later another sub-tribe, the Wuhebat, held a gathering of their own at Sheikh 'Awad. I was told that previously they had not had such gatherings. These gatherings of sub-tribes became a regular annual feature.

A clear pattern emerges here: though the gatherings never ceased, attendance declined when plenty of work was available and when it was expected that the favourable economic and political conditions would continue. This was particularly true for the Muzeneh and Jebaliyeh, who largely depended on wage labour. People who regularly turned up at the gatherings were those who had a predominant interest in herding, and also the former smugglers, who presented themselves as keepers of tradition. When I asked why others did not turn up, I was often told that they were away working and would not jeopardize their jobs. So the men who had an interest in maintaining the tribe showed up at all the meetings and those whose employment was secure did not. After 1973, the employed people also took part in the gatherings. This was the result of a kind of uncertainty. At the time work was plentiful and well paid, but the political future of Sinai was uncertain. The Egyptians and Israelis were negotiating under the aegis of Dr. Kissinger, the Israelis were giving up territory in Sinai and no one could know where this was going to end. The extended negotiations for peacemaking only brought doubts and insecurity for the Bedouin. An Awlad Jindi man employed by the government as driver had often told me that he never attended tribal gatherings. These were for the old people he thought. In 1975 he attended for the first time and explained that his wife had begged him to go and that he could not refuse here wish. He did not admit, perhaps not even to himself, that the future was uncertain and that he might have to rely to a larger extent than hitherto on the help of agnates and tribesmen. At the time he was toying with the idea of setting up a repair shop for motor-cars. Tribesmen could thus become more important even as customers. Since then he has attended the pilgrimage every year.

The two levels of the individual's involvement in the pilgrimage are shown in the eating arrangements. At each gathering there is a communal meal. Several sheep or a young camel are slaughtered and all the men who contributed to the price attend the meal. The animals are bought and cooking arrangements made by an elder of the group. In the late afternoon or evening all the men gather for a festive meal. They pray together and then sit down in a large circle for a meal. Each man's name is announced for all to hear, as a tribesman who contributed to the tribal sacrifice. Then his portion of meat, wrapped in a flap of flat bread, is passed along a chain of servers up to the announcer who hands it to the man. There is no visible leader at these functions, no speeches and announcements are made. Visitors from other tribes are welcome. Their names are announced, and the epithet "guest" added; they too are given portions of meat. Chiefs and notables mingle with other men and no special area is reserved for them. At one of the Muzeneh gatherings the paramount chief of the tribe put in a short appearance, to pay respect to a gathering at which he did not preside. At the Awlad Sa'id gatherings the two tribal chiefs were present all the time and moved among the people. The Jebaliyeh chief did not attend the Awlad Jindi meetings at all; but he was present at those of his own sub-tribe, the Wuhebat.

The chiefs' participation in the proceedings was largely determined by their position in the tribe. While all chiefs are considered to be the representatives of government, this does not count much where government is as distant and quiescent as in South Sinai. The saint is treated as a mediator between the tribe and divine authority precisely because government is so far away and does not assure the Bedouin's basic requirements. Therefore there was no place for the "government" chiefs in the ceremonies. Some of these men were however important in their own right, as organizer of smuggling rings and other economic activities, as powerful leaders of large groups of men, and as mediators in disputes between tribesmen. Such were the chiefs of the Awlad Sa'id and the headmen of the Muzeneh sub-tribes, and they took their rightful place in the ceremonies. Others, like the chiefs of the Jebaliyeh and the Muzeneh, play less important internal roles, and do not need to be present.

The participants in the tribal gathering were at the same time individual pilgrims. All round the saint's tomb related families gathered in small circles. The women began to prepare food for a festive meal. In the late afternoon each man led his family and a sacrifical goat round the tomb, bearing a pan with burning incense and repeating the phrase 'Rely on God' (*ʿtwakkal ʿallāh*). He then recited the opening chapter (*fātiḥa*) of the Quran, dedicating it to the saint, and offered a prayer for the health, wellbeing and livelihood of his family. Thereupon he slaughtered the animal; and while he prepared the meat, the women and children returned to their own circle. The family and its guests, men, women and children shared in a joint meal of meat and other dishes. For once, the order of precedence was dropped and all ate together. The women in particular wore their finest dresses, embroidered with silver and gold thread. The atmosphere was relaxed and the women spoke up freely, even making jokes with sexual innuendos. There was much mutual visiting. The men most of the time made the rounds of friends, now and again returning for a few minutes with their families. At these gatherings people reaffirmed their friendly relations and, incidentally, settled debts and disputes and initiated commercial dealing such as the sale of animals and cars, and other joint activities. Shopkeepers too had arrived and made brisk sales of cola bottles and sweets.

The significance of the tribal pilgrimages has gradually emerged. People attend them for their material and spiritual wellbeing. They hope to meet their relatives and friends, to reaffirm old ties and to forge new ones. Throughout most of the year they had not met many of these people. By participating in the annual tribal muster, and sharing the tribal sacrificial meal, they renew bonds with the tribe, its members and resources. The attendance of guests from other tribes emphasizes the tribes' solidarity with the people of South Sinai, for the preservation of peace, a precondition for access to pastures in the peninsula and for combined smuggling operations. Lastly, they supplicate the saint to forward their prayers to a distant God, in whom they put their trust. Without his help they could not survive in an insecure world, on which they depend in so many ways and over which they have no influence.

V

The significance of the tribal pilgrimages is symbolized in the saints' tombs. I take a 'symbol' to be a sign replete with many interrelated meanings. In this working definition, which bears resemblance to Sapir's (1934:493) characterisation of the 'condensation symbol', I wish to stress the richness of meaning as identifying mark of the symbol, as opposed to the mechanical multiplication of mental associations that may attach to a particular sign. The meanings of the condensation symbol express, as Sapir (1934:493) pointed out, "a condensation of energy, its actual significance being out of all proportion to the apparent triviality of meaning suggested by its mere form". To this I would add that much of the emotional impact of 'condensation symbols' derives from the fact that they evoke numerous meanings simultaneously. The secret of this immediate impact probably lies in the symbol's full integration in the daily routine of its users. Because of this, many students of society today agree that an external observer can tap the multiple meanings of symbols only through intimate knowledge of both native conceptions of their society and of the social contexts in which the symbols are invoked. The whole gamut of a symbol's contextual uses, as well as the associated symbols and contexts, must be explored, before it is properly understood. But once this is done one may find that each segment of the meaning of a symbol has a precise referent and thus appeals directly to communicants.

I shall attempt to unravel three of the major strands in the mesh of meanings attached to the saint's tomb, which have until now remained in the background: the significance of the building erected over the tomb, the tomb itself, and details of the saint's person.

I would argue that the building symbolizes the Bedouin's conception of the tribe's territorial rights whose essence is the tribesman's exclusive right to build a house on tribal land. Geertz's (1968:49) concise description of the Moroccan shrine fits that of South Sinai too: "It is a squat, white, usually dome, block-like stone building set under a tree, on a hilltop, or isolated, like an abandoned pillbox, in the middle of an open plain." (See also Canaan 1927:11). One might add that each shrine has a door, and usually also a small window. Only the dome, often crowned with a crescent, and in a few shrines a prayer niche facing the direction of Mecca, distinguishes the shrine from an ordinary house, and indicates that it serves a religious purpose. We already know that Bedouin consider the building of a house as the exclusive right of tribesmen and do not permit outsiders to build houses in the tribe's territory. The shrine signifies, among other things, the territorial claims of the tribe as whose pilgrimage centre it serves. As other tribes may also visit the shrine, the owning tribe's rights obviously must be limited, while others obtain rights to pass through the tribe's land and to pasture their animals on it. On another level, the use of the saint's tomb as a symbol of tribal ownership indicates that territorial rights are protected by supernatural sanctions, but not by the might of the whole tribe. Bedouin store property, such as tents and farming implements, inside or near the holy tomb, secure in the belief that it is protected by the saint. They recount stories about misfortunes that befell would-be thieves, until they returned the stolen property to the tomb. Construction of a saint's tomb or repairs to one, are acts intended to claim rights in land. When Ghanem Jum'a, a wealthy Muzeneh, built the shrine of Faraj, the tribe's ancestor, in the 1960's, he reasserted the tribe's sovereignty over the area which was at the time becoming the main supply centre in South Sinai, and the major sales depot of the mobile merchants from al-'Arish who control nearly all the commerce in the region. Similarly, Jebaliyeh elders every few years invite their tribesmen to subscribe money for repairs to the shrine of Sheikh 'Awad. This building activity reasserts a tribe's right to the holy tomb, and through it - to territory; and incidentally, in this way all the shrines are kept in a good state of repair.

The saint's tomb occupies the centre of the building, to allow visitors to circumambulate. The tomb rises to a height of about three feet. It is covered by a shroud made of white or green cloth, on which sometimes the Islamic creed and the saint's name are embroidered. There are usually several layers of shrouds, for each time a shroud is worn and torn it remains in place and a new one is placed on top of it. It is always doubtful whether the holy tomb actually contains a human body. While the tomb of Nebi Saleḥ is solidly built and one cannot therefore know whether anyone is buried in it, the tomb of 'Ali Abu Taleb consists of a flimsy wooden frame, just sufficient to carry the layers of embroidered shrouds. Canaan (1927:22) remarks, with regard to Palestinian sanctuaries, that "the tomb is often not in the shrine, but outside of it ... it is not at all necessary that there should be a tomb ... connected with the place to make it a shrine." In South Sinai the Bedouin have gone a step further: they insist that no one is buried in a *maqām*. As proof they cite the "well-known fact that Nebi Saleḥ is buried in Ramla, in Israel, and that even the Sheikhs Habus and Abu Shabib have each two holy tombs. Only one of these holds a grave (*turba*), while the other is a place for gatherings of men (*maqʿad*)." The shrines at which tribes gather could not contain a body, even if the saint had been buried there. For it is common knowledge among Bedouin that the remains of good men dissolve into air (*hawāʾ*) after some time, and only the bodies of ordinary persons remain in their tombs. This attitude releases the saint from his human associations. Shed of his earthly vestiges, he moves into closer communion with God. He becomes distant enough to approach the distant deity.

The saint cannot be a named ancestor because the tribe is not a corporate group, and cannot be represented by a symbol generally reserved for agnatic descent. Most people cannot say anything definite about the saint's person, except that he was a holy man during his lifetime, as proven by instances in which he rescued individuals from various tribes in miraculous ways. Occasionally people hazard guesses about the antecedents of a saint. While some say that Nebi Saleh was a pre-Islamic Arabian prophet, others think that perhaps he was the ancestor of the Sawalha. The same uncertainty seems to have prevailed over a century ago, when Robinson (1841:I, 215) reported: "The history of the Saint is uncertain; but our Arabs held him to be a progenitor of their tribe, the Sawaliha." Sheikh 'Awad is also said by some Jebaliyeh to belong to their tribe, while others claim to know nothing about his origins. Some Muzeneh consider Sheikh Abu Zaid to have been a Sawarka Bedouin (from North Sinai), and others attribute Muzeneh origins to him. The only saint who appears to be an acknowledged tribal ancestor is Faraj of the Muzeneh. But his tomb is not reckoned among the *maqāms*; it is named after a group, the Faranja, and not after the ancestor Faraj; and only in recent years was a shrine built over the tomb. Yet the fact remains that Faranja is one of the Muzeneh's three pilgrimage sites, and one has to conclude that, in a sense, the saint is an emblem of the tribe.

The three holy tombs visited by the Muzeneh allow us to define more clearly the symbolic significance of the saint, for the person of each of the three saints gives special emphasis to one aspect: Faranja symbolizes the unity of the tribe, as well as its descent from the North Arabian Muzeneh (Doughty 1937:II, 381). Nebi Saleḥ represents both the unity of the Tawara, of South Sinai as one region to which all inhabitants have access, and the inclusion of South Sinai in the Islamic world and, by extension, in the state controlling Sinai. Nebi Harun again stands for the connection with the monastery of Saint Catherine's and the privileges associated with it on one hand, and on the other - for the Islamic community. For Moses and Aron are included in Islamic hagiography. I cannot fully explain this continued specialization of the three Muzeneh saints, for in other tribes all the symbolic aspects merge today in a single saint. It may be connected with two facts. First, that the Muzeneh have become the largest and most widely dispersed tribe. They control over half of South Sinai, including most of the east coast, and this encourages a tendency for the proliferation of smuggling rings, with the ensuing competition and strife. The elders of the tribe make special efforts to preserve unity, so as to keep the Muzeneh predominant in the smuggling business. Therefore they stress joint descent and begin the pilgrimage at the tomb of Faraj. Yet competition between rival smuggling rings has several times in recent years erupted violently at the tribal gathering. Second, their exclusive use of the central sanctuary of Nebi Saleḥ, expresses their political dominance among the tribes of South Sinai.

Whether the pilgrimage is made to one or three saints, it always symbolizes the Bedouin's solidarity with three social aggregates. If the saint is to represent all of them, his identity must be indeterminate. He is and he is not a tribesman, a son of Sinai, and an illustrious Moslem.

On a higher level of abstraction, the three Muzeneh saints stand for ideologies that are deeply engrained in Bedouin thought and concern areas of their social life: agnation and territorial organization, kinship and the regionalism of South Sinai, and the universalism of Islam and, by extension, all the external world on which the Bedouin depend and which they do not control. All these ideologies are contained and, to some extent, integrated in a system of thought, in the Bedouin concept "tribe".

The tribal pilgrimage to Saints' Tombs is the Bedouin's answer to some fundamental problems; he came up with this answer because his view of reality is filtered through a theory of society that hinges on the tribe. The Bedouin participates as wage labourer in the wider economy and in a bureaucratic state. Both are distant and leave him an insecure outsider. But he has the tribe to fall back on. The tribe means to him several things: a territorial group owning resources from which he can make a living: land on which he can dig wells, plant orchards and build a house; a political group of agnates, whose members help and defend each other and their territory; and a group whose membership gives access to pastures all over South Sinai. All these together are the Bedouin's basic economy. The pilgrimage brings together the people who help to make this economy, and seeks to re-unite them. At the same time it reflects the fears and uncertainties associated with the distant state, the vagaries of external wage labour, and the problems of life in general.

Thus the cult of saints refers not only to a regionalism more or less confined to the geographical boundaries of South Sinai and to the sharing of natural resources for the benefit of the Tawara and their tribes. It also refers to a larger entity, to the world in which the Bedouin work, and from which they obtain most of their food and other supplies and services. This world is located chiefly outside the borders of South Sinai and, even more importantly, the Bedouin do not exert influence on its activities. A distant government and other external organizations determine much of their lives, but contact with, not to mention influence over, these forces is minimal. For the bureaucratic chain does not fully extend to the Bedouin, and their own appointed representatives, the sheikhs, do not greatly influence officials at the centre. So the Bedouin place their reliance on a 'spiritual' representative, the saint, who is at least close to God and able to influence him. Two worlds are linked through the person of the saint, who is sometimes thought of as the patron of a tribe, perhaps even an ancestor, and at other times as a holy man of Islam. The saint represents both the tribe as conceptualized by the Bedouin, and the wide external world. His function is to mediate between the two worlds which together sustain the Bedouin. I suggest that tribal reunions elsewhere too develop in response to similar situations: in tribal or other economically undifferentiated regions that depend on external forces (natural forces, or an external state and economy) over which they exert little influence. Such societies maintain a pastoral or farming economy on which they fall back in time of need, and maintain the tribe mainly in order to keep control over their territory. A tribal society that is self-sufficient, or that can rely on economic alternatives and on government assistance, does not need tribal reunions.

How does Robertson Smith's argument that there is a correspondence between social organization and religious representations, fare in the the light of this discussion? Warbner tends to reject the "correspondence" theory, because "the 'community of the god' is a conception of boundedness." (Warbner 1977:XVIII). True, Robertson Smith, like the Bedouin themselves, viewed the tribe as a bounded political and territorial entity, perhaps because they considered agnation to be the backbone of the tribe.

The ideology of agnation informs "bounded" activities, such as the control over rights in land, the protection of life and property and the setting up of groups. To this kind of activity applies Robertson Smith's (1854:150) dictum that holiness is "a restriction on the licence of man in the free use of natural things." In the Arabian context, he believed that gods were associated with permanent sanctuaries, and that their powers were confined to a certain territory (ibid.:92). Therefore, "at most sanctuaries embracing a stretch of pasture-ground, the right of grazing was free to the community of the god, but not to outsiders" (ibid.:144).

This prescription did not fit the customary sharing of pastures. Although "every tribe indeed has its own range of plains and valleys, and its own watering-places ... from which it repels aliens by the strong hand, ... not only every tribesman but every covenanted ally has equal and unrestricted right to pitch his tent and drive his cattle where he will" (ibid.:143). The contradiction is immediately explained away: nomads did not claim private property in pastures, and for that reason the local god did not acquire ownership over them.

The material on Saints' Tombs in South Sinai shows that Robertson Smith was mistaken on two accounts. First, the god or saint is not simply associated with one tribe and his influence is not confined to a bounded territory. On the contrary, the "local" god in ancient Arabia, like the saint in South Sinai, symbolizes the interdependence between the tribe and a wider region, particularly where pastures were concerned. Wellhausen shows that many sanctuaries in pre-Islamic Arabia had extensive spheres of influence. For instance, the sanctuary of the goddess Manat was located in Hudhail Territory, but was frequented by Aus and Khazraj tribesmen and by others (Wellhausen

1961:27-28). The sanctuary at Mecca too was not visited by the Quraish only, but attracted pilgrims from various tribes, while the Meccans must have visited other sanctuaries. In this manner, ties were forged between tribes from different regions, which facilitated transit and mutual access to the available pastures, even in the absence of a central government.

Second, for each restriction on the use of resources there must be a corresponding opening up of resources, as exemplified in this statement, also taken from Robertson Smith (1894:111): "The Arabs regard rain as depending on the ... seasons, which affect all tribes alike within a wide range; and so when the showers of heaven are ascribed to a god, that god is Allah, the supreme and non-tribal deity." Evidently these tribesmen reserve certain rights in territory for themselves, but also grant rights to pasture on it to others, on a basis of mutuality. Robertson Smith cannot admit that the "tribal deity" also stands for Allah; to imply that the same people believe in two gods, one tribal and one supreme, at the same time, is as far as he dare go. In South Sinai the saint is clearly associated with God. While he intercedes with God on behalf of his tribe, he also works on behalf of individuals from any tribe, and is thus never an exclusive patron of his own people. He represents both restrictions on the use of the country's resources in favour of some people, and access to the remaining resources to others. There is no paradox in this, for rights are always specific, so that every prohibition has its complementary permission. Thus in South Sinai *certain* rights in land, wells and roads are reserved for tribesmen, and other rights are expressly opened up to all Tawara: land everywhere is available to anyone for pasture, drinking water for men and animals may be drawn from any well, even when surrounded by a fence, and every Bedouin can travel freely anywhere in the peninsula, as long as he does not infringe local privileges of employment or uses another tribe's smuggling route.

Yet, after all is said and done, we are still left with a correspondence, between social reality and its symbolic representation. If the reality is more complex than Robertson Smith's, and if it has many dimensions, that is due to the more detailed ethnography available today. If in addition to bounded social entities today we see networks of relationships, that is due to relatively new theoretical insights. The brilliance of Robertson Smith's original idea, and its eminent usefulness, remain undiminished: symbols refer to a social reality, as seen and interpreted by people. And symbols themselves are taken from daily experience, so that they can be directly apprehended by people.

NOTES

Field work in South Sinai was carried out between 1971 and 1979. I spent a total of twelve months in the field. In 1973-4 Miss Shuli Hartman participated in field work. The Ford Foundation, through the Israel Foundation Trustees, supported the project and this help is gratefully acknowledged. The South Sinai Administration, and especially Moshe Sela, greatly facilitated my work. An earlier version of this essay was presented at the ASA Conference on Regional Cults at Manchester in March 1976 (Marx 1977). The comments of Ernest Gellner, Raymond Firth, Shuli Hartman, Smadar Levie, and Richard Werbner, were of great help in the revision of the essay.

REFERENCES

Ben-David, J.
1972 *Shivte ha-beduim bi-drom Sinai* (The Bedouin Tribes of South Sinai). Jerusalem: Hebrew University, Department of Geography, MA dissertation.

Berque, J.
1955 *Structures sociales du Haut-Atlas*. Paris: Presses Universitaires de France.

Burckhardt, J.L.
1822 *Travels in Syria and the Holy Land.* London: Murray.

Canaan, T.
1927 *Mohammedan Saints and Sanctuaries in Palestine*. London: Luzac.

Christian, William A.
1972 *Person and God in a Spanish Valley*. New York: Seminar Press.

Doughty, C.M.
1937 *Travels in Arabia Deserts*. New York: Random House (first published 1888).

Eickelman, D.F.
1976 *Moroccan Islam; Tradition and Society in a Pilgrimage Center*. Austin, Texas: University of Texas Press.

Ganor, A. et al.
1973 *Aklim Sinai* (The Climate of Sinai). Beth Dagan: Israel Meteorological Service.

Geertz, C.
1968 *Islam Observed; Religious Development in Morocco and Indonesia*. Chicago: University of Chicago Press.

Gellner, E.
1972 Political and Religious Organization of the Berbers of the Central High Atlas, in: E. Gellner and C. Micaud (eds.), *Arabs and Berbers; From Tribe to Nation in North Africa*. London: Duckworth.

Glasener, M.I.
1974 The Bedouin of Southern Sinai under Israeli Administration, *The Geographical Review* 64: 31-60.

Gruenbaum, G.E. von
1951 *Muhammedan Festivals*. New York: Schuman.

Israel, Army
1962 *Beduei Sinai* (The Bedouin of Sinai). Israel: Army, Southern Command.

Kapars, Y.
1975 Ziarat Sheikh Abu Taleb (The Pilgrimage to the Abu Taleb Shrine Shrine), *Teva' Waaretz* 17: 192-194.

Keller, A.
1900 *Eine Sinai-Fahrt*. Frauenfeld: Huber.

Levi, S.
1977 "An Ancient Tradition Regarding the Summit Menegat Musa in Sinai", *Teva Waaretz* 19,4: 173-176. (Hebrew)

Levi, S.
1978 "Deir Arba'in in Bedouin Belief", *Bulletin of Field-School "David Cliffs"* 12: 18-20. (Hebrew)

Levy, R.
1962 *The Social Structure of Islam*. Cambridge: Cambridge University Press.

Linant de Bellefonds, Y.
1974 Kabr. *Encyclopaedia of Islam*, New Edition. Leiden: Brill.

Marx, E.
1977 Communal and Individual Pilgrimage: The Region of Saints' Tombs in South Sinai, in: R.P. Werbner (ed.), *Regional Cults*. London: Academic Press.

Meshel, Z.
1971 *Drom Sinai* (South Sinai). Jerusalem: Sh.H.L.Y.

Murray, G.W.
1935 *Sons of Ishmael; A Study of the Egyptian Bedouin*. London: Routledge.

Musil, A.
1928 *The Manners and Customs of the Rwala Bedouins*. New York: American Geographical Society.

Niebuhr, C.
1799 *Travels Through Arabia and Other Countries in the East*. Perth: Morison.

Palmer, E.H.
1871 *The Desert of the Exodus*. Cambridge: Deighton, Bell.

Palmer, H.S.
1906 *Sinai from the Fourth Egyptian Dynasty to the Present Day*. London: SPCK.

Peters, E.L.
1976 From Particularism to Universalism in the Religion of the Cyrenaica Bedouin, *Bulletin of the British Society for Middle Eastern Studies* 3.

Sapir, E.
1934 Symbolism. *Encyclopaedia of the Social Sciences*. New York: Macmillan.

Smith, W. Robertson
1894 *Lectures on the Religion of the Semites*. London: Black.

Turner, V.
1973 The Center Out There: Pilgrim's Goal, *History of Religions* 12: 191-230.

Wellhausen, J.
1961 *Reste arabischen Heidentums*. Berlin: De Gruyter.
(1887)

Werbner, R.P. (ed.)
1977 *Regional Cults*. (ASA Monograph 16). London: Academic Press.

The Me^{c}ruf of Tamjlocht or the Rite of the Bound Victim

Paul Pascan

Who can tell what the countryside and mountains of this land conceal? The passengers of the long-distance coaches which endlessly travel across the country from North to South, and East to West, have their journeys broken by stops in small rural centres. These are towns which seem to have mushroomed overnight, all similar to each other, as if suddenly born out of a feverish mind. They are sores which scar the countryside; coach stations, petrol pumps, people selling hard-boiled eggs, children offering chewing gum, smoke-filled snack bars, grocershops with their stocks of soft drinks and gas containers greet the eye of the traveller. But each of these travellers belongs to a land somewhere, - to a soil, to a village hidden away and buried in the rolling hills or nestling in the mountains. Rooted there, the memory of the culture of his birthplace is now preserved in the depth of his heart, like a fragile glow; like a smouldering ember, as persistent as the chirring of the cricket on a summer's evening. All is history, told and retold, delving so deeply into the tribal past that no one can claim to be certain about its beginnings.

Production-line worker, stevedore, dustman or navvy on the wet and freezing building sites of Europe, perhaps the migrant worker can only tolerate the intolerable thanks to this hidden memory, - this soft and secret light, the strong and vibrant scent of ineffable experiences which restore him to his people and give him back his identity and his honour.

Only the voyeur will see this as folklore; only someone with no roots of his own will see it as obscurantism.

For those torn away from their village by necessity, the rites have the same effect as Mother Earth on Antaeus or the waters of the Styx on Achilles. They immerse themselves in them again and again to recover their strength, their joy, their reason for living, the power to resist the universe of steel and sweat which is the other (more) apparent side of their life.

The rite is therefore something other than a festival: it is a re-birth, a resurrection, a rehabilitation of the being.

I. As high as one scans the formidable barrier of the Atlas mountains, above Ida U Garyin, on the mountain pastures of Tishka, one sees no sign of a tree along the ridges. The mass of black schist conceals the depths of the valleys. Only by making an effort to search the ravines and by intense concentration can one gradually make out, as they become clearer in this rocky world, the thin whisp of a small wood fire, a few lingering goats clinging to the crumbling slope of a scree, or three moving piles of wood slowly tottering along a rocky path.

From lower down, rising from the darkness of the valley where the seething waters of a torrent are spanned by a couple of twisted tree trunks, one hears the notes of a song sung by a small group.

On looking closer, one can distinguish the people of the valley converging from all directions towards the sanctuary. At the top of a steep rise, some of the villagers who have come to the *me^c^ruf* of Lalla Aziza stop for a rest. The young are dragging along goats; others carry pots of butter or bundles. They are awaiting the arrival of other villagers.

Discrete traces of man's presence on earth have appeared: a barely visible mountain path, a whisp of smoke which slowly dispels, a chant which is lost in the silence of the evening.

II. The SATAS coach rockets into the centre of Imi n'Tanout, screeching and scattering a cloud of dust and greasy paper. An army of young vendors rushes to the coach, offering hard-boiled eggs, cakes and chewing gum. A shish kebab seller throws a lump of fat into the charcoal to fire off a tempting smell. The coach driver climbs down from his seat, carefully wipes the sweat from the steering wheel on his thighs and gives the tyres a hefty kick to check their pressure.

Between the petrol pumps and the water-carriers, the coach disgorges its worn-out passengers, half-asleep and bewildered. Omar, carrying a small case, his *žellaba* rolled up like a scarf and thrown over the shoulder of his wrinkled suit, is directing the unloading of his large trunk which has been carried on the roof of the coach. Taxi drivers shout out their destinations: Bouabout! Douirane! Lalla Aziza!

III. Some twenty or so passengers have taken their place, standing in the back of the lorry, for tomorrow is the market day in the valley. For a price, Omar has obtained the privelege of sitting in the cab next to the driver and Lahsen, who is also going to Zinit. Lahsen's appearance shows that he is a small local grocer from Imi n'Tanout. Along the way, Omar explains to him the tribulations of his journey so far. It is difficult to hear above the noise of the lorry:

"... They searched everything ... even us, with a transistor radio ..."

"the plane ... you can see the town like flies ..."

"... steel ... I work in the steel works ... they say it is for making boats, enormous sheets of steel, as big as that house ..."

"... do you know my Uncle Brahim? ... is he in the valley at the moment?"

The grey barrier of the Atlas mountains opens up ahead on the road. The nose of the lorry drives a rift between the hills, separates the mountains, roots out the villages nestling on the ridges of the valley, plunges through the waters of a ford, then, getting its breath back, it labours up the slopes, sensing out the precipices, attacks the climb, and finally comes to a grinding halt at the Zinit turning, only to set off again in the direction of the mine, leaving behind Lahsen and Omar carrying the trunk. Already children are coming to meet them, then stop and rush happily back to the village to announce the news of the arrivals.

IV. All the pilgrims have gathered at a site above the *zawya* Lalla Aziza. It is a smiling and quiet celebration, disturbed only by children running around in all directions. The arrivals form into groups by age, sex, or social status, without apparent order; they avoid effusive greeting and content themselves with a brief, simple handshake and a few appropriate words.

The *mqeddem* of the shrine pronounces a few words to implore the Saint's blessing for her followers. These holy phrases separate those who have brought offerings from the rest of the crowd: sugar loaves, packets of tea, small packets of nuts placed at the feet of the shrine keeper. The generosity of the assembly calls for a ritual *fatiḥa* which is chanted and taken up by all those present. It is mostly the women, a few children and some shepherds from a distant area and seldom here, who are interested in visiting the shrine.

As the others wait, they exchange news: births, marriages, deaths, sales of trees, fields, livestock, emigration, departures and returns, whilst others prepare the sacrifice.

V. A spurt of blood, a sharp light explodes onto the greyness of life. Blood gushes from the quivering animal. Blood that fascinates the children, makes the men become serious, and encourages the *zġarit* of the women. It ties the mysterious knot of life and death. A sublime moment soon forgotten in the immediate tasks of cutting the animal up, washing the entrails and keeping the dogs away.

As those responsible for the sacrifice work away into the evening, the houses take in the little groups of people invited from other districts, as they are placed without fuss among the inhabitants of Zinit.

VI. We still need another 250 rials for the sacrificial animal! A simple statement of fact. Others join the six organizers of the rite in the small austere room.

The people of this place are not masters of the written word: their calloused hands are used to gripping the plough, the rough goat's hair rope and the handles of their hoes cut from the branches of knotty thuya trees. The pen shakes as it inscribes the sums in large figures next to the names of the representatives of the lineages.

They come in one by one to hand over their contribution: "There's still the Ayt Uchikar, the Ayt Ikru and the Ait Wafaryat to come. And as usual Lahsen ou Ali of Ukraray has not turned up!"

"I've come in his place!" A young twenty year old dressed in a thick woollen *žellaba* hands over a dirty greasy 5 dirham note and a few coins.

Plain dwellings made of mud and stone ... Decoration on the walls is limited to a few posters and pictures: a photo of a son who is a primary school teacher in Casablanca, an old picture of His Majesty Mohammed V, a poster for the Women's Union, strangely out of place here. Through the window three or four young girls bowed under enormous water jars can be seen entering the porch of the house.

Omar enters and greets everybody. He is wearing the *žellaba* which he had thrown over his shoulder in Imi n'Tanout. He can still be recognized as a migrant by his lack of headgear, by his hair, and by the gold-plated watch, obvious seen as he hands the money over to the treasurer:

"I have come for the Ayt Wafaryat; here's what they owe, check that it's all there."

All the lineages participating in the rite are now represented around a glass of hot mint tea. The accounts are proclaimed and amounts due from the previous year are added. Repetitive minute accounting serves to guarantee everyone's participation and also the publicity and the democracy of the organization. Here, there are no edifying speeches, no formal and official announcements. Information is distributed any how and is incidental to the general conversation. Everyone hears rather than listens. Anyone who has an objection will avoid making it explicitly, preferring to ask an innocuous question, which gets a reply seemingly without having demanded it. One can feel that great care is taken not to challenge anything directly for this would be out of place, almost an aggression.

- Ahmed ou Bella says that the sheep which Ali ou Hammou proposes to sell for 2800 rials is a good buy. Do those who have seen it agree?

This is a simple enough question, but one which conceals a whole network of inter-personal relationships, friendly or conflicting, and a whole range of possible or feasible choices, which are difficult to ignore now that the words have been spoken.

The silence which falls on the group is eloquent even though the faces betray nothing. Perhaps we can read their minds. There are at least thirty or forty sheep in the valley as good as Ali ou Hammou's, and any of them could be bought for the same price. Or the sleep could have been bought in the market as in previous years. But it's a bit late now and it doesn't really seem worth starting an argument with Ali's friends.

"So, next Friday, God willing, we shall go the *maqam* of Lalla Aziza in Tamjlocht".

"God willing", everybody replies in unison.

VII. Only close friends stay to share the meal. Once the cousins, relations, allies and neighbours have left, the most intimate friends may still have things to say to one another or, as is more likely, may appreciate the warm reciprocity of mutual silence and listen together to the sounds of the night.

Outside some villagers are celebrating - they have organised an "*aḥwaš*" for the arrival of the people of the district who have come for the *meᶜruf*. The rhythm of drumming and singing gradually takes over from the last sounds of the evening: the plaintive bleating of the goat kids as the flocks are brought in and the call of the *mwedden* to the *cša* (evening) prayer.

Expectation, reserve and hope are the roots of pleasure in life. The *ṭažin* is brought in with simplicity reserved for perfect things. A hidden treasure, in its earthenware cone, which though unseen can already be imagined as hot, succulent, and full of natural aroma. The murmured conversation breaks off, everybody takes his place round the low table. The bread also arrives in its *mendil*, red hot, rough, unrefined, but it too a source of vigour and health. It is shared out and chinks of bread are placed all round the *ṭažin* forming a sort of circle of abundance, this preparation postpones the start of the meal a moment longer.

The master of the house uncovers the steaming plate with a certain flourish. He removes half of the meat and places it in the upturned conical lid: it is not customary here that the host eat with his guests: he is present to serve them and to ensure that everything is to their entire satisfaction and will himself eat the leftovers later on with his family.

The guests' silence and their undivided attention to the meal is ample proof of their satisfaction.

Outside, the dance is at its height: the men's chants come in answer to women's; they sing of love, of war and of life, age-old songs which serve to confirm to them the eternity of their existence as one people.

VIII. The small groups of pilgrims have been climbing the steep path towards Tamjlocht for well over an hour now. In the early, early morning, before the first rays of sun had lit the high peaks of Tinwaline in the west, the men in each of the four villages participating in the rite had sipped their piping hot soup and eaten three good handfuls of nuts as preparation for the tough day ahead. Above the Uchchen *ᶜẓib*, one can see far enough in all directions to recognize the Tamteddit group coming who have just passed the ridge over there; further south two groups Tagounit are starting to climb the Talaat n'Uzru; - lower down still, one can just make out those from Tamzgourt who have come from farther away.

This year it is the lineages of Tinwaline who have volunteered to sacrifice the sheep. For this reason they have to be there well ahead of the others, with two men sent up the day before to get things ready with the sheep, and a mule to carry some wood.

Although he has no part to play in the organisation of the rite this year, Omar has joined up with the first group. They make fun of him a bit.

"You haven'nt got enough wind any more; you're too used to taxis and Mercedes" (laughter).

"Why have you kept those smart city shoes on?"

Indeed, this is the last item of his migrant's dress which he is still wearing. As if dress were the most apparent sign of his readoption into his home land, he has made a change, at each stage of his journey from Imi n'Tanout: the *ṭagiya* has gone, and he has removed his jacket... the legs of his trousers no longer show below his *žellaba*; though he has not gone so far as to wrap a *reẓẓa* round his head, he has covered his head with a woollen cap. But he hesitated to put on the usual open sandals (made from old tyres) since he is not used to them and feared the morning cold. The comfort of his feet is the most important thing he has brought back with him from Europe.

A last effort is necessary to clamber over the rocks which border the site at Tamjlocht. Omar is determined to get there first. He has been twenty times at least to this desolate place which is suspended between heaven and earth. Nevertheless, he is always struck by a sense of mystery. The sea of clouds which for the last hour has been slowly invading the valley now envelopes the peak, ebbs round its slopes and isolates Tamjlocht from the rest of the world. This provides the perfect natural phenomenon to fill the spirit with awe and adoration. It is here, as the elders tell it, that Lalla Aziza pursued by a bold and overzealous shepherd threw herself off the precipice. Her holiness protected her, the story continues, and she flew unharmed to Zinit, like the squawking jackdaws that circle above the site.

Omar rediscovers the small site of the sacrifice: here the tree

Omar rediscovers the small site of the sacrifice: here the tree where the sheep is sacrificed, there the large flat stone where the meat is divided, and, below the rock, the fire-places where the broth is prepared, still visible from the previous year, and finally the room where ...

But the others are already arriving, and they go into the *maqam* to get out the ritual cooking pots.

IX. There are so many different and intertwined scenes in the rite that one can doubt its development from a single origin. The rite follows a spontaneous consensus, with an improvisation of various details which may lend more importance to one sequence, lessen the impact of another, or even conflict with a third. There is an organised chaos which nevertheless brings out in piecemeal fashion the essential points of the ritual. The most important question to be asked is what have the pilgrims come to do? They themselves say they have come to give thanks to Lalla Aziza. But there is no scene actually devoted to her praise. Anthropolatry underlies mysticism and religiosity in all mountainous regions of Morocco - and elsewhere. It was the Almohades who rose against the heresies which had been tolerated by the Almoravides. But here the cult of the Saint Lalla Aziza is rather a call for her intercession with God.

Fundamentally the Seksawa and the people of the rite feel that they are all a people of diverse origins in the process of dispersion. Their unity through their vicissitudes and across centuries has been ideologised in the cult of the virgin. At Tamjlocht, this Friday in March, they wish to reaffirm their alliance by burying their disputes; by atonement for their faults and by the precise distribution of the food produced by all to the stomach of all.

Among these three salient points, everyday life also has its place, there is a little trade though on a tiny scale, and, later, a feverish squabble over the left-overs; and for all there is an opportunity to see people from far away and to discuss business.

This is a very special and subtle atmosphere: joyous but without laughter and show; calm, relaxed, a peace created by the simplicity of an exceptional site: an isolated island in the sky ...

Surely the Imteddan (re)live their ancient golden age during these moments, taken from eternity, and that they spend out of this world.

X. In this georgic world, food results from the relationship, the dialogue between man and his land. Nothing exists that has not been touched by his own hands, extracted, harvested, guarded, processed. What he creates is the physical extension of himself as are his implements, his house, his *saqya* (irrigation canal). By giving, exchanging, or selling, he amputates a part of himself; he foresakes a part of his own being rather than just his possessions. This explains the ceremonious nature of the meeting of men and gods in this Olympus of the Imettdan.

The arrival of people at the summit from all directions precipitates many joyous reunions. The relaxed good-humoured atmosphere in this high place is a break from the cold protocol which is the rule in the valley. The congregation feels its way-pulsating and eddying towards the union in the joint partaking of their food. Each person has brought what he can in the way of unleavened barley bread, butter in jars, red rock salt in plastic bags wrapped in a piece of cloth, and sets them down in the right place without being shown where.

Within the space of a few minutes, the food contributed is collected together, mixed and made indistinguishable. The group will partake collectively of what they have all contributed, so as to become, in a manner of speaking, one single body, since the companions who eat their bread in common will now have their flesh made from the flesh contributed by all.

XI. The sacrifice of the sheep does not attract a large crowd. It is slaughtered early for it must quickly be skinned, cleaned, cut up and put into the pots to be boiled. The meat which is taken off the bone after this first cooking is then divided into the same number of piles as there are contributors, taking into account the number of their family dependents left behind in the village. This entails endless head counts, repeated again and again to ensure that no one has been forgotten. To make all the small individual piles equal, several people volunteer their services to make tiny transfers of the little pieces of meat from pile to pile.

During this time, people bustle about, recognize one another, go up and down carrying wood, water, the pots of rancid butter, bundles of all sorts of utensils.

On a dead tree trunk, the sheep skin, looking strange and fantastic is exposed to the open sky and offered at an auction in which some ten people vie with one another. The amount due from the buyer is credited to the kitty of the next *ma^{c}ruf*. (A purchase on credit, so to speak, with the treasury of the group acting as bank). The title is drawn up straight away by a makeshift scribe. The fleece is said to be blessed by the Saint and it will enhance the place on the buyer's sofa which he offers to guests of rank.

The assistant of the person responsible for sharing out the meat calls out the names of the participants in the order of their drawing lots. They go over to the master of ceremonies to take their little piles which they wrap in a piece of material: the meat which has been distributed (*wzi^{c}a*) is not eaten on the spot: it is sacred and will be taken back home and eaten by those who are absent - the women and children.

Three youths stoke the fires to speed the boiling of the broth where the leftovers of the meat, the bones and the collective butter are thickening.

XII. But a more solemn ceremony interrupts the friendly disorder of the gathering for a moment. On a flat part of the summit, a circle has formed with most of those who are not busy with the fire or in personal discussion with distant cousins.

A *ṭaleb* starts a *fatiḥa* for those who make offerings in the name of the Saint. They approach one by one and put down their money (often a very small amount) whilst in hushed tones the reason for each one seeking the Saint's assistance is whispered round the group. So and so has had ill luck at home; another hopes that the court case will go his way; yet another calls for an end to a dispute. On each occasion, the Saint's intercession is requested to satisfy the wish.

Suddenly someone raises his voice to insist on a *fatiḥa* being said against the thefts of livestock, which have become all too frequent. Everybody knows that a particular problem is being presented under cover of this impersonal reference. Those most closely concerned argue animatedly amongst themselves, making sure not to mention names but giving enough details so that no one can be unaware who is concerned. The hubbub quickly dies down, without the *ṭaleb* playing any role as mediator or peace-maker. People from all sides intervene to quieten the noisy plaintiff whose only objective, in any case, was to publicise his misfortunes and his accusation.

A last *fatiḥa* is said for the protection of all, after which the money is publicy counted. Each person wants to know how much has been collected. Some even want to touch and handle an amount which they seldom have an opportunity to see.

XIII. The communion meal is the most direct means of attaining the consubstantiality to which the group aspires. Each is to be part of the whole, all discord is to disappear since by eating the flesh which belongs to all, all will henceforth be made of one flesh. The tribal communion aims to reinforce the group, not to satisfy individuals. Solidarity takes precedence over personal success, even at the price of impoverishing some.

As we have already seen, the contribution of each person is a part of his being which has been put in common in the mixing of bread loaves, the collective purchase of the sheep, the pile of salt, the butter simmering in the cooking pots. The consumption of these foods is no mundane feast, no profane banquet nor celebration of abundance. On the contrary, it is a ritual meal of food which is not only frugal, but licit and blessed. It is no less than the consumption of the group by the group, a holy self-cannibalism, a reflected collective eucharist.

A dozen earthenware pots of a type not usually found in the valley are left the year round in the *maqam* of Lalla Aziza at Tamjlocht and are reserved for the communal meal. The twelve lineages of the rite invite one another in order to ensure consubstantiality as completely as possible. Those present form into groups of five or six round the sacred pots each group containing people from five or six lineages. They receive their equal share of unleavened bread which has been taken at random from the pile without it being possible to recognize the ones which they themselves brought. The pot is filled with sauce served with a wooden ladel from the three *gedra*-s (large cooking pots) in which the collective butter, meat and salt have been mixed.

Each group retires to a quiet corner to consume slowly and with diligence the bread which they dip in the sauce and a few pieces of meat. A quasi-religious peace and calm reigns over this scene.

XIV. The meal is probably the culminating point of the rite, even if it is not the most important. It is followed by a moment of uncertainty; then the atmosphere changes and suddenly becomes terribly rowdy as the remainder of the sauce is divided out. From a cache or from beneath his garments each produces some sort of recipient, earthware, wooden, iron, plastic - there is great variety of bottles, tin cans and differently shaped containers - to take the rest of the sauce back to the village.

There is ill-controlled pushing and shoving, open competition in an explosion of selfishness which constitutes a complete break with the preceding scene.

Meanwhile, all around, with smiles of complicity, people prepare to play their enigmatic game. Each person present is asked to hand in a token - a twig, leaf or any piece of plant - so that lots may be drawn. The participants try and refuse to comply by showing a kind of repugnance, shamefulness or modesty as if the request shocked their sense of decency.

They are forced to comply both by the Master of the Game and by those who have already placed their token in the folds of the organizer's *žellaba*. When all the tokens have been collected, the group is seized by a feeling of suspense, tinged with anxiety.

The Master of the Game draws a lot at random and shows it to the crowd who force the person chosen to give himself up. He tries to refuse to recognise his lot, and vainly attempts to escape. But finally he resigns himself to the sacrifice and to the fact of being tied up in the *maqam* of Lalla Aziza, bound, and abandoned by the group.

A second lot is drawn to choose who will bind the victim and in this case the person chosen recognises his token straightaway, and shows with appropriate gestures that he will assume his role of tormentor as energetically as the crowd encourages him to do.

Everyone collects up his belongings; the remaining bread is shared out, the ritual pots are washed and put back in the *maqam*.

The person to be bound reluctantly enters the small dark room to undergo his punishment, followed by his tormentor.

An instant later the executioner bursts out of the hut, having supposedly tied the victim up very tightly. His appearance is a sign for the congregation to leave in haste. In a headlong rush without pausing for breath or casting a backward glance, the Imettdan hurry down the slopes of the peak, fleeing towards their villages as if some catastrophe had chased them from the *maqam*.

However they have not reached the first fields before the bound victim, completely free and untroubled, appears and overtakes them. He has been saved by the Saint Lalla Aziza and has returned to join his community. The headlong rush is over; now there is the time to notice the tufts of *Izri*, a type of wild thyme, which is picked and whose perfume is inhaled (a note of mildness after the ferocity of the rite?).

XV. On the way back, Omar has a lively discussion with two companions. A relation seems to want to reason with him:

"You should come back here ... Mohand ou Lahsen wants to sell a bit of land with three nut trees on it. We need a mill in the village, the one in the souk is too far away and too expensive. If "they" stop giving jobs in Europe, the whole valley here is waiting for men able to make something of it ...".

Omar nods and scratches his head beneath the woollen bonnet. It's not quite as simple as all that. Yes, this is good country, but he has growing children who have to go to school, and that means the town.

They approach the village where once again singing and dancing have invaded the central common ground.

Quite naturally, the three or four migrants from the village find themselves sitting together on a few rocks. They talk of Puteaux and Genevilliers: they show each other photos taken outside a metro station, employment and residence cards, a bus pass. Girls pass by them, bowed down under the heavy water jars or enormous piles of wood.

A youth records the *aḥwaš* and then plays it back. His father explains that his son worked in Agadir for a whole year and that he didn't bring back a penny but only this contraption. He adds loud enough to be heard that he would have done better to stay and work in the valley.

The young man is incensed, and calling the migrants as his witness he blurts out: "What interest is there in farming? The land here is too tough, the soil is rocky, it's cold, there's no water, the work is hard. How much can a fit person earn here? He can work the whole year long, from souk to souk, and he won't get more than 500 dirhams. If he goes to town, better still abroad, he can get ten times, a hundred times that amount. His family can stay here and live on what he makes elsewhere. We want dirhams, there's nothing to be gained here."

REFERENCES

This text was written as a preliminary scenario for a film which was made in April 1979 on the actual site of the rite. The only actors were the participants in the ceremony themselves.

Like others, I first learnt of the existencse of the *me^{c}ruf* of Tamjlocht from Jacque Berques' work *Les structures sociales du Haut Atlas* (Paris: Presses Universitaires de France, p. 251, n. 2 and also p. 472, n. 2).

In principle the ceremony is held on the first Friday in the month of March (filahi), (i.e. in the Julian calendar; this means on or after the 13th of March in the Gregorian); but bad weather means that it is often postponed to the 2nd, 3rd or 4th Friday. In fact it can be held on any day except a Thursday (market day), a Saturday or a Sunday. Monday is preferable to other weekdays if there is no Friday possible in March. The participants must have agreed on the day, bought the sacrifical sheep and collected up the funds which comprise:
(1) The receipts from the auctioning "on credit" at the previous year's ceremony of salt, butter and the fleece; (2) the offerings made last year; (3) each person's contribution.

The lineages which join in the rite belong to the four villages which make up the district of Imttdan: Tamṭṭdit, Tagunit, Tiwaline and the Uchchen ^{c}*zib*, Tamzgurt. All these villages are said to be offshoots of one original village: Tamṭṭdit which peopled the Imttdan district. Not all the lineages of these villages participate actively in the rite; they may attend but not officiate, for they are allogenes, that is to say they arrived later than the original group. The dispersion of the lineages - founders of the villages - has followed two axes:

(1) Tamṭṭdit - Tinwaline (and Uchchen) - Tamzgurt
(2) Tamṭṭdit - Tagunit

This was the distribution of lineages (*iġṣan*) and households (*tikatin*) in April 1976 (the lineages officiating at the rite are marked by a cross):

Tamṭṭdit

ayt Warho
a. *muli*
a. *bihi*
(x) a. *wafaryat* (13 households)
(x) a. *mes^c^ud u lehsen* (4 households)

Tagunit

(x) a. *ufqir* (2 households)
(x) a. *ušikar* (2 households)
(x) a. *ikru* (5 households)
a. *uqurm*
a. *šku*
a. *rays*
a. *luh*
a. *batirat*

Tinwaline

(x) a. *uššen* (7 households)
(x) a. *žžamid* (11 households)
(x) a. *u-twirit* (13 households)
(x) a. *ukraray* (15 households)

Tamzgurt

(x) a. *ukraray* (5 households)
a. *sa id*
a. *ḥammu*

Of a total of twenty lineages there are ten who may officiate at the rite representing 77 households. On 16th April 1976, I attended the ceremony and counted 75 households representing 12 lineages.

GLOSSARY OF MOROCCAN WORDS USED IN THE TEXT

aḥwaš	a festive dance in the Western High Atlas.
^c^sa	the night prayer, said about an hour after sunset.
^c^zib	farm, usually in a fairly remote area.
dirham	Moroccan national currency.
fatiḥa	opening chapter of the Koran which is recited to invoke God's blessing.
gedra	earthenware cooking pot.
maqam	a halting place, a place where some famous person, a king of a saint has stayed.
me^c^ruf	an assembly of friends, a gathering in the honour of a saint.
mendil	napkin, piece of cloth in which the bread is wrapped.
mqeddem	one who precedes, the first person, thus a representative or delegate.
mwedden	the person who makes the call to prayer.
ṛeẓẓa	turban of white cloth.

ryal	unit of account used in everyday market dealings equal to five times the national currency unit.
saqya	an open irrigation canal.
suq	weekly market (written in French and English as souk).
ṭagya	small cap in white cotton or embroidered, made in crochet.
ṭažin	meat stew or the earthenware plate in which such a stew simmers.
ṭaleb	a scribe, an educated person.
wzi^{c}a	division, sharing out of meat.
zawya	a sanctuary.
zġarit	women's shouts of joy: ulululation.

The Discrediting of a Sufi Movement in Tunisia*

Kenneth L. Brown

Notes from the field: 6 February 1976

> Last night a lively 'jam session' at the house of X, a local gym teacher. Also there, his ailing father, '*ar-ra'īs*' (a fisherman and musician), Y, another teacher, Z, a young clerk in the Municipality and A, a farmer and former militant of the Néo-Destour and later of the Communist party. There's singing to the accompaniment of *ʿūd* and *darabukka*, and later dancing. After a rendering of the current 'Top of the Pops' - "*ya baba Sidi Mansur*" (the name of Monastir's patron saint and of its finest hotel) - and various improvisations, the melodies of the religious order of Sidi bin 'Isa and of the village's patron saint, Sidi al-Madyuni 'al-Gharbi', are played. Strong, hypnotic sounds. I'm told that only some months ago someone here in the village died who was known for the depth of his trance: upon hearing al-Madyuni's melody, he would bite his flesh, tear at his hair, and generally act wildly whilst in this state of possession. He was the last of the generation of dervishes.
>
> A dramatic performance, the *ḥadra* ('séance') of the Madaniyya order, follows: everyone stands in a circle, holding hands, bowing and straightening up in rhythmic motion and at an accelerating pace, all the while increasing the rate of breathing; on bowing one expels - almost grunts - the sound *ah*, followed by two *ah*-s on straightening up; the tempo builds to a crescendo, almost a frenzy, as A chants a Quranic Verse in counterpoint and guides the performance.

My companions of the evening had pretended by their performance of the *ḥadra* that we were involved in the ritual of *al-ṭarīqa al-madaniyya* - the Madaniyya Order - the corporate pursuit of the 'way' of the Madani Sufis. They had invoked the Divine Name, *Allāh*, by repeating its first and last letters and last syllable - *ah*. Those invocations, till no breath was left, and the accompanying rhythmic motions were means of attaining illumination or direct knowledge of God.

The Madaniyya Sufi Order had its central lodge in a small township in the Sahel region of Tunisia, near Monastir, where I did fieldwork in 1975-76. The Order had been established by a local man who came to be known as Shaikh al-Madani, a disciple in the early years of this century of Shaikh al-'Alawi (Ahmad bin 'Aliwa) of Mostaghanem in Algeria. Until Tunisian independence in 1956, the Madaniyya Order had flourished and been the most important Sufi Order in the Sahel, and it had lodges in major cities and other regions, as well.

In 1976, discussions about the Madaniyya Order still awakened strong feelings of support and opposition. Shortly after independence its founder and shaikh had been publicly humiliated, accused by leaders of the Néo-Destour party of having collaborated with the French protectorate authorities, and not long afterwards he had died. According to some people in the township, his death was a result of the despondency he had suffered following the accusation and humiliation. The *zawiya* or lodge of the order that he had founded and where he was buried seemed to fall into disuse. Nonetheless, two decades after independence, the shaikh's son, then in his late thirties and a social worker and *imām* of the township's main mosque, had gathered around himself a small group of old and new followers who participated in the rituals of the order, in the lodge or by invitation at celebrations of families for the completion of a new house, a circumcision, return from the pilgrimage, etc.

I consider the Madaniyya Order a 'modern' Sufi movement mainly because it came into existence and expanded during the recent past and assumed significance in the township and elsewhere at the same time as, and alongside, the rise of the Old Destour, the Néo-Destour and the Communist parties. Moreover, although the township and Tunisia, as a whole, are undeniably now in a phase of rapid socio-economic and cultural change, the order, however reduced in scope and importance, continues to meet and it has not ceased to trouble and exercise spirits and minds. In discussions in the township about the past or the present, the order has its supporters and detractors. To understand the significance of these points of view, it is necessary to consider the genesis, successes and failures of the Madaniyya, as a social movement and as a particular sort of religious order, and to do so within the context of Tunisia's ongoing process of social change.

The question of modernity has also been posed in regard to the 'Alawiyya Order from which the Madaniyya developed. In the 1930s Augustine Berque characterised Shaikh 'Alawi as a "modernist mystic". Lings' account of the shaikh's life maintained some ambiguity by calling him "A Muslim Saint of the Twentieth Century", but he also contradicted Berque: Shaikh 'Alawi despite his wide and curious intellect, was not a modernist but profoundly conservative and implacably orthodox (1959:48). On the basis of Lings' biography,

Gellner considers the shaikh "an extremely interesting example of the living tradition of sanctity as it is conceived in North Africa" (1968:33); while Jacques Berque refers to Shaikh 'Alawi as "the last great marabout" (1967:74). Nonetheless, the personage of the shaikh remains enigmatic. As Gellner points out, when faced by hostility from the reformist press, 'Alawi replied by the modern form of pamphleteering; but if a modernist, he certainly was not an extreme one and had equal abuse for secularist Turks and reformists. Thus at the time that the Algerian *ʿulamāʾ* pursued and spread their reformist ideas in their press, the shaikh criticised them and the secularists in his own newspapers for "continually yielding to the modern age at the expense of religion" and inveighed against westernization and especially Western clothing. (Cf. Lings in *E.I.*[2]).

Shaikh Madani seems similarly enigmatic: in conflict with the reformists in his own town and country - the Old Destourians, and later with the more secular nationalists - the Néo-Destourians, he employs the same kinds of arguments as did Shaikh 'Alawi. Yet, Shaikh Madani established an institution and attracted followers to it of a sort and in a way that was unprecedented in the Sahel region. The Madaniyya, like the political parties in Tunisia, was a manifestation of the country's 'integration' into the capitalist world economy. In general, the pattern of change in modern North Africa follows those stages outlined by L.C. Brown, *viz.*, 1) the decline, almost collapse of Sufi religious orders, 2) the role of Salafiyya modernism which was *inter alia* the main cause of the orders' decline and 3) the intimate link between Islam - usually in its reformist guise - and the origins and growth of nationalist movements (1966:98). Yet the widespread, simplified and official version of that process in Tunisia - the victory of this-worldly secular nationalism (the Néo-Destour) over the archaic forces of the *ʿulamāʾ* reformism of the salons of the bourgeoisie (the Old Destour) and over the other-world esoterics sullied by their collaboration with colonialism (maraboutism and religious orders) - eliminates the importance of the religious dimension. Seen from the historical vantage point of a township, the victory of secular ideology seems much less stark. Political, cultural and ideological tendencies of great divergence have co-existed and many of the tensions between these divergent tendencies have remained unresolved. The ebbs and flows of the life history of the Madaniyya Sufi Order are a case in point.

Shaikh al-Madani

Muhammad b. Khalifa b. Husayn Hajj 'Umar Khalf Allah 'al-Madani' was born in Ksibet el-Mediouni in 1888 and died there at the age of 71 in 1959. A contemporary notes in his memoirs that he met Madani in 1900 when they studied in a Quranic school in Monastir, and again in 1905 when they were students in the Zaytuna Mosque University of Tunis. Madani remained at the Zaytuna until 1909, and distinguished himself as one of the best students, along with 'Abd al-Hamid Ben Badis of Constantine, the founder of the orthodox reformist movement in Algeria. There their paths split.

In 1909, Ahmad bin 'Aliwa, then a shaikh of the Darqawi Order in Mostaghanem, visited Tunis. While there, a group of Tunisian sufis came to visit him. They were followers of a shaikh who had died a few months previously and whose "spiritual ancestry in the Path of God" led them back through a certain Sidi Muhammad Zafir and his father Sidi Muhammad al-Madani to Mawlay al-'Arabi āl-Darqawi, the famous Sūfi shaikh of 19th century Morocco (who marked that century, as far as mystical orders go, as "The Darqawi century"). The Tunisians introduced themselves as "Madanis", thereby identifying themselves with Darqawi's companion and disciple who had originated from Medina and eventually settled in Tripoli where he established al-Madaniyya al-Darqawiyya, or simply al-Madaniyya, which like many of the well known Sufi orders in Africa was an offshoot of the 13th century Shadhiliyya. The Madaniyya spread quickly and extensively. It was the only competitor of the Sanusiyya among the Bedouin of 19th century Cyrenaica, and had lodges in Morocco, Tunisia, Arabia and Instanbul, where apparently it had close links with the Ottoman Sultan Abdelhamid and his pan-Islamic movement.

The Madani sufis who came to visit Ibn 'Aliwa in Tunis in 1909 were joined by some *ʿulamā'* and students from the Zaytuna, a few of them already initiates of the Darqawiyya while several others entered the order on that occasion. Amongst the visitors was Muhammad b. Khalifa of Ksibet who was, according to his son's biography, so taken with Ibn 'Aliwa that he decided to accompany him back to Mostaghanem where he remained as an initiate and then as the shaikh's secretary until 1912. During the same period, Ibn 'Aliwa sent for the Madanis who had visited him in Tunis and all of them became his disciples. The shaikh had not yet branched off from the Darqawiyya to establish his own order (he did so in 1914), when he sent Muhammad b. Khalifa back to Tunisia to open a lodge. Apparently the shaikh also gave him at that time the name "al-Madani".

The biography of his son recounts that Madani attached himself to the 'Alawiyya way by learning Islamic science and Sufism from the shaikh, received a certificate (*ijāza*) attesting to his tie to the order (*wird*), a specific name (al-Madani) and the secrets of attaining unity with God, and returned to Tunisia to spread Sufism and spend the next forty-nine years in "The remembrance of God's name". His colleague Rukbani describes Madani when he returned from Algeria and began teaching in the Monastir Quranic school: he had grown a heavy beard, wore a black qaftan and a long rosary around his neck (a characteristic of disciples of Shaikh al-'Alawi); he was eloquent, polite, cultivated, wrote prose and poetry, was very religious and encouraged people to participate in remembrances of God. He told his friend that he had joined a shaikh of the Darqawiyya or Madaniyya Order in Mostaghanem and himself become a shaikh of that order. In the school he taught Arabic, religious principles and the biography of the Prophet. At night he would bring together Sufis (*fuqarā'*) and novices (*murīdīn*) and aid and feed them "as the Prophet had done". If he received gifts he would distribute them among his followers whom he also helped with his income from agriculture. Their meetings took place in a lodge or private home after evening prayers. They began and ended with recitations of Quranic verses, followed by simple commentaries by the shaikh. Then they repeated the profession of the unity of God (*tawḥīd*) and the remembrancesof His name (*dhikr*) in the form of "*ah*" (the first and the last letters of Allah), while poems of the pious were recited. The gathering (*ḥalqa*) was rectangular or circular, depending on the place and number of participants, and the shaikh sat amongst them. When he rose and invoked God's name - "*ah*" - everyone stood up, held hands, invoked the name of the Commander - "*ah*" - and began dancing and forgetting everything of this world until they seemed drugged and almost possessed. Then the shaikh recited the opening verse of the Quran and sat down. Everyone did the same. He talked to them about a religious subject, they read a few Quranic verses, and then dispersed. Eventually, according to this account, the shaikh's order had attracted a following of some 10,000 men. (Cf. ms. al-Rukbani.)

Precisely when did Madani establish his order and build the lodge in his hometown of Ksibet? A report by French protectorate authorities in 1893 states that in Ksibet the 'Isawiyya Order has followers. Informants in 1976 remembered how the ᶜIsawiyya in their state of ecstacy violently mistreated themselves to demonstrate their faith. But most followers had left that order which became nothing more than a musical band (*ḥizb*), when Madani's father entered the Darqawiyya-Madaniyya Order in Tunis and soon after established a group in Ksibet. I heard this version from Madani's younger brother, but it was not clear when this had occurred. Their father who died in 1938 at the age of 80 had been a prosperous farmer (owning some 600 olive trees) and fishing captain (introducing the huge Italian nets to the township); but because he was illiterate, he had been unable to attract many followers to the Sufi devotions he organised. The turning point in the fortunes of the order, according to the brother and others in the township but without collaboration from any written source, came some time after Madani's return from Algeria, perhaps in 1917 when Shaikh 'Alawi himself came to visit the town. 'Alawi stayed with Madani in the home of his father and paternal uncle. The latter, nicknamed 'Long' Yusuf, was the man whose word counted in the town, and he purportedly entered the order during that visit.

From French reports, we know that disciples of Madani requested from the authorities his official appointment as shaikh of a *zawiya* in Ksibet in 1919 and again in 1925, without success. Meanwhile a 1921 report ("*Les confréries en Tunisie*") had listed the Madaniyya as a branch of the Darqawiyya with four lodges and less than 200 followers. French authorities obviously had a benevolent eye on the orders, as A. Bernard's book on Morocco in 1922 demonstrated: France, he wrote, "saw in the marabouts nothing but complacency, and in the *ʿulamā'* nothing but independence" (cit. in Waterbury, p. 44). In 1925, in another *mémoire*, the 'Alawiyya are reported to hold meetings in Tunis with the Madaniyya; in the Sahel where a large group in Ksibet has a *zawiya* and frequently receives visitors; and in Souassi, Sfax and Matmata. All told, it has some 2,000 members and is growing. Its shaikh, al-Madani, still teaches in Monastir, has written ten religious works, and has an estimated wealth of 15,000 francs. His father (that too is considered important on the fiche) administers the pious endowments of Ksibet's patron saint, Sidi 'Abd Allah al-Madyuni. Finally, in 1927, the authorities officially appoint Madani as shaikh of the Zawiya of the Shadhiliyya Order in Ksibet, a branch of the mother lodge of the order of Bil Hasan in Tunis. The confusion regarding names of the Order suggests that the French were anxious to prevent orders from hiving off and setting up on their own. In 1933, A. Bernard has a census of the orders in Tunisia carried out: it lists 505 lodges with over 300,000 followers. Of these the Madaniyya have seven lodges and 360 followers, the 'Alawiyya six or seven lodges, including one in Ksibet and some 2,000 members.

By 1940, French reports state that the "Madaniyya-'Alawiyya order, which is in no way political, has spread throughout the country and has great influence in most villages of the Sahel, especially in the province of Souassi." Finally the protectorate archives reveal a document for 1944, a letter from Shaikh Madani to the Resident General in Tunisia, General Mast: Madani introduces himself as the shaikh of a religious order in Ksibet that has "around 60,000 followers in the country" who assemble at religious festivals several times a year, which they have been doing since about 1914. Madani, who undoubtedly greatly exaggerates the number of his followers, requests permission to organize the annual collection of foodstuffs for the poor from farmers in the region who support the order, because many of its followers are underfed and poorly clothed and depend on the *zawiya* to help them. This period probably marked the high point of the order's influence, both among its members and with the French authorities. Many people in the town recounted in bitterness how the shaikh had distributed foodstuffs and served up tea and sugar to thousands of the order's members, most of whom came from outside on visits to the lodge, while the local population suffered hunger and rationing. They believed that only through his connections with the

French had this been possible.

After the war and during the next decade until Tunisian independence, the shaikh and his followers in Ksibet came under increasing attack from their fellow townsmen. From the start the order had awakened criticism and opposition in the town, even while it expanded and attracted supporters from outside; but it had maintained enough local backing among powerful men to withstand the challenges. During the war years, however, the power of those local backers began to diminish significantly. A new and younger generation of entrepreneurs and nationalists had won influence in the town, and they had little sympathy for or indeed outright hostility towards the Madaniyya. After independence they participated in or passively accepted the public humiliation of the shaikh, the order, and all that they stood for.

Religious and Secular Currents in Modern Tunisia

Many Muslim intellectuals today consider Sufism and the religious orders with condescension, an attitude that resembles, as L.C. Brown remarks, the condescension of the 18th century Enlightenment towards the the Middle Ages (1975:174). The Muslim perspective stems from that Enlightenment too, but is more often associated with the legacy of the reformism of the Wahhabis and of the Salafis: their rejection of the other-world piety of the mystic way as an 'accretion' or 'innovation' (*bidʿa*) to the fundamentals of Islam. Nonetheless, in 19th century Tunisia, mysticism and orthodoxy co-existed, and the esoteric doctrines of Sufism manifested themselves both in sophisticated intellectualism and popular maraboutism. Most men, including the learned, frequented one or more religious orders and were attached to a shaikh of some order. The urban bourgeoisie tended to adhere to Shadhiliyya, Qadiriyya or Tijaniyya orders, while provincials venerated local figures known for their or their ascendants' piety or reported miracles. The Beys themselves belonged to *zawiyas* and sometimes financially supported their shaikhs. Local saints as well as the shaikhs of orders might assume political significance as advisors to authorities or themselves fill such positions or act as intermediaries between government and people (*ibid.*:176 f.).

During the same period, reformist currents began to make themselves felt. Despite the lack of scholarly writing on early Islamic modernism in Tunisia, it is clear that since the reign of Ahmad Bey (1837-1855), men in high positions such as Ben Diyaf, Mahmud Kabadu and Muhammad Bayram exercised a reformist influence at the Beys' courts. This tendency was cut short by the exile of the Minister Khayr al-Din in 1877 and by the establishment of the Protectorate in 1881. Yet within a few years reports of the pan-Islamic and reformist movement of Afghani and 'Abduh were being followed in Tunisia. In 1884, 1885 and 1903, 'Abduh visited Tunis at the urging of Muhammad Bayram who had settled in Egypt. Bayram's disciple and friend, Muhammad Snussi, welcomed 'Abduh and introduced him to Tunisian *ʿulamā'*, some of whom joined 'Abduh's secret pan-Islamic society. It was Snussi, then a professor at the Zaytuna Mosque, who led the Bourgeois Movement of Tunis - a series of demonstrations in 1885 against measures adopted by the Protectorate and the first manifestations of political opposition to the colonial regime .(Cf. M-S Lejri ,Vol. I:96 f and 115 f). Though the movement had political, economic, cultural and psychological causes specific to Tunisia's circumstances, it was also marked in its orientation by the external influence of Islamic reformism.

The next stage in the development of political movements in Tunisia is represented by the Young Tunisians' Party of 1907. Among its leaders was another former student of the Zaytuna and a close friend of Ben Badis, 'Abd al-'Aziz Tha'alabi, the editor of the Party's Arabic newspaper and, after the War, the leader of the Destour Party. Tha'alabi's political awakening began with a concern with the dogmas of Islam, influenced by the writings of the Egyptian Muslim nationalist, Mustafa Kamil, founder in 1907 of the Egyptian National Party. Tha'alabi attacked maraboutism in his writings after having travelled for a few years in the Middle East and North Africa and found himself imprisoned for two months in 1907 as a result. Later he participated in student strikes (1910), the Djellaz demonstration (1911) and the boycott of trams (1912) which led to his expulsion from the country until 1914. During the War he militated for the cause of pan-Islam, while at the same time propagating secular and nationalist ideas (Kriem:162 f and Lejri,Vol. I:173 f).

After the War, Tha'alabi helped form the Tunisian Party (1919) and then went to Europe to represent the party in its demands for self-determination before the League of Nations. While in Paris he published the party's programme as *La Tunisie martyr* and mobilized the support of French socialists who went on to lose the national elections. Meanwhile, in early 1920, Tha'alabi's friends in Tunis had established a new party - the Liberal Constitutional Tunisian Party - in short the Destour (Constitution). Within the party, whose broad aims were to obtain equal rights for all those who lived in Tunisia, regardless of religion or nationality, were several tendencies: that of Tha'alabi was characterized as intransigently nationalistic.

There is little in the accounts of political and ideological conflicts between the Destour and the French or within the Destour that relates directl to religious matters. In 1923 the Protectorate authorities again exiled Tha'alabi and he spent the next fourteen years in political activity in various places in the Middle East. Until its split in 1934, the Destour found most of its support mainly in cities among artisans, merchants and landlords. Its leadership, reformers rather than revolutionaries, came from the elite and were pacifists and legalists concerned with self-determination, freedom of the press and individual freedom, and inviolability of property. They maintained their attachment to Islamic reformism, but did not place much emphasis on it.

To be sure, political and religious purposes were not easily separable, especially in mass demonstrations in which religious solidarity joined with outrage at exploitation by foreigners. Thus, the Destour would use religious holidays to organize public demonstrations aimed at expressing and spreading nationalist sentiments, e.g. on the *mawlid*, the Prophet's Birthday, when cortèges would meet and chant litanies like "God controls us. The Destour Party is our support. I am Tunisian and will not change my religion, because though the French want that the Prophet Muhammad does not!". When the French encouraged naturalisation, the Destour tied the question to religion and took the position that to abandon Tunisian nationality for French citizenship was tantamount to apostasy. The connection between Islam and modern nationalism was becoming at the same time closer to the core of Salafiyya thinking.

Another former Zaytuna graduate and leader of the Destour, Ahmad Tawfiq al-Madani, held to Salafiyya ideas and used them to win over the older generation and students to the party. Thus, for example, he used religious sermons to encourage and gain support for the party from workers on strike and bound them to the party by an oath on the Quran. When the Rif war began in 1925, his support of the Rifians in the newspaper that he edited led the French to exile him to Algeria from whence his family had originated. There he became an important figure in the Salafiyya movement of the Algerian *ʿulamāʾ*, which was to play a crucial role in Algeria's struggle for independence.

Another central figure in the political and ideological polemics of this period was Tahar al-Haddad who had studied in the Zaytuna between 1911 and 1920 and become a member of the Central Committee of the Destour in 1923. Haddad also supported the CGT labour union, founded by Muhammad 'Ali, and acted as a member of its Executive Commission. In 1927 he published a book on the subject - *al-ʿumal al-tunisiyyūn*, "The Tunisian Workers" - after having written many articles in the press on the national problem and the union question. In 1930 his second book - *imratunā fi al-sharīʿah wa-'l-mujt* "Our Women in Islamic Law and Society" - appeared and by calling for the emancipation of women caused a scandal. Haddad became the object of hatred and persecution among many of the *ʿulamāʾ* and during the last years of his life (he died of tuberculosis in 1935 at the age of 36) he broke with the party, as well, and remained completely isolated. Haddad was no secularist: he argued that the emancipation of women was consistent with the principles of religion as he understood them. His call for the unveiling of women (which he compares to family treasures covered with dust), his disapproval of polygamy, and acceptance of abortion where doctors fear for the life of a child-bearing woman, were, to his mind, validated by Islam. Indignantly he protests against practises which "we men of the Maghrib cling to despite the beliefs and habits bequeathed to us by our mysterious history, mistakenly quoting the authority of Islam." Haddad's theories were quasi-officially declared heterodoxical. It was a time, as Berque points out, when the pious solemnly discussed whether women ought to learn to write, and the outcry over Haddad's book reveals a "passage from one set of symbols to another: from the ritual to the historic, and correspondingly from introspective withdrawal to expansion" (1962:102f and cf. M. Mutafarrij 1935:201-30). Among the refutations of Haddad's book was one written by Shaikh al-Madani of Ksibet: it was, as we shall see below, replete ith symbols of ritual and introspective withdrawal. In summary, the Destour Party and its generation may be shown to have demonstrated a somewhat eclectic and pragmatic approach to politics and ideology: most means and formulas seemed valuable if they helped the party to attract followers and achieve its ends. They were prepared to indifferently emphasize economic conditions, socialist and communist ideas, unionization and religious fundamentalism.

The Néo-Destour Party that broke off from the Destour in 1934 and became the major force in the independence movement was less eclectic in its methods and indeed indicted the Old Destour for its backward-looking opportunism. It claimed more realism and secularism in its overall orientation. Thus, when Tha'alabi returned to Tunisia in 1937 with the intention of reuniting the parties and regaining leadership, he aimed his criticism at the Néo-Destour's secularism and called for Arab and Muslim solidarity. He had been, as Julien remarks, nourished by the spiritual and unifying ideals of the Arab renaissance and could not accept the fundamentally nationalist conceptions of the Néo-Destour and its secular techniques which used religion as a means rather than an end (p. 82). For Bourguiba and the new party, circumstances in Tunisia were such that concern with religious or Arab unity could only distract the nationalist movement: the primary preoccupation of the party had to be the country's liberation from foreign domination. In that struggle the dominant if never absolute strain was to be secular.

Most of the literature on the modern history of Tunisia sees the Old Destour Party as an extension of the existing political elite and associated with the traditional bourgeoisie, conservative but more progressive than those against whom they reacted. The Néo-Destour, on the other hand, had different social origins, was recruited from amongst those educated in a modern system and those from modest rural backgrounds - small-holders, sharecroppers and wage labourers - "people born from the soil", according to Berque's phrase. The Néo-

Destour are seen as having fundamentally challenged the elite and leading a social revolution, its deliberate populism defending the rural poor and involving it in the organisation of an indigenous trade union. The break with the old party, moreover, contained an attack against the earlier generation's exploitation of Islam (cf. L.C. Brown 1974).

Overall, that view of inter-war Tunisian history carries persuasiveness; but from the micro-sociological perspective some correctives or nuancing seem called for. By the early 1930s, the Old Destour certainly had sunk some roots in the countryside, particularly in the Sahel region. A number of its members transferred their allegiance to the new party in 1934 and with them reformist ideas from the Salafiyya also entered the party's thinking, though, to be sure, they were counterbalanced and sometimes outweighed by secular ideas and policies. The Old Destour did not simply represent the old bourgeoisie led by a traditional elite; its perceptions and utilizations of reformist Islam were more than opportunism; its members shared a world view shaped by earlier circumstances and particular forms of education. By the time the Néo-Destour came onto the scene, the old party had begun already to seriously undermine the status and influence of the religious elite. The new party succeeded to the old in a battle partly won.

The Néo-Destour, for its part, did not eschew the use of religious phrases or slogans for political purposes. Thus, for example, in the struggle for independence in 1949-50, mosques were used for meetings of party cells and as arms caches for those in the *fallāgha*. The party also sounded the call for *jihād*, and as Bourguiba later remarks " some knew nothing about the Destour except that it belonged to Islam" (cited in Debbasch 1962:142). Julien, writing in 1952, keenly observed that Tunisian nationalism seemed inseparable from Islam and that attacks against nationalism increased religious solidarity. Nonetheless, he argues, nationalism represented the greater force; and as it grew stronger, it would become more independent of faith (1972:18). The same line of analysis is pursued by J. Berque: the most significant leaders were also the most ambiguous, the most capable of sudden reversals or double-edged actions. Of these Bourguiba excelled, following "a tortuous logic, making alternate and simultaneous use of the forces of Islam and those of the West ...", a strategy that Berque argues somewhat too neatly, combined loyalty to history and radicalism, rather than the intransigence and opportunism of the Old Destour (Berque 1967:250, 368).

By the time of Tunisian independence, observers and scholars agreed that the status and influence of the religious elite had seriously and permanently declined. Yet during the crisis over internal autonomy in late 1955, religious sentiments had been stirred within the party as well as the country by the opposition of

Ben Youssef and his followers to Bourguiba and his supporters. Ben Youssef did not hesitate to take to the minbar of the Great Mosque of Tunis to mobilize people against the autonomy agreement. When the party expelled him, the religiously conservative are said to have joined his dissident group and to have played an important role in the rebellion against the government.

In part, that conflict with its social and cultural dimension may explain why after independence Bourguiba proclaimed that religion had been a means in the struggle, but that it had since lost its *raison d'être*. He urged the party to take its distance from religion, but the party showed more circumspection and the population little keenness for so drastic a move. Government policy thenceforth was based on pragmatic considerations: as long as religion or religious groups did not interfere with matters of state, the government's attitude would be conciliatory; but if they were found to be an obstacle to the modern state, the government would itself take over the interpretation of religion.

According to the first article of its constitution, Tunisia is a Muslim state, "its religion is Islam". Yet to many, that affirmation seems merely verbal. Legislation has aimed at transforming institutions and structures in order to encourage development and consolidate power by undermining what the Tunisian elite have called "the archaic traditions of Arab-Muslim society". In effect the government has sought to secure the pre-eminence of a modern elite and to destroy the bases of a traditional and religious elite, *viz.*, control over women, *waqf* property, education and justice. Tunisia's Code of Personal Status, interpreted as a struggle of law against morality, indeed is the most modern and secular legislation of any Muslim state especially in its amelioration of the status of women. The Code took effect on 1 January 1957, put an end to separate religious courts and effectively abrogated Shari'ah family law: 1) polygamy was made illegal; 2) repudiation was outlawed; 3) the minimal age of marriage was raised from 'physiological' to 'psychological' maturity, and the explicit consent of both parties and a registered contract were required. Other laws promulgated during the following years complemented these: *waqf* property, both public and private, was disbanded, women received full and equal rights of citizenship, and a series of laws were passed facilitating birth control. (Cf. K. Brown 1978, 1979.)

At the same time as this apparent separation of church and state, the party and government have in some ways appropriated the domain of religion: Bourguiba excercised *ijtihād* (the exerting of knowledge, according to Islamic law, to form a binding legal or theological opinion from first principles) in the general area of public affairs. As President he is to be considered as "responsible for the nation and also holding spiritual authority". Thus, he pronounced on the advisability and legality of a variety of measures, including for example birth control, in respect to Islamic law and common sense. He went so far as to propose that the breaking of the Ramadan fast was justifiable as a *jihad* against poverty, a pronouncement that caused some consternation. The Rector of the Zaytuna (now the Faculty of Theology of the University) resigned rather than condone the advice "to eat to conquer the enemy of poverty as the Prophet had done", while most people grumbled and simply ignored the President and got on with fasting. Some Tunisians, of course, did not fast because they had lost their faith, if they ever had it, and remained indifferent to President and Prophet. The ruling elite, however, shared or at least propagated the modernist view that authentic Islam could not slow progress and that its doctrines were quite compatible with modern science and a modern polity.

The ambiguity that marked the party's struggle against colonialism remained in the government's battles against internal dissension. Thus, Bourguiba has often repeated what he said in late 1958, *viz.* that "unity implies turning a deaf ear to all those attempts by so-called patriots who under the cloak of Arabism and Islam give themselves over to treacherous propaganda. These imposters are more dangerous than the French colonists. Because the latter cannot, for the simple reason of their different religion and race, infiltrate into our ranks, as the others do, to sow disorder and death" (cit. in Debbasch 1962:141). More recently, the government suspended a publication of the integrationist movement which had taken on a new dimension with the events in Iran, because it was considered a threat to the country's stability. M. Sayah, the Director of the Destour Socialist Party, in addressing a party gathering employed similar terms in condemning the "false devotees" and "pseudo-reformers" who under the cover of religion were engaged in subversion. (Cf. *Le Monde*, 9-10.XII.1979). Arguments over 'religion and politics' can and still do stir the sentiments and ideas of many Tunisians, and at the grassroots in the town of Ksibet, the issue of the Madaniyya Order has not been settled.

"No Man is a Prophet in His Own Land"

Shaikh Muhammad b. Khalifa al-Madani built the main *zawiya* of his order in his native town of Ksibet el-Mediouni, but most of his disciples came from elsewhere, particularly from amongst the sedentarized nomads of the Steppes, the hinterland of the Sahel. Ksibet is one of those small, densely populated bourgs of the Sahel, the coastal region that begins some 100 miles south of Tunis and extends from Sousse to Sfax along the coast and about 20 miles inland as far as Kairaouan and the Steppes region. With its olive groves and townships, high human density and relative lack of natural resources, it resembles Andalusia or Sicily. "The Little Casbah of Sidi 'Abd 'Allah al-Madyuni" (Ksibet el-Mediouni) lies six miles south of Monastir; in 1916, it had a male population of somewhat less than 1,500, of whom 90% were considered 'marabouts', i.e. descendants of the four putative sons of the town's patron-saint founder, and thereby classified into 'tribes' (*ᶜarsh* pl. *ᶜurush*). (Variant traditions split the descendants of one son into two 'tribes', or made one 'tribe' descendants of the area's original black inhabitants.) Fifty years later in 1976 when I did fieldwork in the town, it had a population of almost 6,000, about 60% of them claiming descent from Sidi el-Mediouni. Living in an area of less than 7 square kilometres, its human density of 800 km^2 was extremely high, even for the Sahel.

Traditionally, Tunisia has been divided into three sorts of space and specific life styles: *madīna*, *balda* and *ᶜarūbiyya*. The first, 'city', is characterized by its religious institutions, crafts and commerce; the second, 'township' or 'village', by its sedentary argriculture, small-scale crafts, and petty-trade; the third, 'Arab countryside', by its home-steading, transhumance or nomadism (cf. Bouhdiba 1973). Throughout Tunisia's history a pattern and process of geographical and social mobility has taken place: movements from nomadism to sedentarization, from countryside to township, and from village to suburb and city. The middle station, the *balda*, has long been a characteristic of Tunisia, and such communities have synthesized and mediated between countryside and city. In Ksibet, people held a more elemental and Khaldunian dichotomy between themselves, the 'civilized' (*mitmadnin*), and the 'backward' (*mitkhalfin*) or 'primitive' people of the countryside; but they acknowledged their interstitial position between rural and urban ecologies and ways of life. The people of the Sahel were enterprising by need and vocation, and transported their olive oil into the countryside to sell and buy amongst the tribes of the Souassi and the Mthellith and to the north, to Ifriqiya, to invest in crops and herds and run small businesses. In turn, the tribesmen brought their products to the villages and townships and worked in the olive groves. It was along these routes of exchange that the Madaniyya religious order spread.

Many of the shaikh's disciples came from the province and the people of Souassi. Formerly nomads, they had since the turn of the century become gradually sedentarized and taken to individually owning parcels of land. It was this consolidation of private property on lands that had belonged to tribal groupings, a process favoured by the Protectorate, that encouraged the commercialization of land and eventually the proletarianization of labour. The process accelerated the centuries old slow and gradual extension of Sahel landholdersinto the Steppes. The cereal growning areas expanded, some of them gradually giving way to olive groves, and so did the population; and with it came a growing number of sharecroppers and rising volume of loans and sales of land. Where market towns grew, such as

Smala, the centre of the caidat of Souassi, Sahelians (some of them from Ksibet) set up olive presses and permanent shops. Most of the Souassi remained poor and many emigrated permanently to the north. Others, after planting their crops, would go off in small groups to bring in the olive crops in the Sahel for several months during the winter, and to Ifriqiya in the summer (cf. Despois 1955). Shaikh al-Madani attracted most of his 'troops' from these peoples of the Steppes (they were called *mujarradīn* from the same root as 'locusts' and meaning literally "unsheathed (swords)"). He had property and kinsmen from Ksibet at Smala, and some of the tribesmen settled in Ksibet were his permanent 'troops'.

Madani held the allegiance of such men because he had much to offer to them: his teaching, his *baraka* ("the spiritual influence which gives the soul access to divine mysteries", cf. Michon p. 226), the hospitality and companionship of the *zawiya*, and the right to participate in the order's tributary and redistributive 'mode of production'. The shaikh did not grow rich in the process, but he expected and did receive a constant flow of gifts from his followers, and in the distribution of these he demonstrated his generosity. His followers felt that in the *zawiya*, in their brotherhood, there was no distinction among them. As Ksibet's pundit barber put it, and not with malice, "they saw in one another God - they shared, ate and drank together and were equal; they practised real communism, each according to his means, each according to his needs." In effect, some of the shaikh's followers, like those of Shaikh al-'Alawi, became attached to him 'for the blessing of it': those incapable of following a spiritual path or even considering what it might be, and yet with an undefinable urge to benefit from a sacred presence frequently sought the 'initiation of blessing' (cf. Lings 1959:74). In principle, however, the shaikh, like his master, began by teaching the novice the ordinary religious obligations, according to his capacity to learn them. The Souassi, Madani's son told me, were lazy and ignorant, and his father had awakened them to hard work and the understanding of religion. The initiation into the way, the oath of fealty or pact of allegiance, would follow for those considered capable of pursuing it. Then they would learn the litanies of the order and be initiated into the invocation of the Name (*dhikr*).

In Ksibet itself only some of the inhabitants felt the attraction to the shaikh and the order, while others shied away from or positively objected to them. For a long while, Madani enjoyed the protection of his paternal uncle Yusuf, the strong man, petty local leader and benevolent tyrant of the town, who held the contract to provide labour for the nearby French-owned salt mine. Between the Wars, what the Ksibis called "the time of oppression", that position allowed Yusuf to hire and fire men as he pleased. He had influence with the authorities, and struck people with fear. When men were "capable of killing one another over the smell of bread", he alone might feed them. Few dared not to follow Yusuf when he entered the order, or for that matter the ranks of the Néo-Destour for a brief moment in 1934.

One man who took up the challenge of opposing the shaikh and his uncle was a shaikh of a different sort. Muhammad Karkar had also studied in the Zaytuna before being drafted into the French army during the War. Afterwards he had returned to Ksibet and under the influence of Salafiyya ideas and membership in the Destour party opened the first local 'free' school ('free' of government support and inspired by modernist pedagogy). Apparently, Karkar had been an adept or sometime participant in the *ḥadra* of the Madaniyya until, and perhaps after, joining the Destour. One day, according to his wife, he was asked to sign a petition urging the authorities to grant Shaikh Madani a government medal. Madani, himself, made the request. Karkar refused on the grounds that it was incongruous with the shaikh's claim to other-wordliness. From then on, Karkar became an implacable opponent of the shaikh, ceased attending the *zawiya* and proclaimed that Madani was searching for honours and self-agrandizement by endearing himself to the French authorities. Karkar found allies, but Madani's were stronger. When his uncle, Yusuf, publically insulted and struck Karkar, the latter left Ksibet, vowing never to return to that place where he had suffered public humiliation. In fact, he returned less than a decade later in 1934, to be buried in Ksibet's cemetery after having died in a French gaol. In the interim he had become one of the most active propagandists of the Destour throughout the country and, despite his refusal to join the Néo-Destour at Ksar Hellal in 1934, earned the respect of nationalists of all parties.

Madani, meanwhile, saw the number of adherents to his order increase along with the enmity of some people in the town, especially the growing number of men who identified with the Destour, old and new. These conflicts rent the town. Thus in June 1934, the Protectorate Archives reveal that one of Karkar's students was brought to trial for having attacked Yusuf. At the same time, a letter from a group of Ksibis appeared in a Tunis newspaper, stating that the Destourians are taking control of the town, that they fear no one and think that they can refuse God's order to obey their rightful leaders. By 1937, the Archives show Ksibet divided over whether Madani should receive the appointment of *imām* to the main mosque. Letters with hundreds of signatures supporting and opposing his appointment reach the Prime Minister. A long and flowery letter in French, dated 24.1.1938, arrives from Ksibet to the office of the Resident General, attacking Madani for incompetence, immorality, and ignorance: "Our Sufi", it reads, "has gained recognition as a 'holy man' by growing a long beard, praying night and day, gathering around himself the ignorant, giving advice, free lessons, prayer recitations to old marabouts, thousands and thousands of followers from all regions. The educated elite see this araboutism (*sic.*) simply as a way of gathering money and want nothing to do with this man adorned by his partisans and enjoying the favour of the local authorities, because he is of no political party which exists in Tunisia and indeed opposes the parties for he says he has a 'politics' of his own. And yet the local authorities support him for *imām-khaṭīb*. I do not want to pray behind an ignorant man ... who has become rich through his maraboutism. Moreover, outside the political parties of this country, he gives himself over to Mussolinian propaganda and is in contact with people from Tripoli in order to propagate against French and Tunisians of all tendencies. We do not want our religion made a joke of for political purposes, nor innocents used for anti-French propaganda. Do not appoint him."

Madani aroused intense feelings and strong rhetoric among a people who took their religion and politics seriously. He acted correspondingly - opposed the Old Destour for its reformism and hostility to the orders and the Néo-Destour for its secularism and infidel ways. Some of those in the town who used to visit the *zawiya* regularly, who listened to the shaikh's talks, readings and arguments, maintain the conviction that he was a good and decent man. Many express ambiguous judgements about him: on the one hand, they explain, he continued his relationships with some militants in the parties and did not prevent his adherents from joining parties; on the other hand, he did not encourage them to do so and refused to support the independence movement in any way. A more detached view could also be heard: the shaikh's position and influence was enhanced by colonial rule and the colonialists knew how to flatter and manipulate his likes; he wanted colonialism to continue because he believed that it had brought stability to the country and allowed for the spread of religion; he did not consider his countrymen capable of governing themselves; he worried primarily about the good of Islam, and that for him meant opposing the 'Kafir' nationalists who he (correctly) judged as a threat to people like himself. Most people had an anecdote that expressed their respect for the man, sometimes despite themselves. A man who had studied in the shaikh's school as a child and been overheard to curse was punished and told that when he grew older he would be grateful to the shaikh for chastising him and would bring gifts of tea to the *zawiya*. He was and did, while remarking that Madani never gave alms, he only received them. A relative and active nationalist remembers the morning when the shaikh bought a string of fish in the town square and began walking home. His uncle, Yusuf, sitting on a stone bench beside the mosque called to him. The shaikh politely greeted his uncle, who then beckoned him to come over; but he continued walking. Yusuf had him within striking distance, raised his cane and whacked him. The fish went flying. The shaikh with perfect composure and dignity picked up the fish, turned and said "May God guide you my uncle", and continued on his way. The relative concluded the story by declaring that everyone looked up to the shaikh because he had an air of self-respect and was highly intelligent but, unfortunately, he excercised his talents in a useless way.

Few if any of the shaikh's ideas appear to have changed over the years. In the 1930s he had written a violent attack entitled "In Defense of the Veil" against the book of Tahar Haddad and all those who wanted to change the status of women, and in it he argued that modern education turns students into atheists. Two decades later when girls began attending school, he complained to one of the teachers. The teacher replied by quoting a Tradition of the Prophet enjoining the education of girls as well as boys. Madani rejoined that the Tradition was falsified. The teacher concluded that the shaikh probably knew best but that the Tradition had been accepted for over a thousand years and that made it sound enough for him. Madani would never accept that sort of pragmatism.

The Bitter End

The War, especially the German and Italian occupation, undid the influence in Ksibet held by Shaikh Madani and those like his uncle Yusuf. It declined as France's position weakened. During that period, new economic possibilities arose, especially through the black market and the Red Cross, and with them the hold of the old guard over people in the town slackened. They lacked access to new avenues of wealth and power that others managed to find, and they did not share in the widespread realisation during and after the War that Tunisia was bound to win its independence.

Shaikh Madani had received his *Médaille d'Honneur* from the French authorities. Some said that he had kept it a secret, except when he went to Tunis and opened all the doors of the ministries with it. A secret, that is, until the French surrounded the town on a *ratissage* in 1952 and arrested some of the members of the Néo-Destour. Then, he put on his medal, and appeared before the French officer with a request for leniency towards the town. The officer agreed, so the story goes, because he was impressed and because his Algerian translator, the son of an 'Alawi, recognized and respected the shaikh. Others say, more convincingly, that the story is apocryphal, that the French showed leniency towards Ksibet because their actions in a nearby town the previous day had been reported in the New York Times and they feared further publicity. But the link between Madani and the French had become fixed in people's minds by this time, and the taint of collaboration was to strengthen the resentment towards him after independence.

In late 1955, during the struggle against Ben Yusuf, an open meeting was held in Monastir to mobilize followers for the Bourguiba wing of the party. Madani wanted to attend and to speak. Bourguiba anxious, especially in the circumstances, to build alliances with religious personages, agreed. The shaikh's speech in which he urged adherence to an Islamic constitution disturbed many people, including some of the party leaders from Ksar Hellal. The shaikh was very proud of himself, but the politicians were not to forgive him.

In 1957 letters of denunciation against the shaikh began to appear in the press and to arrive at the President's office. Another attempt by him to gain appointment as *imām* failed. The head of the party cell in a letter to Bourguiba accused Madani of trying to undermine the new regime by convincing the population that the government's reforms were anti-religious and that it was composed of atheists (*zanādiqa*) who wanted to unveil women, prevent polygamy, open up the *waqf*, etc. It added that the shaikh had supported colonialism and illegally received property. Newspaper articles called for the expropriation of his property and the making of the *zawiya* into a club for the Youth of Bourguiba. The Ministry of State carried out an investigation but decided that the shaikh had full right to his property.

The following year, the party decided to organize the celebration of the *mawlid*, the Prophet's birthday; Bourguiba would lead the festivities in Kairaouon and cells would carry out local activities. In Ksibet, the party cell ordered the shaikh to appear and informed him of the decision and forbade him to hold the traditional annual celebration of the Madaniyya, normally held on that day. On the *mawlid* a large number of party dignitaries, including those from Ksar Hellal, turned up. A detachment of soldiers and police were there in case of trouble. In the midst of the celebration in the mosque, Shaikh Madani arrived with a group of his followers. Outside, many other adherents of the Madaniyya who had arrived from the countryside waited. As one of the protagonists put it, the shaikh had an instinct to act contrariwise.

The party responsibles began to insult the shaikh and tell him to leave. The microphones in the mosque were open and everyone throughout the town centre could hear what was going on. It became a public trial. Madani was accused of having been a collaborator, of having received large quantities of goods from his followers when these were on ration, etc. Many people believed and feared that he could and would give an order to his devotees to rise up against the authorities, and that a blood bath might ensue. But he remained silent, only responding to the accusations as he walked back and forth in the mosque by constantly repeating "God is most great!", "There is but one God!", and "God alone designates the right path!". Although the accusors had threatened him with imprisonment, the ordeal and humiliation that he suffered (and the dignity of his response) in the end seemed to them sufficient punishment. It shocked most people in the town, however strong their hatred or resentment of the shaikh or what he stood for. Many claimed that the trial had broken his spirit, for afterwards he grew pale, then ceased to leave his house, and not long afterwards he died. In retrospect, people in the town talk about the shaikh and the Madaniyya with mixed feelings, and he remains in their own eyes somewhat enigmatic.

Conclusions

I began by stating that I consider that the shaikh and his order can best be understood within the context of the changes that have taken place within Tunisian society over the past few generations. In the account I have tried to situate them in those changing conditions. The order was not, nor did become anachronistic; but clearly, to a large degree, it did lose authenticity and relevance after the War.

The order's success among the Steppes people fits into the pattern of commercialization of land and protelarianization that was taking place in the region. The order gave them roots - social, economic and religious support. Another element that reflected the mood of the rural and urban populations was the shaikh's abiding anger against usurers and usury, from which both the people of the Steppes and the Sahel suffered. Schematically, it may be said that the Madaniyya were pro-work and discipline, cooperation, knowledge of God, and anti-politics, usury and capitalism. The shaikh expected contributions from members for the good of all, redistribution of tribute and sharing. The order was hardly oriented towards profit and was more 'natural' than capitalism: it did not fully sacrifice gratification of immediate values - material consumption or spiritual fulfillment - for long term economic reward.

Neither was the Madaniyya a deviation from religious orthodoxy, an 'innovation' (*bidʿa*) according to Islamic modernist doctrines: it did not encourage superstitions or those Sufi practices considered as degenerate. Nor was it associated with those features that the reformers condemned in much of Sufism - fatalism, passivity and disdain for rational activity. Thus, for example, the Tunisian historian Muhammada an-Nayyal, who in his book attacks the 'fatalism' of Sufism, excludes from his criticism the 'Alawiyya and the Madaniyya whom he describes as having been characterised by their liveliness, energy, zeal and determination, "misdirected" as these were (1965:341).

Despite the tension and acrimony that sometimes marked the relations between Shaikh Madani and his opponents, there was, on the whole, an absence of total enmity between them. The sources now at our disposal leave no doubt that the French had aided the 'Alawi *zawiya* in Algeria and the *zawiyas* of Shaikh 'Alawi's disciples -

Madani in Tunisia and 'Abd al-Hayy al-Kattani in Morocco (who allied himself with Glawi in the attempt to depose the Sultan in 1953). Yet, Madani never actively supported the French. The brunt of the reproach against him from Tunisians was that he had personally profitted from the *zawiya* and French contributions to it (an accusation never proven) and that he had refused to encourage the nationalists in the struggle for indepedence. That refusal to join the forces of History - the party-led march towards independence - was an unforgivable sin of omission.

In retrospect, the discrediting of the Madaniyya becomes predictable. That it had played an important role between the two Wars has led us to seek understandings of the past of those groups in Tunisian society which it attracted and which, generally, have not found their way into the written records. Local accounts, revealed by ethnographic research, supplement the record and counteract tendencies towards selective historical amnesia. Rich and varied though it is, the nationalist version of Tunisia's modern history neglects those social groups not identified with the victorious political activists who sought to determine the direction of events and, in so doing, appropriated religious symbols to their cause. Shaikh Madani and his followers, for their part, were no less engaged by changing circumstances. The difference in their attitude was that for them religious symbols and religious practices predominated and provided the strength and understanding to cope with circumstances. Such divergent views of the place and significance of religion - secular, fundamentalist and Sufi - have existed in the recent past and to some degree continue to do so in the present.

REFERENCES

Berque, A.
1936 Un mystique moderniste. *Revue Africaine*:691-776.

Berque, J.
1967 *French North Africa. The Maghrib Between Two World Wars*. London.

Bouhdiba, A.
1973 *A la recherche des normes perdues*. Tunis.

Brown, L.C.
1966 The Role of Islam in Modern North Africa. In: L.C. Brown (ed.) *State and Society in North Africa*. Washington D.C.

1974 The Tunisian Path to Modernization. In: M. Milson (ed.) *Society and Political Structure in the Arab World*. Cambridge, Mass.

1975 *The Tunisia of Ahmad Bey 1837-1855*. Princeton.

Brown, K.L.
1979 On the Appropriation of Surplus in Tunisia since the Nineteenth Century. *Dialectical Anthropology*, Vol. 4:57-64.

1981 The Campaign to Encourage Family Planning in Tunisia: In: *Middle Eastern Studies*, Vol.17, no.1 (1981).

Notes on the Significance on Waqf in a Tunisian Zāwiya. In: G. Gilbar (ed.), *Social and Economic Aspects of the Muslim Waqf*. Amsterdam, forthcoming.

Chenoufi, A.
1977 *Un Savant Tunisien du XIXeme Siècle: Muhammad as-Sanūsi*. Tunis.

Debbasch, C.
1962 *La république tunisienne*. Paris.

Despois, J.
1955 *La Tunisie orientale. Sahel et Basse Steppe*. Paris.

Gellner, E.
1968 Santicity, Puritanism, Secularisation and Nationalism in North Africa. A Case Study. In: J.G. Peristiany (ed.) *Contributions to Mediterranean Sociology*. Paris.

Gilsenan, M.
1973 *Saint and Sufi in Modern Egypt*. Oxford.

Julien, C-A.
1972 *L'Afrique d Nord en marche*. Paris, 2nd ed.

Kriem, M.
1976 *Nationalisme et Syndicalisme en Tunisie 1918-1929*. Tunis.

Lejri, M-S.
1974 *Evolution du Mouvement National* (2 Vols.). Tunis.
1978

Le Tourneau, R.
1962 *Evolution politique de l'Afrique du Nord musulmane, 1920-1961*. Paris.

Lings, M.
1959 *The Spiritual Heritage and Legacy of Shaikh Ahmad al-'Alawi, a Twentieth Century Moslem Mystique*. S.O.A.S. Ph.D.-Thesis.

1962 *A Moslem Saint of the Twentieth Century*. London.
"Ibn Aliwa" in *Encyclopaedia of Islam*[2].

Madani, Muhammed b. Khalifa
n.d. *Burhan al-dhakirin*. Tunis.

n.d. *al-lubab fi ithbat al-hijab*. Tunis.

Martin, B.G.
1976 *Muslim Brotherhoods in 19th-Century Africa*. Cambridge.

Merad, A.
1971 *Ibn Badis. Commentateur du Coran*. Paris.

Michon, J-L.
1969 *L'autobiographie (fahrasa) du Soufi Marocain Ahmad Ibn 'Agiba (1747-1809)*. Leiden.

Mitchell, R.
1969 *The Society of the Muslim Brothers*. Africa.

Mutafarrij, M.
1935 Notre femme dans la loi et dans la société de T. Haddad. *R.E.I.*, Vol. 9:201-30.

Nayyal, Muhammad
1965 *al-haqiqa al-ta'rikhiyya lil-tasawwuf al-islami*. Tunis.

Rosenthal, E.J.
1965 *Islam in the Modern National State*. Cambridge.

Rukbani, 'Umar (d. 1968)
n.d. *Mubtada' khabari*. Ms. Monastir.

Trimingham, J.S.
1971 *The Sufi Orders in Islam*. Oxford.

Verdier, J.M.
n.d. Le nouveau droit de la famille en Tunisie. *Cahiers Nord Africains*, No. 77:13-17.

Wallerstein, I.
1979 *The Capitalist World Economy*. Cambridge.

OTHER SOURCES AND DOCUMENTS

Archives of Dar el Bey series A, D, E (Tunis).

NOTE

+I am grateful to the S.S.R.C., London, for support in carrying out research in Tunisia in 1975-76, and to the C.E.R.E.S. in Tunis for its encouragement and lively discussions in the seminar directed by Fredj Stambouli.

Island Puritanism

Katie Platt

The local practice of Islam on the Kerkennah Islands of Tunisia is characterized by two types of puritanism. The first type is a deeply rooted traditionalist puritanism, which emphasizes austerity. The second type is a politically charged, revivalist puritanism, which emphasizes orthodoxy. Both of these religious styles can be described as puritan, because they attempt to achieve a pure, strict, and unelaborated brand of Islam. It is somewhat surprizing to find either of these types of puritanism on these rural islands because both types are normally urban-based religious styles. One would have expected instead a non-orthodox, flamboyant, saint-oriented practice of Islam, which is common in North African rural communities. It is equally surprizing to find these puritanisms harmoniously coexisting on Kerkennah and occasionally collaborating. This is because there are more features, both of character and context, separating the two types than bringing them together. The presence of both types of puritanism on the Kerkennah Islands reveals something about their essential natures, the ways they are opposed to each other, and their potential for reinforcing each other.

These two types of puritanism are generally understood and are of wider concern, because they exist throughout the Arab world. Elsewhere in Tunisia and in other North African countries, the first type of traditionalist puritanism is usually found in literate urban circles that are establishment oriented. The conservatism of this interpretation of Islam is usually accompanied by a social and political conservatism. In contrast, the second type of revivalist puritanism is nowadays largely found among the western educated urban youth who have been heavily exposed to and disturbed by the forces of modernization and westernization (Jansen 1979:123-6). This disturbance often inspires a deeply reactionary impulse of a revolutionary political tone.

In contrast to these two types of puritanism which both have an urban educated character, there is a non-puritanical, rural religious style, which one might have expected to find on Kerkennah, and which is found in rural areas all over North Africa. This interpretation of Islam does not depend on literacy or an educated congregation. It is flamboyant and elaborate in expression and has a capacity to absorb local beliefs and practices which may or may not have had Islamic origins. The most important feature of this flamboyant version of Islam is the central role oflocal saints. The saints, dead or alive, serve as mediators and vessels of holiness. They provide a tangible local focus for people whose religious identity is somewhat confined by a lack of literacy. It is the "excesses" of this exuberant religious style that make more austere styles of puritanism so conspicuous.

Although the two puritanisms both draw on urban, literate populations, they are not usually found in concert. The reasons for this have to do with historical circumstances which favour certain kinds of religious styles to the exclusion of others, and the distinguishing characteristics of the religious styles themselves which put them in competition with each other. Sometimes the styles of puritanism characterize different historical periods and simply follow one another. It often happens that a particular dynasty, regime or government will support one religious style and in this way, prevent the development of alternative styles. This kind of pattern is found in colonial and post-revolutionary Libya. After the Italian suppression of the Sanusi in the 1920s, the dominant and approved religious style for the next forty years was a strict traditionalist conservative puritanism. The military coup of 1969 brought with it an abruptly new revivalist revolutionary puritanism which has dominated ever since (Abun-Nasr 1971:377-392). In this case, one type of puritanism completely replaced the other.

The two types are also commonly separated from each other by an intervening generation, if not by an entire historical period (Demeerseman 1972:22-36). This is the case in the Tunisian cities of Tunis, Sousse,and Sfax, where the elder generation, which practises traditionalist religious austerity, is separated from the younger generation, which practises revivalist orthodoxy, by a liberal secularizing generation. This intervening generation is not typically puritanical. This generation came of age with independence and inherited the control of westernized political and economic apparatus. Their activities were imbued with a nationalistic fervour that had little religious content. This put them in contrast with the puritanical generations on either side of them which were alienated either because the intervening generation was too progressive or not revolutionary enough. In this kind of situation, the puritanisms are separated by a kind of generation gap which inhibits the possibility of their joining forces.

It also sometimes happens that the two puritanisms become indentified with two opposing contemporary political ideologies. An example of this kind of opposition is found in Egypt in the 1930s and 40s. The revivalist puritans who found a voice in the Society of Muslim Brothers launched an attack on the traditionalist puritans who ran the ancient seat of Muslim learning, al-Azhar University. Although the two groups seemed quite close theologically, the Muslim Brothers accused the Azhar *'ulama* of joining forces with the ruling classes and landed interests, of becoming servants of a foreign occupation, and of living "on Islam, as do the germs of bilharzia on the blood of the wretched peasants" (Mitchell 1969:213). Thus, the revivalist Muslim Brothers vociferously repudiated their traditionalist contemporaries whom they called the "civil servant *'ulama*" (Mitchell 1969:214). This is a case where, as peers, the two groups of puritans opposed each other because of their political alignments.

Mundane economic interests are also sometimes involved in the maintenance of discrete boundaries between the two types of puritans. An example of this concerns the traditionalist Ibadi sect of puritans of the island of Djerba in Tunisia and the Mzab oasis in Algeria. Both of these puritan communities are involved in highly successful long distance trade networks, which depend on their exclusive, closed minority positions in the national economies of Tunisia and Algeria. Not only do these communities strictly reject any secularizing influences which might loosen their corporation, but they also will not tolerate Malekite rite reformists in their midst. This emphatic segregation is physically manifest in the carefully planned residence patterns of the towns of Djerba and the Mzab (Alport 1970:225-41; Bourdieu 1962:37-55). Of course, the economic interests are not the only thing that separates these puritans, but it is often the most visible and immediate issue which unifies and closes the group. These are just a few examples of the ways in which traditionalist puritanism and revivalist puritanism tend to be opposed to each other or separated by historical and political context.

The fact that the two puritanisms are usually separated make their occasional occurrence together all the more significant. Because of the local geographical and cultural circumstances of the Kerkennah Islands that I will be discussing here, the two types of puritanism can be found side by side as a regular situation and are occasionally found in intense collaboration. While this is somewhat exceptional in the North African context, other studies suggest that because of realignments in the Islamic world vis-à-vis the west, the collaboration of these two types is becoming more common (Jansen 1979; Brett 1980; Zghal 1973). Thus, the possible interaction between traditionalist puritanism and revivalist puritanism is important both as an independent phenomenon and as an indicator of their essential natures.

Traditionalist religious austerity, as a general North African type and as it is found on Kerkennah, has five main characteristics.

1. It is textually oriented. The Qur'ān is the focal point of religious consciousness and therefore, a high premium is put on scriptural literacy.
2. The Five Pillars of Islam: profession of faith, alms, prayer, fasting and pilgrimage, are the core of religious practice. They are unelaborated and relatively undilluted by local ritual.
3. The operating unit and social level of focus is the local community. The concensus of the community of believers is a morally and legally potent social control device.
4. This interpretation of Islam is comprehensive. It touches all aspects of existence, leaving no room for such a thing as secular life.
5. The aesthetic tone is austere. Possibilities for flamboyance are subsumed by orthodox practice. Maraboutism is low-key, non-charismatic and non-mystical.

While this is a familiar model of religious behaviour, it is striking to find this configuration on the Kerkennah Islands for several reasons. First, austere physical environments in North Africa often manifest a non-austere interpretation of Islam. This desert-like archipelago is nothing if not physically austere. Also, it is expected that rural communities cut off from the urban centers of orthodoxy would turn to a charismatic, exuberant form of Islam. Finally, as well as lacking the urban setting which usually accompanies traditionalist puritanism, Kerkennah also lacks a direct vested interest in the status quo of the political and economic establishment, which is another correlate of traditionalist puritanism.

So why was it possible for traditionalist puritanism to develop on the Kerkennah Islands? The answer lies largely in Kerkennah's paradoxical geographical situation. As a rural area in the sea, Kerkennah is isolated from the "surrounding" rural area and thus immune to the challenges, rivalries and disputes that normally take place in a segmentary rural situation. Because there are no other like units opposing it, it has not needed to subscribe to the "low church" *zawiya* system which often functions as a regional political mediation and dispute settlement institution (Gellner 1972:315). Also, because of its own very poor soil and its remoteness from other rich agricultural areas, Kerkennah has been cut off from the *waqf* land tenure system which traditionally supported charismatic rural maraboutism in Tunisia (Brown 1980).

Kerkennah's geographical position is paradoxical, because although it is cut off from other rural areas and their characteristic institutions, its closest ties are with the major port cities of Sfax, Sousse and Tunis. Its ancient fishing industry has provided it with direct links to the urban centers of orthodoxy where the major fishing ports are. In this sense, Kerkennah's extreme marine isolation has exposed it to a more cosmopolitan view of the world than its less remote mainland rural counterparts. With this exposure to cosmopolitanism came the possibility of a less "rural" religious style.

Because Kerkennah has been cut off from many forums of competition in the mainland economy, it capitalized on scholarship. Kerkennis used the educational system the way other regional groups used trade monopolies and patronage networks. Excelling in school became an important emblem of island identity and a route into the national economy, particularly the civil service. A by-product of this phenomenon of island scholarship was a relatively high level of male literacy. This, of course, gave the population greater access to a scripturally oriented religious style. This textual emphasis was reinforced by the Kerkennis' frequent contacts with urban orthodoxy.

Kerkennah's somewhat unusual tie with the "Great Tradition" of orthodoxy and literacy has been bolstered by its identification with the trade union movement. The first autonomous Tunisian trade movement, the U.G.T.T., was founded in 1946 by a Kerkenni named Farhat Hached. Hached was assassinated by French right wingers in 1952 and thus became a hero of Tunisian nationalism and a local martyr. U.G.T.T. leadership has been held off and on by Kerkennis ever since and the higher echelons have been consistently saturated by Kerkennis. Much of Kerkennah's interest in the U.G.T.T. is based on island loyalty rather than proletarianism, although the two mix quite easily. The effect is that Kerkennah has a local identity with a national manifestation. It has a tie with the "Great Tradition" without having a tie with the status-quo establishment.

Kerkennah's cosmopolitan associations have made possible a kind of cultural and religious sophistication, but its geographical isolation has allowed it to maintain a very stable traditional social structure. This combination predisposed Kerkennah toward a traditionalist puritanical religious style.

While Kerkennah certainly inclines toward a traditionalist puritan style, it deviates from a pure traditionalist model in three ways. First, the pure model would require the seclusion of women and a passive religious role for them. Women on Kerkennah are very much out and about. They are unveiled and have their own public places of congregation. The agricultural sector of the subsistence economy is entirely their domain. As far as the religious division of labour is concerned, they mostly fall under the protection of the religious observation of their menfolk. However, Kerkenni women, both young and old, educated and illiterate, are vociferous about the correct practice of Islam and the religious meaning of human behaviour.

Another deviation from a pure traditionalist model involves Kerkennah's attitude toward maraboutism. Rather than opposing it in the true traditionalist style, Kerkennah has diffused and absorbed it. There are over one hundred maraboutic shrines of various sizes scattered over the islands. For the most part, they commemorate local historical and mythical heroes and are not connected with the maraboutic brotherhoods on the mainland. The Kerkennis stress that these saints are simply "friends" of the Prophet Mohammed. They visit the saints and the women sometimes use them as intercessors, but they do not worship them. The local interpretation is that these are benevolent spirits who have led exemplary lives and that contact with them is beneficial. There is no ecstacy and very little mysticism involved. The saints and their shrines are focal points for village or quarter identity. They are communal gathering places where people go for recreation and where many status change rituals take place (forty days after birth, circumcision, nuptual visits). The shrines almost always have large cisterns built into them which any visitor can use for any purpose, sacred or mundane. This is a very important resource on Kerkennah which has no fresh water wells and where water shortage is a chronic problem. While the numerous island marabouts certainly have a blessed atmosphere about them, they play a limited and down to earth role in Kerkennah life.

The third deviation from a pure traditionalist model is the degree to which Kerkennah Islam is textual but not literate. While Kerkennah religious practice is emphatically textual, for a certain portion of the devout population this emphasis is formal rather than literal. That is to say, that some of the Kerkennah faithful are technically illiterate, but they reproduce the holy text by rote in the same austere style as their scripturally literate brothers. This rote excercise has some of the characteristics of Sufi trance inducing devices. Yet, as in Kerkennah maraboutism, the flamboyant and mystical potential of the rote recitation of the Qur'ān is under-played and controlled within the wider context of the predominantly sober religious style.

All of the main characteristics of the traditionalist model emphasize that it is a style of Islam in which strict practice and community membership supersede any internal individual religious condition. Purity of heart and personal belief are issues that rarely come up for discussion. Whereas, correct practice of the Five Pillars and conformity to the concensus of the community of believers are under constant scrutiny.

Traditionalist puritanism presents a comprehensive social vision in terms of the local community which is its basic level of focus. Outside of this context, it does not provide a social or political model. In fact, the normal traditionalist community response to the secular government, both on Kerkennah and in general, is one of political submission. Any broader utopianism in the traditionalist world view is of an otherworldly sort. The only political aggression associated with traditionalist puritanism is a negative kind, taking the form of a general anti-modernization stance.

Revivalist puritanism is an evolving type that is somewhat less institutionalized than traditionalist puritanism. However, it is quite distinct as a religious style and can be identified by five main characteristics.

1. Although like traditionalist puritanism, revivalist puritanism is textually oriented, in this case the reading of the Text is literal and legalistic in the extreme. That is, there is a resistance to any interpretation, abstraction or metaphorical idiom which might distance the believer from the true and original meaning of the Text. The Text is also treated as a complete and sufficient rulebook for all human situations.
2. Individual piety is an essential condition in this version of Islam. The believer must make manifest his religious intention and purity of heart. This obligation extends to women who have a pious role.
3. The level of focus is supranational, with special emphasis on the international Islamic youth culture. There is a very strong sense of community based on age, education and political disaffection rather than locality or nationality.
4. This religious model is based on a reactionary utopian vision of a religious polity similar to the Islamic community of the Prophet Mohammed's day. This state would use the Qur'ān and the Traditions of the Prophet as constitution, law and social platform.
5. The general tone of this religious style is one of aggression, opposition and striving (*jihād*) rather than submission (*islām*). Illustrative of this tone is the proselytizing behaviour of its subscribers.

Revivalist puritanism in Tunisia came about largely because of government policies that were presented under the general heading of "modernization". There were two aspects of these policies that particularly affected religious identities and styles. These were secularization and monopolization. Soon after independence, the Tunisian government began taking over functions that had previously been performed by religious institutions. This secularization process undermined and made impotent the traditionalist puritans. In addition to this, the government monopolized and centralized many of the functions that had previously been performed at the local level. This deprived people of many areas of control over their own lives. Together, these two processes of secularization and monopolization left a vacuum at the local level which became an hospitable environment for the development of revivalist puritanism.

The secularization process came in many steps. In 1956 the government abolished the *waqf* system and redistributed the holdings of these pious foundations on the principle of economic efficiency. The institutions that had previously been supported by this system were either left to flounder and perish as was the case with many *zawiyas*, or they came under the direct support and control of the government as was the case with many local mosques. In many instances, the Destour Party (Tunisia is a one party system) would actually install itself or one of its secular projects in the shrines and mosques which it had helped to vacate. Local prayer leaders received a small weekly stipend and a "recommended" sermon to deliver on the sabbath from the central government. This was one of the many ways that the local traditionalists were losing control of their own sphere.

Arbitration, ajudication and legislation were thoroughly secularized both at the local level and the national level. Disputes that previously would have been settled by the concensus of the community of believers orchestrated by a local religious leader, were now directed to the police and then to the circuit court system. The court system also undermined Islamic jurisprudence. This was done by incorporating it into, and therefore subordinating it to, the modern Tunisian legal system. The essential differences between the Hanafite and Malekite rites, which had dominated the traditional Islamic legal system in Tunisia, became insignificant in this secular context. The crowning blow to Islamic jurisprudence in Tunisia was the establishment of the Personal Status Code in 1956. This code abolished polygamy, established marriage by voluntary contract, required a minimum age for marriage, ended arbitrary divorce by men, gave women the right to initiate divorce, and recognized female rights to equal inheritance. All of these reforms are counter to traditional Islamic law and were therefore offensive to the traditionalist puritans.

The secularization process had a particularly strong impact on the educational system which the traditionalist puritans had considered one of their most powerful instruments. From independence on, the Zitouna University, which was the bastion of conservative religious learning, was gradually liquidated and replaced in importance by the secular University of Tunis. The primary and secondary education system was centralized in 1958 and the Qur'ānic schools ceased to be assisted by the government. The standardized national curriculum only included one or two hours a week of religious instruction at the primary level and none at all at the secondary level. These policies were especially significant because, in a sense, they cut off the older traditionally educated generation from the younger secularly educated generation (Moore 1965:48-60).

In less sweeping ways, the government also usurped some of the charitable functions of the traditional religious community. Social work became a government activity. The distribution of grain and the management of water during times of shortage, as well as financial assistance to the poor, were rerouted through the government or party, even when these resources originated in the traditional community. In all of these areas, land collectives, law, education, and social administration, traditional religion surrendered its central role to the secular government.

But it was not this secularizing influence alone which undermined the power of the traditional religious community. It was also that the government monopolized several major areas of public life and removed control from the local level to the capital.

Most industries were semi-nationalized, including cottage industries and some peasant activities. The fishing industry came under the Office National du Pêche. This centralization also effected agriculture beyond the subsistence level, the transport industry, and traditional craftwork. All this control and centralization undermined the sense of local identity which supported and was supported by the socially comprehensive traditionalist puritanism.

This erosion of local identity was exacerbated by total governmental control and proliferation of television and radio broadcasts and newspapers. One of the effects of this monopolization of the media is that the population began to acquire Tunisian culture at a distance. The message they were receiving was not one that they could influence by responding. In other words, the concensus of the community was no longer a completely appropriate or relevant mode of cultural expression.

Parallel to governmental control of the means of communication was the control of all political vehicles. All organizations, associations, and unions were required to submit their charters to the government for approval and sponsorship. Any group that deviated from the general aims of the government and the Destour Party was either revamped or abolished. The students' union, which was originally created by the Destour Party, has struggled continuously but unsuccessfully for an autonomous political voice. The only institution somewhat independent of party and governmental control has been the U.G.T.T. But even in this case, the leadership of the U.G.T.T. has undergone major restructuring by the government whenever it has shown signs of becoming a vehicle of political opposition.

The secularization of religious functions, the erosion of local identity, the monopolization of the means of production and the means of communication, and the suppression of dissent are national conditions which have made traditionalist puritanism less satisfying and less effective as a way of dealing with the world than it once was. Traditionalist puritanism has been particularly undermined and has become something of a cultural cul de sac in the urban areas where these conditions have been particularly magnified. In a rural area such as Kerkennah, however, the effect is less pronounced and traditionalist puritanism still has a kind of residual strength.

In addition to these general trends which characterize post-independence Tunisia, there have been a number of secondary developments in the 1970's which have particularly affected the "younger generation", i.e. those who have come of age since independence, and which have created a fertile ground for the development of revivalist puritanism.

The post-independence generations were brought up in a euphoric atmosphere of social and economic optimism. The atmosphere was one of "we can do anything now that we control our own country". This attitude was particularly manifest in the trend toward totally planned socialism which characterized Tunisian government policy during the 1960's. This exhilerating sense of possibility was dissipated by the complete collapse of the socialist cooperatives in 1969 which was accompanied by political purges. The totally planned economy was replaced by a policy of government controlled capitalism with emphasis on the development of export industries. This shifting of gears was demoralizing not only in real economic terms, but also in terms of the ideological momentum behind the socialist movement that had been synonymous with national development. This ideological momentum had to be brought to a dead halt, redefined, and then started up again. Much of the sense of common destiny and corporate energy of the immediate post-independence period was lost.

The Tunisian public was taught to expect the government to become increasingly liberal after an initial stabilization period. The expectation was that there would be increased political choice and an expansion of civil liberties. President Bourguiba loosened the reins slightly during the 1960's, but this trend was emphatically reversed during the 1970's. The shift from socialism to capitalism was accompanied by a shift in emphasis from human rights to state security. The secret police force was given real power and presidential rule became more arbitrary. Bourguiba was made president for life in 1974, and he appointed his own successor. In this way the possibility of true political choice in the form of a free election was delayed indefinitely. Political repression and censorship were increased. The government and party cleansed themselves of critics by major purges in 1970, 1974, and 1977. Potential opponents of the government, especially in the U.G.T.T., were treated more and more harshly. The union newspaper was outlawed in 1977. In 1978, the entire leadership of the U.G.T.T. was imprisoned for treasonous action after a general strike, and the union was crippled by new government controls. The post-independence euphoria was replaced by economic and political disillusionment and a sense of disenfranchisement and betrayal. In nearly every area of self-expression and choice, the public, especially the educated young, felt that they were losing ground.

Meanwhile, among the younger generation, education was increasing, political consciousness was being heightened, and westernized material values were being highlighted without being satisfied. The intensely felt dissonance between Arab culture and western culture was dramatically manifested in the problem of bilingualism. The youth felt that neither language, Arabic nor French, was truly theirs. This compounded the frustration of finding that they had no economic or political voice. The youth felt that the security of a traditional lifestyle was not available to them and that they had been excluded from full participation in the modern secularized system. Hence, they began looking for an alternative ideology that would overcome the problem of cultural dissonance and give them an irrepressible and distinctive voice. Western ideologies were out; alternative political vehicles had been squashed or co-opted by the government; ecstatic religion had been undermined. The only available means of protest and self-expression left was a form of orthodox Islam, of which there were several strong models outside of Tunisia.

The closest and most potent of these external models has been Libya's Colonel Ghaddafi. Oil-rich Libya has been a popular place for young Tunisian men to find work. The young men who go to Lybia tend to be disenchanted in the first place because their homeland has been unable to provide them with a livelihood. In Lybia they are constantly exposed to Ghaddafi's anti-western, arch-Islamic picture of the world via the national media. The promise of an alternative to political and cultural impotence manifested by Ghaddafi's Islamic He-man image is very attractive to the disenfranchised young. Above all, they praise the colonel for being "strong and fearless".

A slightly more "highbrow" model of Islamic self-expression, which has had a significant impact on Tunisian youth, is the Muslim Brotherhood. Exposure to this movement usually takes place at university. Many students who are not actually recruited into the movement are still nevertheless influenced by its propaganda. The appeal of this program, like Ghaddafi's, is that it is supra-nationalistic and aggressively anti-western. By "transcending" the more mundane political issues and institutions, it makes any dangerously overt opposition to the government generally unnecessary. Above all, it stresses education and individual religious commitment. Its immediate focal enemy is any kind of political, economic or social corruption, rather than a particular party, enterprise or institution. This harsh attitude toward corruption strikes a very responsive chord among Tunisia's politically disillusioned and economically disenfranchised youth.

Revivalist puritanism in Tunisia also gains some energy from the more distant Islamic revivalist movements in Iran and Pakistan. These centers of revivalism have turned Tunisia's attention somewhat away from the West and reoriented it toward the Islamic East. None of these external models has actually caused revivalist puritanism to develop in Tunisia. The preconditions and causes all existed within Tunisian society. But realizing that others had chosen a similar course, lends a sense of validity and potential to the Tunisian practitioners of revivalist puritanism.

Revivalist puritanism on Kerkennah is essentially an urban movement that has been imported by the islands' educated youth. The version of it found on Kerkennah differs from the pure revivalist model in that it is not as aggressive in tone or ostentatious in manner. Female revivalist puritans on Kerkennah are disinclined to wear the religious "habit" of some of the mainland revivalists, although they would conform to the same rules of modesty. Also, the revivalist identity on Kerkennah is less dependent on being a pioneering minority; it is not important to them to be an exclusive moral clique. It is also less important to them to have an immediate source of oppression to strike out against. The broader sense of national alienation and broken identity is softened by the persisting vitality of traditional life on the islands.

There are several general points of coincidence between the two religious styles both nationally and on Kerkennah. They share a profound respect for the Holy Book; they both champion strict observance of moral rules; and they both assent to the comprehensiveness of Islam. But these similarities are very general and do not exclude other styles of Islam. More telling are the points of dissonance or divergence between the two. These differences can be summarized in the following way:

TRADITIONALIST PURITANISM	REVIVALIST PURITANISM
1. Emphasizes submission (*islām*)	Emphasizes striving (*jihād*)
2. Moral rules checked by community concensus	Moral rules checked by individual piety
3. Local community frame of reference	Supranational frame of reference
4. Religiously passive role for women	Religiously active role for women
5. A-political	Politically charged

TRADITIONALIST PURITANISM	REVIVALIST PURITANISM
6. Socially conservative	Socially reactionary
7. Anti-modern	Anti-western

Although the actual religious gestures that these two types of puritans perform may often be indistinguishable, the world views that they bring to these gestures and the kinds of worlds that they aspire to are very distinct. As time goes on they would become more distinct.

Given these profound differences in scope, intention, and method, why do these two types of puritanism come together so smoothly on Kerkennah? The answer to this question comes in two parts. One part refers to the long term social context of the islands and the other to recent historical events and alignments.

Social life on Kerkennah has been characterized by an extraordinary degree of continuity over the last three generations. This spans a period when the nation went,through a violent independence struggle, became an independent state, and underwent a rapid modernization process. This local social continuity has been fostered by a number of conditions. First of all, the family structure was prepared for the long and short term emigration of adult males, required by the modern economy, because of the nature of the pre-independence island economy. Long distance fishing and involvement in the marine and rail transport industries had accustomed the Kerkennis to having their able bodied men away for long periods at a time. So when the mainland urban economy opened up after independence and drew workers away from the islands, the family had already developed mechanisms for coping with this. There was no deep modernization blow to the family. This helped to minimize the pre- and post-independence generation gap that particularly rocked the family structure in the mainland cities (Demeerseman 1972).

Kerkennah's relatively isolated geographical position also softened some of the shocks of modernization which often produce a "breakaway" mentality in the younger generation. Western fads and fashions, motor vehicles, and television have been very slow to arrive on Kerkennah. Since these agents of change have been introduced more slowly than on the mainland, there has been more time for the island social structure to absorb the waves of change.

Another stabilizing factor has been the fact that the islands' population size has been almost constant for over thirty years. This is because of the continual process of emigration combined with a high birth rate. It is unusual for a rural area to maintain this kind of population equilibrium over such a long period.

A partial by-product of this constant population size has been that the subsistence sphere of the island economy has been able to remain intact. In other words, in a pinch, the islands could manage to feed its population. This fact plus the remittances from relatives working on the mainland and abroad mean that the islands can absorb most of its unemployed. As in the nation as a whole, this figure on Kerkennah exceeds 25% and much of that figure is young men. The Kerkennah situation is not a question of economic surplus, but the ability of a poor economy to stretch and absorb. The fact that the Kerkennah economy does have this flexibility means that many of the potentially alienated unemployed are not actually alienated from Kerkennah society itself.

Finally, the pre-independence generation, although traditional in most respects, has a self-image of having been part of the political avant-garde. This is because of the Kerkennis' original and continuing role in the trade union movement, an identification which, as stated above, is a much native son regionalism as anything else. No matter the reasons for this self-image, its oppositional character makes it easy for the older generation to identify with the current younger generation's opposition to the present government. A model for this alignment was already built into local social life before the current anti-government rebellion.

Basically, conditions external to Kerkennah created the possibility for revivalist puritanism to arise, and conditions internal to Kerkennah, as delineated above, created an hospitable social environment for it to line up relatively harmoniously with traditionalist puritanism. In addition to this background social context, during the 1970's all the various foci of Kerkennah opposition lined up in such a way that they could be treated as one composite threat. This common external "enemy" reinforced basic Kerkennah solidarity and fostered sympathy and cooperation between the two types of puritans.

This composite focus of opposition resulted from the lining up of four sets of antagonists. The first opposition was based on a traditional rivalry between Kerkennah and the nearby port city of Sfax. On top of this came the opposition of the Muslim traditionalists to the secularizing forces in Tunisian society. These secularizing forces obviously were located in the main urban centers including Sfax, which in some ways is considered to be more modernized, westernized and secularized even than Tunis. The third set was the recently intensified opposition of the U.G.T.T. to the government and the Destour Party. Although there has been a lot of union activity in Sfax, because of its industrial and commercial economy, Sfax is basically managerial and hence, pro-government in its allegiance. Sfax is also the administrative capital of the governorate of which Kerkennah is a part. Because of this, all aspects of governmental control (taxes, military conscription, court proceedings, etc.) are administered to the Kerkennis by the Sfax officialdom. So Sfax has been doubly identified in the eyes of the Kerkennis with the government and the interests of the "patrons", while Kerkennah's identification with the workers, the union and anti-government sentiment has been steadily increasing. Finally, opposition to the political and economic status quo has had an unsurprizing youthful character. This fourth strand of opposition basically amounted to youth vs. the establishment. Although some of the strands of opposition had a national manifestation, the four of them together in the specific context of Kerkennah had a special meaning.

The alignment of oppositions looked like this:

Kerkennah	vs.	Sfax
Religious traditionalists	vs.	Secularizing forces
Union	vs.	Government and party
Youth	vs.	Establishment

At the end of the 1970's, the Kerkennis found that their traditional identity, their religious predisposition, their political alignments, and the orientation of their youth pointed them toward a common composite challenge. Not only were they unified by an external "enemy", they were thrown together even more closely by the fact that this external threat also appeared to be unified. If the challenge from the outside seemed to be coming from many different sources and directions, it would not have provoked a collaborative response from the different groups within Kerkennah society. On a certain level, Sfax, secularization, the central government, and the economic status quo all came to be identified as the same thing from the Kerkenni point of view. The identification of a unified external source of opposition minimized the differences between the two puritanisms and allowed them to support each other and collaborate in a way that would not have been possible otherwise.

This collaboration and support took several different forms. At the most general level, it meant that the older traditionalists sympathized with and encouraged the political activism of the young. This is very significant because often political activism entailed major risks for everyone associated with the activists. These risks included loss of educational grants, expulsion from university and consequent loss of future earnings for the whole family, discrimination by government agencies, imprisonment, and even death if the activism were seen by the government as treasonous. Rather than counselling the cautious approach as one would expect from the older generation, the traditionalists affirmed the honour of taking risks out of conviction. The older generation drew a parallel to their own experiences in the independence struggle when it has been necessary to violate the laws of the French rule. By pointing this out, the traditionalists were giving the young authority to violate the laws of the current establishment.

Backing up this general psychological support, the traditionalists cooperated in the various strikes that were initiated by the young activists, including the revivalists. The traditionalists also assisted the young activists and revivalists by relaying messages from the mainland to Kerkennah and back when formal means of communication seemed too risky. They provided private places to meet and basically smoothed the way for the young to make their revivalist protest as effective as possible.

But this support and cooperation also flowed in the other direction. The traditionalists found many of their ritual practices being taken up by the young revivalists to stir up their own religious identity. Usually the revivalists transformed these practices somewhat by taken them out of their normal communal ceremonial context and enacting them spontaneously and with great individual vigour. This happened with the communal religious sing-alongs, Qur'ān readings and cemetery visits. Even though these traditionalist practices were being reinterpreted in a sense by the revivalists for their own expression, the traditionalists still saw this activity as confirmation of their way of doing things and their picture of the world.

The collaboration of the activist revivalists with the traditionalists is dramatically illustrated by an event that took place during the month of Ramadan, August 1977. A revivalist organization, called the Association for the Protection of the Qur'ān, backed by local traditionalists, demanded that the Sfaxian authorities shut down some cafés which were serving alcoholic drinks during the holy fasting period. The authorities refused to honour this demand because of the interests of the proprietors and clients of these cafés. Consequently, a group of young activists broke up these cafés. They acted both as champions of the trade union protesting the political corruption of the Sfax "patrons" and as champions of Islam protesting the religiously corrupt behaviour of these servers and drinkers of alcohol. This was an instance when religious traditionalists, religious revivalists, and political activists were unified by what they all perceived as a common foe. This pattern of cooperation based on the identification of a common opponent characterizes the relations between the two kinds of Kerkennah puritans.

This kind of collaboration is not entirely new in Tunisia. Like the contemporary traditionalists and revivalists, at the turn of the century, the early nationalists and the established *'ulama* joined forces in resistance against the French. By narrowing their focus down to immediate issues, the two groups were able to ignore their differences and concentrate on their common enemy. When this focus broadened, the perception of a common enemy began to separate out into distinct and uncommon strands of interest. That is, the two groups began to see that they opposed the French for different reasons and that the futures they each envisioned for Tunisian society were radically opposed. The French realized this and changed their policies concerning Islamic reform in order to highlight the difference between the two resistance groups. The result was that the *ʿulamāʾ* dropped out and left the nationalists to fight alone. When the unified enemy atomized, the community of interest disappeared (Green 1978).

On the same principle in contemporary Iran, the most unlikely groups have cooperated in the face of a common source of opposition. The Islamic Revolutionary government of Iran has recognized that internal social coherence depends on the identification of a unified external enemy. Consequently, state propaganda encourages the population to see the Shah, America, Zionism, Iraq, Communism and anything else that threatens Iran as being a single united interest that Iranians must concentrate on defeating. As the distinct and conflicting interests opposing Iran are recognized, Iranian groups will pull apart, each to address its own particular opponent.

In Tunisia, it appears that the new prime minister, Mohammed Mzali, leans toward absorbing some of the impact of the Islamic revival into government policy and that the U.G.T.T. will be allowed to get back on its feet. It also seems that the Libyan aggression in Gafsa in early 1980 dampened some of the enthusiasm of the young for Colonel Ghaddafi and awakened in them a little more nationalistic fervour (Brett 1980). If these things are so, the "alliance" between the puritanisms will probably weaken because the opponent is becoming less unified and less "impure" in terms of the Tunisian and Islamic aspirations of the traditionalist and revivalist puritans.

REFERENCES

Abun-Nasr, J.M.
1971 *A History of the Maghrib*. Cambridge University Press.

Alport, E.A.
1970 'The Mazab'. In: Louise Sweet (ed.), *Peoples and Cultures of the Middle East*. New York: Natural History Press, Vol. 2.

Bourdieu, P.
1962 *The Algerians*. Boston: Beacon Press.

Brett, M.
1980 'Islam and Politics in Tunisia Today'. Unpublished paper.

Brown, K.
'Notes on the significance of Waqf in a Tunesian Zawiya'. In: G. Baer (ed.), *Social and Economic Aspects of the Muslim Waqf*. Forthcoming.

Demeerseman, A.
1972 *La Famille Tunisienne et les Temps Nouveaux*. Tunis: Maison Tunisienne de l'Edition.

Gellner, E.
1969 *Saints of the Atlas*. London: Weidenfeld & Nicholson.

Green, A.
1978 *The Tunisian Ulama 1873-1915*. Leiden: Brill.

Jansen, G.H.
1979 *Militant Islam*. London: Pan Books.

Mitchell, R.
1969 *The Society of Muslim Brothers*. Oxford: Oxford University Press.

Moore, Clement H.
1965 *Tunisia Since Independence*. Berkeley: University of California Press.

Tessler, M.A.
1980 Political Change and the Islamic Revival in Tunisia. *Maghreb Review*, Jan./Feb. 1980.

Zghal, A.
1973 The Reactivation of Tradition in a Post-Traditional Society. *Daedalus*, Winter 1973.

Trajectories of Contemporary Sufism

Michael Gilsenan

In the middle of the 1960s I studied a Sufi Brotherhood (*ṭarīqa*, pl. *ṭuruq*) in Egypt. At the time any talk of Sufism, and certainly of the *ṭuruq*, seemed positively anachronistic. The then Dean of the College of the Foundations of Religion, Sheikh 'Abd el Halim Mahmud (later to become an extremely stern Rector of al Azhar University) told me that I was not studying Islam at all if I wasted my time on the Brotherhoods. Nor did he mean that there were, relatively speaking, so few members left that it was hardly worth my while, though many people were of that opinion. His view was rather the same as that of many others of the *ʿulemā'*, as well as people from many different levels of Egyptian society and particularly the middle classes: that popular Sufism and the Brotherhoods were not truly Islamic. Their practices and beliefs were delusions and distractions from the truth at best, and at worst (and it was implied that the distance between best and worst was not great!) downright superstitious and heretical. This opinion came from someone regarded not only as a stern legist but as one who was well known as a student of mysticism and its paths and who was often identified to me as 'a Sufi'.

Sheikh 'Abd el Halim went on to explain to me that asceticism, about which I had questioned him, was an interior condition of the heart and most secret recesses of the self and not a matter of external show or form of poverty and self-denial. What passed for asceticism to my friends in the *ṭarīqa* was, in his view, a false deluding shape of asceticism without its inward reality. A man could be rich, indeed have millions, and still be an ascetic. The association members of the Brotherhoods sometimes made to me between wealth and not being a true Muslim, said the sheikh, was nonsense. They mistook the form of asceticism for its substance. They were ignorant and my work, as long as it focused on them and took them as in any sense valid representatives of an aspect of Islam, was totally wasted. I should rather go back to the texts, to the lives of the great Sufis and thinkers and leave 'the religion of the streets', as he called it.

One of the ironies of our encounter was that the Sufi Brotherhood that I was particularly studying, the *Hamidiya Shadhiliya*, was exercising enormous care to avoid anything remotely dubious in religious practice and teaching. To this end it had taken on what might be seen as very much the image of its own time. That is to say that it had evolved an immensely elaborate bureaucratic scheme for the administration of the Brotherhood, for a series of offices pyramidally arranged one above the other from the broad base of the humble ordinary member at the bottom to the Sheikh of the Brotherhood himself at the top, passing through half a dozen different positions on the way.

There are rules for disputes, rules for everyday behaviour, rules for ritual comportment and sequence, for the correct way of filling in report forms for the central office of the group, for establishing precedents, for hymn singing, for looking after the shoes at prayer, for eating, dress, and an entire practical and moral order.

The three hundred and twenty nine Laws (*Qānūn*) and the officials charged with ensuring their application were, as part of their function, to guarantee the Brotherhood precisely against attacks such as those made by Sheikh 'Abd el Halim. They were also, in a much less direct way, intended to defend the Brotherhood against specifically political suspicions. The Sufi Orders had been identified in the eyes of many of the Free Army Officers who made the revolution of 1952 in Egypt with too many of the forces in Egyptian society that the Revolution sought to destroy or neutralise.

The Brotherhoods were taken to be too close to powerful, 'feudal' rural class interests, too open to manipulation of the ignorant masses by the British, or the Palace (the regime of the then King Farouk), or the upper bourgeoisie.[1] They were too liable to mystify the people and divert them. Popular Sufism was accused of substituting non-Islamic ecstatic rituals for the political mobilisation and consciousness that the Revolution sought to achieve in the name of the independent nation. And there was a great deal of justice in this view.

This was not all. To many members of the petty bourgeoisie the Sufi Brotherhoods epitomised the ignorance, backwardness and non-Islamic practices from which many members of this very heterogeneous class particularly sought to separate themselves. The Brotherhoods were ferociously opposed by most sections of the Muslim Brothers, for example, a movement whose membership was drawn predominantly from that class. In the rapidly changing urban world, in the new cities that grew from small beginnings or were founded in the late nineteenth and early twentieth century, the Sufi Brotherhoods had few social roots and found it difficult to establish any. I suspect that for many of the clerks, office workers, petty bureaucrats, small shopkeepers and traders, students, young officers and N.C.O.s, and school teachers who were part of this stratum the *ṭuruq* represented forces from which they wished to free themselves. Popular Sufism was associated with what was coming to be seen as a stigma of 'traditionalism' from which this stratum had either liberated itself or hoped to leave behind, along with poverty, clientelism, the power of rural notables, illiteracy, passivity and all that was held to be responsible for Western domination. A certain powerful element of class antagonism was present here.

Where could the Sufi Brotherhoods contribute to Egypt's struggle against imperialism and for the achievement of her national independence? Where did they offer a rethinking or reworking of precept and practice that might bring out the full force of Islam in its 'pure' form against the non-Islamic forms? How, if they were deeply linked with old alliances and social structures in the countryside and the city, could they ever be part of a religious and social renaissance?

In the rural areas, once the sheikhs of the *ṭuruq* had lost much of their control over land in the nineteenth century, political and social forces crystallised in the latter half of that period round a new landed bourgeoisie whose class relations frequently owed little or nothing to such traditional ties and saw them as either manipulable, obstructive, or merely as a useful opiate for the masses. In at least some of the villages also, as Berque notes, the men of religious, political and economic prestige, often associated with leadership of Sufi *ṭuruq*, were increasingly subject to competition from the new educated and professionals whose socio-economic bases became more and more detached from land and local patterns of production and cultural life. Where the labourers and lower peasantry remained profoundly attached to ecstatic *zikr* rituals and the powers of shrines and talismen this too fuelled the opposition, often uncertain and very ambivalent, of the new groups to what they identified as a degraded 'popular religion'.

Given this complex of antagonisms and oppositions it was difficult to preserve, let alone create, a religious and social space for a Brotherhood bij the 1930s. Yet is was precisely at this period of economic and political turmoil that the founder of the *Hamidiya Shadhiliya*, Sheikh Salama ar-Radi, attempted to build up a *tariqa*.

A minor bureaucrat in a government office himself, he followed a double path. On the one hand he began by pursuing a completely traditional andstereotypically rigid form of holy personal activity and behaviour: extreme ascetic practices, endless prayers, seclusion, fasting, self-mortification. He blended into the general image or icon of how a man *becomes* a sheikh, makes himself into another order of being, strips himself of individuality in totally life-transforming practices that absorb him into a picture of holiness. He lived the social imperatives of sacredness, and took on all the signs that might legitimate the founding of his own *ṭarīqa*.

On the other hand, once the Brotherhood was founded after a decade of moving around the poorer quarters of Cairo and the towns and villages of the Nile Delta, he both abandoned extreme forms of asceticism and formulated and produced an innovatory kind of rule within popular Sufism. This was what can only be called the bureaucratic rule. He insisted on a totally orthodox, law bound, theologically correct way, indistinguishable from that of any of the great reformist trends of the nineteenth and twentieth centuries: 'Our way in Holy Law is built on the Quran and the Sunna and it is free from blameable heresy' (law 2). He also constructed an elaborate armour of prescriptions and organising principles that owe perhaps more to his own office and work experience than to tradition. It is not an exaggeration in fact to say that the bulk of *The Laws* are bureaucratic and administrative in nature.

The initial emphasis is the appeal to the poor, precisely the increasingly large numbers existing on the social margin of the new colonial urban and economic order:

Law 4. One of the principles of our way is humility, for it is the wealth of the poor.

Law 11. Sitting with the rich hardens the heart.

Law 16. Helping the poor and being sympathetic to them materially and spiritually as far as possible (is one of the principles of the Brotherhood).

The call is also traditional in its nature. Humility is the capital or resource of the poor. It is a state of being to be poor and it is spiritually blessed. There is no questioning of the social origins and nature of 'the poor'; no suggestion that poverty can be transcended in this world; no indication that humility and the pursuit of the Way might relate to a critique of society or to the kinds of action against the colonial forces that so many groups were undertaking at the time that *The Laws* were written in the thirties.

I shall return to this question of religious ethic and politics shortly. For the moment let me stress that the main emphasis in *The Laws*, as indeed it was in practice during my study in 1964-66, was on order, organisation, efficiency, and a theological and ritual coherence and control which would both give identity to the members (who, unlike all the other Sufi Brotherhoods of Egypt, were expressly forbidden to belong to any other kind of religious organisation) and serve as a defense against authority, political or religious, should it attack popular Sufism.

Perhaps curiously I found myself more personally moved by this attempt to buttress the religion of the street with the instruments of what had become its opponents (the centralising State, bureaucratic control, theological and textual rigour) than by any other element in the *Hamidiya Shadhiliya*. Yet it created an enormous tension. At best it might be a positive and creative tension and combination of elements at the heart of the Brotherhood; between *The Laws*, and the other side of popular Sufism, egalitarian fraternity, ritual performances of huge emotional, psychological and physiological power, intense personal relations and the immediacy of face-to-face contact, brother to brother.

On the other hand it contained the possibility of a clash and contradiction between the bureaucratic principles, and the almost painful desire to see and experience the hand of God working in the grace acts (*karāmāt*) of the now dead holy man, Sheikh Salama. Each seemed to threaten the other. The *rules* might be produced by the Sheikh and maintained by the officials, but the practical meaning of the Brotherhood centres on the *grace* and *power* of the Sheikh and on the experience of his holiness in everyday life that *baraka* and *karāmāt* and the ecstasies and intensity of experience offered by the *zikr* rituals provide.

During my stay (1964-66), when the Brotherhood was headed by Sheikh Ibrahim Salama (one of the founder's sons), it was commonplace to see the officials severely reprimanding those of the members who were seized with ecstasy in the rituals and began to cry out and move violently out of rhythm with the others, shattering the carefully constructed harmony of breath, sound and movement. And the officials also played the classical role of disciples, which I might call 'stopping the little children from coming unto the Lord'. That is to say, they turned away the devout from the Sheikh's presence if he was tired or occupied. They were the ones who prevented the brothers from seizing the Sheikh's hand as he passed, his eyes cast down, his right hand over his heart in silent acknowledgement of their cries and supplications. They pulled back those who wanted to touch the hem of his robe.

The officials created the distance between the faithful and the source of grace without it ever being felt that the source itself, in the person of Sheikh Ibrahim, was denying them. Where the founding holy man had been accessible to his followers, his son, at one remove from the power of his father and with a *ṭarīqa* grown to a far larger size, withdrew into a holy distance which made those rare moments when he did wave the officials aside and require them to admit a child, an old man, a small visiting delegation from a village in the delta, all the more rhapsodic and exalted. Their role was thus both creative and restrictive.

There was, moreover, another associated issue around which certain ambiguities clustered. This related to the notion of hierarchy in a Sufi Brotherhood. In theory hierarchy is a matter of degree of illumination, of having passed through certain stages on the way of mystical knowledge. But it was stressed that the officials were not necessarily in their posts as a spiritual hierarchy in the *Hamidiya Shadhiliya*, but rather for the imperatives of administration. Their bureaucratic status sometimes seemed to combine uneasily with their role as ritual organisers and *de facto* guardians of the Sheikh. The aspect of control occasionally appeared to dominate over direct contact with what is taken to be the real form of life, the pattern of power and blessing lying behind the world's facade.

It should be added that in the many local centres or lodges of the Brotherhood the *khalīfas* (deputies) who run the centres (*zawiya-s*) *are* supposed to be men capable of taking the place of the Sheikh in more than an organisational sense. They have to teach, advise, watch over, serve, coordinate mutual assistance and the practical dimension of fraternity, as well as deal with disputes, guard money, write elaborate reports to the head office, recruit, and defend the group against local opposition where it occurs.

Many of the officers were legitimated, not only by the fact that they had been chosen by the Sheikh, but also by the fact that many of them were still 'first generation' followers and had taken the oath of allegiance to Sheikh Salama himself. They were often poor men themselves, usually workers of different levels, but sometimes teachers in primary schools, clerks (by now often retired) in government offices, shop workers or storekeepers on a very small scale. Such men had the authority of 'first followers', not officials. They were part of, and a link for those younger to, the original mission of Salama ar-Radi himself.

There was, however, another group that had no formal rank but which formed a circle around the Sheikh of a rather ēlite kind. These were mostly business men, small company owners, a senior airline pilot, a high ranking officer and engineer, one or two government officials. They dominate(d) the Sheikh's meetings and the religious discussions. Their own image and understanding of religion is very close to that of reformist and strictly orthodox groups. Their conceptions of the miracles wrought by Sheikh Salama have nothing to do with those of the ordinary members, which are full of astonishing escapes, sudden discoveries of money, dream visions or the voice of the dead but still powerful holy man whispering in the air. Rather they refer to his intellectual gifts, his mastery of Holy Law and his ability to confound the *ʿulemāʾ* who came to challenge him on their own ground, even though he himself had no formal training in law. Their class situation, position in the Brotherhood, and religious perspective were and are, therefore, significantly different from that of the mass of the members.

There existed powerful tensions in the Brotherhood, tensions which arose partly out of the very success of the group and the quality of its internal relations. There were certain critical elements or focal points at which such tensions and distinctions of belief and practice were at least potentially crystallised. What would happen if there were a crisis? Would the organisation be able to ensure a smooth succession? If it came to it, could bureaucracy in fact guarantee and legitimate the supposedly central and determining forces of power and grace?

I was aware, of course, that the Sufi Brotherhoods frequently split into different branches and groupings. Any number of factors may be operating when this occurs, and the multiplication of branches of *ṭuruq* tracing their line of spiritual descent from the same founder but following a specific holy individual who institutes his own branch is totally characteristic. It has been part of the flexibility and responsiveness of Sufism in history.

But in a new group in the context of contemporary Egypt, and given the massive elaboration of the organisational arm everything seemed propitious and a serious split hardly imaginable. Yet there had been one on the death of Sheikh Salama when a large faction refused to follow the choice by some of the followers of one of the Sheikh's sons (the Sheikh Ibrahim referred to) as his successor and united around the man who had been the dead founder's deputy and one of his first disciples. This crisis had gradually been overcome. Sheikh Ibrahim had become undisputed leader, and the central *maglis* (office) of the Brotherhood was notably strengthened in his time to guard against the possibilities of disruption. Such was the situation when I left Cairo in 1966.

My return to the city over a decade later, in 1977, produced several surprises for the complacent anthropologist. After many enquiries at the mosques where large congregations of several hundreds of brothers used regularly to perform the *zikr* had revealed no apparent activity, I was eventually astonished to be directed to a new mosque built in one of the most fashionable and modern luxury areas of Cairo. My surprise was all the greater when I found the half-built shell of a massive construction still covered with scaffolding on what was in effect a huge traffic island behind a chic sporting club and surrounded by a dual lane carriageway.

The doorkeeper brought me in to see the interior of the yet uncompleted prayer hall in beautiful and costly marble brought from Europe. Most significantly, he took me "to see the Sheikh". And I found myself before an ornate tomb that was surrounded by a brass rail and rested on the unfinished concrete. Sheikh Ibrahim had died two years before and his shrine lies in the symbolic centre of the new mosque. I was left alone with him, to be 'in his presence', amidst the wooden poles and supports holding up what will one day be a dome above the shrine. A large empty space beside Sheikh Ibrahim's shrine is reserved for his father, the founding holy man. But, for the moment at least, Sheikh Salama's body remained in the tiny mosque in the old former port quarter of Bulaq, an area which is very much one of the great popular and mass quarters of the city. It was the social centre of the founder's mission in Cairo in the 1930s and of the *mulid* celebrations held every year since his death to commemorate and celebrate his life. His shrine is the core and source of *baraka* and pilgrimage not only for the brothers but for those many persons who seek blessing at the tombs of holy figures.

Now the move to the new mosque was astonishing enough. Nothing could be socially more distant from Bulaq than the ostentatious upper middle class wealth of Zamalek, where the new building is located. This curious transplantation to a high prestige site, the marble carved prayer niche, the plans for a clinic, the teaching centre, a library, all were a very different image of the *tariqa* than had dominated ten years before.

The significance of this shift quickly became apparent. At the sudden death of Sheikh Ibrahim the Brotherhood had split. Part had followed the Sheikh's younger brother, who is a graduate of the Faculty of Commerce and played in the 1960s only a very limited role in the group. The other section was under the joint leadership of a committee composed almost entirely of the inner circle of business men and professionals to which I have referred. The precise sequence of events was difficult to establish. What is important is the extent of the change in the *ṭarīqa* that has occurred.

To understand this we have to realise that there is a conjunction between the crisis of succession and a process of change in Egyptian society as a whole. The division of the Brotherhood is not only an internal question. It relates in part to transformations in the role and attitude of the State, and the global political and social context within which popular Sufism now exists.

Since the economic and military catastrophes of the period from 1965 onwards the policies of Arab socialism and the whole heterogeneous political order and ideology of 'Nasserism' have been under attack. The traumatic defeat of Egypt by Israel in 1967 and the death of Nasser in 1970 were part of a transitional period towards a far more explicitly 'western' model of economic policy. Private enterprise was to be encouraged, economic liberalism and an 'open door' policy to Western goods and interests became part of a reorientation of Egypt's position and relationships in the world at large. State controls were relaxed, the apparatus of intelligence (particularly its military organisation) and the dominance of the Army were diminished. The financial, commercial and industrial wings of the bourgeoisie would be given the opportunity to come to the forefront of the economic and social order.

In the ideological field, with nationalism itself in its Nasserist forms seriously compromised, 'socialism' also identified as having been tried and found wanting, and the regime of President Sadat seeking to distance itself from its own Army and Nasserist legacy, there was a new space for religion and religious movements in State ideology. Groups such as the Muslim Brothers, which had long been prescribed, were tacitly allowed back into public life. Muslim groups were encouraged in the Universities, particularly against any forces identified as being Nasserist or of the Left.

In this context, and with other states such as Libya and Saudi Arabia from their very different perspectives also wishing to encourage Islamic movements cast in their image, there re-emerged an ideological and tacitly political arena for popular Sufism. The *Hamidiya Shadhiliya*, already much the best organised of the Brotherhoods, flowered more freely. The prestigious new mosque was planned, trips to Europe were made by Sheikh Ibrahim and trusted colleagues to arrange the importation of building materials. A site of great social standing was made available and funds acquired. The *ṭarīqa* enjoyed an emergence into official approval as an example of what a true and proper collective form of Sufism might be.

Sheikh Ibrahim's death, however, abruptly posed the problem of succession. The division that followed between the essentially middle class élite of the Brotherhood and those who followed the Sheikh's younger brother occurred with (to me) surprising swiftness. It is significant that the larger fraction of the members, drawn from the social world of Bulaq, outside the benefits of the shift of State policy, most exposed to the economic problems that that policy has entailed for the poor and working classes, should have remained with the Sheikh's brother. A friend who is of a very high position in the Brotherhood, and to whose kindness I owe much, admitted to me regretfully that in the new mosque which he administers, I would no longer find the great crowds that I had known in the difficult years for popular Sufism of the Nasserist regime. Only a minority have made the move to Zamalek. The building has yet to take on any content, and practical significance. There is a kind of social and religious emptiness, despite the tomb of Sheikh Ibrahim and the splendour of the marbled prayer hall.

The ironies are illuminating. The move to Zamalek and into such a mosque was to be a mark of flowering, of new prestige, of social re-emergence into a form of religious practice that would establish Sufism in its *ṭarīqa* forms as once again acceptable and 'respectable'. In fact it helped to divide the Brotherhood and to sharpen cleavages (what were partly divisions of class) that had until the Sheikh's death been contained. The members were ready to follow the Sheikh. They were *not* ready to follow a middle class élite, nor to break with their social and symbolic anchor in Bulaq. The economic divisions in Egyptian society that have both grown and been increasingly revealed in social behaviour in the decade of the 1970s have no doubt exacerbated the real significance of the move to Zamalek and the sense of very contrasting interests within the Brotherhood. The élite of the *ṭarīqa*, by its assertion of dominance, undermined that very dominance.

Furthermore, the whole organised structure - so elaborated, so precisely detailed, so hierarchical, so ambiguous in effect - proved quite unable to hold the *ṭarīqa* together, since it generated as many tensions as it resolved.

The division also intriguingly demonstrates that State support for what might crudely be called a cleaned-up version of the 'religion of the streets' can be *more* productive of contradiction than State disapproval or even quasi-repression. The tacit attempt at an *embourgeoisement* of sectors of popular Sufism in alliance, or what is seen to be an alliance with the State, largely disqualified itself. It failed, and it seems to me that the members were implicitly refusing that kind of incorporation into an ideology and form of Sufism which was alien to them and the position in the social order that the vast majority of them occupy.

Is it reasonable to suggest that what we see here is a renewal in a particular form of the theme of (tacit and muted) opposition between 'the religion of the streets' in its popular Sufism manifestation and the state and central authority? Is it an opposition now felt more from the side of popular Sufism than by the state, in contrast to the whole of the Nasserite period?

I have already remarked as a very general principle, on the subversive and covert elements present in *baraka* and miracles which potentially always threaten to elude religious, not to say political authority, however much effort may be made to strengthen the controls (in the past the banning of saints' days celebrations, with their potent and dangerous concentration of large masses of people; the intimidation of the leaders of the *ṭuruq* or their followers; the removal of shrines or severe government discouragement of 'saint worship').

Yet in the nineteenth century in Egypt many of the leaders of the Brotherhoods were instruments for the channeling and restriction of popular religion by the dominant social strata in the towns and countryside. They were often from those strata and integral to local power structures. In that sense the *ṭuruq* were incorporated by the ruling forces of society and formed an ideological and social bridge to the peasantry and the urban masses.

It was indeed this identification with rural landlords and notables, government manipulation and established political structures that in the twentieth century caused them to be stigmatized both by fundamentalist and reformist groups, who were hostile at once to what they criticised as magical and un-Islamic practices and to the power groups with which Sufism was associated, and by the complex of social forces that went into the Revolution of 1952 which attacked the Brotherhoods as reactionary and 'feudal'. Sufism became more and more peripheral and confined to marginal groupings, excluded from ideological and political space by the development of the independence movement, fundamentalism, nationalism in its different forms, and the association of the colonial and post-colonial state with textual orthodoxy and legalism.

In Egypt, therefore, the Brotherhoods were displaced and lost support in part because of their subservience to the pre-colonial and colonial state. They had not been, as the *ṭuruq* were in the very different social settings of societies such as Algeria, hostile to the emerging forms of the state in the nineteenth century. Even where given local sheikhs or religious notables might, as in the case mentioned by Berque, support the Wafd party in its nationalist programme, this was still a relationship with local rural power structures. So popular Sufism came to be seen as 'traditionalist' and repressive by many elements of the petty bourgeoisie and indeed the middle classes in general, who excluded it from their own organised political and cultural alternatives. At the same time reformist and fundamentalist groups, drawn from those same classes, denied the Brotherhoods' authenticity as practical and theological forms of Islam. Saints' shrines and pilgrimages remained foci any number of different kinds of imagined power, hope, promise, blessing, but the *ṭuruq* were not structurally necessary, even to the saints.

The late 1970s saw the emergence of a different kind of ideology for which the West, and the economic 'opening' were to replace 'Nasserism'. The state and those interests it now represented began to engage in a recuperation of religion as a major ideological support and legitimation. As a small part of that attempted recuperation (of which more in discussion) popular Sufism is to be permitted and even discreetly encouraged. But it proves not always easy to manipulate. Its social base has changed, and it has also diminished. Though its ethic of humility, reliance on the *baraka* of the holy man, acceptance of poverty, proper and scrupulous attention to personal manners and conduct pose no threat, neither does it lead to an identification of the state with religious legitimacy and beneficence. The gulf has widened between social classes whose life chances (in Max Weber's phrase) are becoming more obviously separated and unequal. Since the economic policies of the State do not benefit those classes from which are drawn the members of the *turuq* it is all the more unlikely that the former will be successful in its attempts to use and revitalise this religious form for its own purposes. The *Hamidiya Shadhiliya* divides. The new mosque, splendid on its traffic island amidst the luxury apartment blocks, remains empty.

NOTE

1 In his study of the history of an Egyptian village, Jacques Berque notes that national politics in the shape of the liberal bourgeois natinalist party, the Wafd, came to the community through a committee organised by a local head of the Khalwatiyya order. He organised a campaign of sabotage and boycotts. As Berque says, political agitation and *ṭarīqa* propaganda went hand in hand at this period (the 1920s). *Histoire sociale d'un village egyptien au xxième siècle*, Mouton, 1957, p.66.

The Cult of Saints in North-Western Tunisia[1]; An Analysis of Contemporary Pilgramage Structures

Wim M. J. van Binsbergen

1. Introduction

In this chapter I shall present a description and analysis of the cult of local saints, as a major aspect of contemporary popular religion in the highlands of Khrumiriya[2], north-western Tunisia. This paper is therefore a contribution to the ethnography of religious behaviour in general and that of rural North Africa in particular. As is the case in much of religious anthropology, studies of popular Islam have tended to concentrate on systems of belief and symbolism, with excursions into the relation between religion and the wider social, economic and political context in which that religion occurs. The behavioural aspect of religion has been somewhat neglected, and as a result for some of the most pertinent questions of contextual religious analysis we have had to content ourselves with tentative answers largely founded on intuition and persuasion; the necessary empirical data have often been lacking. A major problem in this connexion is that an empirical, quantitative description of religious behaviour - such as I shall offer towards the end of this chapter - remains meaningless without an adequate discussion of the symbolic and social-organizational aspects of such behaviour.

Having elsewhere dealt with the historical aspects of saintly cults and the interplay between popular and formal Islam in the Khrumiri region (cf. Van Binsbergen 1971a,1980a,1980b)[3], I shall here largely limit myself to the contemporary situation concerning pious visits (*zyāra*) to shrines associated with named local saints - touching on local history only in so far this helps to explain the nature of territorial segmentation today, and refraining from a discussion of such significant aspects of Khrumiri religion as: the veneration of trees and sources; veneration of saints through other rituals than pious visits; the ecstatic cults that are loosely organized in religious brotherhoods and that, although implying saints, form a popular-religious complex somewhat distinct from *zyara*; the symbolic deep structure of such key concepts as sainthood and *barāka*; and finally the formal Islam of the Qur'an, the mosque, the pilgrimage to Mecca. Even so the ethnographic argument will be too lengthy to allow for a more than cursory discussion of the many wider theoretical implications of the Khrumiri data (cf. Van Binsbergen 1971a,1976,in preparation).

2. Regional and historical background

Khrumiriya is a mountainous area in north-western Tunisia, situated between the Tunisian-Algerian border (which is hardly a social and cultural boundary), and the towns of Tabarka and Janduba. The regional capital is the small town of ᶜAin Draham, where the region's only and recently-built mosque is found.

Until the late 19th century, the narrow, densely-forested valleys of this remote region provided a relatively prosperous livelihood for a tent-dwelling population engaging in semi-transhumant animal husbandry (cattle, sheep, goats) and small-scale agriculture (wheat, rye, olives). Each of the scattered homesteads consisted of a core of close agnates, with their wives, children and non-agnatically related adult male dependants (herdsmen, who often became sons-in-law). These residential and productive units existed at the basis of a segmentary system, whose explicit ideology was one of patrilineal descent but in which, in fact, factional allegiance, geographical propinquity, and genealogical manipulation were equally important structuring principles. Localized clans, tribes, and confederations of tribes formed the highest levels of the segmentary model. The segmentary organization regulated: rights over pastures, forest areas and springs; special patronage links between social groups and invisible saints, associated with the numerous shrines scattered over the land; and burial rights in local cemeteries situated around a saintly shrine - although, given the large number of shrines and the very small number of cemeteries per valley, most shrines had no cemetery around them.

On all segmentary levels, complementary segments were in competition with each other over scarce resources, women, and honour. The armed conflicts to which this competition frequently gave rise, were in two ways mitigated by the cult of saints.

First, each higher-level segment (encompassing the majority of the population of a valley) would have a twice-annual saintly festival (*zarda*) near the shrine of its patron saint, located at some conspicuous point in that valley. On this occasion, all members of the local segment (i.e. all inhabitants of the valley) would make a collective visit to the shrine, and would for several days stay near the shrine, chatting, feasting, and being entertained by dancing and singing. Members of feuding segments in neighbouring valleys were likewise under obligation to make a pious visit to the shrine concerned, attending this festival, and sharing in the collective meal there. Temporary lifting of segmentary opposition was achieved not only through this ritual commensality but also through a safe-conduct for all pilgrims, sanctioned by the invisible saint. Also women who, originating from the local segment, had married into a different valley, were under obligation to make the pious visit to the shrine on the occasion of the saintly festival.

Secondly, the major shrines - those that had a twice-annual festival catering for an entire valley - were administered by specialist shrine-keepers. The latter were not considered saints in themselves, but they were pious, pacifist men who had placed themselves outside the feuding system and who, on the basis of a saintly safe-conduct and by virtue of the respect that the shrine's flags commanded, were often successful in quenching violence between segments.

The colonial period in Tunisia, which began with the French conquest of Khrumiriya in 1881, brought tremendous changes in the social, economic and religious structures of the region. It took the colonial state a quarter of a century to impose its monopoly of violence, but from the beginning of the twentieth century an effective stop was put to feuding as the main motor behind segmentary dynamics. Movement of the population was further restricted by state exploitation of the extensive cork-tree forests, the establishment of settler farms (which in Khrumiriya however remained a much more limited phenomenon than in the fertile Tunisian valleys to the south and the east of this mountainous area), and the concentration of land rights in the hands of a few state-appointed chiefs and their families, who were in collusion with the colonial administration. Pressure on the land was exacerbated by dramatic population increase, and massive erosion through over-exploitation of the vulnerable soil system proved inevitable. The economic opportunities in the French-created garrison town of ᶜAin Draham, even after its development into a regional capital and a tourist resort, could not compensate for the decline of the local subsistence economy; neither could, during the colonial period, labour migration directed to areas of capitalist farming, and to urban areas, in Tunisia and Algeria. The reafforesting projects and the umemployment relief work undertaken since Tunisia became independent (1956), did not alter this state of affairs substantially. The ethnographic present of the late 1960s offers the picture of a destitute peasant population, which within the rigid confines of its villages of immobile stone houses and small and fragmented fields, keeps going a transformed neo-traditional social and ritual organization, and a no-longer viable local subsistence economy ineffectively supplemented by unemployment relief projects.

3. Segmentation in Khrumiriya today

The model of a segmentary lineage system has remained the standard idiom by which participants structure their social environment, distinguish between residential groups, and explain relationships between these groups. In the face of the realities of peripheral capitalism, this lineage model became devoid of such economic and political significance as it had in nineteenth-century Khrumiriya. It no longer effectively governs the everyday ongoing social process in the villages. Moreover, as the population has become totally sedentary, and pressure on the land increased, the idiom of patrilineal descent is no longer a device for segmentary mobilization in the competition over scarce resources, but has become merely a folk idiom to describe the pattern of organizational allignment of bounded territorial units such as are manifestly visible in the Khrumiri countryside today - and a means to claim legitimate membership of such units, i.e. rights of residence and rights in land.

From the lowest level upwards, we find (cf. diagram 1)

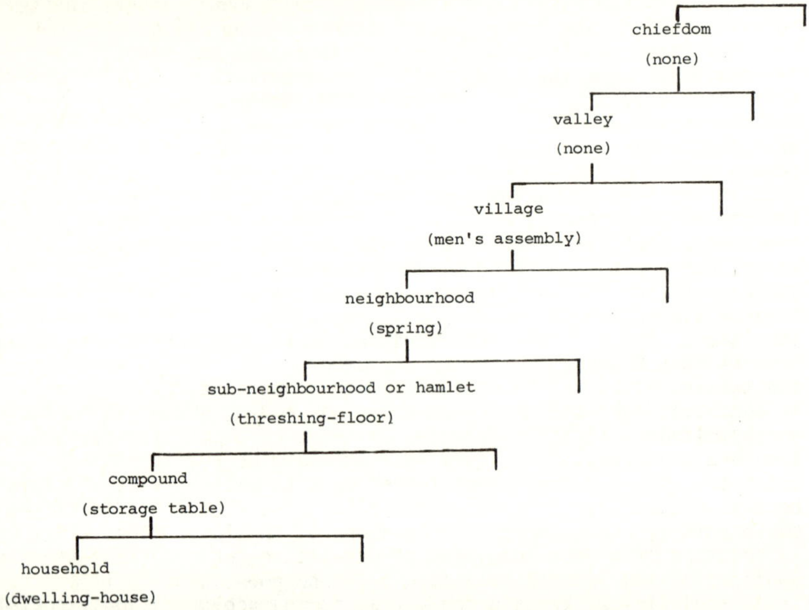

Diagram 1. Schematic representation of territorial segmentation and utilitarian characteristic attributes of segments in Khrumiriya. (Characteristic attributes between brackets.)

households, compounds, sub-neighbourhoods or hamlets, neighbourhoods, villages, valleys, chiefdoms. Each of these is clearly marked, and distinguished from complementary units at the same segmentary level, by unmistakable features in the landscape: the walls of dwelling-houses and the open spaces between houses; the cactus fences between compounds and hamlets; the pastures, fields, shrub-covered fallow areas, and patches of forest between neighbourhoods and between villages; and the steep, forested mountain ranges between valleys and between chiefdoms consisting of a number of valleys.

Most of these units are designated by names derived from human proper names: *Dār ᶜAlī* (ᶜAli's House), *Mhamdīya* (Descendants of Mohammed), *Ulād Ibrahim* (Descendants of Ibrahim), etc. While these labels in fact function as names for residential units, and as toponyms, their evocation of a historical or mythical ancestor from which all born members of that unit are claimed to descend, enables Khrumiri participants to represent their territorial organization today by a patrilineal genealogy encompassing an entire valley and even chiefdom - despite massive oral-historical evidence at my disposal which clearly establishes that, at least in the 12 km^2 that formed the core of my research area, few compounds and hamlets, and no neighbourhoods, villages or higher-level territorial segments, are composed of a homogeneous set of agnates descending from one common ancestor. On the contrary, the population belongs to more than a dozen mutually unrelated patrilineal descent lines, most of which immigrated into their present day territory in the course of the nineteenth and twentieth century; only by virtue of genealogical manipulation can they manage to identify as agnates.

Khrumiri territorial segments have distinctive features beyond their visible boundaries and their proper names evoking ancestors. The extent to which the model of territorial segmentation sketched here is not just a researcher's construct, but a living reality to the participants, is clear from the fact that at each level of territorial segmentation a segment has a characteristic attribute which defines it against complementary segments at the same level. Like the unit boundaries, these attributes are clearly visible in the landscape, and they are a result of human activity. Each household is characterized by its own dwelling-house, which defines the basic unit of human reproduction, since by containing the family bed it sets the scene for sex life, child-birth and child-rearing. A few dwelling-houses combine so as to form one compound; this territorial unit is defined by the storage table, which marks the compound as a basic unit of food processing and consumption.[4] Each hamlet or sub-neighbourhood consisting of a small number of compounds, is characterized by its own threshing-floor, which defines the hamlet as a minimal unit of agricultural production. Neighbourhoods, consisting of a small number of hamlets, each have their own springs, use of which is private to the members of that neighbourhood. The spring defines the neighbourhood as a unit whose members share (for such purposes as water hauling, grazing, collection of firewood, hunting) an overall productive interest in the surrounding countryside, even though the neighbourhood is internally divided into smaller complementary segments with relation to those aspects of production and reproduction that require more prolonged, complicated and socially more intricately-organized tasks. Finally, villages, consisting of a small number of neighbourhoods, are characterized by their own men's assembly: a wind-swept open space overlooking the valley and its main shrines. Here the adult male inhabitants of the village assemble towards the evening, to discuss the ongoing social and political process and to entertain each other with tea-drinking and card-playing. If the village has a store, it is located adjacent to the men's assembly. The men's assembly defines the village as the social unit of sufficient scope and at the same time of sufficient intimacy, to accommodate the ongoing face-to-face social process between people who have widely divergent and conflicting economic interests, as members of lower-level segmentary units. At the men's assembly people meet most of whom, while not strangers to each other, do not automatically share a day-to-day routine of dwelling and working together; thus the men's assembly provides a social and political arena, a more or less external yet inescapable standard for the evaluation of wealth, honour, and propriety, and as such the wider social framework of the interactional processes on which, within the lower-level segmentary units, the organization of production and reproduction depends.

Khrumiri territorial segments thus are not just significant units in the organization of geographical space, they also structure the social and economic space in a way that reflects the vital processes going on in this society. The characteristic attributes by which each segmentary level is marked are, as it were, chosen with great wisdom, and their very nature is suggestive of the social and economic significance of the segments at various hierarchical levels. Not surprisingly, in Khrumiri symbolism the storage table, the dwelling-house, the threshing-floor, the spring and the men's assembly constitute powerful images, around which an important part of the local world-view condensates and finds expression. What is more, each of the characteristic attributes mentioned is conceived as a diffuse, nameless but somewhat personalized, supernatural entity, a distinct power which appears in the dreams of the human members of of the segment with which it is associated, and which can mete out benefits and punishment depending on the degree of propriety and respect people display in the specific activities involving that characteristic attribute. Nor are these activities of an exclusively utilitarian nature: dwelling-house, threshing-floor, spring and men's assembly are in themselves subjected to ritual actions, particularly the burning of incense and the sprinkling of chicken blood. The most important symbolic aspect of these characteristic attributes, and one that in the people's eyes sufficiently explains the animistic overtones alluded to here, is that (as latent or primordial shrines) they are all carriers of *baraka*, the Grace or Life-force through which, under the catalytic effects of morality and good social relations, Man succeeds in sharing the non-human power of Nature and of the Divine.

These characteristic attributes with their rich symbolic elaborations are the visible beacons in a structure of territorial segmentation. But although segmentary dynamics have been stagnant as compared with the turbulent pattern obtaining in the last century, the system of territorial segmentation is by no means entirely static today. Despite rural decline and the pressure on the land, demographic and economic processes are at work which over time propel some lower-level units to higher levels, and vice versa. A compound, while retaining its proper name and ancestral association, may be seen to wax into a neighourhood and even a village in the course of half a century or less. In those cases the named units, as they break through from one segmentary level to a lower or higher one, will shed the characteristic attribute appropriate to the former level and will adopt one appropriate to the new level. Thus the construction, and the sinking in decay, of dwelling-houses, threshing-floors and men's assemblies, and shifts in patterns of water hauling from one spring to another, all mark, again in a way that is visible in the landscape, the waxing and waning of territorial segments.

This is the moment to introduce shrines into our increasingly complex picture of territorial segmentation in contemporary Khrumiriya.

4. Shrines in Khrumiriya

Shrines[5] exist in Khrumiriya in a number of variants. I shall leave aside such non-man-made salient features in the landscape as remarkable trees, rock formations and ferruginous springs[6], which tend to be venerated without being clearly associated with saints. All other shrines are man-made, and considered to be intimately associated with saints: deceased human beings whose *baraka* was and is such that they continue to wield power in the world of man. The association between shrine and saint is conceived in either of the following three ways:

a. the shrine was erected upon the saint's grave;
b. the shrine was erected upon a spot that had a special relation with the saint during his lifetime or shortly after his death: as the place where he rested in the course of his wanderings, or where his body was temporarily put before definitively being put into the grave; and finally
c. the shrine has been secondarily erected upon relics brought from a shrine explained as under a or b. For each shrine there tends

to be some disagreement among participants as to which option (a, b or c) applies in its particular case. The historical dynamics underlying these patterns fall outside our present scope.

Saintly shrines come in a variety of material forms. All mimick more or less the human dwelling-house. Many do so in a very crude form, and consist only of a semi-circle of large rocks covered by another rock or by a slab of cork. This is the type commonly called *mzāra*, although this term (meaning "that which is visited") in principle applies to all shrines. In some shrines the inner room within the ground-plan of rocks is more spacious and of more or less rectangular shape; they may be covered by an elaborate reed roof supported by forked poles carrying a roof-beam. This is the type called *kurbi*, a word otherwise reserved for human dwelling-houses constructed out of arboreal material. The most elaborate type of shrine in Khrumiriya is the *qubba*: a square, stone building with plastered white-washed walls, a domed roof and horned ornaments on the four corners, as commonly found throughout the Islamic world.

All saintly shrines contain minor pious gifts: small amounts of incense wrapped in paper, candles, incense-burners and candle-sticks locally made out of fired clay, and household refuse such as broken teapots and spoons purposely taken to the shrine as token offerings. In addition, the shrines associated with saints that, in the local hierarchy of saints, are considered to rank high, often contain stone balls (*kurra*: the saint is said to have carried them in his life-time, as proof of his sainthood); elaborately decorated flags donated to the shrine as votive gifts; and a wooden chest in which these flags are stored along with other pious gifts, including coins.

Although for the sake of simplicity saints are described here as male, participants acknowledge the existence of female saints. A valley's major saints usually are male. Many saints bear ordinary personal names (e.g. ᶜAbd Allah, Muhammad, Mhammad, ᶜAlī; or women's names: Massaūda, ᶜA'isha, etc.) preceded by the reverential term of address *Sidi* (master, sir; elder brother), *Lalla* (madam, miss, grandmother; elder sister) or *Jaddi* (grandparent). A large number of saints however do not bear human names but derivatives of words denoting natural species: Bu-Kharūba (Man with the Carob-tree), Bu-Qasbaya (Man with the Reed), etc. The Khrumiri saintly cult has an understream of totemism which is also manifest in saintly legends and taboos; but this, however interesting, falls outside our present scope.

Neither can I go into detail here with regard to the relationships deemed to exist between saints. Various structuring principles are invoked to establish some degree of order among the large number of local saints with which each Khrumiri participant is familiar. First, there is a general hierarchy of saints, ranking from Sidi ᶜAbd al-Qādir al-Jilāni (who throughout the Maghreb is considered to be the most powerful saint), through a small number of major saints of more than regional significance (e.g. Sidi ᶜAbd as-Salām ben Mashīsh), to the greatest Khrumiri saints (the ones whose shrines are best known and whose festivals are best frequented: Sidi ᶜAbd Allah bi-Jamāl, Sidi Mhammad, Sidi Bu-Nāqa, Sidi Bu-Kharūba, Sidi Ben-Mtīr), the lesser saints that are only known within a valley and adjacent valleys, and finally the least powerful saints, the ones that are only known and venerated at the village, neighbourhood or even compound level.

This hierarchy very roughly corresponds with the material form of the principal shrines associated with those saints. Whereas the top-ranking international saints do not even have shrines within the region (they are known through hagiographic legends, and as saints featuring in the songs that pertain to the ecstatic ritual of the brotherhoods), the greatest regional saints have long-established *qubbas*, those immediately below them tend to have large *kurbi* shrines or large rock *mzāras*, whereas the smallest *mzāras* and miniature *kurbi* shrines tend to be associated with the least important saints.

Besides this overall hierarchy, saints associated with shrines within the same valley, or in adjacent valleys, tend to be linked to each other in hagiographic legends that claim specific relationships to exist between these saints: they are described as unrelated equals (neighbours, friends), as non-kin involved in a master-servant relation, or - most frequently - as close agnatic kinsmen: father and son, brothers, brother and sister.

The erection of a shrine upon relics brought from an older shrine often creates a situation where, within a valley or adjacent valleys, a number of shrines are associated with and named after one and the same saint. In that case the main shrine (the one that is the most elaborate, and that has the greatest festival) is considered to be the original shrine - although objective historical research would not always bear out the participants' view on this. This shrine is called "the Elder", al-Kabīr, whereas the other shrines bearing the same name are called "the Son" (al-Wilda). Thus in the valley of Sidi Mhammad four shrines of the saint Sidi Mhammad exist: Sidi Mhammad al-Kabir is a *qubba* located on a hill-top overlooking the valley, whereas one *qubba* and two *kurbi* shrines, all three[7] called Sidi Mhammad al-Wilda, are found at a distance of 1 to 1.5 km south of Sidi Mhammad al-Kabir. In the same valley, four shrines associated with the saint Sidi Bu-Qasbaya exist, all of them fairly large *mzaras*; the shrines of Sidi Bu-Qasbaya al-Wilda are situated at 0.3 and 1.5 km south and 0.5 km north of the parental shrine.

Here we encounter a most interesting phenomenon, which occurs time and again in saint worship featuring localized shrines[8]: the material multiplicity of shrines associated with one and the same saint tends to create several more or less autonomous cultic foci, despite the fact that the participants are fully aware that at all these shrines the same saint is venerated. Thus the various shrines of Sidi Mhammad and Bu-Qasbaya are each in their own right objects of ritual attention. Having a relationship with a saint does not mean that one can venerate that saint at just any shrine associated with him; one has also specific relationships with *shrines*. One cannot however visit any of the three shrines Sidi Mhammad al-Wilda unless as part of a ritual cycle which, within the same week or so, also includes a visit to Sidi Mhammad al-Kabir; and the rules of etiquette, which apply in man-saint relationships just as in man-man relationships, would suggest that one visits Sidi Mhammad al-Kabir first. The point is that the shrine, as a material entity, takes on a personalized and autonomous aspect more or less independent from the invisible saint to which it refers; for no participant would maintain that the saint venerated at the shrine of Sidi Mhammad al-Wilda is a son of the saint of the hill-top - *it is the shrine itself which is the child of the other shrine*, and which functions as an irreducible focus of ritual action rather irrespective of the saint with which it is associated. This is summarized in the Khrumiri maxim: "*barāka waḥada; nzūru kūll*" ("it is the same grace, but we visit them all"). And it is precisely the shrines' capability of taking on such cultic autonomy which enables them to function as beacons in the segmentary structure, even when so many shrines bear the same name.

The reader may have noticed that for the highest territorial levels no characteristic attributes have been mentioned. Major shrines, with or without adjacent cemeteries, function as such. As in the nineteenth century, every Khrumiri valley has a major shrine which serves as its characteristic attribute, and which provides a focus for ritual interaction and identification for people whose life-world is contained within the same steep mountain ranges, even though their day-to-day economic, social and political lives, as members of different villages, only infrequently intersect. But there is more. While the attachment of more or less utilitarian characteristic attributes (dwelling-house, threshing-floor, spring, men's assembly) to territorial segments could be seen as a spilling-over, into the symbolic order, of the essentials of the economic and social process, this system is again duplicated in this sense that lesser shrines, in addition to these utilitarian attributes, can be seen to function as ritual attributes of lower-level segments, from the compound level onwards. There are too many territorial segments at the lower levels to make it possible for each segment to be uniquely and exclusively associated with one local shrine. Patterns of shrine ritual are however such that each segment above the household level can be said to be characterized by a fairly unique pattern of saint veneration, in which a number of shrines, venerated with different frequency and intensity, combine in a manner that is manifestly and characteristically different from the combination obtaining in complementary segments. In ways which will become increasingly clear in the course of my argument, shrines are intimately associated with segments; and as can be shown on the basis of a detailed reconstruction of the residential history of the valley of Sidi Mhammad and adjacent valleys since c. 1800, the creation of filial shrines of the saints Sidi Mhammad and Sidi Bu-Qasbaya is a direct reflection of the fission, migration, and relative waxing and waning of social groups in that area since the middle of the last century. These processes occur throughout Khrumiriya, and invariably find expression in the geographical distribution, and nomenclature, of shrines.

However, the fictive genealogy of humans, encompassing all living inhabitants of the valley via the ancestral toponyms of their villages and neighbourhoods, is never systematically mirrored by a fictive genealogy encompassing all saints and shrines in a valley - easily a score or more. The multiplicity of shrines associated with the same saint, and the non-kin relations supposed to exist between many saints whose shrines are situated near each other, render such a saintly genealogy impossible. Shrine and segment are united not through a saintly parallel of human genealogical fictions, but through patterns of pious visits establishing relationships between saints and the living.

5. Saints and the living

Let us therefore now turn from saint-saint relationships to the relationships that the people of Khrumiriya claim to exist between living men, and saints. There is no doubt as to the human nature of saints. However exalted their powers and grace are, the legends about them depict them as recognizable human beings, whose exploits of piety and wonder-working often contain a touch of humour and human weakness. The extremely complex and protean semantic and symbolic properties of sainthood in Khrumiriya cannot be adequately summarized here. For instance, to stress that saints (as indicated by their most frequent designation: *ulī*) are Allah's friends and derive their *baraka* from Him, would underplay the fact that for most practical and ritual purposes Khrumiri saints (not unlike the several shrines with which they are associated) are conceived as autonomous supernatural beings, whose dealings with living humans hardly require Allah's rubber-stamp.

Saints have the power to open up the potentialities of nature and human life for those humans who approach them in the proper manner, i.e. respectfully, sincerely (*qalb bahi*), and with pure intention (*nīya*). There are few provinces of life that are considered to be outside the power of saintly intervention. Saints are invoked to send rain, to assist in the reproduction of domestic animals, to cure madness and reproductory troubles in humans, to enhance the general economic and physical well-being of the family, to control and ward off *jnūn* (spirits of the wilds), to enhance the *baraka* of the house, the threshing-floor, the spring and the men's assembly, to protect people who depart on a long journey, to help people in their careers, to render supernatural sanctions to oaths, to inflict misfortune on humans at the request of their human rivals, etc.

Much of this saintly intervention is taken for granted, as the automatic result of the routine aspects of the saintly cult in which every Khrumiri is involved: the frequent invocation of the names of local saints, the regular dedication of a meal to a specific saint, and the pious visit (*zyara*), at least twice a year, to the local shrine or shrines of that saint. At the latter occasion a small offering of incense and candles is left at the shrine, and specially prepared and dedicated oil cakes are consumed, which after having been consecrated at the shrine, are full of the saint's *baraka*. This ongoing routine of the saintly cult is characterized by great spontaneity, fondness and trustful reliance implied in the main descriptive (as distinct from addressive) kinship term Khrumiri people employ for their local saints: *jaddi*, *jadda* (my grandfather, my grandmother). Although immensely powerful, the saint is not usually thought of as a stern figure of authority, but rather as a grandparent who, like a real grandparent, can afford to spoil his grandchildren, the living humans, since their disciplining is left to an intermediate generation. This quality of fond intimacy stands out clearly when people recount hagiographic legends about their saint, share a meal dedicated to him or her, or when women, in the course of *zyara*, shed their socially-imposed reticence, and in near-ecstacy dance near the shrine, fondle and kiss the walls and the sacred objects there, and exclaim "*jaddi*", "*jaddna*" ("grandad", "our grandad").

While the saint, deceased and invisible, is considered a grandparent, the kinship term *jadda* carries an interesting additional connotation: it also means lineal or collatoral ancestor in general. Supposed (often erroneously) to be buried at the main shrine that carries his or her name, the Khrumiri saint is considered to have lived in the same area in some undefined past, and to be, somehow, among the set of local ancestors. But never is the saint the imputed apical ancestor of a social group, to whom descent is traced through a genealogy. Likewise, the ancestors that gave their names to social and territorial units at various levels of segmentation, are never saints. The two sets of personalized historical symbols do not overlap. In rare cases a saint is claimed to have been a brother of a local apical ancestor, but it turned out to be impossible to let participants pinpoint any living lineal descendants of the saints venerated at local shrines; even when my own historical research convinced me that at least one of these saints, Sidi Mhammad, had actually lived in the area during the nineteenth century, and I thought I could identify his living descendants whose saintly origins had gone lost under the historical and ideological constructions of the contemporary participants.

Outside the ongoing routine of the saintly cult, there are three complementary modalities for the relationship between man and saint, in addition to the trustful intimacy of the grandparent idiom.

First, in particularly important matters the implicit reliance on saintly intervention tends to give way to explicit *supplication*. Reminding the saint of the supplicant's ritual prestations in the past, and stressing the (fictive) kinship relation between man and saint, the supplicant describes his or her plight and entreats the saint to intervene. Such supplication normally takes place at the saint's main shrine, in the course of *zyara*. All the predicaments summed up above may apply. Normally supplication is made to one of the saints associated with the territorial segment to which the supplicant belongs. In rare cases, however, typically having to do with illness and impaired human fertility, supplication may be made at distant shrines, associated with one of the regional saints that are well-known throughout Khrumiriya. On such occasions the usual, small pious gifts are augmented by more substantial offerings, such as: an expensive, elaborately adorned candle; a flag; a meal dedicated to the saint and eaten at home; a similar meal but prepared at the shrine and distributed *gratis* among passers-by; and, as the highest prestation stipulated in the Khrumiri saintly cult, the sacrifice of a domestic animal (chicken, goat, sheep, cow, or bull - in a dramatically increasing order of cost, prestige and supernatural pay-off).

Secondly, the prestations accompanying such supplication often assume a *conditional* aspect. The saint whose special intervention is requested with regard to a specific problem, is promised a substantial offering, only to be made if the saintly intervention turns out to be successful: if a previously barren woman produces a child, if a mental patient regains sanity, etc. Often these conditional promises take on the nature of a gamble. Thus saintly protection over a herd of cattle or a brood of hens is ensured by promising the saint a male specimen of that year's calves or chicks as a sacrifice; if no males are produced, the saint has to accept that his intervention will go unrewarded that year.

Supplications, particularly if of a conditional nature, introduce a contractual element into the man-saint relationship, that stands in some tension with the inclusive, generalized pattern of the grandparent model. Here the saint appears more as a patron. However, both as a patron with whom one has struck a dyadic, conditional contract, and as a grandparent, the man-saint relationship carries, as a third modality, many *obligations* for the people involved. However much a saint is supposed to love his living protégés and clients, however much he is prepared to intercede on their behalf, every saint insists on respectful treatment. The same *baraka* that can, positively, release the possibilities of nature and human life to the people's benefit, is sure to inflict material misfortune, illness and death, should the people fail in respect, and neglect their general and contractual obligations *vis-a-vis* a saint. On the basis of these sanctions, the saint protects the integrity of his shrine, the sacred objects and pious gifts it contains, and the immediately surrounding area. The dead that may be buried there, remain undisturbed; and the trees, plants and animals there are taboo. He also protects his shrine-keepers, and pilgrims in the course of *zyara*. He does not allow people to terminate their relationship with him: whoever has entered, at some point in his life, into a relationship with a saint, is under a life-long obligation to make the twice-annual *zyara* to his shrine and to dedicate meals for him. The saint is supposed to jealously guard his human following against the claims of other saints. Thus the cult of saints acquires an internal momentum of its own which allows it to express and underpin, at its turn, non-religious aspects of life in Khrumiriya.

6. Segmentation and types of zyara

The principal set of people who have a definite relationship with a particular saint are the actual members (i.e. inhabitants) of the territorial segment with which that saint is associated. All these people, male and female, must partake in the routines of the saintly cult, including dedication of meals, at least twice-annual *zyara*, and observance of the saint's festival.

Male members of the segment are not under formal obligations of *zyara*, although many of them do visit, as individuals, the shrines, and attend the festivals, of the major saints in their own valley and adjacent valleys. Some men are involved in the saintly cult as ritual specialists: as shrine-keepers, and as members of the ecstatic cult in whose songs local saints feature along with international saints, and demons. For most purposes, men rely on the women in their households and compounds to deal with the local saints. Yet men who intend to definitively settle elsewhere, in the realm of a different saint, will find their plans crossed by dreams and omens through which the saint protests against their absconding.

Women, through their dedication of meals and their *zyara*, carry the bulk of the saintly cult in Khrumiriya.

This ritual involvement of women is intimately linked to the marriage pattern. Marriage is virilocal: both according to the rule and in c. 95% of actual practice. And since no woman marries into the household in which she was born, every marriage involves a woman's crossing of segmentary boundaries at least at the lowest level of segmentation (in the rare case she marries within the same compound). Like other Islamic societies, an explicit rule as to the preference of agnatic endogamy exists in Khrumiriya. Demographic processes, the dynamics of marital alliance, the essentially bilateral kinship system hiding under the patrilineal idiom, and the intergenerational transfer of property, however, are much more complex than that they could be summarized, at the analytical level, by the participants' ideology of patrilateral parallel-cousin marriage. This is not the place to present my very extensive data on this point. Let it suffice to say that roughly 50% of contemporary marriages involve partners belonging to different villages, each with their own distinct set of local shrines and saints. A village-exogamous marriage means that a woman leaves her original set of village-level local shrines behind and adopts a new set, that of her husband's female consanguineal relatives. It is part of a woman's extensive incorporation into her husband's segment[9] that she fully adopts the shrines of that group. Within the compound, hamlet and neighbourhood, elder women co-ordinate food production, food processing, water hauling and firewood collection. From these female leaders the in-marrying woman will learn about the identity and relative importance of the segment's shrines and saints. She will soon dedicate some of her household meals to these saints, and join the other women in collective *zyara* to the shrines. However, she will not as a rule give up her relationship with the shrines in her original segment. Although a woman will not often leave the immediate environment of the village for the purpose of visiting relatives, the hospital, the market, or diviners, she has an unalienable right to visit her original shrines, and thus her segment of origin and her relatives there, twice a year.

A married woman is involved in two complementary sets of relationship with saints - which mirrors, and in fact sustains, her involvement in both her original segment and that of her husband. The picture is further complicated by the *relative* nature of segmentation. The greater the segmentary distance a woman crosses for marriage, the more different the two sets of shrines will be. If she marries in a different village within the same valley, the two sets will overlap in that the valley's main shrine and festival will be part of both sets; in that case marriage will only add a few lesser shrines of her husband's segment (at the village, neighbourhood, hamlet and compound level) to the woman's pre-existing set. With intra-village local endogamy (c. 50% of all marriages) the differences will be even less significant, and in fact the set of shrines before and after marriage may entirely coincide. The differences are far more conspicuous in the case of a marriage linking people from different valleys or even chiefdoms. But the principles remain the same throughout.

Thus every Khrumiri woman has *zyara* obligations *vis-à-vis* the local shrines associated with the territorial segment (or better: nested hierarchy of segments at various levels) to which she belongs at a given point in time; for descriptive purposes, this type of *zyara* will be called *local zyara*. In addition, all women who have migrated from their segment of birth, i.e. mainly in the context of marriage, retain *zyara* obligations *vis-à-vis* the local shrines in that segment; this type of *zyara* will be called *original zyara*. For the sake of completeness, we should not overlook the fact that marriage is the main, but not the exclusive occasion for a woman to adopt a new set of *zyara* obligations: when the household of which she is a dependent member takes up residence elsewhere, a similar situation obtains regardless of her marital status. However, such cases are so rare as compared with the virtual universality of marriage among Khrumiri women, that they require no separate treatment.

Local zyara comes with actual membership of (i.e. residence in) a territorial segment, and unites all adult women of that segment under a female leader. The latter co-ordinates the collective *zyara* of the segment's women to the local shrines, as part of her general tasks of female leadership. In fact these collective visits to local shrines present an amazing spectacle of territorial segmentation in action. At the occasion of the festival of a valley's or village's main shrine, the various female leaders of segments will have agreed on a time for collective *zyara*. Compound by compound, hamlet by hamlet, neighbourhood by neighbourhood, one will see small groups of women in their best clothes converge along the village path, and team up on their way to the shrine, only to break up again, segment-wise, on their return. Alternatively, the fact that virtually every woman in a compound, hamlet and neighbourhood derives obligations of *original zyara* from her own, unique life history, endows her with an individuality in the religious sphere which she will normally be allowed to maintain despite strong social pressures towards incorporation in her husband's segment. The frequent attribution of misfortune to irate, neglected saints suggests however both the practice of individual shedding of original *zyara* obligations, and the deep-lying tensions in the marital and inter-generational sphere that would seem to attend the incorporation process.

Personal zyara to major regional saints in the context of illness or infertility results, finally, in the third type of women's *zyara* obligations in Khrumiriya. For here again the norm applies that a living human cannot at his or her own initiative terminate a relationship with a saint once entered into. For a variety of reasons (which seem to include female under-nutrition; a very low marital age of women before marital legislation was revised in the 1960s; and a repressive sexual culture instilling profound fears and sexual inhibitions in young people of both sexes) many Khrumiri women are recorded to have suffered from impaired fertility in the first years of their marriage. In order to remedy this complaint, women would often resort to pilgrimage to distant shrines of regional saints outside the set of shrines falling under local or original *zyara* obligations. The personal relationship between a woman and a regional saint invoked for reproductory troubles would ideally last a lifetime; in later years, as a woman would take her daughters and daughters-in-law with her on this personal *zyara*, the younger generation would automatically inherit this relationship, even though the regional shrine would be too distant to be listed among the territorial segment's local *zyara* obligations.

Numerous are the cases when material misfortune, illness and even death are attributed (via various techniques of divination) to irate saints revenging humans' lack of respect, breach of promises, failure to dedicate meals and make pious visits, or neglect of duties *vis-à-vis* one saint while honouring the expectations of another saint. Since Khrumiri saints are shown to embody, on the one hand, concepts of intra-kin intimacy and inter-generational relations, on the other hand a structure of complementary opposition of segments, it will be obvious - even without a discussion of specific cases - that the social, mental and psycho-somatic dramas enacted in such cases reveal deeply-rooted tensions and contradictions within the Khrumiri social process and symbolic order. However, an explanation of misfortune like the Khrumiri one would represent a welcome escape clause in any religious system: given a certain degree of recognized non-observance of rules and of opportunism[10] among the living humans involved, the supernatural entities invoked are free to honour or to ignore human requests without succumbing to their professional disease: credibility gap. In fact, not all Khrumiri women attend to their original and personal *zyara* obligations with equal zeal; the factors apparently determining this variation in religious behaviour will be discussed below.

In modern anthropology, paradigmatic consistency and elegance have become reasons for healthy mistrust. Therefore, the above generalized description of the saintly cult, and particularly of *zyara*, in contemporary Khrumiriya needs to be substantiated with evidence on actual religious behaviour as stipulated by the models and rules described here. We find ourselves here in the somewhat exceptional situation that such evidence is, in fact, available, and that it corroborates the generalized description with amazing precision.

7. Local zyara in the valley of Sidi Mhammad

In the remaining sections of this chapter I shall describe the patterns of local, original and personal *zyara* as found among the adult women inhabiting the villages of Sidi Mhammad and Mayzīya, in the valley of Sidi Mhammad.

The data were collected in 1968, at a point in my field-work when I had sufficiently mastered the principles of Khrumiri popular religion and society to phrase my questions properly; and when my stay in the village of Sidi Mhammad had generated a sufficient amount of trust and rapport to allow me to systematically interview the majority of the adult female population in both villages. In Sidi Mhammad, of the total population of 42 resident adult women, 35 (=83%) were thus interviewed. The 17% non-response could be shown to form an a-select sample from the total population of 42, with regard to important background variables: relative economic position of their household; number of years of their marriage had lasted; geographical distance across which their marriage had been contracted. (See Table 1, p.217). My data on Mayziya are less complete: they adequately cover local *zyara*, but show gaps with regard to original and personal *zyara*. The analysis of the latter two types (section 8) will exclusively be based on Sidi Mhammad data.

Zyara is public behaviour and moreover a source of prestige and *baraka*. It is therefore discussed without reticence, even when the interviewer is a young male foreigner. The interview data were checked against: observational data concerning the various types of *zyara*; systematically elicited statements about the *zyara* behaviour of neighbours; and many accidental statements uttered during everyday conversations or open-ended interviews. The correspondence between these data proved to be almost 100%. Moreover the data show great internal consistency, particularly in the extent to which the responses and observational data on local *zyara* converge for the several women of each segment. This convergence could hardly be a research artifact, because when I collected the data I was not even beginning to realize that Khrumiri social organization could be described with a model of territorial segmentation. For all these reasons I consider the data to be of good quality, and amenable to such non-parametric statistical tests as I shall perform upon them.[11]

The valley of Sidi Mhammad stretches from south to north along the Wad al-Kabīr, a river whose tributaries have their sources at the highest peaks of Khrumiriya, and which flows into the Mediterranean near the town of Tabarka, c. 15 km north of Sidi Mhammad.

Diagram 2 (see p.218) shows the wider surroundings of the valley. This diagram conveys the remarkably small geographical scale of the phenomena at hand. The valley of Sidi Mhammad has an area of about 10 km^2, and comprises only six villages: Sidi Mhammad, Mayziya, Tra^{c}āya-sud, Tra^{c}āya-bīdh, Fīdh al-Missāy and Raml al-^{c}Atrūs; together these villages comprise c. 600 inhabitants. Movement between villages is mainly on foot, and here the mountainous terrain imposes severe constraints. Thus from Sidi Mhammad it takes people half a day to

(a) duration of marriage (years)*

		2	3	6	8	10	16	18	20	23	24	25	28	30	33	38	total
number of women	in response group	1	0	1	1	1	0	1	1	1	1	1	1	1	1	1	13
	in non-response group	0	1	0	1	0	1	0	0	0	0	1	0	0	0	0	4

Mann-Whitney U-test, corrected for ties: z = 1.13; p = .13

(b) distance across which marriage was contracted (km)

		.0	.1	.2	.3	.4	.5	.6	.7	1.1	1.3	1.4	1.8	2.3	2.5	2.6	3.0	3.5	6.2	7.8	10.2	total
number of women	in response group	0	7	6	4	2	3	2	0	1	1	1	0	2	0	2	1	1	1	1	0	35
	in non-response group	1	0	0	0	0	0	1	1	1	0	0	1	0	1	0	0	0	0	0	1	7

Mann-Whitney U-test, corrected for ties: z = -1.36; p = .09

(c) relative economic position of household ⊕

		poor	medium	wealthy	total
number of women	in response group	21	11	3	35
	in non-response group	2	2	2	6

Mann-Whitney U-test, corrected for ties: z = 1.11; p = .13

*the analysis is limited to women resident in the village of Sidi Mhammad but born in a different village

⊕one woman was omitted from the analysis since the wealth of her household could not be assessed with certainty

Table 1. Zyara among women resident in the village of Sidi Mhammad: comparison of response and non-response groups.

N.B. Homran and Sidi Bu-Naqa of Homran not shown in exact location

Diagram 2. Selected shrines in Khrumiriya.

reach the major regional shrine of Sidi ^{c}Abd Allah bi-Jamal, a distance of barely 10 km as the crow flies. Such a distance forms in fact the effective maximal radius for most purposes of inter-village contacts, including *zyara* and marriage. While illustrating this point, table 2 suggests that structures of *zyara*, and the affinal networks created by marriage, together constitute one relational region, of the sort which Meillassoux has called a marriage field (*aire matrimoniale*, Meillassoux 1964:11 and *passim*).

	range (km)	median (km)
distance across which marriages are contracted	.1 - 7.8	.45
distance across which shrines are visited (all types of *zyara* combined)	.0 - 10.1	.55

Table 2. A comparison of geographical distances across which women resident in the village of Sidi Mhammad visit shrines and across which the marriages of these women have been contracted.

Like Sidi ^{c}Abd Allah bi-Jamal, Sidi Mhammad is a regional saint. The latter's twice-annual festival lasts for several days and nights. In addition to the people of the valley itself, who are under obligations of local *zyara*, the festival attracts, from all over Khrumiriya, scores of women who are under obligation of original or personal *zyara*, and moreover scores of male pilgrims, as well as musicians, showmen, ecstatic dancers, butchers, and peddlers in sweets, candles, incense, haberdashery, etc. While the saint Sidi Mhammad is locally represented by no less than four shrines including two *qubbas*, he is by no means the only saint of the valley. Diagram 3 (see p.220) shows, in their relative position *vis-à-vis* the dwelling-houses, the location of the eighteen shrines that are found in the immediate environment of the villages of Sidi Mhammad and Mayziya alone. Table 3 summarizes the names and physical characteristics of these shrines (see p.221).

A minority of the local shrines are surrounded by cemeteries, and a segment's right to bury its dead in a particular cemetery, i.e. near a particular shrine, is an important expression of the segmentary structure. However, this aspect is not dealt with in my present argument, which concentrates on *zyara*. Of the shrines listed in table 3, the numbers 1 and 8 are surrounded by cemeteries that are still in

Diagram 3. Shrines and dwelling-houses in the villages of Sidi Mhammad and Mayziya.

no. in diagram 3	name	physical characteristics
1	Sidi Mhammad al-Kabir	*qubba*
2	Sidi Mhammad al-Wilda	*qubba*
3	Sidi Mhammad (al-Wilda)	*kurbi*
4	Sidi Mhammad (al-Wilda)	*kurbi*
5	Sidi Bu-Qasbaya al-Kabir	*mzara*
6	Sidi Bu-Qasbaya al-Wilda	*mzara*
7	Sidi Bu-Qasbaya al-Wilda	*mzara*
8	Sidi Rhūma	*mzara*
9	Sidi Bu-Naqa	*mzara*
10	ᶜA'isha	*mzara*
11	Mzara ᶜAin Raml	*mzara*
12	Hashārat al-Brīk	*mzara*
13	Sidi Hamād	*mzara*
14	Sidi Bel-Ahsīn	*mzara*
15	Jadda Massauda	*mzara*
16	ᶜAli ᶜAbu 'l-Qāssim	*mzara*
17	Sidi Bu-Kharuba	*mzara*
18	Hashārat al-Fras	*mzara*

Table 3. Names and physical characteristics of shrines in the villages of Sidi Mhammad and Mayziya.

use, whereas abandoned cemeteries are found around the shrines 5 and 7, as well as several hundred meters south of 9 and 13.

Moreover, many of the saints listed in table 3 have shrines elsewhere, outside the villages of Sidi Mhammad and Mayziya; those distant shrines are not listed here. The local *zyara* pattern in those two villages is confined to the eighteen shrines of table 3.[12]

In order to assess whether the pattern of local *zyara* as found in these two villages is in fact governed by territorial segmentation, we have to go through a number of steps. First, the dwelling-houses, representing the lowest level of segmentation, have to be clustered into higher-level segments, according to their location, to the visible boundaries by which they are surrounded, and to the distribution of utilitarian characteristic attributes (threshing-floors, springs, men's assemblies) over the clusters thus formed. The outcome of this exercise is shown in diagram 4 (see p.222).

The following step is the tracing of the specific pattern of local *zyara* which obtains in each of the territorial segments thus distinguished. A problem arising at this point is that there are far fewer local shrines than territorial segments. The choice is further limited by the fact that not all shrines are vailable in the same

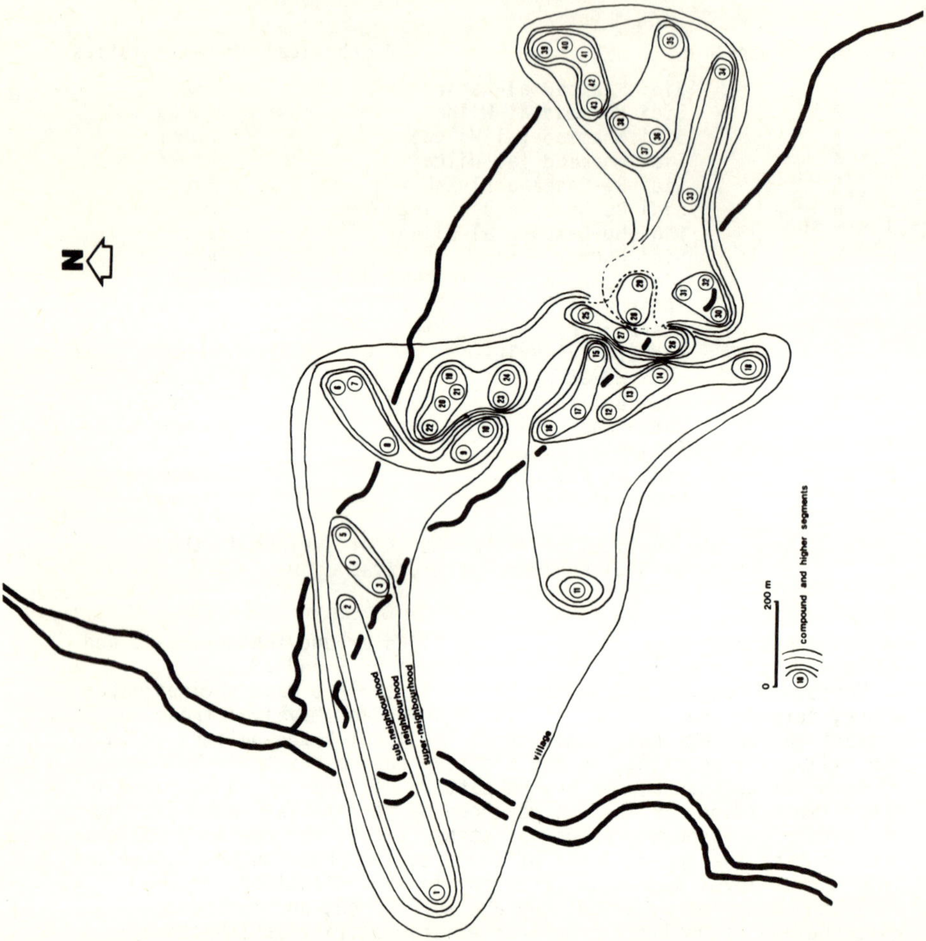

Diagram 4. Territorial segments in the villages of Sidi Mhammad and Mayziya.

degree as additional, religious attributes of segments. For two adjacent lower-level territorial segments, which are complementary in that they both form part of a higher segment at the next hierarchical level, it would be impossible to express their segmentary opposition by differential patronage of some very minor shrine situated at a considerable distance, say at the other end of the village: the catchment area of that shrine would be too small to reach as far as these segments. Similarly, these segments could not distinguish themselves by differential patronage of the village's or valley's main shrine, for that shrine would already function as the additional, religious attribute of a higher segment encompassing both lower-level segments.

Two devices combine so as to solve these dilemmas. First, non-patronage, even of a nearby shrine or combination of nearby shrines, can mark a territorial segment just as much as positive local *zyara*. Secondly, segments can distinguish among themselves not only through the selection or non-selection of local shrines in a particular combination, but also through differences in *frequency* with which the selected shrines are actually visited. Twice-annual *zyara* constitutes a minimal frequency for any shrine; four times a year is an average frequency for shrines that are visited with more than minimal zeal. As marking devices, non-patronage and differential frequency dramatically increase the number of possible combinations given a limited number of shrines; yet it must be admitted that differential frequency introduces a non-discrete element that somewhat spoils the neat, digital combinatory logic of the segmentation model.

These devices are clearly at work in the pattern of local *zyara* in the village of Sidi Mhammad and Mayziya, as shown in diagram 5 (see p.224). Here for all compounds of both villages the associated patterns of local *zyara* are shown, on the basis of the interview and observational data discussed above. Combining the information of diagrams 4 and 5 results in diagram 6, which presents the segment's differential local *zyara* patterns in the familiar dendrogram format (see p.225).

A number of conclusions can be based on diagram 6. Clearly, territorial segmentation provides the key to existing structures of local *zyara*. Territorial segments, whose existence is marked by visible boundaries and the distribution of utilitarian characteristic attributes, distinguish themselves in the religious sphere by the veneration of specific combinations of local shrines, in specific frequencies. What emanates clearly from diagram 6 is the fact that complementary opposition in segmentation only refers to one level at the same time, irrespective of the distribution of distinctive features at higher or lower levels. Thus segments 1.1.2 and 1.2.2 can afford to be both associated with shrines 1, 2 and 3, which both segments visit frequently. There is no direct complementary opposition

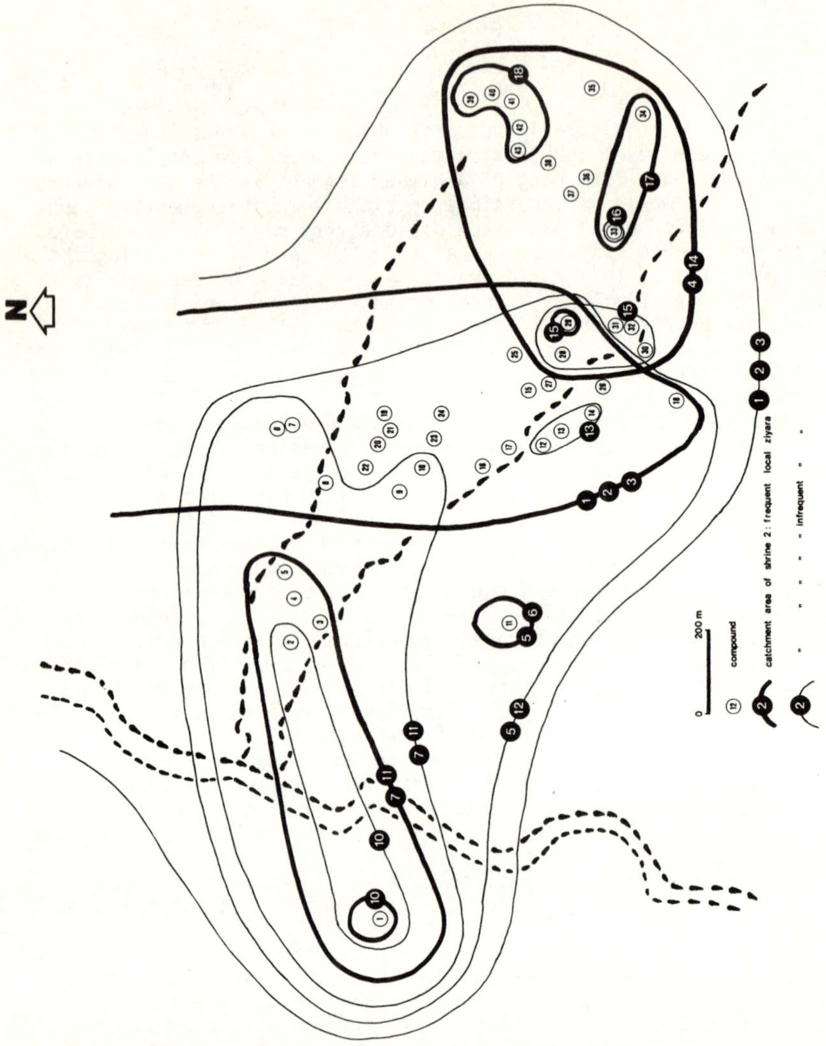

Diagram 5. Shrines' catchment areas with regard to local *zyara*, in the villages of Sidi Mhammad and Mayziya.

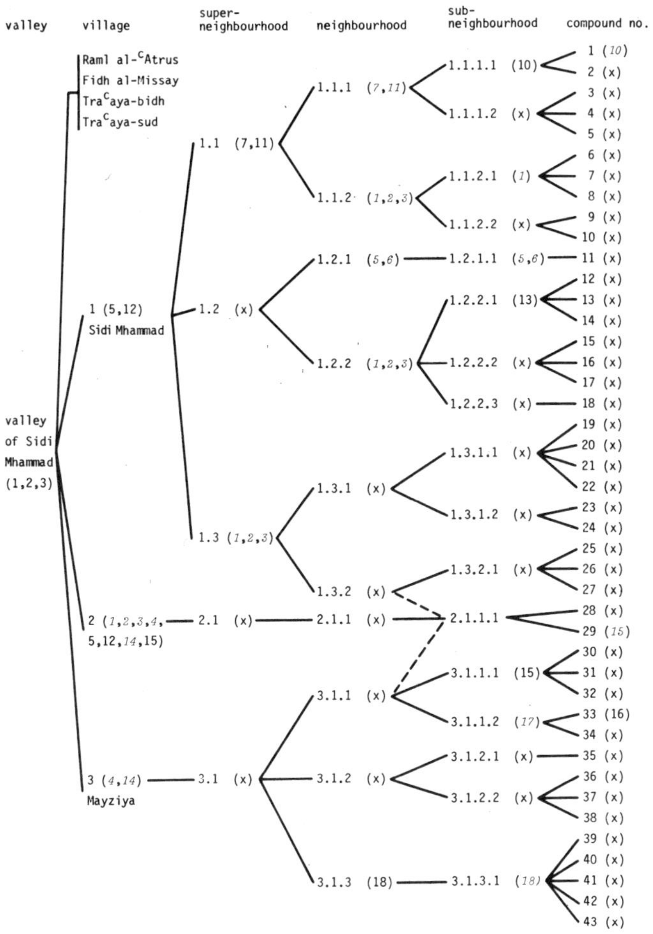

Diagram 6. Dendrogram representation of the differential patterns of local *zyara* among the territorial segments in the villages of Sidi Mhammad and Mayziya.

Key: Compounds and shrines are numbered as in diagrams 3, 4 and 5; the numerical coding of higher-level segments is self-explanatory. The numbers between brackets following a segment's numerical code indicate a shrine or shrines which the members of that segment visit frequently (shrine code italicized) or infrequently (shrine code in roman). (x) indicates that no specific positive *zyara* behaviour, but rather its absence, characterizes the segment in question at that hierarchical level.

between these two segments, since they belong to different higher-level segments (1.1 and 1.2 respectively), and the difference between the latter is marked by shrines 7 and 11. The complementary segment of 1.1.2 is 1.1.1 (this difference is marked by frequent visiting of shrines 7 and 11, as against shrines 1, 2 and 3); the complementary segment of 1.2.2. is 1.2.1, with differences being marked by frequent visiting of shrines 5 and 6 as against 1, 2 and 3, respectively. The inclusion of complementary segments in higher-level segments renders the combinatory logic of characteristic attributes more complicated, but does not destroy it.

However, while the model fits empirical reality amazingly well, the fit is, of course, not 100%. Not all complementary segments at all levels are marked by differential local *zyara*. Thus the sub-neighbourhoods 1.2.2.3, 1.3.1.1, 1.3.1.2 and 1.3.2.1 have an identical pattern of local *zyara*.

Moreover it turns out that, insofar local *zyara* is concerned, three and not two segmentary levels are to be distinguished between compound level and village level; this is particularly the case in the village of Sidi Mhammad. Environmental conditions and the ongoing dynamics of territorial segmentation can explain these deviations from the simpler model. Permanent water supplies are scarcer in Sidi Mhammad than in Mayziya: in the former village there are 9 to 17 households to one permanent water source, against only 8 to 9 in Mayziya. Hence the spring-defined neighbourhoods are in fact considerably larger in Sidi Mhammad than in Mayziya, and begin to approach villages. This process of segmentation also manifests itself in the erection of a separate men's assembly in the southern part of the village of Sidi Mhammad (super-neighbourhood 1.1, called Qā^{c}a-Raml), and in the growing expression of antagonism between people from that part and the rest of the village. The complex historical background, involving competition between rival clans, aspirations of political leadership, the vicissitudes of marriage alliances, the effects of the establishment of a colonist's farm near Qa^{c}a-Raml, and the differential use of cemeteries, cannot be elaborated upon here (Van Binsbergen 1971a, 1980a, 1980b).

The ongoing segmentation process also explains the ambiguous position sub-neighbourhood 2.1.1.1 occupies in the dendrogram. But here we encounter not fission (as in the Qa^{c}a-Raml case), but fusion: the segment in question, straddling the boundary between the two villages, historically forms part of Mayziya, but its members have established strong ties of marriage and clientship with their present neighbours, the administrative chief's family; the latter's residence in the village of Sidi Mhammad dates back to the 1910s.[13]

Rather than upsetting the model of territorial segmentation as governing local *zyara*, these deviations show that model to be dynamic, and capable of responding to the realities of the social and ecological process. Let us now turn to the quantitative data concerning original and personal *zyara*: forms of religious behaviour that cut across, instead of express, the pattern of territorial segmentation.

8. Original and personal zyara in the village of Sidi Mhammad

Turning now to non-local *zyara*, we should first assess the relative incidence of the three types of *zyara*.

The 35 systematically interviewed women in Sidi Mhammad observed between them 232 *zyara* obligations *vis-à-vis* shrines in Khrumiriya. Of these, 219 (=94%) involved local *zyara*. Each woman observed an average of 6.6 *zyara* obligations, the total range stretching from 5 to 10. Of this average of 6.6, an average 6.3 involved local *zyara* (range 5-8, as can be read from diagram 6). The fact that many shrines are associated with the same saint, means that the number of observed *zyara* obligations *vis-à-vis* different saints is lower than that *vis-à-vis* shrines. The women of the sample have an average of 4.1 (range 3-7) observed *zyara* relations with saints, out of which an average of 3.7 (range 3-5) involve saints associated with the local segments these women belong to at the several hierarchical levels. These data on *zyara relationships* can be converted into figures on *actual pious visits made*, by taking differential frequency into account. Per period of six months, the women of the sample make 342 *zyaras* between them, of which 329 (=96%) are local *zyaras*, 10 (=3%) are originial *zyaras*, and only 4 (=1%) are personal *zyaras*. These figures must be considered estimates. Yet they convincingly demonstrate the overwhelming preponderance of local *zyara*, as stipulated by the structure of territorial segmentation, over the non-local forms that cut across the segmentary structure.

It is virtually impossible for a woman to resist the strong social pressure and the supernatural sanctions that prompt her participation in the collective local *zyara* of the segment in which she is resident. Original and personal *zyara*, however, are a more individual matter, and here observance of existing obligations shows considerable variation.

The positive data on *personal zyara* are too limited to allow statistical analysis. The three women concerned are between forty and sixty years old. They have exceptionally high prestige and power because of their age, their very close kinship relations with administrative chiefs, and the wealth of their households. Two are effective female leaders of their neighbourhoods, and as such co-ordinate local *zyara*. Their maintaining of personal *zyara* relations with distant shrines, nearly all of which are of regional importance, adds to their local prestige, and renders further independence to their religious and social behaviour as individuals. Moreover, they would hardly be able to fulfil their personal *zyara* obligations if their social position did not provide them with the financial means to undertake a long journey, and with an extensive regional network of social contacts on which they can rely during that journey and at the distant shrine. The data strongly suggest that many other women in the sample contracted personal *zyara* obligations at some time in their lives, but had to drop them because of their less exalted social position within their segments of residence.

Original zyara is a somewhat more common phenomenon. Here we can draw on two sets of data: data on the women resident in Sidi Mhammad; and on the set of women who originate from that village and who (according to the converging evidence of observational data and interviews) either observe, or fail to observe, their obligations of original *zyara vis-à-vis* the regional shrines of Sidi Mhammad.

Since about 50% of all marriages are contracted within the same village, and since (cf. diagram 6) not all segments within a village differ as to the set of shrines to which local *zyara* is directed (although frequencies of *zyara* tend to differ), not all women in the sample acquired obligations of original *zyara* at marriage. In fact, only 14 women in the sample did so (=40%); for the remaining 60%, local *zyara* and original *zyara* entirely coincide.

Of these 14 women, 7 (=50%) observe their original *zyara* obligations, while 7 (=50%) do not. Table 4 makes clear that the relative importance of shrines is a crucial factor here. Such importance is measured by the following indicators: the segmentary level at which the shrine functions as an additional, religious attribute; the physical characteristics of the shrine (*qubba*, *kurbi* or *mzara*); and the existence of a twice-annual festival for that shrine.

importance	range of geographical distance (km)	number of observances	number of non-observances	total
high	2.6 - 8.8	8	1	9
middle	.8 - 3.2	1	7	8
low	.1 - 2.1	0	5	5

Table 4. The observance of obligations of original *zyara* among women resident in the village of Sidi Mhammad, as a function of the importance of the original shrine, and of the geographical distance between that shrine and a woman's current place of residence.

Further statistical analysis (Van Binsbergen 1971a:286f) demonstrates that such conceivable factors as wealth, prestige, and the number of years elapsed since the woman, by marrying and taking up residence in her present segment, acquired obligations of original *zyara*, do not have a statistically significant impact on the observance of original *zyara* among the resident women of Sidi Mhammad.

These data are supplemented by those on women who, originating from Sidi Mhammad, have married outside and therefore are under obligations of original *zyara* focusing on the valley of Sidi Mhammad. The festival of Sidi Mhammad is the only occasion at which the necessary observational data can be collected; moreover it is by far the most important occasion for women to observe their original *zyara* obligations. For these reasons I shall concentrate here on *zyara* to the major, regional shrines of Sidi Mhammad, and ignore *zyara* to lesser shrines in the same valley. A fortunate implication is that thus importance of shrines as a factor determining observance of original *zyara* is kept constant, so that other factors may stand out more clearly. It is important to realize that in these cases we are dealing with women who have married not only outside the village, but also outside the valley of Sidi Mhammad - for all villages of that valley would make the pious visit to the shrines of Sidi Mhammad as part of their *local zyara* obligations.

On the basis of my village census and genealogies the full set of women involved can be identified. Limiting the analysis to those who currently live within a distance of 20 km (original *zyara* across wider distances would be practically impossible anyway), the set consists of 22 individuals, 15 of whom (=68%) actually observe original *zyara*, while 7 (=32%) do not.

While no data are available as to the wealth and prestige of these out-marrying women in their present, distant places of residence, the data reveal that the number of years elapsed since marriage (i.e. since the departure from the original segment) is significantly associated with observance of original *zyara* (table 5). All women who

		duration of marriage (years)									
		3	4	5	7	8	10	12	15	25	total
number of women	observing	1	1	4	2	2	2	1	1	1	15
	not observing	0	0	0	0	0	1	2	2	2	7

Mann-Whitney U-test, corrected for ties: $z = -2.81$; $p = .003$

Table 5. Observance of original *zyara* obligations among out-marrying women from Sidi Mhammad, as a function of the duration of marriage.

left the village for marriage ten years ago or less, stick to the rule; those who left longer ago, tend to drop observance. Duration of marriage seems to be a surface factor, underneath which a more important one is hidden: the residence, in the segment of origin, of a surviving parent (table 6). Of course, the longer a marriage has lasted, the older a woman is and the less likely she will have surviving parents.

	at least one parent alive, and resident in Sidi Mhammad	no parent resident in Sidi Mhammad	total
observance	12	3	15
non-observance	0	7	7
total	12	10	22

l=15.30; df=1; $p < .001$. The l-statistic has the same distribution as χ^2; cf. Spitz 1961.

Table 6. Observance of original *zyara* obligations, among out-marrying women from Sidi Mhammad, as a function of parents' residence in the segment of origin.

This factor points to the social functions of original *zyara*, as a unique opportunity to visit living kinsmen. Additional statistical analysis (Van Binsbergen 1971a:288f) however suggests that, besides sociability and psychological kin support in the vicissitudes of marriage and virilocal incorporation, another structural theme is involved here: the inter-generational transfer of property rights (particularly in relation with land, a scarce asset in Khrumiriya). The wish to keep in touch with consanguineal relatives around the original shrine is not a sufficient reason for original *zyara*; for observance of this type of *zyara* is not significantly associated with the residence, in the segment of origin, of an outmarrying woman's *brothers* - whatever the wealth of the latter. The continued residence of parents suggests an undivided patrimony. By keeping up visits to her segment of origin, the woman, in accordance with Khrumiri views on land tenure, asserts her right to a share equal to that of her male siblings. *De facto* these rights are waived as, after the father's death, the surviving sons administer the patrimony on their own behalf: initially under the direction of the eldest sons, until such time when fraternal rivalry necessitates division. At that point a reversal of visiting obligations can be seen: more fully incorporated in her husband's segment, the woman tends to drop her original *zyara* obligations, but instead her brothers are under obligation to visit her with presents at the day of the Great Festival (*ᶜĪd al-Kabīr, ᶜĪd al-Ādha*). The woman's sons, however, retain a latent right in the land administered by the mother's brothers, and in exceptional cases these rights are actually exercised, leading to a man's matrilocal residence.

Combining the evidence on Sidi Mhammad's resident women and out-marrying women, the main factors determining observance of original *zyara* obligations may be summarized as in diagram 7:

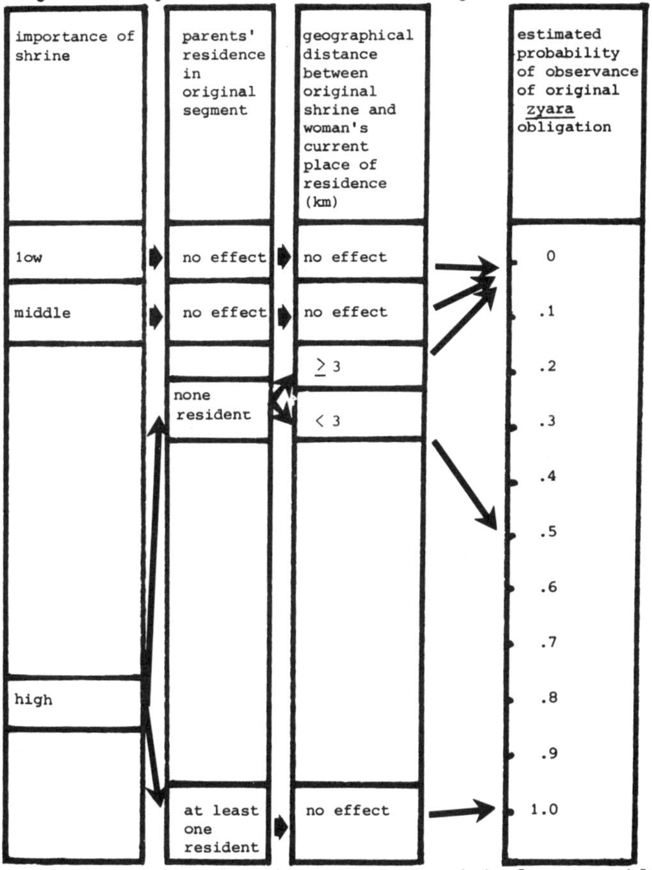

Diagram 7. Factors affecting observance of original *zyara* obligations.

9. Conclusion

The ethnography presented here clearly has many interesting openings towards central theoretical concerns in the social science of religion.

There is a striking Durkheimian suggestion of one-to-one correspondence in the extent to which the saint and his shrine seem to function, at all levels of social and ritual organization and experience, as a straightforward symbol of the social group with which they are associated. Alternatively, such cutting-across the overall structure of segmentation as can be seen in original and personal *zyara*, points to the potential of religion to provide alternatives to the structural arrangements that govern the more secular aspects of social life.

This calls to mind the theories of pilgrimage and regional cults as advanced by the Turners and by Richard Werbner (Turner 1974; Turner & Turner 1978; Werbner 1977). The possible contribution of the Khrumiri data to the further development of these theories would at first glance appear to be somewhat negative. Werbner, in an attempt to get away from the classic correspondence paradigm in religious anthropology, has stressed cultic regions' autonomy *vis-à-vis* processes of material production, secular social organization, and political structure. The Khrumiri case (of predominantly local *zyara*) however would be an example of extreme correspondence between cult and the secular societal process. Moreover, except in the relatively rare cases of original and personal *zyara*, which cut across segmentation, the more massive manifestations of the cult (at the village and valley level, and culminating in festivals) do not seem to involve principles different from those operating at the lowest level: the cult of inconspicuous *mzaras* that are tucked away in some corner of a compound and hamlet, and that have virtually no relevance beyond these small territorial units. In this respect the Khrumiri cult of saints, while clearly a regional cult in terms of geographical scope and number of people involved, would not stand out as one when its organizational structure is considered.

Similarly, it is only in personal *zyara* to distant saints - the expression of an atomized devotion - that the shrine appears, in Turner's terms, as the "Center Out There", and that his generalizations apply as to pilgrimage as a distinct social process in its own right. In local *zyara*, which constitutes the vast majority of pious visits in Khrumiriya, the shrine is not a distant place visited at the end of a long and arduous physical and spiritual journey across unknown parts - it has more the nature of a visit to a close and dearly-loved relative, involving a short passage through familiar surroundings, in the company of people one knows well and identifies with. It is for this reason that I have refrained, in this essay, from using the term *pilgrimage* - except in the title, for signalling purposes only.

Finally, while both authors would stress the dialectics of

inclusiveness/exclusiveness or universalism/particularism as the crux of the cults they describe, the Khrumiri data would suggest that this dialectic could hardly be adequately analysed on the level of popular religion alone. On the one hand the very same dialectic underlies the secular structure of segmentation (where the opposition of complementary segments is resolved at the next level of segmentary inclusion). On the other hand it is on this dialectic that the interplay revolves between formal and popular Islam (which the saints straddle, as epitomes of the former and yet cornerstones of the latter) (Van Binsbergen 1980a).

Another obvious dimension of the Khrumiri data concerns the dialectics between socio-economic structure and the symbolic order (Van Binsbergen 1981). The embeddedness of most of the cult of saints, through patterns of local *zyara*, in a segmentary organizational structure of localized social units entrusted with material production, biological reproduction, and with the regulation of the social relations upon which these fundamental processes depend, would suggest that in the cult
production find expression, and are in themselves being reproduced. Too little could be said here about these contradictions (mainly: those between men and women; and between human patrons and clients) to indicate their relation to the cult of saints. Moreover, the virtual coincidence (table 1) in Khrumiriya between the cultic regions as created by various types of *zyara*, and the area within which the biological reproduction of the human population takes place (as indicated by the distances across which marriages are contracted), suggests that the relation between religion and societal reproduction operates at an even profounder level than the sheer underpinning of the structures of segmentary organization, and of authority, that govern the local subsistence economy. The saints' involvement in women's reproductory troubles points in the same direction. Marital relations, and more in general the tension between male and female, would seem to constitute a dominant axis in the Khrumiri cult of saints (cf. Fernea & Fernea 1972; Dwyer 1978; Davis 1979)[14].

Meanwhile at least one other contradiction would have to be considered, that between the state-supported rural elite (administrative chiefs, officers of the unemployment relief work organization, teachers) and the peasants. The dialectics of their relationships must be understood in the light of the relation between the peasants' less and less viable subsistence economy (with its manifold links with the cult of saints), and the capitalist economy into which Tunisia is increasingly drawn - with as its latest local manifestation the massive labour migration to Libya of Khrumiri men in the 1970s. This interplay of competing relations of production seems to offer, finally, a setting for the persistence of Khrumiri popular religion, with the cult of saints as its major manifestation, despite the inroad of formal Islam.

Popular religion lives on at least to the extent to which the non-capitalist local subsistence economy lives on - albeit that the symbolic order tends to either lag behind, or anticipate, the development of economic relations.

I shall, however, resist here the temptation of jumping to theoretical conclusions; these will hopefully be drawn elsewhere, at greater length and against a fuller background of historical and ethnographic data, and theoretical considerations.

NOTES

1. Field-work was conducted in north-western Tunisia in 1968, 1970, and 1979. Although the 1979 field-trip has convinced me that the religious patterns described in this paper have by and large persisted through the 1970s, the ethnographic present in this chapter refers to the late 1960s. I am indebted to the Municipal University of Amsterdam, and to the Free University, Amsterdam, for grants towards my 1968 and 1979 field-trips respectively, and to the Musée des Traditions Populaires, Tunis, for local support. I am moreover indebted to: the people of Khrumiriya, Hasnawi b. Tahar, Douwe Jongmans, Jeremy Boissevain, Klaas van der Veen, and Henny van Rijn, for substantial contributions to my analysis of Khrumiri popular religion. An earlier version of this paper was written and presented in 1980, when I was a Simon Visiting Professor at Manchester University; I am indebted to the participants in the anthropology seminar, and particularly to Emrys Peters, Richard Werbner and Kenneth Brown, for helpful criticism made on that occasion. Finally I wish to thank Daan Meijers and Jojada Verrips for organizing the conference out of which the present volume has emerged; Ernest Gellner and Katie Platt for going out of their way in order to accommodate this chapter in that volume; Adrienne van Wijngaarden and Wilma Keijzer for typing successive drafts; and F. de Jong for advice on translitteration.

2. For the rendering of place-names (including the name Khrumiriya), Arabic terms and plurals, cf. Van Binsbergen 1980b:71, n.7. The system adopted is merely intended to approximate the Khrumiri dialect and obviously obscures many of the orthographic and phonetic distinctions. Long vowels in Arabic words are indicated by a stroke whenever the word appears for the first time. In Khrumiriya the personal names Muhammad and Mhammad are clearly distinct, with the first "a" in Muhammad tending towards the Italian "a", in Mhammad towards the French "ê".

Earlier ethnographic sources on the cult of saints in Khrumiriya include: Dornier 1950; Demeerseman 1938, 1939-40, 1964; Dallet 1939-40; Ferchiou 1972. I shrink from citing here the enormous literature on maghrebine rural popular religion. For a recent bibliographical survey with particular reference to Tunisia, cf. Louis 1977. Studies of maghrebine rural religious behaviour applying the canons of modern social science are, however, extremely scarce. A useful, though more islamological than anthropological, recent survey of popular Islam is: Waardenburg 1979.

3. The contentious model of territorial segmentation presented here is argued at great length in Van Binsbergen 1970 and 1971a. This model could not have been formulated but for Gellner's (1969) stimulating study of saints and segmentation in the Moroccan High Atlas; cf. Hammoudi 1974 and Van Binsbergen 1971b. For another interesting case of the distribution of religious centres following secular segmentation, cf. Evans-Pritchard 1949, ch.3.

4. While this reflects the historical ideal, the breaking-up of commensality between co-residing kin has led to a situation where households, rather than compounds, are in the possession of their own storage table.

5. For a definition of shrine, and a theory of shrines in relation to social organization and the natural environment, cf. Van Binsbergen 1981.

6. In Khrumiriya, springs emanating from soil with a high iron content contain reddish foam; these springs, which are relatively rare, are invariably the object of a cult.

7. The puzzling status of shrines 3 and 4 as filial branches of shrine 1 is discussed in Van Binsbergen 1971a:281f and 1980b:71, n.15.

8. For a striking parallel in Andes popular religion, cf. Sallnow 1981.

9. An indication of this incorporation is that very few widows ever move back to their village of origin; for a set of indicators of female incorporation in a context of marriage, cf. Lewis 1965.

10. Cf. Köbben 1975, who in fact cites the Khrumiri case.

11. These tests are not affected by the relatively small number of

cases, nor do they imply assumptions as to the scale level (interval, ordinal, nominal) of the variables; cf. Siegel, n.d. The short questionnaire, in colloquial Arabic, used to collect (in addition to observational materials) the quantitative data on *zyara* and other types of religious performance, will be included in Van Binsbergen, in preparation.

12. Of the 18 shrines, the numbers 8 and 9 are not visited by any inhabitant of either village: 9 is, however, visited by inhabitants of the neighbouring village of Tra^c^aya-bidh.

13. A peculiarity of the *zyara* pattern of the village of Mayziya, and one that is not easily accommodated within our tripartite typology of Khrumiri *zyara*, is that virtually all adult women resident in that village have an infrequent *zyara* relationship with the shrines of Sidi Bu-Kharuba and Sidi Bu-Zarura in the adjacent valley of Saydiya, c. 4 km east of Mayziya. Here again segmentary fission provides the explanation: these distant shrines are collectively visited because the majority of the present-day inhabitants of Mayziya are recent immigrants from Saydiya; their migration from that valley has been too recent than that religious and secular ties with that relatively distant place of origin could already have been severed entirely. Khrumiri history offers numerous cases of emigrants cutting off such ties after a few decades.

14. Davis's juxtaposition of pious men in Islam versus pious women in mediterranean Christianity seems scarcely to apply to Khrumiri popular Islam.

REFERENCES

Dallet, J.
1939- Les "mzaras" de Kroumirie. *IBLA (Institut des Belles Lettres*
1940 *Arabes)*, 3:323-42.

Davis, J.
1979 The Sexual Division of Religious Labour in the Mediterranean, paper read at the Conference on Religion and Religious Movements in the Mediterranean Area, Amsterdam: Municipal University of Amsterdam/Free University.

Demeerseman, A.
1938- Le culte des saints en Kroumirie. *IBLA (Institut des Belles*
1939 *Lettres Arabes)*, 1:3-28 (1938), 2:3-27 (1939).

Demeerseman, A.
1939-1940 Les croyances relatives aux "Oualis" des mzaras en Kroumirie. *IBLA (Institut des Belles Lettres Arabes)*, 3:3-39.

1964 Le culte des walis en Kroumirie. *IBLA (Institut des Belles Lettres Arabes)*, 27:119-66.

Dornier, P.
1950 Le recours aux oualis dans les campagnes du Nord de la Tunisie. *IBLA (Institut des Belles Lettres Arabes)* 13:392-396.

Dwyer, D.H.
1978 Women, Sufism and Decision-making in Moroccan Islam. In: L. Beck & N. Keddie (eds.), *Women in the Muslim World*, Cambridge (Mass.)/London: Harvard University Press, pp. 595-598.

Evans-Pritchard, E.E.
1949 *The Sanusi of Cyrenaica*. Oxford: Clarendon Press.

Ferchiou, S.
1972 Survivances mystiques et culte de possession dans le maraboutisme tunisien, *L'Homme*, 12, 3:47-69.

Fernea, R.A. & E.W. Fernea
1972 Variation in Religious Observance among Islamic Women. In: L. Beck & N. Keddie (eds.), *Women in the Muslim World*, Cambridge (Mass.)/London: Harvard University Press, pp. 385-401.

Gellner, E.
1969 *Saints of the Atlas*, London: Weidenfeld & Nicholson.

Keddie, N.R. (ed.)
1972 *Scholars, Saints and Sufis*, Berkeley/Los Angeles/London: University of California Press.

Köbben, A.J.F.
1975 Opportunism in Religious Behaviour. In: W.E.A. van Beek & J.H. Scherer (eds.), *Explorations in the Anthropology of Religion*, The Hague: Nijhoff, pp. 46-54.

Lewis, I.M.
1965 Problems in the Comparative Study of Unilineal Descent. In: M. Banton (ed.), *The Relevance of Models for Social Anthropology*, London: Tavistock, pp. 87-112.

Louis, A.
1977 *Bibliographie ethno-sociologique de la Tunisie*, Tunis: IBLA (Institut des Belles Lettres Arabes).

Meillassoux, C.
1964 *Anthropologie économique des Gouro*, Paris/The Hague: Mouton.

Sallnow, M.
1981 Devotional Pluralism in the Andes, paper read at the Symposium on Plurality in Religion, IUEAS (International Union of Anthropological and Ethnological Sciences) Intercongress, Amsterdam.

Siegel, S.
n.d. *Nonparametric Statistics*, New York etc./Tokyo: McGraw-Hill/ Kōgakusha.

Spitz, J.C.
1961 De 1-toets en de 1'-toets, *Nederlands Tijdschrift voor de Psychologie*, 16:68-88.

Turner, V.W.
1974 *Dramas, Field and Metaphors*, Ithaca/London: Cornell University Press.

Turner, V.W. & E. Turner
1978 *Image and Pilgrimage in Christian Culture*, Oxford: Blackwell.

Van Binsbergen, W.M.J.
1970 Verwantschap en territorialiteit in de sociale structuur van het bergland van noordwest Tunesië, drs.soc.sc. thesis, Amsterdam: Municipal University of Amsterdam.

1971a Religie en samenleving: Een studie over het bergland van noordwest Tunesië, drs.soc.sc. thesis, Amsterdam: Municipal University of Amsterdam.

1971b "Saints of the Atlas": Ernest Gellner, *Cahiers des Arts et Traditions Populaires*, 4:203-211.

1976 Shrine Cult and Society in North and Central Africa, paper read at the Annual Conference, Association of Social Anthropologists of Great Britain and the Commonwealth, Manchester.

1980a Popular and Formal Islam, and Supra-local Relations: The Highlands of North-Western Tunisia, 1800-1970, *Middle Eastern Studies*, 20:71-91.

1980b Interpreting the Myth of Sidi Mhammad. In: K. Brown & M. Roberts (eds.), *Using Oral Sources: Vansina and Beyond*, special issue, *Social Analysis*, 4, Adelaide: University of Adelaide, pp.51-73. Also in: *Proceedings of the International Oral History Conference, 24-26 October 1980*, Amsterdam: Historisch Seminarium, Municipal University of Amsterdam,

Van Binsbergen, W.M.J.
1980b (cont.) vol.II:511-547.

1981 *Religious Change in Zambia*, London/Boston: Kegan Paul International.

in prep. *Shrines and Ecstasy in the Social Structure of North-Western Tunisia.*

Waardenburg, J.
1979 Official and Popular Religion as a Problem in Islamic Studies. In: P.H. Vrijhof & J. Waardenburg (eds.), *Official and Popular Religion*, The Hague/Paris: Mouton, pp. 340-386.

Werbner, R.P. (ed.)
1977 *Regional Cults*, London/New York: Academic Press.

The Contemporary Situation of the Muslim Mystic Orders in Yugoslavia

Alexandre Popovic

The Muslim mystic orders of the South-Eastern European countries have scarcely been the object of study until the present time, for the following obvious reasons: lack of available documentation, difficulty of access to the sources (manuscript and archival documents) and above all, difficulty in approaching these more or less closed societies for a non-Muslim historian, not to mention the distinctive situation of each of these orders with respect to period and country.

In the post-Ottoman period, these orders promptly disappeared in Hungary, but they have continued to exist for some time in Bulgaria, Greece and Rumania, before disappearing in these countries as well. Those of Albania have had varied fortunes (especially the Bektachis), but they finally disappeared as well, afflicted by the "cultural revolution" of 1967. Yugoslavia is altogether a case of its own, and deserves our full attention, for the Muslim mystic orders of this country have not only continued to exist, but moreover seem to be characterised by a renewal that is very curious and at the very least unexpected. This is all the more so as these orders, after a difficult survival at the end of the nineteenth and the first half of the present century, tend to disappear from 1945 onwards. In fact, since 1952, all the *tekke*-s lodges of Bosnia and Herzegovina have been closed and all the existing orders forbidden[1] while those of Kosovo and Macedonia were semi-clandestine.

From that time, and especially from 1970 onwards, it has become evident that the mystic orders of Bosnia and Herzegovina have never really disappeared (in spite of the official prohibition of 1952) and that those of Kosovo and Macedonia were still functioning.

But, for a better understanding of the present situation, it is necessary to have a look at the documentation concerning the Muslim mystic orders of Yugoslavia since the end of the Second World War.[2]

I. The period 1945-1960

To my knowledge, only four publications concerning our subject appeared between 1945 and 1960, and two of them deal with the period prior to 1945. This is especially the case in the brief article of M.S. Filipović (1954) on the Bektachis of the Strumica region (Eastern Macedonia) based on the information collected locally before the Second World War, and that of V. Boškov and F. Ishak (1958) on the *tekke* of the Rifā'īs at Skopje, in which the two authors very briefly present the history of this *tekke*, before analysing the four inscriptions found there, as well as the text of the *waqf-nāme* of the foundation of the *tekke*, dated 1233/1818.

More information, however, on the situation of the Muslim mystic orders of that time is to be found in the other two publications, the one of K. Halimi (1957) - on the various orders of the Kosovo - and the one of G. Palikruševa (1958/1959) - on the Khalwetis of Macedonia.

Principally based on his personal investigations, K. Halimi describes the various *turbe*-s of the town of Gnjilane (situated in the eastern part of the Kosovo) as well as the two communities of dervishes of the town: the Sa'dīs (comprising at that time about twenty people) and the Rifā'īs (a community of about fifteen people). But the author also supplies much data on the history of the two orders in question and on several other *turbe*-s shrines and *tekke*-s of the various villages of the region: Nosaljac, Rogačica, Toponica, Kitka, Daždinci, Djuriševac, Marevci, Zajčevac, Gornja Burdriga, Novo Brdo, etc.

As for the article of Mrs G. Palikruševa, this is a first-hand survey, not merely on the situation at the time, but also on the history, the ramifications and the ritual (*dhikr*) of the order of the Khalwetis, which remains, even today, the most widespread Muslim mystic order of Macedonia.[3] She informs us mainly of the *tekke*-s of Skopje, Ohrid, Struga, Kičevo, Štip and of several other towns and villages of Macedonia, but at the same time she informs us of those of Prizren and those of several other places outside of Macedonia.

Finally, it is to be noted that an attentive analysis of the principal (official) Yugoslavian Muslim publication, entitled "Bulletin of the supreme Islamic Authority" (*GVIS*) allows us to complete our knowledge a little in this field, and especially concerning the number of functioning *tekke*-s, the number of sheiks and dervishes according to region, the situation of the various orders, etc.[4]

II. The period 1960-1970

Not many texts have appeared on our subject during this decade. Besides, some of them hardly deal with the contemporary situation of the Muslim mystic orders.

This is precisely the case with two of the three principal publications of this period, that of G. Palikruševa and K. Tomovski (1965) on the *tekke*-s of Macedonia in the 18th and 19th century, and that of L. Bogojcvič (1965) - on the *turbe*-s of Skopje. However, these two publications also contain some information on the more or less recent history of certain Macedonian *tekke*-s and especially on the most beautiful of all, that of Harabati Baba of Tetovo (formerly Kalkandelen), that has belonged to the order of the Bektachis and is transformed now into a motel.

Much more important for us is the short article of J.F. Trifunoski (1965) on the *tekke*-s of the basin of the river Bregalnica in Eastern Macedonia. It is a succinct but very accurate description of the situation at the time of about fifteen *tekke*-s (all abandoned because of the emigration of the Turkish inhabitants of the region) in the following villages: Penuš, Hadži-Hamzali, Čreška, Češmedere, Enešobe, Bečirlija, Testemelci, Dobrošan, Sofilar, Adži-Suli and Kišin. Considering the quality of the information, it is to be regretted that the author has not extended his research to the whole of Macedonia.

The last text that appeared during this period is a curious but very interesting article on the few survivors of the Rifā'īs order of the town of Kosovska Mitrovica in Serbia published by the journalist of a weekly magazine from Belgrade (Mladenovič 1967).

Finally, scraps of information on the Khalwetīs of Ohrid and Prizren and on the Rifā'īs and the Sa'dīs of Djakovica are to be found in a review by H. Kaleši which was published in 1969.[5]

Other information of this kind, or sometimes even more substantial information, can be obtained from the "Bulletin of the Supreme Islamic Authority" (*GVIS*) of the years 1961-1970.[6]

III. The period 1971-1979

Since 1971, we have been witnessing a flood of publications (besides some documentary films) on the Yugoslavian dervishes. In a relatively short space of time, these publications and films deeply enriched our knowledge in this field, nevertheless without allowing us to have a very precise idea of the actual situation on the spot.

a) Firstly, attention should be called to a remarkable article/ testimony on the Naqshbandīs of Bosnia (believed to have disappeared since the 1952 prohibition), by one of the best specialists of the present time on the Naqshbandīya in general, Hamid Algar of Berkeley, California (Algar 1972).[7]

Having stayed for some time among the dervishes of this order, H. Algar presents the history of the principal centres of the Naqshbandīya of Bosnia, before describing in detail the *tekke*-s of Živčiči, Oglavak and Visoko (that are all still actively functioning); finally, he pays great attention to the peculiarities of their *dhikr*, comparing it to the *dhikr* of other centres of the Naqshbandīs in the world. In addition, much information is given on the life of this order in Bosnia and its relations - that are rather difficult, to be sure - with the official Sunni centres. The appendix shows a choice of the *ilâhîs*, of the three principal local representatives (Sirri Baba, Mejli Baba and Šejh Behaedin Hadžimejlić).

b) The indefatigable activities of the late Hasan Kaleši have formed a second source of information for us. He was particularly well acquainted with the situation on site, especially at Kosovo and in Western Macedonia.[8]

It concerns two of his communications, the first on the Khalwatīya in Yugoslavia (presented at the 13th PIAC-congress in Strassburg, June 1970)[9], and the second (cf. Popovic 1978)[10] on the order of the Sa'dīya in Yugoslavia (presented on the occasion of the 29th International Congress of Orientalists in Paris, July 1973). Both have supplied much information of an historical, religious and social kind, be it on the implantation of the two orders (at Kosovo, in Southern Serbia, in Macedonia and in Northern Albania), their ramifications and evolution or on their present situation, the details concerning their *dhikr*, etc.

The second group of contributions of H. Kaleši in this field, consists of a series of texts, intended to accompany the documentary films on the various Muslim mystic orders of Kosovo. These films were realized (in October 1975) by Professor Hans Joachim Kissling of Munich (for the Institute of Scientific Films of Göttingen), thanks to the preparatory work of H. Kaleši and his mediation for those concerned (Majer 1976:219-220).[11] It concerns texts/films on the following orders: the Bektachis of Kosovo and their leader, Baba Kiazim of Djakovica[12] (but part of the text is also devoted to the history of the Bektachis of Albania, who are - for at least certain periods - hardly dissociable from those of Kosovo); the history of the order of the Khalwetīs in Southern Serbia, at Kosovo and in Macedonia, and the *tekke* of the Khalwetīs of Prizren[13] and finally the Melāmīya order, their *tekke* of Orahovac, their *dhikr* and their founder Muhammad Nūr al-'Arabī, also known in these regions by the name of Arap Hodža.[14]

c) A certain amount of information can also be found in two recent publications of Nimetullah Hafiz who is actively working in this field and who has already gathered important documentation. The first of these publications, which appeared in 1976, concerns the *tekke*-s of the Bektachis in Yugoslavia (Hafiz 1976:57-67) the second, which appeared in 1978, concerns those of the Mewlewīs (Hafiz 1978:173-178).

d) The publication of the thesis of Džemal Ćehajić on the Muslim mystic in Yugoslavia (presented recently at Sarajevo) is awaited with interest. The author is one of the most important researchers in this field at present and, though his approach is rather historical (he is chiefly interested in the Ottoman period), his work would most certainly afford at least some data concerning the modern and contemporary period. Džemal Ćehajić has already published several articles in this particular field, always from a historical perspective and centred on the Ottoman period (Ćehajić 1973, 1976, 1978 etc.).[15]

e) Finally, it is to be noted that the - very particular - *dhikr* of the Rifā'īs[16] has recently attracted the attention of several Yugoslavian cineasts and journalists. As a result, at least three documentary films were made (the first two of which were realized by the television team of Priština and that of "Kosovo film", and the third by a Belgrade cineast[17]), besides an abundantly illustrated reportage in one of the principal weekly newspapers of Belgrade (Mladenović 1973). These documents are of great value and, as far as I know, unique.

f) This being said, it must be stressed first of all that there is a new source of firsthand documentation, namely the publication of an "Information Bulletin" entitled *Hu*, edited by the Yugoslavian dervishes themselves.

Indeed, a decisive stage in the Yugoslavian Muslim mystic movement was reached in November 1974 by the creation of a community by the name of *SIDRA* (Savez islamskih dervišhkih redova Alijje u SFRJ)[18], grouping all the Muslim mystic orders of Yugoslavia (which is a practically unprecedented phenomenon in the history of the Muslim world).[19] The SIDRA has edited the first issue of the Bulletin *Hu* on the occasion of its creation.[20] In 1978 this community changed its name to ZIDRA (Zajednica islamskih derviških redova Alijje u SFRJ)[21] and edited (in the course of 1978) three new issues of the Bulletin *Hu* (in Serbo-Croatian in Albanian).

The religious authorities of the official (Sunni) Muslim community reacted very violently, at first. They reacted on the one hand against the creation of this second Muslim community in the country, that in fact presents itself simply as a 'parallel' community (following a felicitous expression of A. Bennigsen, talking about Soviet Islam), and on the other hand against the publication of the Bulletin.[22]

However, after a short while, and for obvious reasons, this intolerant attitude was replaced by more moderate reactions, to such an extent that the leaders of the official Muslim community organized a meeting on the highest level (Sarajevo, March 17, 18, 1979) in order to examine the new situation, its consequences and the steps to be taken.[23]

The relations between the two Muslim communities seem to be the more complex at present as a number of Muslim leaders of the highest level, belonging to the official Sunni community, have just undergone a series of attacks in the principal Yugoslavian newspapers. These attacks are extremely serious[24], no doubt issuing from the decisions taken in the high governmental spheres and of which the consequences for the two Muslim communities are at present impossible to foresee. It must be added that the leaders at whom the criticism is aimed, and who are reproached for their conduct among other things during the

Second World War, have enjoyed their positions for..... about twenty, or even thirty years!

g) Since I have been interested, for a number of years now, in the survival of the Muslim mystic orders of South-Eastern Europe in the post-Ottoman period, I have been able to carry out two study-tours to Kosovo and Western Macedonia in the course of 1979.[25] During these tours I have visited about forty *tekke*-s, belonging to nine different orders.[26] I have been able to talk for a long time with many dervishes and their sheiks, to collect a great variety of information and to form an opinion on the current situation of these orders.

The documentation that I have been able to gather on site is still hardly utilizable, and its classification still demands several months' work. On the other hand, it is clear that only frequent and prolonged visits to these centres over a period of time will allow a proper understanding of the situation, which is, to say once again, of a rare complexity. Nevertheless, I will try to present some data here, besides some reflections, that are certainly susceptible to revision.

IV. Some notes on the present situation

There are nine Muslim mystic orders in Yugoslavia today; at Kosovo, in Macedonia and in Bosnia and Herzegovina. They are (in order of importance and number of surviving *tekke*-s): the Khalwetīs, the Sa'dīs, the Rifā'īs, the Kaderīs, the Naqšibendīs, the Melāmīs, the Bektašīs, the Sinānīs, and the Shādhilīs. Some of these orders are divided into several branches, others have only one. Some other orders have also existed before, but have disappeared for a longer or shorter period, like, for example, the Mewlewīs and the Bayramīs.

Although it is impossible to give exact figures, the number of *tekke*-s is believed to be between sixty and a hundred.[27] The number of sheiks is about forty at the most, while that of the dervishes will be as high as several tens of thousands of people.[28]

The ZIDRA community contains twelve recognized orders. To the ones mentioned above (with the exception of the Melamīs) the Mewlewīs, the Bedewīs, the Desūkīs and the Bayramīs must be added.

For complex reasons that demand further explanation, the Melāmīya Nūrīya order (of which at least three *tekke*-s are at Kosovo at present) does not take part in the ZIDRA.

The majority of *tekke*-s are more or less officially counted and their sheiks are well-known. There are, however, other *tekke*-s (especially recent ones) of which even the ZIDRA-office does not have exact information. This is so particularly because amongst the Romis (gipsies) of Macedonia, for complex reasons connected with the hierachy issue between the various nationalisms in Yugoslavia, a flourishing of *tekke*-s and sheiks now takes place. Their emergence and names escape all control by the ZIDRA-authorities.

The son succeeds his father as a sheik, according to the 'evladiyet'-system. If the sheik does not have a son, his brother generally takes the vacant place, but, of course, there has been some evasion of this rule.

All the *tekke*-s of an order are equal and there is no hierarchy among them, except that there is a chief house for each order, called the 'asitane'. In the asitane the future sheiks are instructed and nominated. On this occasion and according to the habitual terminology, they will have "taken the hand" of the sheik of the asitane in question. May it be added that the asitane-s of certain Yugoslavian orders are sometimes located outside the country, e.g. in Damascus or in Istanbul. At present there is little contact between the *tekke*-s of the various regions of Yugoslavia, and still less contact, or none at all, with those abroad, which has not always been the case.

Nowadays, the majority of sheiks, and with still more reason, almost the totality of dervishes, practise a profession. In the country they are in general agriculturists, and in the towns craftsmen, merchants or employees. However, some sheiks have no other profession. In this case it concerns either sheiks leading a principal *tekke* of one of the important orders, or elderly persons.

This reason and others explain why there is practically no community life in the *tekke*-s. One knows, in fact, that in the past the dervishes often used to live together, exploiting the lands belonging to their *tekke*, exactly in the same way as a Christian monastery. The most typical example for Yugoslavia was that of the large *tekke* of the Bektachis of Tetovo, already mentioned above. These days seem to belong definitely to the past. However, there are some examples of an intermediate kind today. It concerns, of course, the *tekke*-s , the most famous and the most in view, where a small community life continues to exist in the old style (e.g. the *tekke* of the Bektachis of Djakovica), or those in which a community life survived, thanks to a certain number of "permanent ones" or people coming to perform their duty in turn, sometimes from villages and towns at a distance of tens of kilometres (e.g. the *tekke* of the Khalwetīs of Prizren, that of the Rifā'īs of Prizren, etc.).

Some orders have survived better than others. There may be a great number of reasons for this state of affairs, but one should be careful, I think, of making hasty judgements, for, if certain *tekke*-s have disappeared, this is sometimes quite simply because of the sheik's departure to Turkey or elsewhere, having in some cases taken all the *türbe*-s of the *tekke*, that is to say the graves of his ancestors, with him.

In any case, we have several types of *tekke*-s at present: those that are more or less in ruins (as for example one of the *tekke*-s of the Sinānīs of Prizren, in spite of all the efforts of the descendants who did their utmost to try and prevent expiration) or those who have been completely done up like new (like, for instance, the *tekke* of the Rifā'īs of Prizren or of the Bektachis of Djakovica). Finally and fortunately, there are still some examples of ancient *tekke*-s in full splendour, like the one of the Khalwetīs and of the Kaderīs of Prizren, the one of the Khalwetīs of Orahovac, and that of the Rifā'īs of Djakovica, etc.

Many of the *tekke*-s possess small libraries, where one should be able to find important manuscripts, concerning their respective order. The most valuable library I have seen (yet without having been able to consult the books and manuscripts) is the one of the Bektachis of Djakovica.

One can note the fact that the majority of *tekke*-s are situated in the small towns: Djakovica, Prizren, Orahovac, Kičevo, etc. There are, however, many *tekke*-s located in the villages, in Kosovo as well as in Macedonia and in Bosnia and Herzegovina. One may well ask furthermore, to what extent Muslim mystic life now tends to be gradually moving to the country. But this remains to be established.

One of the most important, and at the same time most interesting points obviously concerns the present (and past) role of the Muslim mystic orders in a particular region, or even the role of a fixed *tekke*, on its members and sympathizers, as well as that of the function and the limits of the sheik's power. This is a complex question and I think it is too early to answer. Simply, according to what I have been able to observe (in the case of the large brotherhoods which are deeply rooted in the population of the area) it is by no means a religious affair only, but it concerns a very complex situation (which changes according to the circumstances) including many problems of spiritual life, indeed, but also those of everyday material life. I will explain myself: in many cases one would not undertake a serious affair (e.g. the marriage of one's son, the building of a house or any important transaction) without having asked the sheik for advice. One may therefore rightly wonder in what respect the sheik has considerably more power than is generally believed. I think, without trying to generalize or maximize my assertion, that in certain cases at least it is correct. The decisive role that may be played by the sheik of Kosovo in the settlement of a vendetta, which is still a current phenomenon today in this region, may serve as an example. The examples of this kind are multiple and probably may be extended to economical, political and other areas.

I do not wish to enter into the spiritual or theological considerations of the sheiks and dervishes whom I met.[29] For one thing, I only spent a short while in their company, and for another, the publication of the *Hu*-bulletin provides us with some first-hand examples for such an analysis. I would prefer to emphasize a simple fact that demands consideration, namely that the Muslim mystic is anything but dead in Europe, and moreover in a socialist country in which, on the one hand, the Communist Party has been in power since 1945, and on the other hand the leaders of the official Muslim community have done all they could to prohibit it. So there are still today in Yugoslavia people who need the *tekke*-s, the *dhikr* and a certain form of monastic and community life for self-fulfilment and sublimation. It is a phenomenon that deserves interest and research on a historical level, as well as on the levels of sociology, religious sociology and other sciences.

Of course, I cannot predict the evolution in the years to come of the Muslim mystic orders of Yugoslavia, and their relation to the official Muslim community and the public authorities. What is certain, on the other hand, is that our future research in this field has a particularly vast scope:

a) Collecting and publishing all the basic texts that are to be found on site.
b) Collecting and analysing all the testimonies available on the situation of these mystic orders in the recent and remote past.
c) Undertaking as many study-tours and study-visits on site as possible, to gather all possible information and testimonies.
d) Finally, working in this interesting but difficult field, trying to understand with the head as well as with the heart, and without any prejudice.

But I do not wish to conclude my paper without presenting a testimony of my own, that is very dear to me. In a great majority of cases, I have been welcomed by the dervishes and sheiks of Kosovo and of Macedonia in an extremely warm and friendly way. I have been able to talk very openly with them about the problems I am interested in, and I could ask all the questions that came to mind. In one word, I have been received in societies that are much less closed than I personally had imagined before making my first journey.

NOTES

1. Cf. 'Odluka o prestanku rada tekija u NRBiH', in: *Glasnik Vrhovnog Islamkog Starješinstva*, (henceforth *GVIS*), maj-juli 1952, III/ 5-7:199.
2. I am in the process of preparing an article on the Muslim mystic orders of Eastern Europe (Albania, Bulgaria, Greece, Hungary, Rumania and Yugoslavia) in the post-Ottoman period, in which one finds the complete bibliography on the subject, whereas the present communication only treats the case of Yugoslavia, and this solely in the period 1945-1979.

3. In 1939 there would have been 25 *tekke*-s of the Khalwetīs in Kosovo and in Macedonia, of which about ten at least are still functioning today.

4. The following may serve as an example:
In 1951, there would have been 45 sheiks 'in function' in Kosovo and 62 *tekke*-s (all active?) (cf. *GVIS*, juli-september 1951, II/7-9:316). In 1956, there would have been 48 open *tekke*-s in Macedonia with about thirty sheiks and about 3000 dervishes (cf. *GVIS*, 1957, VIII:50). In 1958, there would have been 48 open *tekke*-s in Macedonia with 25 sheiks and about 2500 dervishes (cf. *GVIS*, 1959, X:65-66).
In 1959, the *tekke*-s of Ohrid, Struga and Kičevo (all of the order of the Khalwetīs) were authorized to function normally. The ten other *tekke*-s of Macedonia (amounting to 706 dervishes) are not considered to be under the authority of '*Ulema Medžlis*' of Yugoslavia (cf. *GVIS*, 1960, XI:49).
In October 1959, the *Reis ul-ulema* of Yugoslavia Hadži Sulejman Kemura (chief of the Yugoslavian Muslim community) was received in the *tekke* of the Khalwetīs of Ohrid, whereas he did not visit any other *tekke* during his tour in Macedonia (cf. *GVIS*, 1960, XI:210).

5. Cf. *Prilozi za orijentalnu filologiju*, 1964-1965, XIV-XV, Sarajevo, 1969:468.

6. The following may serve as an example:
In 1960, there would have been 11 open *tekke*-s in Macedonia, with 11 sheiks and 704 dervishes (cf. *GVIS*, 1961, XII:102). At that time The Supreme Islamic Authority of Yugoslavia disapproved very firmly of the existence of Muslim mystic orders and tried to prohibit them in Serbia (Kosovo) and in Macedonia, as it did in 1952 with the orders of Bosnia and Herzegovina (cf. *GVIS*, 1962, XIII:186).
In September 1962 (as in October 1959), the chief of the Yugoslavian Muslim community Hadži Sulejman Kemura did visit the *tekke* of the Khalwetīs of Ohrid, whereas he would not visit any other *tekke* during his trip to Kosovo and Macedonia (cf. *GVIS*, 1962, XIII:381).
In 1962, there would have been 4 (open?) *tekke*-s in the city of Skopje (cf. *GVIS*, 1963, XXVI:354). In 1967, the chief of the Yugoslavian Muslim community, Hadži Sulejman Kemura visited the ancient *tekke* of the Bektachis of Tetovo, without visiting the other *tekke*-s of Kosovo and Macedonia (cf. *GVIS*, 1967, XXX:533).

7. I have not yet been able to see his article bearing the same title that was published in 1975 (in *Studies in Comparative Religion*, Bedfont-Middlesex 1975, 9:69-96), but I suppose that it simply concerns a re-edition. Cf. also his article 'The naqshbandī order: a preliminary survey of its history and significance' (Algar 1976 - more especially p.130 and pp.146-147).

8. Cf. on this engaging personality *Turcica*,1978, IX/2-X:7-8, and *Journal Asiatique*, 1972, CCLX/3-4:387ff.

9. Hasan Kaleshi, *L'ordre des Halvetīya en Yougoslavie*, unpublished. In spite of all my efforts (since the death of the author), I have been unable to obtain the manuscript of this valuable text.

10. The summary of this communication had previously appeared in the fascicle "XXIXe Congrès International des Orientalistes, Paris, 1973, Résumés des communications, Sections 6-7", p.36.

11. Thanks to the kindness of Dr Klaus Kreiser of the German Archeological Institute of Instanbul, whom I would like to deeply thank here, it was possible for me to receive a copy of these texts.

12. Baba Kiazim of Djakovica (Kosovo) and Baba Rexhepi of the Bektachi *tekke* of Detroit (USA) are at present the two main representatives of the Bektachis in the world.

13. The film on the *dhikr* of the Khalwetīs of Prizren was shown in Paris, at the Guimet Museum, at the time of the Congress of the Orientalists in 1973.

14. The order of Melāmīya Nūrīya is concerned here, as one can see. We have found with Mr Darko Tanasković of the Belgrade University (at the library of the University) three manuscripts of Muhammad Nūr al-'Arabī, which we hope to publish in the years to come.

15. There are, of course, many other publications on the Muslim mystic orders in Yugoslavia in former periods, either on a historical level (cf. especially the works of M. Kalabić, G. Elezović, Š. Sikirić, R. Muderizović, M. Handžić, F. Hadžibajrić, M. Hadžijahić, etc.) or on the level of the history of art and architecture (cf. the work of A. Bejtić, Dž. Čelić, M. Mujezinović, M. Bećirbegović, etc.). The references are to be found in my article on the Muslim mystic orders of Eastern Europe in the post-Ottoman period (cf. *supra*, note nr.2).

16. In this particular case the Rifā'īs of Prizren are concerned. Furthermore, a recording of their *dhikr* has existed for several years (cf. Mauguin 1975).

17. Several times, I have had the opportunity of seeing one of these colour films, entitled 'The Blood of Spring', made by Kosovo film of Priština in 1977. It is in every respect a remarkable film.

18. 'Union' of the orders of the dervishes.

19. The only precedent that I know of is the Union of the mystic

orders created in Albania in 1936. (Yet it could not group all the mystic orders, because of the fact that the Albanian Bektachis did not adhere to this organisation.)

"On March 3, 1936, the delegates of the sects (Kadiri, Rifai, Saadi, Tidjani) of the Moslem Community of Albania met at Tirana and formed a common organization called Drita Hyjnore (The Divine Light), which aimed to secure "the exercise of spiritual duties" and "to strengthen the morals of the faithful through sermons" (Skendi 1958:288).

20. The first issue of the *Hu*-Bulletin is dated November 12, 1975.

21. "Community" of the orders of the dervishes ..... Therefore it certainly concerns a new community, entirely comparable to the official Yugoslavian Muslim community.

22. Cf. e.g. the Muslim newspaper *Preporod* of Sarajevo, nr.17 (192) of August 20, 1978:7, and nr.2 (202) of January 15-31, 1979:9.
It concerns a seemingly belated reaction, but one that is easily explained. It is a reaction to the publication of the second issue of the *Hu*-Bulletin, because the first issue had remained more or less confidential, as it had not been officially published. Cf. also the official report on the problem presented by the regional Sunni Muslim authorities of Kosovo to the General Assembly of the Muslim Authorities of Yugoslavia (held in Sarajevo, May 17, 1975) in *GVIS*, Sarajevo, May-June 1975, XXXVIII, 5-6:296.

23. Cf. with respect to this meeting *GVIS*, 1979, 2:195-200, and especially the subsequent issue (*GVIS*, 1979/3) devoted for a large part to the Muslim mystic orders of Yugoslavia. One will find especially *in extenso* the principal reports presented at the meeting of March: H. Djozo, 'Pravi put i stramputice tesavufa'; F. Hadžibajrić, 'Tesavuf tarikat i tekije na području Starješinstva IZ BiH danas' (it contains an excellent account on the mystic orders and the *tekke*-s of Bosnia and Herzegovina, besides details on the creation of the SIDRA/ZIDRA); Dž. Salihspahić, 'Neke negativne pojave kod pristalica tesavufa'; and finally, Š. Ahmeti, 'Kosovska pseudo učenja tesavufa' (which contains some details on the present orders of Kosovo but in a purely negative perspective).
Cf. also the summary of this meeting in the global report on the year 1978/1979, published in *GVIS* 1979/4:371-372.
With regard to the Muslim mystic orders of Yugoslavia, one must stress, however, that some other articles have appeared previously in the Yugoslavian Muslim press, written in a resolute, but more reconciling manner. Cf. e.g. that of N. Šukrić, in

Preporod 3 (178) of February 1-15, 1978:4.

For the same reasons one has greatly emphasized the attitude of one of the most famous Muslim scholars of Bosnia and Herzegovina, Mehmed Handžić (1906-1944), towards the local mystic orders. His main article on this subject has been reprinted. (Cf. in particular an article by M. Traljić in *GVIS*, 1975, XXXVIII 7/8 :387-389, and the reprint in question in *GVIS*, 1979, XLII/3 :263-270.

Let us note the recent publication of several theoretical texts on the *Tariqat*-s in Islam, as for instance the one of F. Djidjić, in *GVIS*, 1977/2 :127-130; Dž. Cehajić in *GVIS*, 1978/2 :109-112; F. Hadžibajrić, in *GVIS*, 1978/3 :242-247; and finally a whole set of articles in the *GVIS*, 1979/3, that have already been dealt with at length above.

24. The starting point for these attacks has been given by the publication of a series of abstracts that appeared in the *Oslobodjenje*-newspaper of Sarajevo (in the course of August, September, October and November 1979), taken from a work entitled *Parergon*, by D. Sušić.

25. In April and October 1979 to be precise.

26. If I have the occasion, I hope to pursue my journeys in the years to come, not only visiting the dervishes with whom I am acquainted, but also those of Eastern Macedonia and of Bosnia and Herzegovina.

27. In one of the reports (of 1976), a total of 67 *tekke*-s is given for Kosovo alone (cf. *GVIS*, 1976/3 :299).

28. There have, of course, never been statistics nor precise accounts of the number of dervishes. On the one hand, no *tekke* has kept registers of this kind, and on the other hand the distinction between "full-time" dervishes and the innumerable sympathizing dervishes has always been extremely vague. The leaders of the ZIDRA-community give a total of "more than 50,000 dervishes" for the present time (cf. *Hu*, Prizren, 1978, nr.2:2).

29. However, as soon as possible one should undertake the analysis of the theorists of these orders, in the way this has been done by Ernst Bannerth on the Khalwatiyya and the Rifa'iyya in Egypt (cf. MIDEO, 1964-1966, vol.8 :1-74, and 1968, vol.10 :1-35).

REFERENCES

Ahmeti, S.
1979 Kosovska pseudo ucenja tesavufa. *Glasnik Vrhovnog Islamskog Starješinstva* (GVIS), 2/3:282-285.

Algar, Hamid
1972 Some notes on the Naqshbandī tarīqat in Bosnia. *Die Welt des Islams*, vol.13:168-203. (Also published in *Studies in Comparative Religion*, 9, Bedfont-Middlesex 1975:69-96.)

1976 The naqshbandī order: a preliminary survey of its history and significance. *Studia Islamica*, vol.44:123-152.

Bogojević, Lidija
1965 Les turbé-s de Skopje. *Atti del Secondo Congresso Internazionale di Arte Turca* (Venezia, 26-29/9/1963), Napoli, Instituto Universitario Orientale, pp.203-211.

Boškov, Vančo & Fetah Ishak
1958 Rifaiskoto teke vo Skopje. *Glasnik na Institutot za nacionalna Istorija*, II/1:179-191.

Ćehajić, D.
1973 Dželaluddin Rumi i mevlevizam u Bosni i Hercegovini. *Izraz*, XVII/10, Serajevo, October.

1974 (1976) Neke karakteristike učenja Ǧalāluddīn Rūmija i nastanak derviškog reda mevlevija, mevlevije u Bosni i Hercegovini. *Prilozi za orijentalnu filologiju*, XXIV.

1978 Bektashis and Islam in Bosnia and Hercegovina. *Anali Gazo Husrevbegove biblioteke*, V-VI, Serajevo, pp.83-90.

Djozo, H.
1979 Pravi put i stramputice tesavufa. *GVIS*, 3:235-241.

Filipović, Milenko S.
1954 The Bektashi of the District of Strumica (Macedonia). *Man*, 54:10-13.

Hadžibajric, F.
1979 Tesavuf tarikat i tekija na području Starješinstva IZ BiH danas. *GVIS*, 3:271-277.

Hafiz, Nimetullah
1976 Yugoslavya'da Bektaşi tekkeleri. *Çevren*, IV/11, Pristina, pp.57-67.

1978 Yugoslavya'da Mevlevi tekkeleri. In: Fevzi Halici (ed.), *Mevlâna ve yaşama sevinci*. Ankara: Konya Turizm Derneği Yayini, pp.173-178.

Halimi, Kadri
1957 Derviški redovi i njihova kultna mesta na Kosovu i Metohiji. *Glasnik Muzeja Kosova i Metohije*, 2, Priština:193-206 (with seven photos).

Majer, H-G.
1976 Arbeitsschwerpunkte der deutschen Osmanistik. In: K.D. Grothusen (ed.), *Südosteuropa und Südosteuropa-Forschung*, Hamburg, pp.219-220.

Mauguin, B.
1975 *Islamic Ritual from Yugoslavia.* Zikr of the Rufa'i Brotherhood. Philips, Holland (=Unesco, Collection 'Musical Sources', Platte und Studie).

Mladenović, M.
1967 Šta će Alahu merdevine (Jedno veče u tekiji poslednijih der derviša). *Ilustrovana Politika*, Belgrade, November, 28:26-27.

1973 Noć derviša. *Ilustrovana Politika*, nr.754, Belgrade, April, 17:30-33.

Palikruševa, Galaba
1958/1959 Derviškiot red halveti vo Makedonija. *Zbornik na štipskiot Naroden Muzej*, I, Štip, pp.105-119.

Palikruševa, Galaba & Krum Tomovski
1965 Les tekke-s en Macédoine aux XVIII et XIXe siècle. *Atti del Secondo Congresso Internazionale di Arte Turca*, Napoli, Instituto Universitario Orientale, pp.203-211.

Popovic, A.
1978 Un texte inédit de Hasan Kaleshi: 'L'ordre des Sa'dīya en Yougoslavie. In: R. Dor & M. Nicolas (eds.), *Quand le crible était dans la paille* (presented to Pertev Naili Boratav). Paris: G-P. Maisonneuve et Larose, pp.335-348.

Salihspahić, Dž.
1979 Neke negativne pojave kod pristalica tesavufa. *GVIS*, 3:278-281.

Skendi, S. (ed.)
1958 *Albania.* New York: Praeger.

Trifunoski, Jovan, F.
1965 O tekijama u donjem slivu Bregalnice. *Prilozi za orijentalnu filologiju*, XII-XIII, 1962-1963:255-258.

The History of Religious Politics in the Lebanon

Anton Wessels

The mass media in the western world have described the Lebanese civil war of 1975-76 - often now called 'the two year war' - as one between Christians and Muslims, and therefore as a religious or holy war. The use of such shorthand devices to represent historical events is by no means an unfamiliar phenomenon, as the current reporting on Iran in the West makes abundantly clear. Moreover, this has been true throughout history.

On both the Christian and the Islamic side examples can be adduced of how in the past a particular struggle was presented as a religious war: a *crusade* on the one hand, a *holy war* on the other.

Time and again it seems that struggles which are (or were) both political, economic, social and religious in nature are experienced and represented as being first and foremost of a religious character. Often one notices that in assessing past events people are tempted to read back into history that which took place only centuries later.

In the struggles of the eighth and ninth centuries in Spain we are told that religious ambition was not nearly as great as it became later. Both Muslims and Christians had family members on either side of the dividing line. Even until late in the tenth century there was a common culture in which secular elements dominated over religious ones.

It was not until the eleventh century during the struggle for the extension of the Northern kingdoms in Spain that the identification between political contestation and the extension of Christianity took place. Not long afterwards the Muslims, too, began to see themselves as 'defenders' of their (Islamic) territory (Watt 1972:46-47). It is interesting to note that it was at about the same time, the eleventh century, that relationships between Muslims and Christians began to take a polemical turn (De Elpalza 1971:100). This tendency to over-emphasize the religious element in such a way that what is basically political-economic strife is 'elevated' to the status of religious struggle between Christians and Muslims can be illustrated from both Islamic and Christian epic poetry. These poems were often written long after a particular event took place. The famous *Chanson de*

Roland, for instance, was written in the eleventh century for the purpose of glorifying an expedition of Charlemagne to Saragossa in the year 778. Charlemagne was unsuccessful in taking Saragossa, and what he did accomplish militarily seems to have been nothing more than the unimportant defeat of a rearguard in Roncevalles. It appears that he was not so much interested in further conquests in Spain but rather in exploiting internal feuds there in order to expand Frankish authority.

But in *Chanson de Roland* the expedition is portrayed as a struggle for the Christian *reconquista* of Spain: the ideal of the Frankish knight ranged in holy battle against the Saracen. In actual fact, the relationship between Charlemagne and the Muslims seems not to have been that bad; it certainly could not have been if, as is related, he was in contact with the famous *caliph* Harun al-Rashid.

A similar kind of epic originated around the exploits of a Spanish knight from Castile, Rodrigo Diaz de Vivar. After a row with the Christian king Alfonso VI, he offered his services as military leader to the Muslim king of Saragossa and ended up as independent military leader of the Muslim city of Valencia. But this Spanish knight *El Cid* (*al-Sayyid*) became in the poem *El poema del Cid* the model of knighthood and honour, the great champion of Christendom.

There is no doubt that in the case of Spain the *reconquista*, coupled with the increase of African inroads in the south, made the relationship between Christians and Muslims worse. It is then that the polemical activity really begins and that one can observe the phenomenon of deteriorating political relationships effecting the breakdown of religious ones. Originally, the nature of the struggle in the Iberian peninsula was connected with 'tribal' rivalries and not promted by religious factors. By the second half of the eleventh century, it is true, these relations had become profoundly influenced by the politicizing of religion. Nevertheless, the religious impulses of the *reconquista* did not make it a religious struggle (Watt 1965:170).

The same can be said in some instances about the Islamic approach. There is an epic in the language which is widely spoken in East-Africa, Swahili, under the title *Heraklios, The Struggle of Muhammad against the Christians*.[1] Heraklios is the name of the Byzantine emperor during the lifetime of the Prophet Muhammad. Although towards the end of Muhammad's life the first skirmishes between the Muslims and the Byzantines had begun, there was never a direct battle between Muhammad and the emperor. It would not be until the year 1453 that Byzantium would fall before the Muslim onslaught, and then not of Arab but of Turkish troupes.

According to the Islamic understanding, war against Christians is not the intention as such, since these latter, like the Jews, are 'people of the book'. They are supposed to be tolerated and respected in their religious freedom. One cannot deny, though, that the Islamic countries did not always live up to that rule, and that 'people of the book' suffered discriminatory measures - the pact of 'Umar - and were sometimes even persecuted within their borders.

In this epic poem, the first of its kind according to Jan Knappert, there is no doubt about the legitimacy of a struggle against Christians on the grounds that they venerate idols and statues and are drunkards, a subject on which Muslims, who are supposed to be teetotallers, are fond of attacking Christians (Andrae 1926:30). In the words of the epic:

"This was the army of those people (Byzantines)
Statues made from dust
Thirteen in number
All of them drunkards" (Knappert 1977:114).

About the Byzantine fighters is said:

"They had small statues
Many-coloured, on their breast
Everyone of them had one,
Each of the ten thousand men." (ibid.:106).

One is reminded here of the custom of the members of the Maronite militia in Lebanon, who decorated their breasts and even their tanks with crosses, crucifixes and pictures of Mary. This was of course already the case with the crusaders who fixed a red cross on their shoulders, a custom which originated in the army of Constantine: *In hoc signo vinces*, 'In that sign thou shalt conquer'!(Altheim 1975: 110).

Something similar can be said about the Islamic reaction towards the crusades. It is clear that later experience during the colonial period led to a reinterpretation of the earlier clashes during the time of the crusades as being 'religious', which in its turn gave rise to an assessment of the colonial enterprise as a new wave of crusades.

The Muslim writer Muhammad al-Bahay, for instance, views colonial activity as having risen from the wish to take revenge for the defeat of the crusades in the thirteenth century.[2]

But Christians sometimes interpreted the colonial enterprise from this perspective too. The well-known story repeated again and again in the Arab press has it that the British general Allenby, who conquered Jerusalem in 1917, said after arriving at the temple square: "The crusades ended today".[3] Another story concerns the French general Gouraud, who conquered Damascus about this same time; arriving at the grave of Saladin he is supposed to have said: "Here we are Saladin (Nous voilà Saladin)".

Although one does not find this statement by Allenby in either comtemporary English or Arabic sources of the time, the comment is ascribed to him in the Arab press of today. There is no trace of this comment in the offical proclamation.[4] Nevertheless, it is not unthinkable that Allenby did express himself in this way, though it apparently irritated him whenever anyone referred to his campaign as a crusade since an important part of his forces consisted of Muslims. Major Vivian Gilbert wrote in his *The Romance of the Last Crusade with Allenby to Jerusalem* (New York 1923): "At last Jerusalem was in our hands! In all ten crusades organized and equipped to free the Holy City, only two were really successful, the first led by Godfrey de Bouillon, and the last under Edmund Allenby." When Jerusalem fell, Allenby's name was on everyone's lips. The *New York Times* said that Allenby was worth "to be remembered along the greatest of the crusaders in the Middle Ages" (Gardner 1965:127, 153, 160, 253; cf. Wessels 1972:160, 161).

One cannot help but see the similarities between this and the way sources from both within and without Lebanon treat the civil war there as a religious struggle between Christians and Muslims.

Historically, Lebanon has been a haven for 'dissenters' both from the Christian Church - the Maronites and from Sunni-Islam - the Shi'ites, Druzes and Nusayri's. Lebanese history is one of peaceful coexistence between these different groups as well as one of conflicts.

Before the First World War Lebanon had in actual fact become a kind of mainly Christian enclave. In its mountains Christians, Greek-Orthodox and some Druzes were living together under the aegis of the Ottoman empire.

When in the seventh century the Arab Muslims began to conquer the Middle East, the Maronites put up resistance to the Arab influx. Apparently the caliphs were not really aware of the strategic importance of the mountains of Syria/Lebanon. The Maronites built their monasteries there as places of refuge for times of persecution. The mountains formed a kind of island in 'the sea of the Islam' where Christians - but also others - could take refuge, either to escape paying taxes or to avoid other discriminatory measures of various Islamic princes. When the pressure and threat became great, there were regular waves of emigration from Lebanon. The nearest place to go was Cyprus, where as early as the beginning of the ninth century a Maronite monastery was built in surroundings very similar to those of Lebanon. Many Maronites went there after the 'fall' of Jerusalem in 1192. Until the 'events' of 1975 5,000 Maronites were living in Cyprus whose numbers increased drastically for a time during the critical months of the Lebanese civil war in the middle of 1976.

In earlier times Maronites had functioned as guides for the

crusaders. In addition to the ruins of their fortresses the crusaders left behind other traces of their presence in the names of some important Maronite families, such as Salībī (crusader!) or Franji (the name of the Lebanese president from 1970 until 1976). Beginning with the Middle Ages a special relationship between France and Lebanon began to develop which continues to a certain extent even today. A statement of King Saint Louis IX dating from 21st May 1250 may illustrate this: "We are convinced that this nation which was founded under the name of Saint Maron is a part of the French nation."[5]

After the so-called massacres of 1860 the allies, led by the French under Napoleon III (who saw himself as the defender of the Catholics in the Ottoman Empire), forced a solution for Lebanon upon the Ottomans.

During the nineteenth century especially Maronites and Druzes were fighting for hegemony in 'Mont Liban' or *Jabal Lubnān*. This led to bloody conflicts in the fourties and seventies of that century. After frequent European interventions in the affairs of the empire of 'the sick man at the Bosporus', Lebanon gained a form of independence within the Ottoman Empire. The mainly Christian north received a Christian governor assisted by a council in which the religious groups were equally represented. Of the twelve members four were Maronite, three Druzes, two Greek-Orthodox, two Shi'ite Muslims and one Greek-Catholic (Melkite). This division according to confession was destined to play a large role in the later history of the Lebanon. The earlier clashes between Christians (mainly Maronites) on the one hand and Muslims on the other, can throw some light on the conflicts in our time. The way in which both Muslims and Christians read history and evaluate current events and past history varies greatly. Some read it as proof that coexistence of Christians and Muslims is not really possible; others understand the same history or events as being of a largely non-religious nature and not as a proof that life together is impossible. The Christians in the East differ among themselves, as do the Muslims, in accordance with their differences of experience and insight.

Some quotations from a book by a certain Colonel Churchill, who spent more than ten years in the Lebanon during the disturbances last century, illustrate the difference in the analysis and the response to the conflicts at that time by the Greek-Orthodox as compared with the Maronites. During the disturbances of the fourties the Greek-Orthodox "declared their preference for Druze rule over them, thus belying the constantly repeated assertion of the Maronites that the Christians could never be happy under the Druzes, and that death would be preferable to submitting to their intolerable tyranny" (Churchill 1863:81). "This preference on the part of the Greek Christians is a most important and instructive fact. It proves that

Druze resistance, and even violence, was not so much directed against Christianity as against Maronite ambition and presumption, and the domineering views of an intolerant priesthood." (ibid.:82). Churchill relates that weeks and months passed in vain endeavours to find common ground between the two sects: "The Maronites, excited by their clergy, talked loudly of the intolerable yoke of Druze oppression, and declared their determination never to submit to it again." ibid.:82, 83). The Maronites in the mixed Maronite-Druze districts explained: "We cannot exist with the Druzes, either they or we must be destroyed or leave the country." (ibid.:85). Instructions to that effect were given by the Maronites to their co-religionists in Dayr al-Qamar, "In pain of death, not to enter into friendly or indeed not any intercourse whatever with the rival sect." ... "Knowing that the great body of Maronites would not engage in a war, simply to destroy the political rights of the Druzes, the justice of which, indeed, the more dispassionate amongst them were ready to admit, he made of a war of party a war of religion. The Druzes, the enemies of the cross, the infidels, were to be exterminated or driven out of the land." (ibid.:85-86).

Speaking about the events of the year 1860, Churchill observes, "The Moslems hourly vowed death to the Christians ... An on the Christian side the men of Zachle etc. ... were written to be of good cheer; this was a war of religion." "The standard of the cross, blessed by their priests, had been elevated amidst enthusiastic rejoicings. The Maronites had embroidered the cross on the sleeves of their right arms." (ibid.:90). One of the letters was intercepted by the Druzes. They said, "This then is a 'war of religion'. So let it be." (ibid.:90, 91).

In order to understand the attitude of especially the Maronite Christians towards the Muslims in the Arab world in general and in Lebanon in particular, one has to ask how they see 'arabism'. How do they view Arab identity. At the beginning of the twentieth century the Maronite Negib Azoury wrote his famous *Réveil de la Nation Arabe* (1905). In it he declares that there is only one Arab nation including both Christians and Muslims. He sees the religious problems at issue between Muslims and Christians as in reality political in nature and exploited by outside powers (Hourani 1962:277 ff.)

It is true that in the struggle against the Turks, Christians and Muslims fought side by side and that not only in Lebanon. In the heart of Beirut one finds an area called Martyr Square. On the 6th of May 1916 both Muslims and Christians fell together! A Lebanese author, Tawfiq Yusif 'Awwad, describes in his novel *Al-Raghīf* (*A Loaf of Bread*):

> "There are no Muslims who fight against Muslims or against non-Muslims, but Arabs who fight against Turks to gain freedom, and Turks who fight against Arabs in order to keep them under control. Today the True Arab nation is born. She is born from the revolt wherein I participate; I, an Arab Christian, next to Arab Muslims, fighting a common enemy, the Turk, whether he is an adherent of Muhammad, Christ or the devil ... The Turks have persecuted us because we are Arabs and not because we are Muslims who believe in the *Qur'an* or Christians who believe in the Gospel."
> "You Kamal (who has spoken in the novel about *jihad* between Arabs and Turks, *A.W.*), you spoke like that because you were inspired by your past, the most part of which is based on Islam. In the past, religion was for all people the binding element determining their national character. In our time it would be a shame if we were to base our state on religion. Today the Arab nation is born, which cares as little about the caliphate as the Italians do about the papacy ..." (Makarius, R. and L. 1964:84-89).

There remains as fundamental a difference of opinion among Christians in this century as in the nineteenth century concerning their own identity and their relationship with the Muslims. Are they really *Arab* Christians or ought one speak about Nestorians (Assyrians), Armenians, Copts and Maronites in the Arab world? Are they and do they feel themselves to be an integral part of the Arab world or are they a national body in a world which is basically alien to them? Christians in the East differ fundamentally on this matter. Undoubtedly Christians have played an important, if not crucial part in the so-called *Arab Awakening*. One has only to call to mind the title and the book of Georges Antonius, *The Arab Awakening*, although it is true that soon the initiative was taken over by the Muslims.

But the question remains as to whether Muslims and Christians are talking about the same thing when they speak in favour of the Arab Nation and Arab Nationalism. Does what they are talking about have to do with a nationalism which transcends religious controversies or is it something intrinsically bound up with Islam? From the Christian side - as we heard from the novel of 'Awwad, one learns not to identify Arabism and Islam. The fundamental question remains, though, whether the Muslims likewise are prepared not to make that identification.

Not a few Christians, many of whom have done a great deal for the sake of Arab nationalism and the 'Arab cause' in the recent past, feel frustrated by the recent developments and the civil war in Lebanon. They have the feeling that they are confronted with a forced identitification between Arabs and Muslims and they see themselves excluded, as it were. The pronouncements of Al-Qadhafi in 1980 saying that an Arab cannot be a Christian corroborated this view. Maronites in the para-military group of the Falangists confront their Muslim opponents with the reproach that in the end their loyalty is not Lebanon but the Arab community (*umma*) in general, understood as a muslim *umma*. They believe that when Muslims talk about an *Arab* Lebanon they mean in actual fact a *Muslim* Lebanon. They see Lebanon as the only place left in the Arab world where Christians still have political freedom; and they want to defend this at whatever cost.

The way in which the Maronites see the civil war of 1975 and 1976 can be illustrated by a few quotations from pamphlets which were brought out by the well-known Maronite center Kaslik (The University of the Holy Spirit). Speaking about the mass of people rallying to the anti-Lebanese cause, one of these pamphlets - whose anonymous writer refers to this cause as anti-Christian - states:

> "... and beginning as a political-social crisis, it turned into a religious war ... On the Christian side the fighters carried the cross. A childish manifestation. But significant. Against Islam, they defended the last fortress of Christianity in the Arab world. Everywhere else in this Muslim world which surrounds us, Christians are not full citizens."

> "Holy war on both sides, one could say. But with two essential differences. The Christian here has only the mountain or the sea, that is to say, the choice of striking roots in spite of all opposition or emigration, while the Muslim of Beirut or Tripoli, of 'Akkar, of Beka, feels supported by the whole interior of this part of the world: by the Arab world despite its divisions, and larger still by the whole Islamic world."[6]

> "The Christians, in particular the Maronites, will sacrifice to the utmost rather than surrender to live as *dhimmi's* in the Muslim empire."[7]

In is striking to see that in this century, like in the nineteenth century, there is a different interpretation of current events by other Christians such as Greek-Orthodox as compared to the Maronites, which is not to say that there are not also Maronites who hold the same opinion. This became clear on the 23rd of August, when a Message of the Holy Orthodox Antiochene Assembly to the Orthodox Christians in Lebanon stated, among other things:

> "By deepening your awareness of your country's problems everyone far and wide will be aware that you have entrusted your own defense to no one. You have lived here in the Middle East for 2000 years in continuous strength and with a spirit of deep-

> rooted ancestry; you are neither vagabonds nor of abject origin. You have received from him who stood up for knowledge and prestige the conviction that you should loath every "Christian" ghetto and every "Christian" existence for Lebanon, for any closing of the ranks must be nationwide, motivated by our common destiniy. In your awareness of that you have borne, together with other citizens, the torch of national (*qawmi*) liberation since the last century. Since the dawn of Arab history you have been a continual shining presence within Christianity as a whole. You have had your share in the transmission of the ancient heritage to Arab civilization. Throughout all aspects of Arab life you have disseminated graciousness, human understanding, and sympathy." (CEMAM-Reports 1976:60).

One can ask the question: Which of these Christian or Muslim attitudes will prevail in the end? That depends on both Muslims and Christians of course. Much depends on whether or not something like a nationalist identity can be developed in Lebanon, which whether secular or not, would in any case transcend confessional differences. During the Lebanese civil war slogans appeared on the walls of buildings in west Beirut - the so-called progressive Palestinian part of the city - which read: "No to confessionalism and yes to secularisation" (*ʿilmaniyya*). This expression was intended as a rejection of the confessional system upon which the Lebanese republic has been built since its independence in 1943. This is a system whereby sixteen different minorities of Muslims and Christians get a fixed share but Maronites a definite preponderance of positions in political, social and economic fields. The already mentioned Lebanese author Tawfiq Yusuf 'Awwad more recently published a book under the title (in English) *Death in Beirut*. He records the voices of protesting students as one could hear them shortly before the war, who were shouting opposition against the worn-out feudal system, in which religious affiliation made the forming of a really democratic socio-political system impossible. "Shout in their faces: 'We don't want your broken down crutches! We don't want your system! And we reject your counterfeit religions!'" ('Awwad 1976:114).

But will a 'non-confessional' secular state materialize in Lebanon? Or must we believe that other slogan, written on another wall in the same quarter of Beirut: "No to confessionalism, yes to Islam"? Will the confessional arguments and sensibilities on both the Muslim and Christian sides prevail and increase the polarization of the struggle so that it does evolve from a social political to a religious one? Will both Muslims and Christians be able to withstand the temptation to exploit religious labels in order to hide the real issues (the injustice structures of society?) for which *all* Lebanese citizens together are responsible? The same author 'Awwad quotes

> "God is one of our great problems. The God that Moslems and Christians divide among themselves, that we divide between us, the God of the confessionalism, of politics and the sharing out of official jobs. The God that stands between us to prevent mixed marriages between different religions or raises his hand in protest at civil marriages. That kind of God ought to be dealt and done away with ..." ('Awwad 1976:128).

The question remains as to whether that is what really is going to happen. It was said of the Falangists in the sixties that they stood for a modernizing party who favoured national integration and social reform. But in the seventies they returned to their original beginnings and began recalling their deep anti-Muslim prejudices (Entelis 1974).

Something comparable is happening on the Muslim side via what today is often called the revival of a fundamentalistic form of Islam. Many Muslims of the 'Muslim Brotherhood'-type see the whole development of Arab nationalism and Arab socialism and secularization in the Arab and Islamic world, as well as the division of religion and state so widely favoured and supported by Christians, as a 'Western trick' to divide and weaken Islam and the Islamic world.

On of the dangerous potential consequences on both sides is that the controversies will become consciously or unconsciously polarized along religious lines, thus eliminating all progressive forces which could contribute to a more just society in which there is permanent room for permanent coexistence between people of varying ethnic and religious backgrounds. Only a process of de-polarization and de-confessionalization on both sides of the controversy can end the continiung 'innere und aussere' emigration of Christians and the misuse of religious labels to disguise the real social and political issues.

It is obvious that the real issue in the Middle East is the Palestine problem and not only since the Israelis invasion of Lebanon in 1982 - the first real Israeli-Palestine war. The Lebanese problem has become indefinitely related to the Palestian. No solution for the Lebanese problems is in sight when there will not be a *political* solution of the Palestine issue.

NOTES

1 J. Knappert, Heraklios. *De strijd van Muhammed tegen de Christenen.* Swahili epos. Amsterdam 1977 (De Oosterse bibliotheek).

2 *Al-Fikr al-islāmī -l- hadith wa silātuhu bi'l isti mār al-gharbi.*

Cairo 1960. Cf. J. Jomier, M.I.D.E.O. VII, 376.

3 For instance M.H. Haykal, *Hayāt Muhammad*, Cairo 1935, 253.

4 Cf. *The Times*, December 1912, 1917.

5 For the details of the Lebanese history we used P.K. Hitti *Lebanon in History*, New York 1967[3], 321.

6 *Liban 1975-1976. Qu'avons-nous fait en que faire* (6) 1976, 10, 11.

7 *La crise libanaise dans ses principales dimensions*, 1.

REFERENCES

Altheim, F.
1975 *Der unbesiegte Gott, Heidentum und Christentum*. Hamburg.

Andrae, T.
1926 *Der Ursprung des Islams und das Christentum*. Uppsala.

'Awwad, Tawfiq Yusuf
1976 *Death in Beirut*. London.

CEMAM-Reports
1976 *Religion, State and Ideology*. Beirut.

Churchill
1862 *The Druzes and the Maronites*. London.

De Elpaza, M.
1971 Notes pour une histoire des polêmiques anti-chrêtienne dans l'occident musulman. *Arabica* XVII.

Entelis, J.P.
1974 *Pluralism and Party Transformation in Lebanon: al-Kata'ib 1936-1970*. Leiden.

Gardner, B.
1965 *Allenby*. London.

Gilbert, V.
1923 *The Romance of the Last Crusade with Allenby to Jerusalem*. New York.

Hitti, P.K.
1973[3] *Lebanon in History*. New York.

Hourani, A.
1962 *Arabic Thought in the Liberal Age 1789-1939*. London.

Jomier, J.
1960 *Mélanges de l'Institut Dominicain d'Etudes Orientales*, VII.

Knappert, J.
1977 *De strijd van Muhammed tegen de christenen*. Swahili epos. (De Oosterse bibliotheek), Amsterdam.

Makarius, Raoul & Laura
1964 *Anthology de la Littérature Arabe Contemporaine*. Paris.

Watt, W.M.
1965 *A History of Islamic Spain*. Edinburgh.

1972 *The Influence of Islam on Medieval Europe*. Edinburgh.

Wessels, A.
1972 *A Modern Arabic Biography of Muhammed*. Leiden.

Aspects of the Changing Nature of Lebanese Confessional Politics: Al-Murabitun, 1958-1979[1]

Marion Farouk-Sluglett and Peter Sluglett

Almost all recent studies of Lebanon have begun to challenge the rather bland and almost self-congratulatory view of the country put forward by social scientists in the early and middle 1960's. This approach, exemplified by the collective volume edited by Binder[2] has clearly proved inadequate in the face of the most violent internal conflict in recent Middle Eastern history; the notions of 'balance' and 'harmony' between the religious communities, and the idea of an equitable sharing out of power between them, now have to be, and have been, substantially revised.[3] More detailed studies, especially the careful analysis of Dubar and Nasr[4], have begun to correct the balance, and see Lebanese society less in terms of an agglomeration of 'primordial loyalties'[5] than of a grouping of fundamentally antagonistic classes whose inherent contradictions have been almost concealed by the facade of the 'traditional' political system. The received wisdom of communal harmony has demonstrated its own inadequacy, not only by the fact of interconfessional conflict, but also by the failures of the traditional bonds of unity and loyalty within the sects themselves. To a very great extent, Lebanese politics over the last ten years have emerged, very painfully, out of the ideological strait-jacket into which the constitutional arrangements of the 1940's had managed to confine them.

In this paper we shall examine the changing nature of Lebanese confessional politics through a study of *al-Murābitūn,* whose members form the Independent Nasserist Movement based in Beirut.[6] Although the organisation is almost entirely composed of Sunni Muslims, it is not a confessional movement, in that it does not seek to promote the ideology or interests of a religious confession *per se*. It is thus a movement of Sunnis, but not a Sunni movement. In order to understand this distinction we must first look at Lebanese history over the past fifty years, and also at part of the history of the Arab world, to which many Lebanese claim not to belong, but of which perhaps rather more feel themselves to be an integral part.

Present day Lebanon was put together by the French in 1920, by enlarging the former Ottoman *mutaṣarrifiyya* to include the coastal towns of Tripoli, Tyre, Sidon and their hinterlands, and the plains of the Biqa' and the 'Akkar. The *mutaṣarrifiyya* had consisted principally of Mount Lebanon and Beirut, whose population was very largely Maronite and Druze, while the regions added in 1920 were preponderantly Sunni and Shi'i:

Mount Lebanon

Christians		*Muslims*	
Maronites	156,000	Druzes	34,181
Greek Orthodox	40,689	Sunnis	18,573
Greek Catholic	16,468	Shi'is	19,898
Other Christian	2,400		72,562
	215,557		

Areas Added

Christians		*Muslims*	
Maronites	43,000	Sunnis	160,213
Greeek Orthodox	40,720	Shi'is	85,049
Greek Catholic	25,994	Druzes	9,552
Other Christian	7,618		200,814[7]
	117,332		

Hence, although the Maronites remained the largest single community, they no longer enjoyed their previously considerable numerical preeminence. Furthermore, while many of the Maronites of the Mountain in the 1920's were smallholders, the vast majority of the Sunni and Shi'i populations on the periphery were sharecroppers, largely because of the different forms of cultivation and the different social relations prevailing in these areas. In addition, the main beneficiaries of the penetration of European capital in the mid-nineteenth century had been the Maronites of Beirut and the Mountain, although a small but important stratum of Sunni merchants from Tripoli and Beirut also participated in the process. Finally, the Christians' 'head start' was also reinforced by their more direct access to education: throughout most of the period of the Mandate (1920-1946) education was still substantially in the hands of foreign missions, and thus more specifically directed towards the Christian population. Even in 1968, 62% of all school-children attended private, that is largely Christian, schools.[8]

AlbertHourani has described the various ideologies which form an important *Leitmotiv* within the political culture of the main communities[9]. Probably the strongest of these is the Maronite belief expressed here in a quotation from the seventeenth century patriarch Istifan al-Duwayhi: "The Maronite community's history is a continuous struggle to maintain national and religious identity in a dominant Moslem environment"[10], signifying the ever-present fear of drowning in a Muslim sea. This notion has been supplemented, and for some Maronites replaced, by a more populist ideology propounded by the *Katā'ib*, a political party founded by Pierre Gemayel in 1936. Other Christian groups were also attracted to the *Katā'ib*, although many of them joined the more universalist associations such as the *Parti Populaire Syrien* (*PPS*), founded in 1932, and the various Communist parties.[11]

Among the Muslims, and specifically among the Sunnis, political articulation developed more slowly and less cohesively. With the possible exception of the Druzes, Muslim communal solidarity is and was less strongly felt than that of the Maronites, and there have been other important focuses of loyalty. The sense of an embattled community is of course not present, since the Sunnis especially have always been aware of their membership of a wider Sunni world beyond the borders of Lebanon. In fact, for most of the period of the French Mandate the Sunnis refused to accept the idea of Lebanon as a permanent entity, hoping that the country would eventually be reabsorbed into Syria. Ultimately, however, the Sunni leadership was persuaded to give up this particular aspiration in return for a promise on the part of the Maronites to forfeit the safeguard of French protection: Lebanon was to be independent, neither part of Syria nor a French protectorate. This arrangement was enshrined in the unwritten National Pact of 1943, between the Maronite President Bishara al-Khuri and the Sunni Prime Minister Riyadh al-Sulh, which maintained the principle of confessionalism in the various offices of state and at all levels of the civil service as well as in the armed forces. On the basis that the Maronites were the largest single community, they were given the key offices of the Presidency and Commander in Chief of the Army. In addition, the Christian/Muslim balance in offices and in the Chamber of Deputies was to be maintained at a fixed ratio of 6 Christians to every 5 Muslims. The Pact had the direct or indirect effect of preventing or at least hindering the growth of forms of political life based on matters of ideology or principle, and the view of it expressed in the pages of *al-Murābit* and by the leaders of the Independent Nasserist Movement as the 'Lebanese Company Limited' is not far from the truth.[12]

The arrangement thus arrived at, of a horizontal alliance which facilitated the vertical distribution of patronage of various kinds in return for votes at elections worked, after a fashion, until the middle 1950's. One of the reasons for this was the system through which influence and control was exerted at the lower levels of the patronage ladder, since the political bosses (*zā'im*, plural *zu'amā'*) employed strong-arm men to control their (normally confessional) following, as described by Johnson for the Sunni quarters of Beirut.[13] These *qabadayat*, or petty to medium gangsters, were instrumental in articulating the *zā'im's* relations with his clients, and it is incidentally significant that the power structures in West Beirut have undergone what seems to be a major transformation partly because of the breakdown of this relationship.

Hence, apart from the *Katā'ib*, the *PPS* and the Communist party, political parties as such hardly existed in Lebanon until comparatively recently. There is thus much truth in the description of pre-Civil War Lebanon as a society where "there is little or no class consciousness and political parties are weak to the point of insignificance, as are trade unions and other interest groups".[14] Instead, the notables of all the communities were linked with one another in a complex system of bargaining, whose main objective was to ensure their dominance within their community or region, and, as a class, within the system as a whole.[15] They were able to maintain their position by a virtual monopoly of patronage in the fields of political favours, the direction of contracts, employment, education and so forth.

In a certain sense, the Christian, and in particular the Maronite, *za'im* had an easier task than his Muslim counterpart in the course of the 1950's, when the Arab world was experiencing a period of rapid political change. The system, with its built-in implications of Christian superiority, was relatively easy to maintain among a Maronite clientêle, and although it also suited the Sunni political leaders, it could scarcely expect to find wide approval among their less fortunate co-religionists. The first signs of a major challenge to the status quo began to come to the surface in the mid-1950's, with Nasser's successful seizure of power in Egypt, which coincided with the beginnings of the oil boom and the consequent increase in the self-confidence and economic power of the Sunni bourgeoisie, whose commercial links with the Arab hinterland had always remained strong.[16] Here we can see the beginnings of a certain tension within the Sunni community; the leaders were consolidating their wealth from their position of advantage within the Lebanese economy, while the bulk of the community were eagerly following Nasser's progress and hoping that a closer integration of Lebanon with the rest of the Arab world might result.

Eventually the greater radicalism of the Sunni 'street' had a decisive effect on forcing at least the semblance of change of attitude at the 'top'. The rank and file of the Sunni community increasingly identified themselves with Arabism and Nasserism, and there were mass demonstrations against the Baghdad Pact, in support of the nationalisation of the Suez Canal, and against the 'Tripartite Aggression' of 1956. Even fairly conservative quarters began to identify themselves publicly with Nasserism; on 8 November 1955 the Mufti of Lebanon sent Nasser a telegram addressed to the "Arab Muslim President Jamal 'Abd al-Nasir ... In the name of the Muslims of Lebanon we greet you and endorse your magnificant stand ... and your defence of the Arab cause and Islam".[17] On the occasion of the nationalisation of the Canal, 30,000 signatures of support were collected in Tripoli alone, and popular pressure was so great that the Prime Minister, 'Abdullah al-Yafi', and his colleague Sa'ib Salam, both prominent Sunni *zu'amā'*, were virtually forced to resign from office when President Cham'un refused to break off diplomatic relations with Britain and France in November 1956.

As the appeal of Nasserism grew stronger, the various Sunni leaders, particularly Sa'ib Salam and Rashid Karami, resorted to "promoting their popularity within the community by competing for identification with Nasser [18]". More significantly, perhaps, Nasserism became the political expression of popular Sunni opposition to the status quo; Nasser was upheld as the hero (*baṭal*) who had successfully defied imperialism, an aspect of his achievement to which *al-Murābit* magazine still makes constant reference. The Egyptian leader's popularity was even further boosted by the declaration of the United Arab Republic of Egypt and Syria in February 1958. *al-Muqāsid*, a Sunni educational and welfare charity virtually controlled by the Salam family for the bulk of the period between 1920 and 1970[19] declared the day a national holiday, and three hundred thousand Lebanese were reported to have visited President Quwatli in Damascus;[20] banners in Tripoli proclaimed "We want immediate unity with the revolutionary Jamal 'Abd al-Nasir."

In this highly charged atmosphere President Cham'un let it be known that he would attempt to introduce a constitutional amendment which would permit him to succeed himself as President for a second six year term. On 8 May 1958, a prominent opponent of Cham'un, the journalist Nasib al-Matni, was assassinated by the President's supporters, and fighting immediately broke out. Cham'un's opponents were partly motivated, on a popular level, by grievances relating to the underprivileged status of the Muslim community, and by the President's anti-Arab and pro-Western stance, while the *zu'amā'* feared the consequences of another six years of exclusion from office and the inevitable limitations on their access to patronage.

Eventually, the Lebanese government took the dispute to the United Nations, on the grounds that the opposition was being armed by the UAR. Landings of United States troops on 15 July, the day after the Iraqi revolution, had the effect of separating the fighting factions, and a 'neutral' candidate, General Fu'ad Shihab, the Commander in Chief of the Army, was elected President on 31 July.

This episode is of importance not so much for any positive results but because of the immense jolt which it gave to the system and the impact it had on the generation which participated in it. Ibrahim Qulailat traces the foundation of the Independent Nasserist Movement to his experiences in 1958, when he was 17; the Lebanese Communist Party also gained experience of guerilla fighting, as did the followers of Kamal Jumblatt, who became the nucleus of the Progressive Socialist Party. For our present purposes it is highly significant that the Muslim *zu'amā'* seem to have been pushed into a position of opposition to the State structure partly for reasons of self-interest, but also as a consequence of pressure from their 'supporters', showing even at this early stage that notions of clientelism and 'primordial loyalties' were already in need of review.

Shihab's presidency from 1958 to 1964 was marked by attempts to extend the activities of the Lebanese state, and to introduce an altogether more *dirigiste* and reformist style of government. Both Shihab and his successor Charles Helou (1964-1970) concentrated on developing the regions somewhat at the expense of the capital, and both attempted to curb the political influence of the *zu'amā'*, whose "Byzantine and internecine factionalism"[21] had certainly been an important factor in 1958. In foreign affairs, Shihab came to a tacit agreement with President Nasser in 1959 whereby he undertook to follow a generally pro-Egyptian foreign policy while being permitted to contain the Nasserist movement inside Lebanon. The latter process encouraged the expansion of the *deuxième bureau* whose intelligence activities began to press heavily on both Christian and Muslim *zu'amā'*, which encouraged greater cooperation between the leaders for the purpose of warding off the unwelcome encroachments of the state. This development in its turn permitted or assisted the *zu'amā'* to reassert their dominance over their communities. The rise to power of the Ba'thist regimes in Syria and Iraq did not mobilise any significant degree of support among the Lebanese population, whose notions of *waḥda* (unity) remained almost inextricably bound up with the person of Nasser. In the 1960's many intellectuals became increasingly critical of the more oppressive aspects of Nasserist rule, although the popular cult of Nasser as a charismatic leader does not seem to have diminished; indeed, as will be seen, it continues to have remarkable vigour even today.

Although Nasser's foreign policy setbacks in the 1960's and his partial withdrawal from inter-Arab politics had some effect on Sunni militancy in Lebanon and reduced the capacity of the rank and file to exert the kinds of pressure on their leaders that we have seen operating in the 1950's, Nasser's support of the Palestinians after 1965, and even more the devastating defeat of June 1967, had the joint effect of strengthening his following in Lebanon. To the

Arab nationalists and Nasserists the Palestian guerillas represented the main hope of Arab regeneration. The Israeli attack on Beirut airport in 1968 served to polarise Lebanese opinion yet again, the Muslims demanding a stronger army and freedom for the Palestinians to operate from Lebenese territory, while most of the Chirstians supported curbing Palestinian activity to prevent Israeli reprisals.

In spite of the very considerable tensions which have been described above, the *laisser-faire* political and economic features of the Lebanese state enabled the political system to survive, greatly to the benefit of those who controlled it, until the beginning of the 1970's. Since the basis of both the constitution and the system of patronage were confessional, the structure appeared to imply, and of necessity reinforced, confessional solidarity on the part of participants at all levels, while concealing its fundamentally exploitative nature. The endemic weaknesses of the system were thus successfully concealed, or at least glossed over, until the period immediately before the Civil War of 1975-76, when a combination of galloping inflation, economic dislocation, political frustration, the exigencies of the Arab-Israeli situation and the problems arising from the presence of large numbers of armed Palestinians within the country, came together to deal it a mortal blow.

The imbalances within the economy[22] are reflected in the enormous size of the service sector, which generated 62% of GDP in 1960, and 72% in 1972, and in Lebanon's function as a kind of staging post for foreign banks, through which deposits drained out of the country to Western money markets. In 1972, only 15 out of the country's 80 banks were controlled by Lebanese majority interests: three fifths were subsidiaries of Western banks, and the other fifth was controlled by non-Lebanese Arab interests. The equivalent of between 50 and 60% of GDP left the country annually through the banking and financial system, while far smaller sums were invested locally. Here again the pre-eminence of the non-productive part of the economy must be underscored; of these investments, 4.3% went to agriculture, 16% to industry and 53% to commerce.

Industry and agriculture showed similar tendencies. In 1970, textiles, food and construction material accounted for 70% of all industrial production, the remaining 30% consisting largely of the assembly of products imported from outside for onward export to the Arab world. Of 25 large firms, 17 were controlled by members of the Christian *grande bourgeoisie*, and 7 by their Muslim counterparts, while foreign capital accounted for 41% of investment in these companies as a whole. Furthermore, seven family groups controlled ten of the largest firms. Over the past 30 years, agriculture has suffered an immense decline; nearly 50% of the active population were employed on the land in 1959, and only 18.9% in 1970. Agriculture provided 33% of exports in 1965 and 16.5% in 1972. In the period immediately before the Civil War, two large firms monopolised the importation of all fertilisers and insecticides, while at the other end of the process 25 merchants were responsible for the purchase of almost all agricultural produce.

Hence many smallholders on Mount Lebanon were forced to sell up because of rising costs and leave the land, or become wage labourers. Elsewhere, sharecroppers were gradually forced to leave the land because of increasing mechanisation. One of the results of the decline in agricultural employment was that by 1974 half the families in Lebanon lived in greater Beirut. The effects of this major movement of population on the labour market can easily be imagined; industrial wages could be kept low, and trade unions were either repressed altogether, made legal but kept extremely weak, or controlled by the employers. An enormous sub-proletariat came into existence, participating occasionally in the service sector. Most of the migrants have come from the peripheral areas, the Sunni north or the Shi'i south and east. Emigration abroad, Lebanon's traditional safety valve, has tended to slacken off, and in any case the Gulf States and Sa'udi Arabia need businessmen or technocrats rather than ex-peasants.

The tensions arising from this recent influx of uprooted rural migrants were further compounded by the presence of nearly 300,000 Palestinians on Lebanese territory, half of whom have entered the country since 1967.[23] The Palestinian resistance first began to show real muscle after the defeat of the Arab armies in 1967, producing great tension and instability in the countries where the Palestinians were based. Guerilla raids into Israel provoked reprisals, with Israel accusing the host countries of being unwilling to control their 'guests'. Furthermore, particularly in Jordan and Lebanon, it was clear that the Palestinians were having a radicalising and thus disturbing effect on the local population. In the late 1960's, Palestinian raids from Lebanon attracted a sharp response from Israel, and the resentment of segments of Lebanese society found expression in the major clashes between the Lebanese Army and the Palestinians which came to a head in November 1969.

As a result of Egyptian mediation, a Lebanese-Palestinian agreement was signed in Cairo, which legitimised the Palestinian presence and facilitated commando activities in Lebanon, regulating their relations with the authorities in such a way as to uphold Lebanese sovereignty. While the agreement was welcomed by the more 'radical' forces, it was roundly condemned by the *Kata'ib* on the grounds that Lebanese sovereignty was being violated, and in the early 1970's the *Katā'ib* and ex-President Cham'un's National Liberal Party began to set up training camps for their militias, making a showdown more or less inevitable. Relations
between 1970 and 1974, and added to the growing social tensions

within the country, which came to the boil in the spring of 1975. The clashes between the Lebanese Army and demonstrators at Sa'ida in which the popular deputy Ma'ruf Sa'd was killed were followed in April by a shooting incident involving members of the *Katā'ib* and the Palestinian resistance at 'Ain Rummana, which is generally taken to mark the beginning of the Civil War.

It was against the backcloth of the 1975-76 Civil War that the Independent Nasserists Movement and its military wing *al-Murābitūn* first rose to prominence on the Lebanese stage, although its ideological foundations had been laid some twenty-five years before. So far, we have described the considerable dislocations that emerged within the Lebanese economy, and the increasingly apparent limitations of the political system. In a sense the appearance of phenomena like *al-Murābitūn* can be seen as one of the consequences of the virtual collapse of both these sectors during the Civil War. Of course, as they have emerged from this background they inevitably reflect certain features of it. However, they represent, in a functional sense, an important break with the past, and a new type of formation within Lebanese politics. In this, of course, they are not alone; *al-Murābitūn* are one of fifteen political organisations which combined to form the Lebanese National Movement (LNM) which itself, together with the Palestinians, was one of the two 'sides' in the Civil War. The LNM and the Palestinians have been virtually ruling West Beirut, Tripoli and parts of South Lebanon since 1976, following the *de facto* division of the country which followed the intervention of the Syrian Army in May 1976.

al-Murābitūn describe the Civil War and the continuing tensions in Lebanon as a battle between the forces of progress and democracy against the 'isolationist establishment' (*al-mu'assasa al-in'izalia*), Imperialism and Zionism, a view which gains more credibility from the clear evidence of Israeli assistance to the *Katā'ib* and other Christian militias in South Lebanon, against the forces of the LNM and the Palestinians. Their own vision for the future of Lebanon, frequently reiterated in conversation and in their weekly *al-Murābit*, is for an independent secular democratic Arab state, in which, they claim, they would put up their own candidates for election.

The Independent Nasserist Movement was founded by its present leader, Ibrahim Qulailat, in 1958. Qulailat himself comes from a lower middle class Sunni family from West Beirut, and became an activist in the course of the earlier (1958) Civil War, which broke out during his last year at secondary school. Although it is difficult to trace his career precisely, it seems that he was imprisoned several times in the 1960's for various acts of violence, as well as being detained in Riyadh in 1960 on suspicion of involvement in a plot to assassinate king Sa'ud of Sa'udi Arabia, who was apparently himself trying to assassinate Nasser at that time. Qulailat's own account of the incident is colourful but somewhat mysterious. In 1966 he was arrested again in Beirut on suspicion of the murder of an anti-Nasser and pro-Sa'udi newspaper editor, but the charges were dropped after what appears to have been some high level intervention on his behalf. He was once associated with Sa'ib Salam, but cut off links with him after the latter's abandonment of Nasserism in the 1960's.

When he was released from prison in 1967, Qulailat claims that he had gathered some 6,000 supporters around him. Although this figure seems farfetched, it is probably true that his organisation was the largest Nasserist association in Lebanon. In that year the Movement became closely linked to *Fataḥ*, and it was to play a major role in the clashes which culminated the Cairo accords of 1969. After Nasser's death in 1970 there were a number of splits in the Nasserist ranks, caused largely by Sadat's apparent jettisoning of Nasser's legacy in 1971, and the links forged by various groups with Syria and Lybia. The Independent Nasserist Movement began to make serious military preparations after further clashes between the Palestinians and the Lebanese Army in 1973, and by the time of the Civil War in 1975 it could field some 3,000 armed men.[24] During the war itself they came to prominence particularly in the course of the fierce reaction to the appalling massacres of Muslims perpetrated by the *Katā'ib* and the Cham'unists in Beirut on Black Saturday, 8 December 1975. "While every possible measure was taken to secure the safety of unarmed Christians living in the Muslim sectors of Beirut",[25] *al-Murābitūn* occupied the hotel area in the north west of the city together with other militias, and engaged the 'isolationists' in fierce fighting for several days.

al-Murābitūn continued to play an important role throughout the fighting in 1976, particularly at Dammur and on Mount Lebanon. Though they have become grudgingly reconciled to the presence of the Syrian Army, its arrival in May 1976 was not at all to their liking: in Sinan Barraj's words: "When we were just about to win, the Syrian invasion came to stop us, and to strangle the Lebanese National Movement, and to have better relations with the isolationists. Without Syrian assistance Tall Za'atar would not have fallen (in August 1976). They went there to kill them" (Interview, September 1979). The numerical strength of the forces of *al-Murābitūn* ensured that they would become an important part of the Lebanese National Movement, which assumed formal organisational structure in July 1976, under the presidency of the late Kamal Jumblatt.

Within the National Movement, which has itself never been officially recognised by the Lebanese government, *al-Murābitūn* consider themselves 'hardliners'; despite the LNM's reconciliation with Damascus in September 1977, Qulailat himself did not go to see 'Asad until October 1978, and *al-Murābitūn* have also opposed any overt support for the government of President Sarkis. They are also particularly critical of the new Army Law, which they see as a means of building up the Lebanese Army as an instrument which the 'rightists' will be able to use to smash the forces of the 'left' and the Palestinians. Here, however, it is important to preserve a sense of proportion, since the capacity of *al-Murābitūn* to influence the course of Lebanese politics is extremely limited, and they can only act within the framework of the National Movement as a whole.

In theory, *al-Murābitūn* are organised on a cell basis; the organisation as a whole knows who the members are, but the individuals themselves only know their own cell members, with the exception of the link to the higher level. In fact, there is a *Murābitūn* office in each quarter controlled by the National Movement, with a library and games room, and on this level the movement functions more as a social than a political organisation. There is an elected supreme 'leadership council', a weekly magazine, *al-Murābit*, and a radio station, the Voice of Arab Lebanon (compare *Sawt al-ʿArab*, the Voice of the Arabs, Nasser's name for Cairo radio), which can be heard in most parts of Lebanon. Their Beirut headquarters, near al-Jama'a al-'Arabiyya in Abu Shakir Street (Abu Shakir is Qulailat's father) was impressively organised, and guarded, like the other National Movement offices, by armed militiamen. The building had spacious offices, with Qur'anic quotations on the walls and pictures of Qulailat and Nasser together.

In private, Qulailat seemed rather shy and diffident. Although content to be built up as a leader, he seemed to entrust political work, and *al-Murābitūn*'s regular representation on the National Movement Council, to his deputies, nicknamed *al-dakātira*, the doctors, by other Beirutis - Dr. Samir Sabbagh, Dr. Ziad al-Hafiz, and Mr. Sinan Barraj, all of whom are or have been practising lawyers. Qulailat is projected by the organisation and in its magazine as a tireless fighter for freedom, a man who has devoted his life to the 'anti-imperialist' struggle, a close friend and confidant of Nasser, a thoughtful man who weighs his words carefully, but also a man with whom his followers can identify; the *dakātira* are clearly, by their language and style, middle class figures, while Qulailat is the hero of the Sunni 'Street' - the essentially service nature of the Lebanese economy making the use of the term 'working class' almost meaningless in this context.

The movement vigorously promotes the cult of Nasser's personality; the leaders say '*Lama ghaba ʿAbd al-Nāsir*', when Abd al-Nasir *disappeared* (sc. from this world), and refer to him as *al-shahīd*, the martyr, meaning the martyr to the Arab cause. Qulailat referred in conversation to Nasser's life as '*al-sīra al-mutakāmila, al-sīra al-farida*', meaning perfect conduct, unique life; the word *sīra* is generally used in the context of the biography of the prophet Muhammad. Qulailat himself is built up as it were apposition to

Nasser, whose picture and sayings appear in every issue of *al-Murābit*. The movement's slogans are the Nasserist 'unity, freedom and socialism', but both the leaders and the magazine are somewhat imprecise when it comes to matters of practical strategy and politics, particularly in the immediate Lebanese context. Not surprisingly, they have not made any serious analysis of the Nasserist period in Egypt and take it for granted that 'democracy' and 'socialism' actually existed in Egypt in the 1950's and 1960's. Hence Sadat is the betrayer (*khā'in*) of Nasser's heritage, and is ritually lampooned, denounced and caricatured in the magazine.

al-Murābitūn both represent and try to appeal to very wide strata of the Lebanese population, and this is reflected in the vagueness of their political programme. An important feature of their writings and declarations is that the external conflict (Zionism/Imperialism) and the image of the external enemy are constantly utilised in an attempt to be acceptable to the various disparate social groups to which their potential 'constituents' might belong. However much the social or economic interests of these strata may otherwise differ, their own recent experience has led them to range themselves against 'Zionism and Imperialism'. Concentration on this very real issue has the effect of glossing over class differences, but such "very real issues" are the *fons et origo* of nationalist parties.

This appeal for unity against an essentially external enemy is also a vital component of the programme of the Lebanese National Movement as a whole, and an important feature of its avowedly cross-confessional message. More specifically, *al-Murābitūn*, along with the rest of the National Movement, want electoral reform and the end of confessional representation in parliament and the civil service. Although these may seem fairly modest demands, it will be clear by now that in the Lebanese context it would mean that the traditional ruling classes, the Muslim and Christian *zu'ama*, would inevitably lose much of their influence, which would be almost tantamount to a revolution.

However, a striking feature of the ideology of *al-Murābitūn* - and of most of the other nationalist parties - is an almost mystical belief that because they are all Arabs (or all Syrians in the case of the *PPS*), once the external battle is won, social justice will reign, and the internal class conflict will somehow be overcome by peaceful means. "Who are the people (*al-sha'b*)?", asks Samir Sabbagh (*al-Murābit*, 5/11/77). The people are "the producers, the workers, the revolutionary intelligentsia, the soldiers and that part of the national bourgeoisie which accepts state planning and control by popular institutions. The 'great' capitalists are not the people." The social revolution which will follow political reform will abolish 'capitalist exploitation' (14/9/77); its leaders will come from the ranks of the masses (*al-jamāhīr*), and class distinctions will melt (*tadhwīb*) in the face of the unifying power of Arabism (3/12/77).

In order to differentiate themselves from the Communist Party, and to pre-empt the fears of Communism which may exist among their actual or potential supporters, *al-Murābitūn* are at pains to emphasize the difference between exploitative and non-exploitative private property (9/9/78). As Nasser has shown, it is pointed out, not all the means of production have to be nationalised; private property is not to be abolished, nor are the rights of inheritance to be touched. A public sector must be created to work out a development plan, but as the private sector also contributes to the nation (*al-watan*) it participates as well, although of course under the control of the people (*al-shaʿb*) (9/9/78). As Nasser has shown, it is pointed out, not all the means that they were neither Marxists nor Communists, and that their alliance with the Communist groupings in the LNM was 'political' and not 'ideological'. On the occasion of the sixtieth anniversary of the 1917 Revolution, *al-Murābit* magazine devoted a long article to the 'Great October Revolution' (29/10/77), which pointed out that the Socialist countries are and have been the only true friends of the Arabs, both in their support of Nasser and in their opposition to Israel. This said, however, *al-Murābit* hastened to point out that the movement's friendship with the Soviet Union is based on strategic, that is, tactical, solidarity (cf. the issue of 5/11/77), a term which is regularly used when the leadership is defining its position *vis-à-vis* the Socialist countries.

It will be clear from our description of the political system that apart from the older political groupings (notably the Communists and the *Parti Populaire Syrien*) which have themselves only recently been free to operate openly in Lebanon, the formulae set out in the National Pact of 1943 have generally had the effect of maintaining and reinforcing confessional alliances, and in making confessionalism an integral feature of political life, both on the 'left' and on the 'right'. Thus the Shi'is are particularly numerous in the Communist Party, the Druzes in Jumblatt's PSP, and (although this tendency has been greatly modified) the Greek Orthodox in the *PPS*. In spite of the fact that the Lebanese National Movement as a whole and the individual parties by themselves are profoundly committed to the secularization of political life, the practical constraints on this are considerable. Thus the Nasserists, including *al-Murābitūn*, confront the particular difficulty that Nasserism as such appeals primarily to Sunni Muslims. Although the leaders of *al-Murābitūn* claim that the Druze and Shi'i communities are well represented within their movement, it is clear that the Sunnis form the overwhelming majority.

The main reasons for this are first, the role that Nasser has played in Lebanese history, which has already been described, and secondly the strongly Islamic connotations of Arabism, *ʿurūba*, in Lebanon. In order to counter this, and to make *ʿurūba* acceptable to other religious sects, *al-Murābitūn* emphasize that although "Religion is part of the Arab nation" (*al-umma al-ʿarabiyya*) and "Islam is a spiritual bond; this bond is not in conflict with the national bond which links the sons of the nation in language, culture, history, heritage and common interest." (15/5/76). Thus Arabism and the Arab nation (*al-watan al-ʿarabī*) is considered to precede Islam. However, in stressing the need for secularization, the movement finds itself in a vicious circle; its main supporters *are* Sunni Muslims, and concessions in this direction must be made. Thus many issues of *al-Murābit* carry pictures of the leaders in conversation with Shaikh Hasan Khalid, the Mufti of Lebanon, to convince their readers that the movement is not anti-religious, while *al-Murābitūn* emphasize, and their political programme clearly shows, that they are an ideological and not a confessional party. Thus, however sincere their attempts to overcome confessionalism may be, they are seen by the other communities as essentially a Sunni movement, and find it difficult to gain adherents elsewhere. This paradox underscores the immense obstacles facing all Lebanese political parties trying to break away from the confessional tradition.

It may be alleged that the leaders of *Murābitūn* are gradually becoming, or are seeking to become, the new *zu'amā'*. However, the main effect of the *zā'im - qabaḍā'i* relationship was the maintenance of vertical social and political control and the rule of the traditional establishment. Certainly, a number of deeprooted and persistent features of the old system still combine to prevent the emergence of a less personal and more formal *voie hiérarchique*, and the leadership has to a certain extent taken over some of the mediating function of the traditional *zu'amā'*; they have the necessary *wāsṭa* (back door influence, means of access) to ministers and other influential personalities. Nevertheless the movement as a whole stands firmly against the notion of the 'Lebanese Company Limited', and its continued existence is dependent on the extent to which it does oppose confessionalism in politics; although, in common with many other parties in the National Movement, it finds it difficult to reach members of all religious confessions, it is none the less a *political* party. However, if the present virtual stalemate in Lebanon continues, such parties may ultimately find themselves absorbed by the force of the underlying continuity of traditional political practices. *al-Murābitūn* are of course a manifestation of aspirations on the part of the less privileged and generally non-Maronite members of Lebanese society to participate in a more integrated political system. It is clear that radical changes will be necessary before they will be able to do so.

POSTSCRIPT, AUGUST 1983

As we have indicated, the research on which this paper is based was carried out in the course of a visit to Lebanon in September 1979. Since then, and specifically in the aftermath of the Israeli invasion of 1982, in which *Murābitūn* militia played an important part in the defence of Beirut, Lebanese politics have undergone a series of dramatic convulsions. In the first place, the expulsion of the Palestinians has gravely weakened the Lebanese National Movement, although the skeleton organisation still survives. The presence of the multinational peacekeeping force and the Lebanese Army in West Beirut is evidence of attempts to promote the authority of the Lebanese government there, but Lebanon has now become divided *de facto* between the Israelis and their client Major Haddad in the South, the Syrians in the North and East, hostile Palestinian factions in the Biqa', and the Lebanese government under President Amin Gemayel controlling Beirut, parts of Mount Lebanon and the coast as far North as Jounieh. Fierce fighting is taking place in the Shuf between the *Katā'ib* and Druzes attached to Walid Jumblatt's Progressive Socialist Party; Jumblatt, Rashid Karami and Sulaiman Franjiyyeh have recently announced a United Front against Gemayel's government on the grounds that its claim to be a government of national reconciliation is a sham. In these confused circumstances, the aspirations of many ordinary Lebanese for a peaceful secular democratic state seem as far away from fulfilment as ever.

FOOTNOTES

*This article is a revised version of a paper originally presented at a conference in Amsterdam in December 1979 on 'Religion and Religious Movements in the Mediterranean', sponsored by the University of Amsterdam and the Free University of Amsterdam. Although it has been revised substantially in the light of comments received from colleagues and friends, we should like to emphasize that it was written well before the tragic events of the summer of 1982.

1 The research on which the paper is based was made possible by a travel grant from the Centre for Middle Eastern and Islamic Studies, Durham University, which is gratefully acknowledged.

We should also like to thank several individuals for their assistance, both in Beirut and in London. We are particularly indebted to the leaders of *al-Murābitūn*, notably Messrs. Ibrahim Qulailat, Samir Sabbagh and Sinan Barraj, who gave us several interviews as well as a complete set of the weekly *al-Murabit* from April 1976 to September 1979. We should like to thank them and other leading members of the Lebanese National Movement, particularly Mr. In'am Ra'd of the *PPS*, who also gave generously of their time. We are especially grateful to Dr. Faisal al-Darraj for his stimulating and cordial hospitality, and to Dr. Rashid al-Khalidi, Mr. Husain Agha, Mr. Ahmad al-Khalidi and in particular Mr. 'Abbas Chiblak, for their ready assistance.

2 L. Binder (ed.) *Politics in Lebanon*, New York 1966.

3 A.H. Hourani 'Ideologies of the Mountain and the City', in: R. Owen (ed.) *Essays on the Crisis in Lebanon*, London 1976, pp. 33-42.

4 C. Dubar and S. Nasr *Les Classes Sociales au Liban*, Paris 1976.

5 S. Khalaf 'Primordial Ties and Politics in Lebanon', *Middle Eastern Studies*, 1968, Vol. IV, No. 3, pp. 243-269.

6 We have used *al-Murabitun* as a convenient shorthand throughout to refer to the Independent Nasserist Movement, although strictly speaking *al-Murabitun* refers only to members of its military wing.

7 Dubar and Nasr *op.cit.*, p. 24.

8 N. Hachem *Libanon, sozio-ökonomische Grundlagen*, Opladen 1969, p. 35.

9 Hourani *op. cit.*

10 Quoted in T. Khalaf 'The Phalange and the Maronite Community', in: R. Owen *Essays on the Crisis in Lebanon*, London 1976, pp. 43-48.

11 For the *Kata'ib* see J.P. Entelis *Pluralism and Party Transformation in Lebanon; al-Kata'ib, 1936-1970*, Leiden 1974; For the *PPS* see L.Z. Yamak *The Syrian Social Nationalist Party; an Ideological Analysis*, Cambridge, Mass. 1966. It should be pointed out that the *PPS* leaderschip has transformed the political orientation of the party very profoundly since 1969; in the 1958 Civil War, for example, it fought alongside the Cham'unists, while in the 1973 -75 Civil War it emerged as an important component of the National Movement. Yamak's useful monograph appeared well before this development. There is no comprehensive study of the Lebanese Communist Party in any European language.

12 In 1944-45, members of the Lebanese cabinet included 'Abd al-Hamid Karami, Camille Cham'un, Majid Arslan and Salim Takla; in 1975, they included Rashid Karami, Camille Cham'un, Majid Arslan and Philippe Takla.

13 M. Johnson 'Political bosses and their gangs; *Zu'ama* and Qabadayat in the Sunni Muslim quarters of Beirut', in E. Gellner and J. Waterbury *Patrons and Clients in Mediterranean Societies*, London 1977, pp. 207-224.

14 *Ibid.*, p. 210.

15 M. Gilsenan 'Against Patron-Client Relations', in: Gellner and Waterbury *op.cit.*, pp. 167-184.

16 N. 'Atiyah *The Attitude of the Sunnis toward the State of Lebanon*, unpublished Ph.D. thesis, London 1973, p. 240.

17 *Ibid.*, p. 253.

18 *Ibid.*, p. 280.

19 See M. Johnson 'Factional Politics in Lebanon: the case of the "Islamic Society of Benevolent Intentions" (*al-Maqasid*) in Beirut', *Middle Eastern Studies* 1978, Vol. XIV, No. 1, pp. 56-75.

20 F.I. Qubain *Crisis in Lebanon*, Washington 1961, p. 61.

21 M. Johnson 'Factional Politics ...', *op.cit.*

22 This discussion of the economy is based on Dubar and Nasr *op.cit.*, pp. 51-117.

23 See H. Sirriyeh 'The Palestinian Armed Presence in Lebanon since 1967', in: R. Owen *op.cit.*, pp. 73-89.

24 See J. Chami and G. Castoriades *Days of Tragedy Lebanon 1975-76*, Nicosia 1977, p. 2.

25 K. Salibi *Cross-Roads to Civil War: Lebanon 1958-1976*, New York 1976, p. 147.

Indexes

There are three indexes, listing proper names, subject matter and foreign words (mainly Arabic). The spelling of the proper names in the first index reproduces the spelling used by the authors in their papers. The spelling of Arabic words in the third index as well as in italics in the text has been unified according to a common system of transliteration recognizable for Arabists. It could not be entirely consistent because of the presence of words from different dialects.

The indexes were made by Hans van der Kerke, a student at the University of Utrecht.

Index 1: Proper Names

Abbasids 31
'Abd al-'Aziz Tha'alabi 153, 155
'Abd al-Hamid Ben Bādīs 149
'Abd al Hamid Karami 282n
'Abd al Hayy al-Kattani 166
'Abd Allah 206
'Abduh, Muhammad 14, 32, 80, 82, 84, 101, 152
'Abdullah al-Yafi 271
Abu Rudes 114
Abu Taleb 120
Abu Znema 108
al-Afghani, Jamal al-Din 14, 28, 80, 152
Afghanistan 97
Africa 68n
Ahmad b. Khuja 80, 81
Ahmad Bey 75, 79, 152
Ahmad Tawfiq al Madni 154
'Ain Draham 200, 201
'Ain Rummana 275
'Akkar 262, 268
'Alawiyya 147, 149, 151, 165
Albania 240, 243, 251n
'Alequat 104, 110, 112, 114, 119
Algeria 77, 78, 82, 83, 99, 147, 148, 149, 150, 154, 165, 171, 197, 200, 201
'Ali Ibn Abu (i) Taleb 104, 124
'Ali Bey 76, 79
'Allal al-Fasi 83
Allenby (general) 257, 258
Almohads 31, 138
Almoravides 138
Arabia 33, 149
Arabian Peninsula 18
Arabs 27
Arabs (Christian) 37
al-'Arish 124
Aristotle 99
Armenians 261
Aron 104, 120, 125
'Asad (President) 73, 276
Asia 63
Atatürk, Kemal Pasha 15, 20
Atlas Mountains 133, 134
Aus 127
Awlad Jindi 120, 121
Awlad Sa'id 104, 109-121

Awlad Sidi 'Ubayd 78

Baba Kiazim 243, 250n
Baba Rexhepi 250n
Baghdad 31
Balkan 9
al-Baydawi 80
Bayramîs 245
Bayrams 76
Bedewîs 245
Beirut 260-263, 268-277, 281
Beka (Biqā^{c}) 262, 268, 281
Bektachis 204 - 251n
Bektašîs 245
Ben Bādīs 153
Ben Diyāf 152
Bengladesh 98
Beni Wāsel 110, 112
Ben Youssef 157
Ben Yūsuf 164
Berber 82
Bergson 100
Bernstein 49
Bīr ^{c}Oqda 108
Bīr Zrer 108
Bishāra al-Khūrī 269
Bosnia 82, 84, 155-157, 164, 178
Britain 67n, 271
Buddhist 52
Bū-Kharūba 206, 207, 221, 236n
Būlāq 193, 194, 195
Bulgaria 240
Bū-Qasbāya 207, 208, 209
Byzantium 256
Bourguiba 82, 84, 155-157, 164, 178
Cairo 31, 64, 84,86, 190, 193, 194, 274-277
Calvary 63
Calvinists 16
Chad 98
Cham^{c}ūn 271, 274
Cham^{c}ūn Camille 282n
Chanson de Roland 255, 256
Charlemagne 256
Christ 12
Christians 36, 255-264, 268, 273, 276

Church of England 16
Cid, El 256
Constantine 257
Copts 261
Cromer (Lord) 80, 81
Cromwell 16
Cyprus 258
Cyrenaica 107, 149

Damascus 31, 246, 257, 271, 276
Dammūr 276
Dār al-[c]Ulūm 86
Darqawiyya 149, 151
Desûkîs 245
Djakovica 242, 243, 246, 247, 250n
Djerba 171
Druzes 258-260, 268, 269, 279, 281
Durkheim 5, 6, 68n, 232
Dutch Reformed Church 16

East 102
East-Africa 256
Egypt 1, 16, 32, 33, 38, 58, 73, 74, 75, 78-81, 84-87, 95, 96, 98, 101, 108, 112-115, 119, 153, 170, 187-190, 193-198n, 270, 271, 274, 278
Egyptians 65, 108, 120
Engels, F. 49
Europe 1, 2, 58, 67n, 73-75, 102

Falangists 262, 264
Faraḥ Dība 17
Faraj 124, 125
Faranja 125
Farḥat Hached 173
Farȯuk (King) 188
al-Fataḥ 276
Fătimidṡ 31
Ferḥāt [c]Abbās 82
Firȧn 112
France 100, 151, 259, 271
Franji 259
French (in Tunisia) 150-154, 158-166, 173, 184, 185, 201
Freud, S. 57
Fu'ad Shibab 271, 272

Gafsa 185
Gallawi 100
Gambon, Paul 81
Gautama 53
Gemayel, Amin 281
Gemayel, Pierre 269
Ghaddaffi (president) 15, 73, 89, 179, 185, 261
Ghanem Jum'a 124
Al-Ghazzali 56
Gibbon, Edward 5
al-Glawi 166
Gnjilane 241
Gouraud (general) 257
Goux 66
Greece 240
Greek-Catholic/Melkite 259
Greek-Orthodox 258, 259, 262, 279
Greeks 99
Gulf States 274

Haddad (major) 281
Hadži Sulejman Kemura 249n
Hamada 104, 110, 112, 119
Hamadsha 57-60, 63, 66
Ḥamidiya Shadhiliya 64, 65, 188-197
Ḣammuda Bey 79
Hanafite 79, 176
Hanbal, Ahmad b. 31
Hanbalites 31
Harabati Baba 242
Harun al-Rashid 256
Hasan al-Banna 86, 95
al-Hashash 104
Heidegger 100
Helou, Charles 272
Heraklios 256
Herzegovina 240, 245, 247, 249n, 251n, 252n
Hindus 99
Ḥizb al-Taḥrir (Liberation Party) 87
Ḣudhail 127
Hugh of St. Cher 63
Hungary 240
Husayn b. 'Ali 76
Husserl 100
Huwetat 110, 112

Ibn Al-Arabi 56
Ibn Khuja 82
Ibn Taimîya 31
Ibrahim ar-Riyahi 76
Ida U Garyin 133
Ifriqiya 159, 160
Imamites 31
Imettdan 138, 139, 142, 143
Imi n' Tanout 133, 135, 137
Indonesia 16
Iran 10, 14, 16, 17, 21, 31, 34, 73, 84, 89, 90, 91n, 94, 99-101, 158, 180, 185, 255
Iraq 84, 185, 272
Isawi tariqa 65
Isawiyya 150
Ismailis 31
Israel 1, 11, 28, 29, 37, 95, 114, 115, 119, 124, 129n, 194, 274, 279, 281
Israelis 16, 108, 120
Istanbul 75, 149, 246
Istifan al-Duwayhi 269
Izri 142

Jainist 52
Janduba 200
J'ayyit 84
Jebaliyeh 104, 109-125
Jebel Katarina 107
Jebel Meneja 117
Jebel Musa 117, 118
Jerusalem 98, 257, 258
Jesus 49, 53, 68n
Jews 1, 36, 76, 256
Jordan 274
Jounieh 281
Jumblatt, Kamal 272, 276
Jumblatt, Walid 279, 281

al-Kâbir 207
Kaderîs 245, 247
Kairaouan 158, 164
Kaslik 262
Kautsky 49
Kerkennah Islands 169-174, 178-184
Khadiyah 53

Khalwatiyya 198n, 243
Khalwetîs 241-250n
Kharijites 31
Khayr ad-Din 80, 81, 152
Khazraj 127
Khomeyni 16, 17, 90
Khrumiri 199-216, 230-236n
Khrumiriya 199-206, 209-219, 227, 230, 233-235n
Kosovo 240-252n
Kosovska Mitrovica 242
Ksar Hellal 161, 165
Ksibet el-Mediouni 148-152, 155, 158-164

Lalla Aziza 133-142
Lebanon 1, 7, 9, 29, 84, 257-263, 267-281
Lēvi-Strauss, C. 66
Libya 15, 16, 21, 34, 73, 170, 179, 185, 195, 233, 276
Lyautey 81

Macedonia 240-252n
Madanis 149
Madani Sufis 146
Madaniyya 147-152, 161, 164-166
Maghreb 1, 75, 78, 82, 83, 155, 206
Mahdiyya 101
Mahmudiyya 86
Mahmud Kabadu 152
Majid Arslam 282n
al-Majlîs al-Akbar 79
al-Majlîs ash-Shar^{c}i 80
Malamatiyyah 67
Malays 4
Malikites 79, 176
Manāt 127
Maronite 257-263, 268-270
Ma^{c}ruf, Sa'd 275
Marx, Karl 4, 49, 50, 66
Massaûda 206
Matmata 151
Mawlay al-'Arabi al-Darqawi 149
Mayziya 219, 220, 236
Mayzîza 215, 216, 221-226
Mecca 89, 91n, 98, 117, 118, 123, 128, 199

Medina 31, 42, 98, 149
Mediterranean 1, 4, 8
Mejli Baba 243
Melâmîs 245
Melâmîya 243
Melâmîya Nûrîya 245, 250n
Mewlewîs 243, 245
Middle Ages 152
Middle East 10, 14, 58, 153
Moghul (empire) 41
Mohammed V 135
Monastir 146-148, 151, 159
Morocco 63, 67n, 77, 82-84, 98, 100, 107, 123, 138, 149, 151, 166
Moses 104, 114, 117, 125
Mostaghanem 147, 149, 150
Mount Lebanon 268, 274, 276, 281
Mount Sinai 107-110, 115
Mourides 68n
Mthellith 159
Muhammad 12, 24, 29, 31, 36, 41, 49, 53, 63, 174, 175, 206, 234n, 256, 277
Muhammad 'Ali 75, 154
Muhammad al-Bahay 257
Muhammad Bayram 152, 153
Muhammad Bayram IV 79, 80
Muhammad Bayram V 80
Muhammad Bey 79
Muhammad Karkar 161
Muhammad Mzali 185
Muhammad Nûr al-'Arabî/Arap Hodźa 243, 250n
Muhammad Snussi 153
al-Murabitun 267, 275-281, 282n
Mustafa Kamil 153
Mustafa as-Sîba'i 89
Muᶜtazilites 31
Muzeneh 104, 109-113, 116-126
Mzab 171

Nafta 78
Najaf 90
Napoleon III 259
Naqshbandî 242, 245, 249n
Nasib al-Matni 271
Nasser (President of Egypt) 9, 87, 194, 270-272, 275-279

Near East 1
Nebi Harun 104, 120, 125
Nebi Saleh 104, 118, 120, 124, 125
Nestorians 261
Nietzsche 100
Nile Delta 58, 190
North Africa 31, 58, 59, 148, 153, 169, 171, 172, 199
North Yemen 7
Nosaljac 241
Nuqrashi 87
Nusayri's 258

Oglavak 242
Ohrid 241, 242, 249n
Orahovac 243, 247
Osman dan Fodio 4
Ottoman Empire 42, 75, 258, 259

Pakistan 4, 16, 21, 33, 34, 38, 180
Palestine 1, 98, 124, 264
Palestinians 29, 87, 272-277, 281
Paul (Saint) 33
Persian Empire 102
Persians 99
Plato 99
Plotinus 99
Prizren 241-247, 250n

Qa'a-Raml 226
Qararsha 104, 110-114, 118, 119
Qayrawan 77
Qulailat 272, 275-277, 281n
Quraish 128
Quwatli 271

Ramla 124
Rashid Karami 271, 281, 282n
Rashidûn (caliphs) 31
Red Sea 108
Renaissance 20
Rida, Rashid 14, 74, 84-86, 101
Rifâ'îs 241-247, 250n
Rifians 154
Riyadh al-Sulh 269, 275

Rodrigo Diaz de Vivar 256
Roman Catholic Church 63, 67n
Roman Empire 102
Romans 99
Romis 245
Roncevalles 256
Rumania 240

Sadat, Anwar 73, 194, 276, 278
Sa'dis 241, 242, 245
Sa'diya 243
Safavid (dynasty) 42
Sahel 147-151, 156-160, 165
Sa'ib Salam 271, 276
Sa'ida 275
Saint Catherine 108, 111, 113, 117, 120, 125
Saint Maron 259
Saladin 257, 258
Salafis 152
Salafiyya 14, 33, 73, 74, 75, 82-88, 101, 154, 156, 161
Salama Ibn Hassan Salama 64
Saleḫ (nebi) 104
Salîbî 259
Salim Takla 282n
Samir Sabbagh 277, 278, 281n
Samuelson 53
Sanusi 170
Sanusiyya 101, 149
Saracen 256
Saragossa 256
Sarkis 276
Sartre 100
Sa'ud (King) 275
Sa'udi Arabia 89, 94, 98, 101, 112, 195, 274, 275
Sawalha 104, 110, 112, 118, 125
Sawarka Bedouin 125
Sayah, M. 158
Saydiya 236n
al-Sayyid 256
Sayyid Qutb 86
Scheler 100
Seksawa 138
Senegal 68n
Serbia 242, 243, 249n

Sfax 151, 158, 170, 172, 182-184
Shadhiliyya 149
Shah 17, 20, 73, 89, 100, 101, 185
Shaikh 'Abd el Halim Mahmud 187, 188
Shaikh Abu Shabib 124
Shaikh Abu Zaid 125
Shaikh Ahmad al-'Alawi 64, 65, 147-150, 160, 165
Shaikh 'Awad 104, 118, 120, 124, 125
Shaikh Habus 118, 124
Shaikh Hasan Khalid 280
Shaikh Ibrahim Salama 191-195
Shaikh al-Islam 79
Shaikh al-Madani 147-151, 155-166
Shaikh Salama ar-Radi 65, 189-193
Shaikh Suliman Nfe'i 104
Shaikh Qra'i 104
Shaw, Bernard 2
Shekha Swerha 104
Shi^{c}i 268, 274, 279
Shi^{c}ite 31, 258, 259
Shuf 281
Sidi 'Abd Allah bi-Jamal 207, 219
Sidi 'Abd as-Salam ben Mashîsh 207
Sidi 'Abd al-Qadir al-Jilâni 206
Sidi Mhammad 206-210, 215-231
Sidi Muhammad al-Madani 149
Sidi Muhammad Zafir 149
Sidon 268
Siloam 63
Sinai 107, 112-115, 119, 120, 125, 126
Sinai, South 104-109, 117-129n
Sinan Barraj 276, 277, 281n
Sinǎnǐs 246
Sirri Baba 243
Skopje 241, 242, 249n
Smala 160
Smith, Adam 4
Sofilar 242
Somalis 4
Souassi 151, 159, 160
Sousse 158, 170, 172
South-Eastern Europe 240, 245
Soviet Union 39, 73, 98, 279
Spain 31, 105, 255, 256
Spengler 99

Struga	241, 249n
Strumica	241
Sudan	32, 98
Suez Canal	96, 271
Sūfis	25, 51, 54, 150, 187
Sulaiman Franjiyyeh	281
Sultan Abdül Hamid II	28, 149
Sunnis	31, 90, 267-269, 274-280
Syria	1, 33, 73, 84, 89, 258, 269, 271, 272, 276
Syrians	281
Tabarka	200
Tagounit	137, 143
Tahar al-Haddad	154, 155, 163
Takla, Philippe	282
Tall Za'atar	276
Talaat n' Uzra	137
Tamjlocht	136-143
Tamteddit	137, 143
Tamzgourt	137, 143
Taqiyy ad-Din an-Nabhani	87
Tawara	110, 125, 126, 128
Testemelci	242
Tetovo	242, 246, 249n
Tih Plateau	107
Tinwaline	137, 143
Tishka	133
Toponica	241
Tripoli	84, 149, 162, 262, 268, 271, 275
Tunis	76, 79, 80, 84, 149-153, 157, 158, 163, 170, 172, 182
Tunisia	73-84, 90n, 147-185, 199-201, 233
Tunisian Djerid	78
Tunisians	158
al-Tūr	108, 112, 113
Turkey	15, 16, 20, 98
Turks	27, 148, 260, 261
Tyre	268
Uchchen	137, 143
cUmar	257
Umayyads	31
United Arab Republic of Egypt and Syria	271

United States	73, 100, 185, 271
Valencia	256
Virgin Mary	105, 257
Visoko	242
Wadi Firan	108, 117, 119
Wadi Leja	117
Wadi Nasb	108
Wadi Rahaba	116
Wadi Slaf	116
Wahhâbi	4, 31, 33, 152
Weber, Marianne	49
Weber, Max	7, 49-56, 61-68n, 197
West	94, 95, 99-102
al-Wilda	207
Wuhebat	120, 121
Yemen	89, 97
Yugoslavia	9, 240-251n
Yusuf Sahib at-Taba^c	76
Yusuf, uncle of Shaikh Madani	150, 160-163
Zamalek	194, 195
Ziad al-Hafiz	277
Zinit	133, 134

Index 2: Subject Matter

agglomeration of "primordial loyalties" (in Lebanon) 276
annual migratory cycle (of Bedouin) 116
Arabism and Islam 261
Arab movements of protest 37
Arab nationalism 261, 264
Arab socialism 15, 194, 264
Army Law (in Lebanon) 277
ascetism 50-54, 64, 187
ascetism, Sufi 54, 55
ascetics, Christian 54
Ash'arism 101
asitane, chief house for mystic orders in Yugoslavia 246
Association for the Protection of the Qur'ân 184
awakening of Islam 94
al-Azhar University 86, 90n, 102, 171, 187

Baghdad Pact 270
Bahai-ism 13
Bathist regimes 272
Bedouin 104-128, 149
Bedouin basic economy 115, 119, 126
ben Nasriy order 61
Beylical family 75
Bible 12, 14
bidonvilles 59, 60, 65
Bil Hasan order 151
British occupation (of Egypt) 74
British occupation of the Suez Canal 95
brotherhood, Hamidiya Shadhiliya, the administration 188
brotherhood, Hamidiya Shadhiliya, antagonisms and oppositions 189
brotherhood, Hamidiya Shadhiliya, the bureaucratic rule 190
brotherhood, Hamidiya Shadhiliya, contrasting interests 195
brotherhood, Hamidiya Shadhiliya, division 194, 195
brotherhood, Hamidiya Shadhiliya, helping the poor 190
brotherhood, Hamidiya Shadhiliya, the notion of hierarchy 191
brotherhood, Hamidiya Shadhiliya, practical meaning 191
brotherhood, Hamidiya Shadhiliya, polotical suspicions 188
brotherhood, Hamidiya Shadhiliya, reactionary and "feudal" 196

brotherhood, Hamidiya Shadhiliya, tensions	192
Buddhism	11, 20, 62
Buddhism, Hinayana	50
capitalims (in Tunisia)	178
Catholicism	50, 54
charisma	49-55, 63, 66, 68n
Christianity	5, 8, 11, 13, 14, 20, 22, 23, 29, 51, 53, 62, 63, 65, 67, 68n, 255, 256, 260, 262, 263
Christianity, fundamentalist groups	10
Christianity, radical	11
Christian minorities	1
Christians in the East	261
civil war (in Lebanon)	258-263, 270, 273, 275, 276, 282n
clashes between Christians and Muslims (in Lebanon)	259
Code of Personal Status (of Tunisia)	157, 176
collaboration	163
collaborator	164
colonial period in Tunisia	201
communion meal	140, 141
communism	185
Communist Party (in Lebanon)	269, 270, 272, 279
Communist Party (in Tunisia)	146, 147
community life in the tekke	246
compatibility of Islam with modern civilization	81
conditional aspect of the saintly cult	211
confederation (of tribes)	110
confessionalism (in Lebanon)	263, 264, 269, 279, 280
confessional system (in Lebanon)	263
conflicts in Ksibet	161
Confucianism	49
counter movements	27, 30, 36
crisis of the East	102
crisis of the West	102
Crusaders	259

Crusades	99, 255, 258
Crusades, Islamic reaction	257
cult of Nasser	272, 277
cult of the Saint Lalla Aziza	138
cult of saints	105-107, 126, 199, 200, 210-215, 232, 233
cult of saints, ritual involvement of women	212
cult of saints, routine aspects	210
Darqawiy order	61, 149, 150
Darqawiyya - Madaniyya order	150
decline of the West	100
decolonization	56
Demerdashiya Khalwatiya order	68n
denasserization	95
Destour Party	153, 154, 176, 177, 182
Destour Party, pragmatic approach to politics	155
Destour Socialist Party	158
development	33
development, Islamic notion	30
dialectic	26
dialectics between rural elite and peasants	233
dialectics between socio-economic structure and symbolic order	233
dialectics of inclusiveness/exclusiveness	232-233
differences in religious styles	60
differentiation, religious	61
differentiation of religious markets in services	59
different interpretation of events, Greek-Orthodox and Maronites	262
different response to the conflicts, Greek-Orthodox and Maronites	259
dissonance between Arab culture and Western culture	179
divinization	26
dominating West	42
domination, imperialist	14
domination, Jewish	27
domination, Western	26
economic dimension	60
economic interests	50
economic relations	50, 52

economic model of aintship 64
economic support 53, 62
Egyptian National Party 153
Enlightenment 152
European-American interests 88
European influences 75, 78, 80
European penetration 88
European threat 74
exchange relations 59
exchange theory of saint cults 67

Feast of the Sacrifices 104
Five Pillars of Islam 172
folk religion 56
formal Islam 233
Free Army Officers 188
French and British military intervention (in Tunisia), the threat 79
French occupation (of Egypt) 75
French protectorate (Tunisia) 81, 147
fundamentalism 10, 11
fundamentalism, Islamic 21
fundamentalism, Muslim 18
fundamentalist form of religion 1
fundamentalist groups 196
fundamentalist sects 68n
fundamentalists, Islamic 20
fundamentalists, modern 14

geographical and social mobility (in Tunisia) 159
German and Italian occupation (of Tunisia) 163
government policies (in Tunisia), aspects 175
Grand Mosque of Mecca 89, 91n
Great Mosque of Tunis 157
Great Tradition 26

Hanafite chief 76
Hanafite School of Law 75, 76
Hasafiyya brotherhood 86
Hindu cults 50
Hinduism 11, 20, 49
holiness and economic activity 77, 78
Holy Orthodox Antiochene Assembly 262
Holy War 255, 262
humane values 35

human rights 24, 35
Husaynid dynasty 76
Husaynid period 75, 76
Husaynid state 79

Ibadi sect 171
ideal character of the Sharî^{c}a 34
identification between Arabs and Muslims 261
ideologies of the main communities (in Lebanon) 269
ideologization of Islam 42
idolatry 26
illness 56-62, 67n
illness, social distribution 58
imperialism 27
independence (of Tunisia) 147, 152, 156, 157, 163, 166, 170, 175-184
independence movement (in Tunisia) 162
Independent Nasserist Movement 267-282
Independent Nasserist Movement, foundation and leader 275
Independent Nasserist Movement, ideology 278
Independent Nasserist Movement, military preparations 276
Independent Nasserist Movement, need for secularization 280
Independent Nasserist Movement, organization 277
Independent Nasserist Movement, political programme 278
indigenous powers (of Islam) 100, 101
industrialization 1, 2, 6
inferiority complex 100
integrative functions (of the ulama) 75
interconfessional conflict 267
Iranian Constitution 14
Iraqi Revolution 271
Isawiyya order 150
Islam, concept 41
Islam, conversions to 22
Islam, critical use or function 22
Islam and development 30
Islam, foundation 22
Islam, fundamentalist revival 10
Islam, the great Arab protest movements 37
Islam, ideological use 28
Islam, indefinable character 40
Islam, militant 73
Islam, mystical 25

Islam, normative	25, 26
Islam, only viable political system for the Muslims	101
Islam, in a privileged position to express protest	41
Islam, protest against foreign culture	28
Islam, protest function	22
Islam, a rational progressive religion	74
Islam, a rational religion compatible with progress	84
Islam, reformed	7
Islam as a religion	29
Islam as a religious culture	24, 25
Islam, religious sectors	24
Islam, revelation and reason	32
Islam, rural and urban forms	60
Islam, symbolic meaning	23
Islamic Ethics	95
Islamic faith	23, 25
Islamic fundamentalism	94, 97-103
Islamic fundamentalist revival	21
Islamic fundamentalist state	98
Islamic modernism in Tunisia	152
Islamic movements	26
Islamic orthodoxy, new	84
Islamic protest	28
Islamic reformation	8
Islamic reformism	154
Islamic revival	185
Islamic revolution	33, 34, 39
Islamic saints	62, 67n
Islamic socialism	89, 96
Islamic state	33, 37, 38, 41
Islamic Sufism	66
Islamic tolerant openness	81
Israeli invasion of 1982	281
Israeli-Palestine war	264
Jewish minorities	1
Jewish nationalism	11
Jilaliy order	61
Judaism	11, 13, 14, 20, 22, 27, 54, 68n
Kata'ib Party	269-282n
Laws, the (of Sheikh Salama ar-Radi)	190, 191
Lebanese civil war (see: civil war)	255

Lebanese history, the past fifty years	267
Lebanese National Movement (LNM)	275-282n
Lebanese National Movement, appeal for unity	278
Lebanese National Movement, secularization of political life	279
Lebanese state, the laisser-faire political and economic features	273
Liberation Party	87
lineage model (in north-western Tunisia)	202
lineages (of Tinwaline)	137, 144
lineages, dispersion	143
lineages, distribution	143
lineages, participating in the rite	135
lineages, which join in the rite	143
local subsistence economy (in north-western Tunisia)	201, 233, 234
local zyara	214, 215, 223-232
Madaniyya order	146-150, 158
Madaniyya order, a modern Sufi movement	147
Madaniyya order, spreading	159
Mahdist movements	32
Mahdist state	32
Malikite ᶜālim	80
Malikite chief	76
Malikite ᶜulamā'	76
Mamluk domination	75
al-Manār, periodical	84
Mandate, French (in Lebanon)	269
Mandate-period (in Lebanon)	268
maraboutism	148, 152, 153, 162, 172, 173, 174
marabouts	77, 78, 83, 148, 151, 159, 162, 174
marriage field	219
Marxism-Leninism	97
Marxism, traditional	97
Marxists	96, 98
masculinity	57
mass religion	49
mass religiosity	51, 54, 56, 66

material interests 49, 50
militant Islam 78, 85-89
militant Muslims 73, 79, 85-90
minority Islam 9
misjudgements (of Islam) 99
missions, Christian 29
modernization 1, 6
modernization (in Tunisia) 181
modernism 35
modernist movement 35
modernists 83
modernity 147
modern North Africa, pattern of change 148
Monastir Quranic school 148, 149
monopolization (in Tunisia) 177
Mufti of Lebanon 271, 280
al-Murābit, magazine 269, 271, 275-281n
Muslim communities (in Yugoslavia), relations 244
Muslim mystic orders (in south-eastern Europe) 240-252
Muslim mystic orders (in south-eastern Europe), documentation 240-245
Muslim mystic orders, function of the sheikh's power 247
Muslim mystic orders, present situation 245
Muslim protest movements 36
Muslim revolutionaries 96
Mu'tazilism 101
mystical Islam 85
mystical Path 24, 25, 34
mysticism 12, 51, 52, 62, 138, 174, 187
mysticism, Islamic 56
mysticism and orthodoxy (in Tunisia) 152
mysticism, philosophy and gnosis 35
mysticism, Sufi 59
mystics 34
mythical society 97
mythology 12, 13, 16

Nasserism 194, 197, 270, 271, 276, 279
Nasserist regime 195
Nasserists 273
Nasserites 96

National Liberal Party 274
Nationalism 1-4, 8, 9
nationalism, Arab 3
nationalism (in Egypt) 197
nationalism, Tunisian 154, 156
nationalist élites 85, 88
nationalist identity in Lebanon 263
nationalist leaders 83, 84
nationalists (in Tunisia) 148, 152, 161, 162, 166, 184, 185
National Pact of 1943 (in Lebanon) 269, 279
Néo-Destour Party 146-148, 155, 156, 161, 162, 163
Néo-Destour Party, nationalist conceptions 155
Néo-Destour Party, social origins 155
neo-orthodox movements 33
new orthodoxy 85

official Muslim community (of Yugoslavia) 244, 248
Old-Destour Party 147, 148, 156, 162
opposition (Kerkennah Islands) 182, 183
Organization of the Muslim Brethren 32, 33, 37, 82, 85, 86, 87, 89, 95, 96, 171, 179, 188, 195, 264
Organization of the Muslim Brethren, the teachings 86
orientalism 29, 55, 99
orientalists 55
original zyara 214, 215, 219, 227-232
original zyara, main factors determining its observance 231
original zyara, two sets of data 228
orthodox Judaism 11
orthodoxy 21

Palestinians on Lebanese territory 274
Pan-Islamic movement 28
Parti Populaire Syrien (PPS) 269, 270, 279, 282n
People of the Book 256, 257
personal and institutionalized baraka 63

personal zyara 214, 215, 219, 227, 232
personal zyara, high prestige 227
pilgrimage 104, 106, 107, 112, 118-121, 125, 126
pilgrimage centres (in Sinai) 119, 123
pilgrimages, individual 117
pilgrimages, significance 122
pilgrimage, two levels of the individual's involvement 121
pilgrimage, tribal 111
pilgrims (of Lalla Aziza) 134, 137, 138
pious visits (in north-western Tunisia) 199-201, 209, 210, 227
political action 33
popular belief 57
popular Islam 65, 199, 233
popular and official Islam 55
popular and official religion 56
popular religion 55, 56, 65, 189, 196, 199, 215, 233-235n
popular religiosity 54
popular Sufism 55, 188-197
popular Sufism, recuperation 197
popular Sunni opposition (in Lebanon) 271
Progressive Socialist Party 272, 279, 281
protest in the Arab world 38
protest dimension (of Islam) 36
protest, expressions 40
protest function of Islam 22
protest, religious dimension 25
protest, usefulness of the notion 23
protest, which appeals to Islam 23
Protestantism 1, 2, 49, 54
Protestantism, European 3
Protestant scripturalism 3
Protestant sects 50
public trial (against Sheikh Madani) 164
puritanism 4
puritanism of Islam 9
puritanism, Muslim 3
puritanism, two types 169, 171
puritanisms (two), alliance 185

puritanisms, distinguishing characteristics 170

Qadiriyya order 78, 152

Rahmaniyya brotherhood 78
Reconquista of Spain, religious impulses 256
reform 8, 81, 82
reformation 1
reformation, European 8
reformers 5, 14, 165
reformism 1, 8, 152, 162
reformism, Islamic 99
reformism, puritan 56
reformism, puritanical and scripturalist 8
reformist 81, 85, 148, 192
reformist doctrine 80
reformist and fundamentalist groups 197
reformist groups 196
reformist ideas 156
reformist Islam 156
reformists, Malekite 171
reformist movement 32, 101, 152
reformist trends 190
reformist ulama 74, 78, 80
reform movement, liberal 13
reform movements 30
reform movements (from above) 15
reforms, Turkish Tanzimat 14
rejection of European civilization 73
relationship with a saint 212
religio-nationalist resentment 89, 90
religion, behavioural aspect 199
religion, minimum definition 11, 12, 13
religious austerity, characteristics 171
religious conservatism 94, 97-101
religious dimension 24
religious experience 35
religious labels, to hide the real issues 263
religious labels, misuse 264
religious pluralism 1
religious protest movements, non-Sunni 31
religious reformism 98
religious struggle 256
religious struggle between Christians and Muslims 255, 258

religious war 260, 262
resistance movements 27
revival of Islam 87, 88
revivalists 31, 41, 184
revivalist puritanism 169-171, 178-182
revivalist puritanism, characteristics 175
revivalist puritanism, differences on Kerkennah Islands 180
revivalist puritans 171, 185
revolution (in Egypt) 188, 196
revolutionary movements 33
rite (of Lalla Aziza) 137, 142
rite (of Lalla Aziza), a rebirth 132
rite (of Lalla Aziza), twelve lineages 141
rural religious style 169
sacrifice, the fact of being tied up in the maqam of Lalla Aziza 141
sacrifice of the sheep 139
sacrifice work 134
sacrificial animal 135
sacrificial sheep 143
Sahel 147-151, 156, 160, 165
saint, antecedents 125
saint/devotee relationship 62
saint, he intercedes with God 128
saint and man, relationship: supplication; conditional aspect, obligations 211
saintly mediation 106
saint, a mediator 121
saint, symbolic significance 125
saints, contemporary 64
saints, equality 118
saints, their function to mediate 126
saints, intercessors 174
saints, intercessors with God 118
saints and the living, relationships 209
saints, mediation 105
saints, mediators 170
Salafiyya conception of reform 74
Salafiyya doctrine 74, 78, 79, 82
Salafiyya leaders 74, 78, 82
Salafiyya modernism 148
Salafiyya movement 154

Salafiyya movement, reformist 73
Salafiyya school 83
Salafiyya teachings 84, 85
Salafiyya teachings, transformed into a nationalist ideology 81
Salafiyya ulama 78, 82
Sanusiya lodges 66
scholarly studies (of Islam) 29
secularization (in Lebanon) 263
secularization (in Tunisia) 176, 183
secularization and monopolization (in Tunisia) 175, 177
secularization and urbanization 65
segmentary lineage system 201
segmentary opposition 200, 223
segmentary system (in north-western Tunisia) 200
segmentation, opposition in 223
segments, characteristic attributes (in north-western Tunisia) 202, 203, 204, 221, 223
segments, characteristic attributes as a distinct power 204
segments, characteristic attributes as the Grace or Life-force 205
segments, characteristic attributes of the highest territorial levels 208
segments, characteristic attributes and their symbolic elaborations 205
self-defense 24, 27
self-purification of Islam 4, 5
separation of church and state (in Tunisia) 157
Shadhiliyya order 151, 152
Sheikh Madani, decline of influence 163
Shi[c]ite– Isma[c]ili belief 90
shrines (of saints in Sinai) 104, 107, 117, 118, 123-125
shrines (in north-western Tunisia) 199-201, 205-208, 213, 214, 219, 221, 227-229
shrines, associated with segments 209
shrines, cultic autonomy 208
shrines, hierarchy 207
shrines, material forms 206
shrines, material multiplicity 207
shrines, pious gifts 206

shrines, ritual attributes of lower-level segments 208
shrines, a theory 235n
shrines, zyara obligations of women: local zyara, original zyara, personal zyara 213
shrine and saint, association 205
shrine, a symbol of the territorial claims of the tribe 123
SIDRA/ZIDRA 244-246, 251n, 252n
socialist movement (in Tunisia) 178
social tensions (in Lebanon) 274
socio-economic doctrine, Muslim 18
sociology 49
sociology of religion 49, 51
state socialism 95, 96
steppes 158, 159, 160, 165
story of Lalla Aziza 137
stratification 51, 53
stratification of Buddhism 53
stratification of charisma 59
stratification, charismatic 66
stratification of the population 59
stratification, secular 66
struggle against Christians 257
struggle against the Turks (in Lebanon) 260
struggle, presented as a religious war (crusade / Holy War) 255
sub-proletariat (in Lebanon) 274
Sufi brotherhoods 56, 76-78, 85, 187-193
Sufi brotherhoods, ignorance, non-Islamic practices 188
Sufi lodges 59, 66
Sufi movement 54
Sufi orders 61, 65, 147, 148, 188
Sufi saints 64
Sufi shaikhs 76
Sufis 25, 51, 54, 150, 187
Sufism 9, 54, 55, 67, 86, 149, 152, 165, 195, 196
Sufism, anachronistic 187
Sufism, responsiveness 193
Sufi trance 174

Sunni Islam	31, 65, 258
Sunni movement	267, 280
Sunni political leaders	270
superiority-inferiority complexes	99
supplication aspect of the saintly cult	211
Supreme Islamic Authority of Yugoslavia	249n
symbol	122, 123, 128
symbolic character of protest	39
symbolism	12, 13
Tawara, alliance	110
Tayyibiyya brotherhood	77
tekke	240-252n
tension within the Sunni community (of Lebanon)	270
territorial segment, dynamics	226
territorial segment, local zyara	214
territorial segment, relationship with a saint	212
territorial segmentation (in north-western Tunisia)	202, 203, 216, 235n
territorial segmentation, original and personal zyara	227
territorial segmentation, pattern of local zyara	221
territorial segmentation, segmentary dynamics	205
territorial segmentation, structures of local zyara	223
territorial segments	203, 208, 211, 221
territorial segments, social and economic significance	204
theories of pilgrimage and regional cults	232
Tijanniyya order	61, 152
tombs of saints (in Sinai)	104, 105, 112, 118, 122-127
tombs, meanings	123
traditional bourgeoisie	15, 16
traditionalist believers	35
traditionalist faithful	34
traditionalist model, characteristics	174
traditionalist model, deviation on Kerkennah Islands	174
traditionalist Muslims	39
traditionalist puritanism	169-182
traditionalist puritanism, development on Kerkennah Islands	172
traditionalist puritans	171, 176, 185
traditionalist puritan style, deviation on Kerkennah Islands	173
traditionalists	183, 184
traditionalists and revivalists, Sunni	32

Traditionalists, Sunni 31
traditional orthodoxy 20
traditional rural Muslim community 6
transformation of the role of the saint 64
tribal gatherings (in Sinai) 104, 105, 112, 116-122
tribal gatherings, attendance 120
tribal gatherings, date 119
tribal ritualism 98
tribe, an administrative unit 111
tribe, a political organization 110
tribe, a segmentary political organization 111
tribe, a territorial organization 109
tribe/tribesmen 104-129
Tripartite Aggression 271
Tunisian Party 153
turbe 241, 242
Turkish troops (in Tunisia) 75
two puritanisms, support 183, 184
two religious styles, differences on Kerkennah Islands 180
two religious styles, general points of coincidence 180
two types of puritanism 181
two types of puritanism, collaboration 171
two types of puritanism, cooperation 182
two types of puritans 171
two types of puritans, cooperation 184
types of tekke-s 246

UGTT, Tunisian trade movement 173, 177, 178, 182-185
^{c}ulamā', integrative functions 81
^{c}ulamā', as intermediaries between the rulers and the ruled 76
^{c}ulamā', marabouts, shaikhs, an integral part of the socio-political leadership 78
^{c}ulamā' and the modern world 81
^{c}ulamā', power and wealth 80
^{c}ulamā', role in economic life 77
^{c}ulamā', as social regulators 77
^{c}ulamā', subordinate function 83
^{c}ulamā', subordinate role 88
Union of the mystic orders in Albania 250n
University of the Holy Spirit in Kaslik 262

virtuosi, Buddhist 62
virtuosi, mystical 62

virtuosity 54, 61, 65-67
virtuoso/mass dichotomy 53
virtuoso-mass model 67
virtuoso and mass religion 50
virtuoso/mass religiosity 52
virtuoso model 61
virtuoso religion 50, 52, 64, 66
virtuoso religiosity 51
virtuoso religious groups 59

Wafd party 197, 198n
wage labour (of Bedouin) 109, 113-116, 120, 126
wage labourer 114, 126
Wahhabism 98
Western intrusion 24
western liberalism 95
western model of economic policy (in Egypt) 194
western youth culture 17
women's zyara obligations 214
worker-saint 65, 66

Yugoslavian Muslim community 249n, 251n
Young Tunisians' Party 153

Zaytuna Mosque (University) 76, 79, 149, 153, 154, 158, 161, 176
Zionism 11, 27, 28, 29, 37, 185, 275, 278
Zionist movement 11, 29

Index 3: Foreign Words

^{c}adl	notary	77
agurram		68n
ahl al-bilād	(native Tunisians)	75
ahl al-dhimma	*protégés* of the Islamic state	99, 262
aḥwaš	a festive dance in the Western High Atlas	136, 142, 144
ajram, anabasis (shrub)		107
^{c}arsh/ pl. *^{c}urush*	"tribes"	159
^{c}arūbiyya	countryside	159
balda	township/village	159
baraka	charisma	55-59, 62-68n, 160, 191, 194-199, 205, 208-212, 216
baṭal	hero	271
ba^{c}tharan, artemisia (shrub)		107
bid^{c}a	innovation	152, 165
darabukka	hand drum	146
darwīsh		54
dawla	state	86
dhikr	liturgy	65, 86, 160, 189-193, 241-244, 248, 250n
dhimmī	*protégé* of the Isl. state	99, 262
dīn	religion	86
dirham	Moroccan national currency	144
dīya	blood compensation	111
'eleh	a family	110
fallāgha		156
faqīhs, Shī'ite ^{c}ulamā'		89, 90
fara^{c}/ pl. *furū^{c}*	a branch of a tribe	111
fātiḥa/fatīḥa	opening chapter of the Quran	122, 134, 140, 144
fatwā	legal decision	81
fiqh	jurisprudence	34, 74, 83-87, 101
al- fuqarā' (sg. *faqīr)*	the poor, adepts of a saint	54, 60, 62, 150

gedra	earthenware cooking pot	141, 144
ḥabūs, waqf	religious bequest	76-79
ḥadīth	tradition on sayings and actions by the prophet	12, 29, 83-86
ḥaḍra	ecstatic dance, seance	57, 60, 62, 65, 146, 161
ḥajj	pilgrimage to Mecca	12, 117
ḥalqa	gathering	150
hawā'	dissolving of the remains of good men into air	124
ḥizb	musical band, group	150
ḥizb al-taḥrīr al-islāmī jund Allāh	Islamic movement in Egypt	38
ᶜid al-aḍḥā	feast of the sacrifices	104
(al-) ᶜid al-kabīr	great festival	231
iġṣan	lineages	143
ijāza	certificate	149
ijmāᶜ	consensus	85, 105
ijtihād	personal effort to arrive at knowledge from the sources of religion	83, 86, 87, 157
ikhwān	brethren or members of an order	39
(al-) ikhwān al-muslimīn	the Muslim Brotherhood	33, 38
ilahis		243
ᶜilmaniyya	secularization	263
imām	leader of prayer	76, 90, 147, 161, 164
imām khaṭīb	preacher	162
iṣlāḥ	reform	32, 33, 35
islām	abandonment of oneself to God	26, 175, 180
jaddī	grandparent	206, 210
Jāhilīya	pre-Islamic age of ignorance	36
Jamāᶜat-i-islāmi	Islamic movement in Pakistan	38
al-Jamāᶜa al-islamiyya	Islamic movement in Egypt	38, 96
Jamāᶜat at- takfīr wa'l-hijra	Islamic movement in Egypt	38
al-jamāhīr	the masses	278
al-Jihād	Islamic movement in Egypt	38

jihād	holy war	24, 27, 42, 49, 156, 158, 175, 180, 261
jinn	spirits	12, 57, 58
jnūn	spirits of the wilds	62, 210
jizya	poll-tax	76
karāmāt	acts of grace	191
khā'in	betrayer	278
khalīfa	deputy	87, 192
kulughlis	sons of Turkish soldiers and Tunisian women	75, 90n
kurbi	type of shrine, dwelling-house	206, 207, 221, 228
kurra	stone balls	206
lalla	madam, miss, grandmother, elder sister	206
laṭīf	prayers	82
madīna	city	76
madrasa	school	76, 79
majlis	office of a *tarīqa*	193
mahdī	eschatological figure	32
majlis shūrā	consultative assembly	87
maq^cad	place for gatherings of men	124
maqām	(holy) place	104, 124, 125, 136, 138, 141-144
maṣīf	harvest	119
maṣlaḥa	principle of general utility	84, 85
mawlid (mulid)	birthday of the prophet or of a saint	154, 164, 194
ma'zūr	possessed male	58
ma'zūra	possessed female	58
mendīl	napkin, piece of cloth in which the bread is wrapped	136, 144
me^cruf	gathering in the honour of a saint	133, 136, 139, 143, 144
mitkhalfin	the backward people of the countryside	159

mitmadnin	the civilized people	159
mizwar	leader of a saint's lineage group	62, 63
mqeddem	one who precedes, a representative	134, 144
mudarris	teacher in a mosque	79, 80
muftī	legal adviser	75, 76, 79, 80, 84
muḥibbīn	devotees	60, 62
Munaẓẓamat al-Ikhwān al-Muslimīn	Organization of the Muslim Brethren	85
murīdīn	novices	150
musem	pilgrimage	57
mutaṣarrifiyya	province	268
mwedden	person who makes the call to prayer	136, 144
mzāra	type of shrine	206, 207, 221, 228, 232
nabadh	nickname	110
Nahda	Arab cultural revival movement	14, 15
naqba	nickname	110
nīya	pure intention	209
qabaḍāi	strong arm men	280
qabaḍāyāt	petty gangsters	270
qāḍī	Islamic judge	74-77
qalb bahi	respectfully, sincerely	209
qānūn	laws of a *tarīqa*	188
qawm	folk	54, 263
qubba	type of shrine	206, 207, 219, 221, 228
rabī^{c}	spring	116
al-ra'īs	the chief	146
ratam	broom	113
reẓẓa	turban of white cloth	137, 144
rīḥ	musical formula	58
rizq	livelihood	115
ruba^{c}/pl. *rubu*^{c}	quarter (of a tribe)	111
ryāl	unit of account used in everyday market dealings (Morocco)	145

sāqya	an open irrigation canal	138, 145
al-salāf al-ṣāliḥ	the pious forefathers	74
seyāl	acacias	113
^{c}sā	the night prayer	136, 144
al-sha^{c}b	the people	278, 279
shabāb Muḥammad	Islamic movement in Egypt	38
shahīd	witness, martyr	77, 277
shaykh	oldest, religious chief	39, 76-78
sharī^{c}a	religious law	14, 25, 33, 34, 41, 84-90
shirk	sin of idolatry	4, 8, 26, 41
sīdī	master, sir, elder brother	206
sīra	life (of the Prophet)	277
subṭān al-deir	children of the monastery	114
ṣūf	undyed woollen garment	54
sunna	early tradition	25, 26, 30-36
sūq	weekly market	145
tadhwīb	dissolution	279
tafsīr	exegesis	80
ṭagya	small cap	137, 145
ṭaleb	a scribe, an educated person	140, 145
taqlīd	passive loyalty to tradition	83
tarfā'	tamarisks	113
ṭarīqa (pl. *ṭuruq*)	religious mystical group	25, 39, 64, 65, 146, 187-198n
al-tasāmuḥ al-islāmī	Islamic tolerant openness	81
tawhīd	oneness of God	82, 150
ṭažin	meat stew or the plate in which such a stew simmers	136, 145
thrayya	Canopus (star)	119
tikatin	households	143
turba	a shrine	104, 124
'twakkal ^{c}Allāh'	rely on God	122

ᶜūd	lute	146
ᶜulamā' (sg. *ᶜālim)*	religious scholar	18, 25, 31, 39, 59, 65, 74-91n, 102, 148-154, 171, 184-187, 192
ulī	saints	209
umma	community of believers	88, 97, 262
ᶜurūba	Arabism	280
ᶜusūl al-fiqh	sources of the law	34, 74, 80, 101
ᶜuzr	excuse	58
waḥda	unity	272
wakīl	superintendent	77, 79
waqf	pious foundation	157, 164, 172, 176
waqf-nāme	certificate establishing a *waqf*	241
wāsṭa	back door influence	280
al-waṭan	the nation	279
wird	link to a *tarīqa*	149
wulād siyyid	descendants of a saint	62, 63
wziᶜa	division, sharing out of meat	139, 145
zahir (dahir)	decree of Berber law codification	82
zaᶜīm/pl. *zuᶜamā'*	leader	270, 271, 272, 278, 280, 283
zakāt	alms	86
zanādiqa	atheists	164
zār	a ceremony connected with *ᶜuzr*	58, 65
zarda	saintly festival	200
zāwiya	brotherhood, lodge	60, 61, 76-79, 134, 147, 151, 152, 158, 160-166, 172, 176, 192
zawya	sanctuary	145
žellāba	a loose shirtlike garment	133, 135, 137, 141
zġārīṭ	women's shouts of joy: ululation	134, 145
ᶜzib	farm, usually in a fairly remote area	137, 143, 144
zyāra	pious visits	117, 199, 210-233, 236n